ENCYCLOPAEDIA
OF
RURAL SOCIOLOGY

ENCYCLOPAEDIA
OF
RURAL SOCIOLOGY

Vol. 4
TRANSFORMATION OF RURAL SOCIETY

Editor-in-Chief
ARVIND KUMAR

INSTITUTE FOR SUSTAINABLE DEVELOPMENT
LUCKNOW

&

ANMOL PUBLICATIONS PVT. LTD.
NEW DELHI-110 002 (INDIA)

ANMOL PUBLICATIONS PVT. LTD.
4374/4B, Ansari Road, Daryaganj
New Delhi-110 002

Encyclopaedia of Rural Sociology
Copyright © Institute for Sustainable Development, Lucknow.
First Edition 1998

ISBN 81-261-0004-4 (Vol. 4)
ISBN 81-261-0000-1 (Set)

PRINTED IN INDIA

Published by J. L. Kumar for Anmol Publications Pvt. Ltd., New Delhi-110 002 and Printed at Mehra Offset Press, Delhi.

Contents

Preface

In India, a number of systematic studies on rural life has been made after Independence. Most of these studies were made by social anthropologists. Anthropologists, who preoccupied themselves earlier with the studies of primitive or aboriginal people, latter shifted their focus on the village life. Several other studies of Indian villages were also made during the last three decades by rural sociologists, social anthropologists, sociologists and agricultural economists. It can be hoped that in the near future, the discipline will have deep roots in other agricultural universities and traditional universities of the country.

The question of the importance in Rural Sociology today is not a question of whether or not we should have it but a question of how the knowledge acquired by it can be used. It is this phenomenon in its varied dimensions which the different volumes of this Encyclopaedia have tried to explore. The titles of different volumes are: Rural Sociology: An Introduction; Social Stratification in Rural Society; Rural Industrial Sociology; Transformation of Rural Society; Social Inequalities in Rural Areas.

As is obvious, the works, encyclopaedic in nature, are basically drawn from the writings of different authorities in the field, we owe our gratitude to all the academics, social scientists and writers, whose writings are cited or substantially made use of in the present encyclopaedia.

We are also indebted to Shri J. L. Kumar, Managing Director, Anmol Publications Pvt. Ltd., New Delhi for agreeing to publish this work.

We are solely responsible for any shortcoming, if crept in the work.

—**Arvind Kumar**

1

The New World Order or Disorder? An Option Before the World

Patterns of Global Change

E.H. Carr writing in his celebrated essay *"What is History?"* said: "Nothing is history is inevitable, except in the formal sense that for it to have happened otherwise the antecedent causes would have had to be different."

Even Carr would have been surprised at the recent dramatic changes in the world and the frequency and rapidity with which they have taken place. It has been a stormy world since the end of the Second World War. Marx believed that quantitative change goes on building until it turns into a qualitative change, but the world since 1940 seems to be plunging into one qualitative change after another, first after every 10 years and now it seems after every 5 years.

Let us take a look at the phenomenal changes that have been taking place in the last half a century. The world that emerged after the last world war was an entirely different world from the one preceding it. It became virtually one world dominated by the United States. Both military and economic power were concentrated in Washington. This power was exercised, in the ultimate analysis, by one person, the President of the United States. He alone had his finger on the buttons that could release death and destruction, the nuclear weapons. That is why his office came to be styled as the *Imperial* Presidency of the United States.

No king or emperor before him had the awsome power which he had at his command. The United States by positioning nuclear weapons strategically in different parts of the world ensured its dominance over the international system. Washington also came to be the economic nerve-centre with it producing about 40 per cent of the world's wealth. Indeed, the world was increasingly become a unified, capitalist one world market.

Yet two counter-trends also appeared bringing about yet another qualitative change in the situation. First a socialist world had emerged, defying the writ of Washington, with its nerve centre in Moscow. Smaller in size and very much less developed than the capitalist world, the USSR, nevertheless, broke the nuclear monopoloy of the West and acquired various attributes of power. It began challenging the West, resulting in one crisis after another in various parts of the globe. Economically, the socialist world was much weaker and could not provide an alternative world market. And yet it provided the much-needed countervailing power to the Western bloc and put demonstrable restraints on the freedom of action of the Western countries.

The second counter-trend was the collapse of the imperialist system and of colonialism and the rise of independent countries. Weak economically and without any military clout, many defied attempts to dictate policies on them. Some of them succumbed and joined the Western bandwagon, but many kept the flag of independence flying. This struggle for independence and independent economic development led to the rise of the non-aligned movement, which under the inspiration of Jawaharlal Nehru joined by Tito and Nasser, emerged as a significant factor in international relations. Their efforts were aided by the military balance between the Western and the Eastern worlds. The availability of a counter-balancing force in the Soviet Union made it easier for the non-aligned countries to strengthen their independence.

Yet another phenomenon was the emergence of superpowers. Some states had accumulated so much power, particularly military power, that they could operate all over the world. Essentially, there were just two superpowers, the USA and the USSR. Both believed they had global interests; they had to intervene in every situation to checkmate the other. Their relative strength was determined by their willingness and capacity to invest their resources into escalating development of nuclear weaponry—one might extend it to nuclear weaponology. No other state could match the range, accuracy and lethality of their weapons, as they alone had the power to destroy the world many times over.

But they became overextended. In certain situations they could not used all the awsome power that they possessed. There were limits to the use of their prowess. The Americans got the experience of this mortification in Vietnam and the Soviets later in Afghanistan.

Synchronously, other trends were emerging. It was not just overextension that was hurting the superpowers, it was also overinvestment in newer and smarter weapon-technology and weaponry. Consequently, for the first time, a dissonance developed between military power and economic power. Germany and Japan began rising as economic giants. The share of the USA in world production declined from 40 per cent to 20 per cent and Japan's economy reached an incredulous $2.8 trillion mark. Certain other countries notched up accelerated economic growth in the late 1970s and 1980s. This included not only industrial Europe but also countries like South Korea, Thailand, Singapore, Taiwan and Hong Kong.

A Major Qualitative Restructuring

Just when the world was believed to be moving towards pluralism, other qualitative changes took place transforming the world situation. Not only did the superpower-protected countries with replicas of the system tumble one after another, but even more incredibly a superpower itself began disintegrating. Mikhail Gorbachev's 'perestroika' and 'glasnost' shook not just the capitalist world but the socialist world too; and finally Gorbachev himself. Few would have anticipated the collapse of the Soviet Union and its splitting into 13 independent countries apart from the three Baltic states that broke away earlier. One American academic foe of communism called it the end of history.

This is not the occasion for any systematic and detailed analysis of why the socialist world broke up. Suffice it to say that politically the system was too backward for the times and economically too ahead of the times. In any case, the collapse of the socialist world was an event of tremendous magnitude underlying *a basic disorder* in the international system. The Tiananmen uprising in Beijing and the internal uprisings in various republics of the erstwhile Soviet Union were evidence of the deep-seated maladies and the continuing problems. The process was taken by some as the end of history as they believed the last cold war was the last ideological confrontation in which socialism had lost and capitalism had triumphed. To others, this appeared to provide an opportunity for creating a new world order as a consequence of the end of the cold war. To still others, it meant the defeat of Russia and the reassertion of the United States as "the only superpower" in the world. Each of them was, perhaps, looking at the multi-faceted reality from distorted angles and coloured prisms.

It shattered many old myths and created new ones. And then came the Gulf War. Gulf War represented both the ambition and latent turbulence in the region. President Saddam Hussein tried to enact the role of a superman. There was no justification for the annexation of Kuwait which was a member of the United Nations. But an important underlying issue was oil, its supply, availability and control. Overlaid were the Arab-Israeli disputes and the clash of President Saddam Hussein's ambition in the region against the assertion of American supremacy.

Iraq fought a wrong war on a wrong issue and had the entire international community either against it or paralysed into helpless passivity.

The promise that detente held had almost gone awry. It turned into a demonstration of the withering away of the Soviet Union and the strength of the United States. The world also witnessed an inflated rise of American nationalism. The threat of a unipolar world loomed large. All countries were being made to pay the price for the Gulf War and the American claim to leadership. The Third World has since been treated with indifference. The Republics of the Erstwhile Soviet Union are the recipients of patronising assistance from the West. Germany and Japan were presented with angry demands to fork out more money for the Western military involvements. In fact, a major share of the cost of war was met by these and some other countries, including Saudi Arabia.

The Emergence of Sole Superpower

As an American analyst put it, "America has embarked on an aggressive assertion of strategic independence; the deployments in the Persian Gulf represent a new birth of ambitious American unilateralism, appropriate to the status of the sole remaining superpower, as is heard repeatedly these days." The content of the new Bush doctrine would be that the United States, as the lone superpower survivor of the Cold War, could afford to retrench somewhat in its tangible military power and defence budgets but would still need to keep a great deal of force in order to wield decisive influence. This interpretation "harbours an actual disdain by the United States for allies and for the processes of international organisations, but it masks such attitudes in the rhetoric and institutions of collective security."

Many American academics believe that there are influential sections in Washington, who, in the wake of the disappearance of the bipolar competition with the Soviet Union and with the end of the Soviet Union as it existed earlier, believe that the U.S. strategy could now be directed to active intervention to resolve conflicts in other regions on terms favourable to American interests, and that those interests themselves were to be defined broadly as the maintenance of "stability" and "order" in all regions of the world.

This was, indeed, the message contained in what was supposed to be a confidential document prepared in the Pentagon, but became highly publicised with its leakage in the *New York Times*. The American administration tried to pass it off as a low-level position paper that did not have the sanction of the highest level policy-makers. It was, however, far from the truth.

The truth was that it was a 46-page document prepared at a senior level under the supervision of Paul D. Wolfowitz, the Pentagon's Under Secretary for Policy, in consultation with senior national security advisers of the President as well as with the National Security Council. The document of the Defence Department asserted that the U.S. political and military mission in the post-Cold War era would be to ensure that no rival superpower was allowed to emerge in Western Europe, Asia or the territory of the former Soviet Union.

The document was to be released by the Defence Secretary, Dick Cheney, later but its premature leakage and the furore it created led to an official disclaimer stating that it had yet to be approved by the President an his senior colleagues. There need be no doubt that the thesis presented in the document reflects at least one very strong view within the U.S. administration and the administration-associated academia. The document would warn that a part of the U.S. mission should be "convincing potential competitors that they need not aspire to a greater role or pursue a more aggressive posture to protect their interests". It makes the case for a world dominated by one superpower whose position could be perpetuated by constructive behaviour and sufficient military might to deter any nation or group of nations from challenging the U.S. supremacy.

To perpetuate this role, the United States was asked to be prepared to "sufficiently account for the interests of the advanced industrial nations to discourage them from challenging our leadership or seeking to overturn the established political and economic order."

As was noted by the *New York Times*, with its focus on this concept of benevolent domination by one power, the Pentagon document "articulates the clearest rejection to-date of collective internationalism, the strategy that emerged from World War II when the five victorious powers sought to form a United Nations that could mediate disputes and police outbreaks of violence."

Implicitly as well, the Pentagon position foresees building up of a world security arrangement that would preempt Germany and Japan from pursuing the course of substantial rearmament, especially nuclear armament, in the future. Hence it places a strong emphasis on using military force, if necessary, to prevent the proliferation of nuclear weapons and other weapons of mass destruction in such countries as North Korea, Iraq, some of the former Soviet Republics and Europe.

It states quite bluntly that the world order "is ultimately backed by the U.S." and that "the United States should be postured to act independently when collective action cannot be orchestrated" or in a crisis that demands quick response.

The Indian newspapers have published those parts of the documents which ask for a constructive military relationship with Pakistan and for restraining what the document describes as Indian hegemonistic ambitions.

Skewed Order to Disorder

Undoubtedly, the world is an considerable disorder and there is no new world order on the horizon as yet that would be universally acceptable. Since the collapse of the Soviet Union. American officials have been busy looking for alternative rationales for U.S. interventionism in a post Cold War world and they have displayed, to use the phraseology of the director of the foreign policy studies at the Washington-based Cato Institute, "an astounding degree of creativity in formulating new missions". They have particularly highlighted two missions for the USA: preserving international "stability" and leading a world-wide movement for democracy. In this scenario, Washington would be either "the social worker" or the "policeman of the planet" or both. Thus the end of the Cold War would usher in not a "peace dividend" but a "defacto peace penalty". He has described the goal of seeking global stability as equivalent to the search for the Holy Grail.

President George Bush had a tremendous opportunity to strive for a new world order based on the United Nations and on justice and equality. As many American analysts have noted, he could have cast himself in the role of Woodrow Wilson or Franklin Delano Roosevelt, who were driven by a vision of a violence-free, just, democratic international order. But influential segments of the U.S. administration seem to have opted for the course advocated by Teddy Roosevelt who believed in the manifest destiny of America.

This seems to conjure up a rather forebidding scenario of one superpower using its whiplash at all others and making them fall in line. The irony is that if this were possible, it would have at least brought about a single world order ruled over by one hegemonic power. But it has little chance of bring successful as the two-super power syndrome was. That is where the duality of the situation lies. There are a large number of corrective, countervailing trends in the United States in the world in general for one-power hegemony to survive or last.

Costs of World Supremacy

For one, history does not afford any example, as many American academics have been quick to concede, that a unipolar world could be sustained for any significant length of time. Historically, the second echelon of countries always tend to come together to counter-balance the power of the hegemon, especially if that hegemonic power becomes overbearing. For another, the costs of attaining such a goal would be unacceptably high for the American people.

There is little to suggest in the U.S. situation that the American people are anxious and willing to undergo the risks and costs that are involved in maintaining the military force levels, expenditures and commitments required for the kind of role that some people are envisioning for the United States. Walter Lipmann had warned that the American foreign policy to survive must be a solvent foreign policy, that is, one that operates at a level of risks and costs that the American people would find acceptable. Already the euphoria of the victory in the Gulf War has quickly faded, as the American people struggle with a sluggish economy and a rising breadline. In a situation in which a high level of unemployment and a real fall in the living standards of close to 40 per cent of population is a fact of life, it is rather wishful to expect that the American public would endorse a hyperactivist U.S. rule that would entangle the country "in multiple conflicts that will cause haemorrhage of lives and wealth."

The Gulf War came in the context of a very peculiar international situation, highly unlikely to be repeated. I am not speaking here of the military aspects, although they are important, but much more of the political and economic dimensions, it is extremely unlikely that subsequent interventions in future conflicts could be as low-cost to the United States as the Gulf War was. Indeed, if they turned out to be difficult and sanguanary, the Vietnam syndrome could once again trouble the American political scene. The expectation that the United States could pursue global "order and democracy" without frequent interventions is too fanciful to believe.

The Gulf War incurred a total expenditure from the Western side of some $61 billion, of which the American contribution totaled only $7 billion. The rest came from the allies of the United States, Germany, Japan, U.K., Saudi Arabia and others. It is questionable that such large contributions would be available in future interventions unless they were seen to be central to the security of the Western alliance countries.

The Countervailing Factors

In addition there are other countervailing trends that cannot be ignored. The hiatus between military power and economic power has only been getting wider and wider. The economic centres of power have moved further away from the military centres. One does not have to underline this point; the whole world knows about the rise of Germany and Japan, and even some other "little dragons" of Asia (South Korea, Taiwan, Singapore, Hong Kong) because they are not carrying the burden of the world on their shoulders. Already many people are talking about the 21st century as the Century of Europe. What is equally significant is that the domestic forces within, say, Germany and Japan are in a large measure against military solutions. In any case, the trends that set their face against military solutions in those countries are stronger than those which would like to use economic muscle for other purposes. The hawks in the Pentagon could find themselves stymied by domestic opinion in the United States as well as in Germany and Japan.

Add to this the economic difficulties that are troubling not only the United States but have begun to surface in Germany and Japan too. In Japan they are already talking about the bursting of the bubble and of recessionary trends in Germany. It is easy to exaggerate these trends but they cannot be ignored. The economic troubles are hardly likely to encourage greater military spending and interventionist trends.

We may also notice in passing what I may call the regionalisation of power. Regional power centres have been arising not always contributing to tranquility in the respective regions. It is hard to imagine one or two big powers being able to suppress all the regional discordancies. There will be a difficulty regional balance of power in the foreseeable future continually challenging the world balance of power.

One might end by nothing that even Russia is an imponderable factor. It may be down and out at present, but it remains to be a huge military power. There is nothing is Russian history to sustain the view that Russia will remain quiescent and subordinate, a junior partner of Washington, for any good length of time. It may take a decade, but the rise of Russia again over the long run can hardly be doubted. It is too early to say what kind of role it would then play.

Thus the world threatens to continue to be restless, disorderly and non-tranquil and a new world order cannot be ushered in by the attempt of any one or two countries to dominate it. Any quest for a just and lasting world order must address itself to the strengthening of the United Nations, its collective action structures, and its reorganisation and democratisation so that it can truly reflect the will of the peoples of the world.

2
Transforming Indian Rural Society:
An Overview

India is subcontinent with fourteen major languages and is divided by several religions, castes and customs. Together with joint family system and village community, these institutions have governed whole gamut of social and economic life of Indian people in the past 'Even amids upheavals, these have served to sustain and retain the basic character of Indian society'. These institutions have been evolved in the long course of history primarily with a purpose to ensure security, stability and survival of the society as a whole rather than of the individual. Any action that threaten these institutions or their status quo met with strong opposition from the whole society or group. It is only after British rule was established that these institutions were called upon to play a role quite different from one for which they were created and maintained viz. progress, change and development. Those which could not adapt to the new role were viewed as inimical to development and in most cases, they were treated so. Consequently, in order to affect change and development host of institutions including those concerning science, technology, education, economic, law, administration, government land tenurial and the like were borrowed from the advanced countries and transplanted in the Indian soil. This has provided a parallel and sometimes conflucting structure of institutions whose roots lie somewhere else in the Western world. As expected, they being alien to the Indian people, were not only opposed but proved relatively far less effective than in the country of their origin. The roots of failure and ineffectiveness, if any, therefore, can be traced in basic attributes of their parent society.

The interaction that took place over the years between alien and native institutions has generated a process of change and accommodation on the past of both and redefinition of role of each vis-a-vis the other. In this, the process of accommodation to the alien institutions as also to the newly emerged needs of the society proved more painful for the native institutions. The constitutional provisions, legislative measures, planned development strategies and similar developments introduced after attaining Independence have all made it necessary to induce fundamental alteration in the character and function of the existing institutions, so that these may better serve for achieving the goal of rapid economic development with social justice, the one we set for ourselves.

How far these institutions have been able to bring fundamental change in their character and to what extent these have worked as instruments of social change and development rather than survival and security is a matter of serious controversy. But the fact remains that the present period in India's long history signifies a period of profound transition in the institutional structure and in the relationship this structure has with Indian Society and its stability or change. The colonial theorists often argue that since the inherited institutional structure, which were evolved for an altogether different purpose, is not suited to the task of bringing social change and achieving economic development, it should be radically transformed.

It is in this perspective, that India's plans from the very beginning set for themselves the twin-goals of economic growth and social justice to be attained through structural transformation of society and economy, what is popularly known as the "Socialistic pattern of society." It is assumed that the two goals are inseparable and that neither of the two can be achieved independently through in practice one may receive primacy over the other. Pandit Nehru, the architect of the economic planning in India also viewed the existing socio-economic structure inimical to achieve the aforesaid goal and noted. Our economic and social structure have outlived their days and it has become a matter for us to refashion them so that they may promote the happiness of all our people in things material and spectial...we must aim of class less society based on cooperative effort with opportunities for all."[1]

In order to bring such a structural transformation, two sets of forces are commonly recognised: external and internal. Scholars, however, differ about their relative role. In fact, the stability and change in the Indian society were greatly influenced by both external and internal factors and more and more social scientist have come to hold this view though it may not be easy for them to isolate their effects because of close interlinkages between them.[2] For examples, those holdings external factors responsible for the Indian society's development or underdevelopment would agree that the inequalities based on caste and class were not invented by the Britishers nor they much to transform them. What they infact contributed was the weakening of the unity and solidarity of the village communities through privatisation of landholdings, destruction of rural crafts and improverishment of artisans. The influence on regional inequalities is better demonstrated through the differential policies pursued by the Britishers in different parts of India. Punjab and Bihar are known to have good resource base for agriculture but today former turned into the riches and the latter poorest among the Indian States. The clue to these differences despite similar starting point lies in different policies pursued in respect of the two States: Punjab came under British Rule in 1849 while Bihar in 1757. In Bihar, Britishers followed the policy of maximisation of tax revenue through ruthless methods which resulted in the concentration of lands in a few hands and increased dependency of landless poor peasants on the land-owners. In Punjab, in contrast, Sikh persisted during 1750-1849 and paved way for relatively equal distribution of land. When Britishers took over Punjab, their main objective was to ensure flow of supply of raw material for their industries in England rather than to maximise the taxes; they rather helped in weakening the power of the large landowners, the process initiated in the Sikh Rule itself.[3] In latter phase, this helped Punjab to reap the benefits of green revolution more than Bihar.

British influence is evident also in the absence of commitment on the part of the dominant ruling classes and weakness of the administrative machinery created for implementing the development programmes. In order to gain first control over the country, Britishers replaced the traditional administrative and legal framework by new type of bureaucratic and legal system with power and responsibility concentrated at the top. Their apathy and attitude were such that without direct intervention or bribery no action was possible. In the post-independence era it inherited almost the same style of functioning. The attempts to change the mould and prejudices of the civil servants and make them capable to cope with the problems has seldom gone beyond peripheral limits.

While laying emphasis on the internal forces, scholars have pointed towards institutional adaptation to the changed requirements or reduction in the socio-economic inequalities and associated exploitative structural arrangements. Those favouring adaptation on the part of existing institutional framework believe that the underlying beliefs and attitudes exert adverse influence on the economic behaviour and thereby retard economic development. Though the ways in which these institutions govern economic behaviour have always been a matter of controversy among social scientists, their influence on almost—all aspects of lives of the Indian people including their attempts for material advancement has been recognised. The notion of 'economic man' is now no longer held valid and the unity of social life is well recognised in which different social, economic, cultural and ethical aspects are inseparably integrated. The Planning Commission, for example, noted: 'The existing social and economic institutions have.....to be appraised from time to time in relation to their role in nations' development. To the extent they...fail to secure the economic aims of planned development they have to be replaced or transformed."[3]

Scholars are however not unanimous about the role of such social forces in the process of economic transformation and industrial development. The major influencing factors that were identified by different social Scientists include, besides others, "relations of individual to society,"[4] secularism, egalitarianism, and nationalism,[5] personality attributes,[6] religion[7] and education.[8] In the context of India's social development, the most widely discussed factors are religious values such as attitudes towards present and life after death, institutional framework of caste and joint family system, social customs, education, regionalism and political factors and institutions.

The social factors affect economic development through influencing human behaviour. In order to satisfy one's desires individuals make efforts which result in promotion of goods and services which are consumed or accumulated for further investment. It is these factors i.e. desires, efforts, production, consumption, saving etc. that result in economic and material advancement and it is these factors which are also affected by religious values and similar other social factors. The religion affects economic development through influencing these factors. The role of religion in development has always been a matter of controversy. Lewis observes: "If religion lays stress upon material values, upon work, upon thrift, and productive investment, upon honestly in commercial relations, upon experimentation and risk bearing, and upon equality of opportunity, it will be helpful to growth whereas in so far as it is hostile to these things, it tends to inhibit growth."[9]

With respect to India, it is generally believed that, Hinduism which is followed by majority of Indians, proved to be an obstacle to economic development through providing such values as ascetism, fatalism, rigidity of castes acceptance of one's status as a result of *Karma* discounting material things and the like.[10]

The Hinduism promotes such values as fatalism, asceticism and other worldness and these are the forces which tend to retard economic development in India. The belief in the theory of *Karma* and cycles of births and rebirth tended to breed fatalistic and helpless attitude. The individual loses confidence in his own abilities and capacities to achieve progress. The thought of transitory nature of life develops feeling of self-contentment and withdrawl that tend to work against economic effort for development. The motivation of pursue economic activity, which is a pre-requisite for development, is generally marred by the non-attachment to worldly things and to the fruits of one's action.

Many, however, argue that religion dues not always act as impediment to developments, it also promotes development. For example, *Gita* has laid emphasis on notion by actively and seriously performing one's duty without expecting reward. The doctrine of *Purushartha* lays stress on *artha* which prescribes acquisition and use of material means for sustaining life. *Karma* is also a part of *purushartha* which urges fulfilment of common desires of body i.e. food, drink and through material means obtained. Weber[11] asserted that India and China would have achieved industrial revolution as quickly as Europe if protestant ethics prevailed there. Though only a few world endorse this view, Myrdal noted retarding role of the religion.[12]

Our social life is greatly influenced by two major social institutions, namely, joint family and caste system and their influence on the process of development has been formidable. The ideal form of joint family system is based on sharing of work and income, among members, acceptance of the authority of the oldest male as the head in the matters of property, marriage etc. joint ownership of property. Reverence or even worshipping of the living as well as dead elders is a part of *Dharma*. According to the doctrine of *Ashrama* (stages of life) to marry and to secure continuity of family life through the birth of a son is a religious duty.

Though joint family system provided security to minors, sick, old and disabled and helped in saving by avoiding wasteful duplication of consumption articles and equipment, it acted against promoting individual initiative and development of self-confidence, the attributes necessary for promoting development. Besides, it promoted idleness and voluntary unemployment and encouraged high fertility rates by placing high values on male child.

Our inability to induct fundamental change in the socio-economic structure particularly in family institution was also responsible for continued and growing unemployment. India's economy is essentially rural with over three-fourth of its labour force concentrated in agriculture. In agriculture as also in cottage and small-scale industries, the traditional joint family system happens to be the unit of operation. All the members of the family are associated in varying degrees with the production process of the family-operated farm or non-farm enterprise. The members tend to adapt themselves to the requirement of the enterprise and earning is often pooled to meet the common needs. Such a family system has important implications for employment pattern. While individual way not be involved in "full time work", he may feel that he is employed even if his withdrawl may not affect produ tion or income. If commonly accepted criteria of unemployment is used, he will be classed as employed since he is not seeking work. However, from economic considerations, he is "unemployed" or what is referred as "disguised unemployment" and magnitude of such unemployment is quite high and growing. This is the case of all the family operated enterprises and no estimate of the problem does take into account this problem. What is often accounted for is the involuntary unemployment which is characteristic of the urban population. Besides, glorification of the role of women as a housewife has also adversely affected the problem of unemployment among them. The employment data suggests that the incidence of chronic employment, those who remained unemployed, throughout the year, is higher among women than among men and higher in urban households than among rural ones. The daily status unemployment was found highest among agricultural labourers and lowest among self-employed households in both farm as well as non-farm sectors.

Another social institution which has contributed great deal in shaping of the socio-economic life of Indian people is the caste system. Though part of Hindu Society, caste system has influenced other religious communities as well. Besides determining social status of different groups in the society, it tends to mould the behaviour pattern of people and regulate interpersonal relations and communication between different groups. The most severe criticism against caste system was made on the ground that it is inimical to economic development. The rigidity between castes and occupations presented occupational mobility which is crucial for economic development and industrial growth. While changes in occupations are needed to improve efficiency based on once capacity and skill they are believed to endanger ones social and caste status. The system also prevented people of certain section from using technologies that may improve health or productivity. It prevents use of bones, right soil and fish as manures; or from killing insects and pests, it also prevents certain scientific faculty from handling of dead animals etc. in laboratories. Adherence to one's occupation is often interfered with supply and demand of labour in the economy and even where there are job opportunities people do not accept work on account of caste prejudices. It is why, there is more unemployment among higher castes. It also obstructs formation of functional groups of workers belonging to different castes.... Besides, polarisation of society, resultant discrimination and segregation based on castes still continues particularly in rural areas. However, some do not agree with the rigid links between caste and occupations particularly in modern times when more and more favourable opportunities are available and people irrespective of their caste affiliations are found in the same occupational category. Organised sectors, agricultural, and army no longer remain prerogative of any one caste. While changes are discernible on the above lines, it is common to find more low caste members working an agricultural labourers or share croppers or performing class IV jobs in offices than those of upper castes.

The problem of social transformation is discussed in terms of an all-inclusive concept of "modernisation" also which is varying defined as technological advancement, institutional innovation or modification and rational value orientation. These interconnected dimensions combine in themselves whole process of economic and industrial development; the economic growth can not be taken achieved without affecting improvement in technology; the adoption the later needs institutional/structural modification of the existing one or creation of the new and human behaviour that is compatible to development demands and these cannot be achieved unless values and attaches of the people undergo fundamental change. In this perspective, Indian traditional institutional framework and other related attributes of Indian society are believed to be inimical to modernisation and therefore needed transformation syndrome.

Associated with the modification or creation of institutional framework is the problem of socio-economic inequality which has always remained in the forefront of any discussion among social scientists as well as development practitioners. All the measures initiated for development address themselves without failing, towards reduction of socio-economic inequalities. This syndrome consists mainly of inequalities of income distribution, landholding and social stratification. Myrdal also noted that the inequality in the rural setting is "mainly question of landownership with such associated leisure, enjoyment of status and authority."[13] The off-repeated issue of inequalities between rich and poor is compounded by the other two forms of inequalities, namely, land distribution and caste and class hierarchies. It is the socio-economic inequality syndrom which is central to widely discussed development models which assumes that it is not so much of development which produces change in the structure as it is the transformation of the structure which permits effective development.[14] "The promotion of social and economic equality" Myrdal also argues. "is a precondition for attaining substantial long term increases in production.[15]

The planning in India, initiated in right earnest, intended to achieve institutional transformation and reduction in socio-economic inequalities while seeking rapid development. In pursuance of the constitutional provisions and Directive principles of State policy on the subject, our Five Year Plans set for themselves the goal of achieving rapid economic growth and reducing economic inequalities. The draft Fourth Plan emphatically states: "the basic goal is a rapid increase in the standard of living of the people......emphasis is placed on the common man, the weaker sections and the less priviledged......" and the concentration of income, wealth and power should be progressively reduced.[16] The twin-goal was sought to be achieved through such measures as growth of public sector or nationalisation, land reforms and redistributive policy to reduce inequalities in and concentration of income and wealth. In the context of rural areas, this goal was sought to be achieved by launching of a multifaceted community development programme in 1952, a programme of self-governing units of Panchayati Raj institutions with an intent to bring all-round development of the community as a whole. However, its failure on the food front and mounting food crisis resulted in the major shift in the policy in favour of the development of the agriculture alone. The new policy addressed itself to the landed class and the well-endowed regions and groups thus setting the stage for regional imbalance and economic inequalities. In the process, the land reform measures initiated to provide security to tillers and to change the feudal agrarian structure were also relegated to the background and the production gain was sought through application of improved technology. It was somehow wrongly assumed that agriculture, production was independent of production relations. This was also viewed as one of the means to reduce our dependence on advanced countries. The resultant account of the new agricultural strategy was shifted to techno-economic factors and this transition took place with the arrival from Mexico "wonder seed". The approach was peculiar in its selectivity—selection of crops, regions, technology, and even farmers. The result was unbalanced development of regions and increase in disparities between regions and groups.

The techno-economic approach to development, far from removing inequalities, gave rise to a dualistic structure all over viz. urban versus rural, industry versus agriculture, rich versus poor and the like. With each successive plan, this dualistic character, got strengthened. Within agricultural sector, such a structure was deliberately fostered through policy measures in favour of irrigated and well-developed areas and regions covering Punjab, Haryana and Western Uttar Pradesh. The effect of green revolution virtually confined to this region, which, though accounts only for 15 per cent of the total cultivated area, provides over 80 per cent of the total procurement of wheat and rice for central pool. Likewise, the share of the irrigated agriculture which account for only 30 per cent of the total cultivated area, works out to be 57 per cent in the total agricultural produce; the corresponding share of the rest of the 70 per cent rainfed area was only 43 per cent.[17]

The major controversy which has been raging since long concerns with efficacy of the development strategy to alter inherited igantarian socio-economic structure while registering appreciable success in the field of food production, industrial development and other related areas affecting GNP. All evidence suggest that the socio-economic inequalities far from being reduced, have further accentuated as reflected in the distribution of income, landholding, assets, consumer expenditure pattern, and relative contribution of different sectors in the economy and the like.

The pattern of income distribution and respective share of different classes remained more or less unaltered during the process of development.[18] Lydall's estimates showed that in 1955-56 the share of top 20 per cent of the households in national income was 34 per cent as against 9.6 per cent of the bottom 25 per cent of the households. According to Iyngar and Mukherji, top 10 per cent claimed 35 per cent share whereas bottom 24 per cent claimed only 8.5 per cent in 1956-57. Almost same income distribution was noted after two decades i.e. 1975-76 wherein lowest 20 per cent received 7 per cent and top 10 per cent received 40 per cent. The present income distribution is not likely to be very different.

Some structural changes in the economy as a consequence of development are reflected in contribution of various sectors in the national income. In 1950-51, the respective share of primary, secondary and tertiary sectors in GDP was 59.61 per cent, 14.47 per cent and 25.92 per cent; the corresponding figures for 1980-81 were 41.52, 21.60 and 36.92 and for 1985-86, 36.92, 21.92 and 41.16.[19]

Evidently, with development there has been a corresponding decline in the share of primary sector and rapid rise in the share of tertiary or service sector. However, the share of industrial sector did register increase but not in proportion with which the share of primary sector declined. The sluggish growth of industrial sector becomes more glaring when construction, electricity, gas and water supply, presently included in this sector, are treated as part of services sector as done in many advanced countries. In that event, the services sector would account for about 46 per cent of GDP in 1985-86. It is the growth of this sector which has benefitted the middle class more than any other group and this is the main reason also of the rise of this class. In this, the inter-relationship between ruling middle class and country's economic structure can also be discerned in which both have worked in the interest of each other throughout the process of development.

The experience of industrially advanced national revealed that the increased development is followed by gradual shift of work force from agricultural sector to industrial and service sectors. However, no major change has taken place in India in this regard. Since 1921, the sectoral composition of labour force in agriculture remained more or less stagnant despite rapid growth of industrialisation in the country. The Sixth Five Year Plan noted with concern: "It is historically unique fact that over the last six decennial Censuses, in spite of impressive development of large scale manufacturing and infrastructure sectors, the share of agriculture in the work force has not diminished at all. It was 73% in 1921, 73% in 1961 and 73% in 1971.[20] In almost all countries, economic development is associated with a significant decrease in this share. Even during the decade 1965-75, the share declined in 13 Asian countries. But in India, fairly rapid growth in the non-agricultural sectors in the last 25 years of planned development has completely failed to make any noticeable impact on the industrial distribution of workforce."

The extreme inequalities found in the distribution of landownership also did not register any decline since mid-fifties: 22 per cent owned no land at all; another 25 per cent owned less than one acre; another 14 per cent owned uneconomic or marginal holdings ranging from 1.0-2.5 acres.

This means, majority of households comprising 61 per cent either owned to land or uneconomic and marginal holdings of one acre or less comprising of only 8 per cent of the total area. Most of these are unemployed or underemployed and living at the subsistence level or below. It contrast, the upper 13 per cent of the all households owning more than 10 acres of land owned about 64 per cent of total area and upper 5 per cent with 20 acres or more own 41 per cent of the area.[21]

The, poverty estimates are quite often made in terms of money, changes in poverty are essessed also in terms of ownership and distribution of assets, consumer expenditures, employment etc.[22] For example, Seventh Plan noted decline in proportion of people below poverty line from 48.3 in 1978-79 to 36.9 in 1984-85 and is likely to come down further to 25.8 by 1989-90 but evidence showed that despite this, the inequality measured in terms of ownership of assets or consumer expenditures has either persisted or is likely to increase. Percentage distribution of assets of rural and urban households as revealed by 37th roujd of NSS (July 1981 to June 1982) showed that 40 per cent of the households with assets worth less that Rs. 10,000 owned just 4.3 per cent of total assets; in contrast, only 8.4 per cent of households owing assets worth Rs. 1 lakh and over owned as much as 48.4 per cent of assets. The asset distribution in 1981-82 was not only highly skewed, but over the period of two decades, the distribution pattern does not show any improvement. The inequality appears to have increased when measured with reference to the pattern of consumer expenditures of rural households.[23] The share of lower 50 per cent of households, in total consumer expenditure has declined from 33.1 per cent in 1971-72 to 31.3 per cent in 1983. In contrast, the share of upper 30 per cent during the period increased from 45.5 to 49.8 per cent. The deterioration in the structure of land ownership and composition of rural labour force was also noted. The percentage of marginal holdings (1 ha. and below) in the total operational holdings has increased from 50.6 in 1970-71 to 56.5 in 1980-81. At this rate, the percentages of small and marginal holdings (2 ha. and below) in total operated land which was 74.5 in 1980-81 will not be less that 85 or 90 by the end of this century.

Our failure to accommodate the increased labour force as owners or operators of land is also brought out by the fact that between 1973 and 1983, there has been a progressive and sustantial decline in the proportion of male workers in the self-employment category. Clearly, there has been a progressive rise in the share of wage labour in the work-force from 34 per cent to 40 per cent in case of males and from 36 per cent to 38 per cent among females. Another significant trend is growing casualisation of wage labour; the tendency being more pronounced among males; male casual labourers as a proportion of male wage labourers rose from 64 per cent in 1972-73 to 73 per cent in 1983.[24] While assessing the employment effects of the new technology, Parathasarthy[25] has noted that the wage labour and its casualisation is on the increase primarily because of the entry of marginal farmers and artisans in the labour market. The evidence are also available of the declining trends in labour absorption effects of new farm technology as measured in terms growing unemployment and increasing employment per unit area under HYV.

Evidently, the land reforms and other measures introduced from time to time also did not result in any discernible improvement of the rural poor as a whole. Besides class-based inequalities are manifested also in differential skills, education, power and authority etc. In addition, caste system has also made co-operative effort and solidarity difficult. Though caste does not ensure economic ranking, it tends to influence rights to land and attitudes towards ownership. Despite some mobility in the system, landless share owners and workers seldom move upward. Thus caste and class-based inequalities tend to reinforce each other.[26]

The experience of Green Revolution particularly of Punjab indicates that growth is not synonymous with development and that a technologically-fulled growth model, when superimposed on a society based on inequality, led large farmers to expend their economic base despited land ceilings and drive poor farmers into landless category, thus increasing polarisation in the countryside in view of inherent contradictions in the development. Scholars lamented that the whole approach represents a circuitous route to rural development i.e. first to create disparities and then to launch target-group oriented programmes to reduce these disparities.[28] Evidently development strategy adopted India to has failed in general to transform the socio-economic structure, explained by the thesis advanced by *Sinha* at all which states that a direct attack on povery without an equally direct attact on structure, which had bred poverty and continues to do so, is illusion at best, a fraud at worst.[29] The recent studies lent support to this.[30] The structural change asserts, Dantwala does not involve land reforms or land distribution; beside there are several policy and other measures which can make agrarian structure more agalitarian. These include other assets, skill etc. as will.[31] However, no marked change took place in these respects.

Scheduled Castes and Scheduled Tribes constitute two most important underdeveloped communities. In the past they were always subjected to exploitation and assigned low social status in the society. The development goals include improvement in their status also. There have been several attempts made to improve their socio-economic conditions including special development programmes in addition to constitutional and legislative measure. However, their continued backwardness becomes evident when we find that over half of the working population of scheduled castes work as labourers and 28 per cent as farmers. Among those classified as agricultural labourers in 1971, about one-third belonged to scheduled castes, far above their strength in the total population. Further, as against 59 for general population only 36 per thousand persons from scheduled castes were in the industrial sector and 13 per thousand in trade and industry as against 36 for the country as a whole. The policy of reservation also did not benefit them much. This becomes clear when we find that the representation of scheduled castes in classes I, II, III and IV services in 1964 were 1.64%, 2.82%, 8.88% and 17.75% respectively, this was improved in 1980 with respective percentage of 4.83%, 8.07%, 11.54% and 19.16%. Thus, they are concentrated more in class IV service followed by class III.

The incidence of landlessness among scheduled caste agricultural households was also highest in Northern states with 83.3 per cent of them having no land. Despite their higher proportion in Punjab and Haryana, they are essentially landless with about 93 per cent of them landless.

Development could not help them much even in increasing literacy rates where they lag far behind the general population. For the two communities, respective literacy rates were found to be 21.38 and 16.35 in 1981 as against 36.23 for the general population. Disparities and literacy rates are far more glaring with regard to the female population. In 1971, only 6.4 per cent females of the scheduled castes were literate as against 18.7 per cent literate females in the country.

By initiating different measures to improve the conditions of scheduled castes and to remove social disabilities and discrimination it was often assumed that the problem in theory is solved. This view is reflected in abandoning the recording of caste in censuses and other occasions, viewing caste as deterimental to development, belief among the educated among urbanised folk about the disappearance of caste system. However, this is far from the reality, Srinivas[32] opined that developed programmes and its benefits have given rise to an unknown competition among beneficiaries to be classified as backward" for figuring in the list of beneficiaries and by its reckoning, about three-quarters of our people may be backward.

One of the ways often used to bring about socio-economic transformation in India was to expand education. A commandable headway has been made over the years in providing educational facilities at all levels. The annual growth rate of education at different levels suggests a remarkable progress over ten years (1960-70): 5.4% of primary and middle level, 7.1% at secondary level and 11.0% at college level.[33]

In view of the assumed high correlation between education and economic development a mixed response in Indian case is perplexing. It is generally believed that education, besides modernising outlook tends to build up capacity for positive economic activity but this did not happen. There are about 55000 unemployed engineers in India and only 30 per cent of the total technical manpower is gainfully employed. Many attribute such a consequence to "overproduction" of graduates. Being unemployed these graduates could not contribute anything to economic development.

Two significant and disquieting tendencies have emerged regarding unemployment of educated manpower: (1) rate of unemployment of educated manpower: (1) rate of unemployment paradoxically tended to increase with the level of education, i.e., unemployment was greater among college educated than among holders of high on higher secondary school diploma,[34] and (2) rate of unemployment tended to increase also with economic development, increased industrialisation and growth of tertiary sector. In other words, there is no decline in the educated employees. This suggests that the expansion of education beyond secondary level does not contribute much to bring economic transformation. What is needed is to assess the requirement of developmental tasks and match them with the needed number of educated persons. The number to be passed out should not be allowed to exceed the demand for requisite skills and services. However, no effort has so far been made to change the educational system towards making it conducive to socio-economic development.

Thus, during the plan period, economic imbalances have been intensified which is manifested in dualism all around: the development of metropolitan centres as 'growth poles' with simultaneous existence of vast tract of backward areas; sophisticated and advanced technologies in strategic and goods industries existing with primitive type of agriculture; minority group of elites and professionals emulating western life style with a vast group of poverty stricken and rustic population and some industrial show-pieces and "prestige projects" with ill-organised sector of village and small-scale industries. This divides the country into the zones of poverty and prosperity. The social implications of this state of affairs are more dangerous than economic. Already unrest and agitations among deprived classes have become matter of concern. Apparently, all the classes seem to have benefited from development particularly from green revolution but the relative gains accrued to them became a bone of contention. Large farmers evidently gained in term of increased production and thereby incomes; with profits from cultivation rising, they tended to lease in more land than lease out; those who lease out some land now demand high rents as compared to past; because of higher production per unit, sharecroppers are now offered lower share of produce instead of half.

The situation of the landless agricultural labourers at a first glance looks more favourable. Intensive cropping, increased irrigation, labour intensive practices and diversification of cropping have created additional demand of labour and this provided landless work for longer periods in a year. This has also shot up wage rates and bargaining capacity of the labour. More the labour asserted for higher wages more landowners became resentful of labourers' blackmailing tactics: land-owners, while agreeing to pay higher wages have often retaliated by applying other economic pressures, important among them are: (i) denying labourers to take fodder from the fields, (ii) refusal to allow to take agricultural waste as fuel; (iii) withdrawal of additional payments in kind particularly vegetables from the fields, and (iv) refusal to advance interest free loans which was a usual practice in the past. A far more serious consequence has been the determined attempt of the land-owners to make all kinds of payments in cash instead of kind interview of the rising prices of grain and other agricultural produce. Equally serious is the diseparate attempt of the landowners to mechanise as quickly as possible farm operations and to get ride of their dependence on the labourers. The extent landowners succeeded in their attempts, labourers will have lost their major advantage accured from green revolution.

Our failure to transform Indian Society as envisaged can be explained through the paradox with which our plans suffer. While there had been continued emphasis on the promotion of cottage and small scale industries to increase employment opportunity, process of mechanisation and labour saving measures were allowed unchecked thereby reducing the growth of employment. Likewise while justifying mechanisation of agricultural on the ground of promoting multiple cropping in Punjab, Haryana and Western Uttar Pradesh the use of labour displacing machines for other operations provides no rationale.

It would, however, be wrong to say that there has been no progress since Independence in improving the over all conditions of the poor masses. The provision of educational and health facilities development of roads and communication and growth of industries etc. have had positive effects on the conditions of the poor. But what is of crucial significance is the fact that despite many-sided developments, the goal of socio-economic transformation of the society still remains a far cry.

The explanation of continued poverty is often provided in the political process typified by both internal and external forces. India is among a few nations known to practice democratic rule since its Independence. Different conceptions of the democracy view it as an instrument to provide solutions which express the interests of the majority of the electorate. In India, rural and urban poor constitute the single largest group but the functioning of democracy hardly reflects the interests of the poor thereby suggesting its failure. It is mainly so because rural poor are dependent for their livelihood on the elites. This dependence gives the elites power to decide the voting of the poor as well and thereby paralyse the political system and prevent any reform that threatens their position. Preventing taxation of surplus agriculture and implementation of land reforms provides evidence to this effect. The failure of the poor to challenge the hegemony of the land owing elites lies in the internal cleavages among the poor based on caste dividing Harijan poor from members of the backward and other castes and classes. Frankel observes, "The poor peasantry who had numbers on their side, found it impossible to built across kinship, caste and functional groups for common political action in larger areas when their own fortunes inside the village were still intimately tied to good relations with members of the landowing elites"[35] Many attribute the problem to the weakness of the poor, economically, organisationally and politically. Some doubt if the increased political awareness and strength among the poor, if it is realised at all can be effectively used to promote their interest against the wishes of the powerful social forces. It is why many advocate in favour of non-democratic options to effect structural reforms favouring the poor.[36]

The picture is not, however, completely static. The government programmes, expansion of education, outside exposure etc. have contributed in varying degrees to overcome the cultural impediments and to improve the conditions of the poor. Many of these elements are of internal origin. The external factors have only strengthened or weakened these elements. It is, therefore, argued that a direct attack on poverty without a direct attack on inegalitarian structure and traditional institutional framework, which bred poverty and under development, is not going to yield desired results. "The promotion of social and economic equality," argues Myrdal, "is a precondition for attaining substantial long term increases in production."[37]

REFERENCES

1. Cf. Uppal, J.S. (1975), *India's Economic Problems*, Tata-McGraw Hill, New Delhi, pp. 144-45.
2. Sorensen, George (1988), "Internal and External Interwined: Five Obstacles to Development in India", *G.N.D. Journal Society*, 9(1), April 24-25.
3. Govt. of India (1961), Third Five Year Plan, Planning Commission, New Delhi, p. 8.
4. Parsons, Talcott (1951), *Towards a General Theory of Action*, Harvard University Press, Cambridge.
5. Kuznets, Simson (1966), *Modern Economic Growth*, Yale University Press, New Heaven.
6. Hagen, E. (1962), *On Theory of Social Change; How Economic Growth Begins*, Dorsey Press, Homewood; Mc Cleland, Davis (1961) *The Achieving Society*, D. Van Nostrand, Princeton.
7. Weber, Max (1956), *Protestant Ethic and Spirit of Capitalism*, Shriber, New York; Tawney, R.H. (1952), *Religion and Rise of Capitalism*, Harcourt and Brass, New York.
8. Denison E. (1962), *The Structure of Economic Growth in the U.S. and the Alternative Before the U.S.*, Committee for Economic Development, New York.
9. Lewis, W.A. (1963), *The Theory of Economic Growth*, Unwin, London.
10. Singer, M. (1968), "Religion and Social Change in India: The Max Weber Thesis Phase Three *"Economic Development and Cultural Change"* 14(4), July 1-3, Srinivas, M.N. (1968), A note on Mr. Goheens note *"Economic Development and Cultural Change"*, October: 3-6; Karve, D.C. (1958), "Comments", Economic Development and Cultural Change, Vol. 7, October 7-9.
11. Weber Max (1956), op. cit.
12. Myrdal, Gunner (1968), *Asian Drama: An Inquiry into the Poverty of Nations*, Pantheon, New York.
13. Ibid.
14. Frank, A.G. (1967), "Capitalism and Underdevelopment in Latin America; Historical Studies of Chile and Brazil," *Monthly Review.*, Press, New York.
15. Myrdal, Gunner (1968), op. cit.
16. Govt. of India (1969), Fourth Five Year Plan, Planning Commission, New Delhi.
17. Bhatia, B.M. (1990), India's Political Economy since Independence, *Hindustan Times*, Republican Day Feature, Dated 26.1.1990.
18. Bhatia, B.M. (1990), Ibid.
19. Bhatia, B.M. (1990), Ibid.
20. Govt. of India (1980), Sixth Five Year Plan, Planning Commission, New Delhi.
21. Frankel, Francis (1978), India's Political Economy, 1947-77. The Gradual Revolution, Princeton.
22. Rath, N. (1988), "A note on possible numbers of poor people and households in Rural India in 1988-89" in *National Seminor on Poverty Alleviation*, Department of Rural Development, Govt. of India, New Delhi.
23. Dandekar, V.M., (1986), "Agriculture. Employment, and Poverty, *Economic and Political Weekly*, 21 (38 and 39), September 20-27.
24. Dantwala, M.L. (1986), Equality: The Forgotton Ideal, 2nd National Conference of Indian Association of Social Science Institutions, Ahmedabad.
25. Parthasarthy, G. (1988), "Poverty, Alleviation Programmes: Lessons of the Past and Issues for the Future" in *National Seminar on Poverty Alleviation*, Ibid.
26. Beteille, Andre (1969), *Caste, Class and Power Changing Patterns of Stratification in Tanjore Village*, Oxford University Press, Bombay; Dak, T.M. (1982), *Social Inequalities and Rural Development*, National Publishing Houses, New Delhi; Myrdal (1968), op. cit.
27. Haque, Wahidual, Mehra, Niranjan, et. al. (1977), "Towards a Theory of Rural Development, *Development Dialogue*, 2, p. 23.
28. Frankel, Francis (1972), *India's Green Revolution: Economic Gain and Political Cost*, Princeton University Press, New Jersey.

29. Sinha, R., et al. (1979), *Income Distribution, Growth and Basic Needs in India*, Croom Helm, London.

30. Dak, T.M. (1982), *op. cit.*

31. Dantwala, M.L. (1986), *op. cit.*

32. Srinivas, M.N. (1962), *Caste in Modern India and Other Essays*, Asia Publishing House, London, p. 40.

33. United Nations (1963), *Economic Survey of Asia and Far East*, Bangkok, p. 40.

34. Govt. of India (1981), *op. cit.*, 1980-85, p. 206.

35. Frankel, Francis (1978), *op. cit.*

36. Petras, James (1978), *Critical Perspectives on Imperialism and Social Class in the Third World*, New York, p. 73.

37. Myrdal Gunnar (1968), *op. cit.*

3

Contemporary Social Transformation in India: Processes and Contradictions

Significant changes have taken place in India since the four decades of Independence. These changes offer today numerous challenges. Their analysis is necessary to evaluate and to set out new policy directions to augment the processes of change. The social sciences are, however, at their weakest in formulating a 'theory' of social change. They have achieved substantial credibility in postulating a theory of social structure, forms of kinship, family, linguistic structures and modes of economy. In the analysis of change, however, social scientists encounter formidable challenges.

To understand the sociological dimensions of change in India it is necessary to grasp the concrete process of restructuration going on in society. These processes have been set in motion under specific historical contexts of social forces, public policy and national ideology. Historical social forces define the initial social conditions from which the processes of social transformation and restructuration began in India. One has to draw both from history and sociology in order to understand the shape of these initial conditions. Its main feature has been the principle of inter-structural autonomy in the social system. The concerned main structures are social stratification, political system and cultural ideology.

Caste comprises the central principle of social stratification, and traditionally it enjoyed a great deal of internal autonomy. Being regional in character, the caste panchayats functioned as relatively autonomous economic, cultural and judicial systems well upto the nineteen-thirties. Only in exceptional circumstances did the members of a caste go in for appeal to the institutions of the state (king) for redressal of grievances. The relationship between the state and the representatives of the cultural tradition, the priests, was also governed by relative autonomy. Indian polity was never a theodicy; it always accommodated plural cultural and religious traditions. The process of social charge ushered in by British rule set in motion social and cultural dynamics that started a reorganisation of this pattern.

Social Resilience and Change

The inter-structural autonomy of the social components in traditional Indian society has deeply influenced the nature and direction of its social change. Their role could be evaluated through various stages of historical transformation. The first stage coincided with the beginning of the Western contact through British Rule which set the pace for cultural renaissance, initial industrialisation and the growth of a new political consciousness culminating in the national freedom movement.

These forces brought about major changes in Indian society, especially in the areas of institution-building for a civic society, the growth of modern education and judicial-administrative structures. It was marked paradoxically by a process of de-industrialisation and ruralisation of the economy on the one hand and the emergence of a colonial mode of industrialisation and modernisation on the other. These innovations convulsed the traditional social structure, led to the downward mobility of several privileged classes and families and the upward mobility of others drawn from the traditional business classes and feudal nobility. The social mobility created new classes of educationist, administrators, professionals, businessmen, company agents and others who took advantage of the opportunities available in the early phases of colonial transformation.

The emergence of these social groups, together with the cultural awakening and reform movements in various parts of the country, prepared the ground for political awareness and the national movement. This became a potent source of social and ideological mobilisation Intensifying the sense of collective self-awareness. The strategy not only for political independence but social, economic and cultural modernisation of society was evolved. The emphasis on the involvement of women, members of the weaker sections, peasants and workers reflected this ideological perspective. Political leadership at the local, regional and national level emerged. Leadership also emerged from among the weaker sections, women and tribal groups.

A substantial section of the middle classes comprising of educationist, professionals, bureaucrats and businessmen had already set forth a new process of social mobility. This process of change, however, had a segmentary character. It did not affect large parts of the rural peasantry, working classes, scheduled castes and tribes. The national movement too, in many ways, had a segmentary character, despite periods of mass mobilisation. This is being highlighted by recent studies in subaltern history. The tiner-structural autonomy of the Indian social system was possibly responsible for this. It made it possible that selective modernisation could take place. Among with enclaves of rapid social transformation it left massive areas of society untouched by winds of change.

This elitist or segmentary nature of social change had its positive features. It helped galvanise social energies of the people to fight against foreign rule without maximising internal schisms. The British policy of divide and rule only partially succeeded. The evolution of a constitutional and democratic strategy of social transformation has been possible also due to this social feature. It kept the pace of transformation within the tolerance limit of culture and society. The process of change could start and filter down without a major breakdown in the social structure, and without the loss of cultural identity.

Independence and New Forces of Change

The strategy of social change after independence underwent fundamental changes. The state took upon itself the responsibility of conscious planning of social transformation. Its objectives were the creation of a society based on democratic political participation, social justice and cultural and religious pluralism within the framework of a secular state. Steps were taken to abolish institutions which traditionally perpetuated exploitation and inequality. A policy framework was introduced to strengthen institutions which served the objectives of justice in society. It meant also the abolition of the age-old principles of inter-structural autonomy in Indian society. The principles of inequality based on caste, birth, religion and sex were, in a normative sense, derecognised, if not successfully abolished. The new institutions which sought to replace them implied changes in society which had very revolutionary implications.

The Constitution of India broadly lays down these objectives. In some areas the policy of change began to show immediate results. These were electoral politics, agrarian reforms, industrial and economic expansion and investment in education, science and technology. All these coincided with an expanding role of communication and media participation. Electoral politics, apart from its liberating psychological effects on the mind of people, released new social energy in society. This was compounded by the abolition of intermediary rights in land and the introduction of panchayat raj and community development schemes in the villages. The rural areas were this exposed to major forces of social change.

Social Development and Inequalities

However, the nature of social change in India's village during the fifties and sixties indicates an uneven impact on its social structure. The domination of the traditional castes and classes continued despite social and economic reforms. The lectoral challenges from the lower castes, the ex-tenantry, working classes and the weaker sections did not alter the traditional power structure. The benefits of extension work in agriculture, animal husbandry, irrigation, marketing, credit and cooperative were monopolised by the traditional upper caste rich strata. More significant changes in the power structure of the rural society took place in the southern states than in the northern ones, because of the differences in caste demography. In this region too, spectacular patterns of changes emerged later as a investment made during the fifties and sixties matured in the seventies and eighties. Social mobility during the first two decades after independence was slow and mainly confined to the upper castes and classes. The poorer sections of peasantry, agricultural workers and Harijans did feel the liberating impact of the new reforms, psychologically, and in some measure culturally but their overall impact on their social status and power and income remained marginal.

Similar processes had been taking place in urban centres. The urban change during this period has been termed as 'over urbanisation.' It meant city-ward migration of population without its occupational integration in the urban industrial work force. It led to urban degradation, exploitation and impoverishment. The increase in entrepreneurship and industrial investment was confined to the upper classes. The opportunities of education, especially in science, technology, medicine and professions continued to be the preserve of the privileged groups. Some openings were, however, found by the agricultural labourers, peasants, scheduled castes and tribes to send their children to the primary and secondary schools and a very small proportion of them went to colleges or institutions of higher education. Few among them could survive upto the university level of education. Socio-logically, however, even the school and college drop-outs severed an important function later as catalysers of social, economic and cultural change in their society.

Change and Social Structuration

Thus, the changes during the first two decades after independence were also segmentary as in the past. There were, however, some major differences; the scope and potential of the social transformation now was much larger and the aspiration for social mobility had ceased to be segmentary. It had assumed a truly structural dimension engulfing the whole of society. This, with the rising population, preponderance of the young in society, greater political participation, exposure to the media, such as radio, newspapers magazines and public meetings led to a new social and political awareness. The welfare policies of reservations for the scheduled castes and tribes, land reforms and developmental planning led to the emergence of a category of people from among the lower strata who were self-conscious of their deprivation, could assume a leadership role for their community and mobilise them for organisation and protest.

The release of these social forces also coincided with major investment in science and technology, in agriculture industry and health. The cumulative result of these showed results during the seventies and eighties. In many rural regions there took place the 'green-revolution', and the rise of new peasant middle classes. In the urban-industrial domain a new mercantile entrepreneurial class has emerged. However, in the realm of culture and national ideology, the values of secularism, social justice, consensus and participation have increasingly come under strain. These spell out serious consequences for the political culture and its future in India. We have to understand these forces, redefine our strategies and plan for the future.

Today, the changes in rural India, which constitutes the dominant sector of our society, are bringing about a process of rapid social restructuration. It is leading to a breakdown in the segmentary mode of social change, a rise of new middle classes to power, massive absorption of science and technology in agriculture and substantial changes in beliefs. The green revolution signifies not merely growth in agricultural production but also the use of new technology and new social relationships in production processes. These developments make this phase of changes in rural economy and society distinctive. A new interaction among technology, social relationship and culture is now taking place in rural society. This has resulted in social mobility, emergence of new power structure and modes of exploitation of the deprived classes. It has generated new contradictions in society.

Socially, the green revolution has been basically a contribution of the middle caste peasantry, who have had traditionally, a strong attachment to land and agriculture as a mode of work and livelihood. The Jats, Kurmis, Yadavas in the north, the Kunbis, Patels and Patidars in Gujarat, the Maratha in Maharashtra, the Kammas, Reddis and Rajus in Andhra Pradesh, the Vanniyars and Nadars in Tamil Nadu etc., have been the leaders of the green revolution.

It is anchored in the traditional peasant caste structure. Yet, the green revolution marks a basic departure from the traditional pattern. The family made of production continues, but authority has passed from the older to the younger generation. The new agriculture requires the skill in the peasant to negotiate with banks, revenue authorities, police police administration, marketing bodies and block development administration. One is required to consult the experts and technicians for irrigation, soil testing, fertilisers and seeds. This could not be handled with facility by the older generation of peasants. This role is increasingly being performed by the younger generation, college or school educated or even a drop-out from these institutions. This change is also reflected in the panchayat elections and the rural electoral politics in general.

The green revolution has led to the consolidation of the status of the middle peasantry as a dominant class. But the rural poor too have got more organised. They too have now a youthful leadership which deals with agencies of development, political parties and institutions of law and order. The upper caste-class groups who traditionally dominated have now been either replaced by the middle peasantry or have to compete with them to maintain their traditional status and power. They employ a variety of strategies of coopration, compromises and occasional confrontations to remain in power. These triangular sets of social forces in rural society, which are particularly prominent in the northern states lead increasingly to social polarisation, large scale migration to cities, social tensions and erosion of political culture. The quality of relationship between the middle caste peasantry and the lower castes has particularly declined and is marked by exploitation and violence.

The peasantry have had a tradition of Bhakti movements or other reform movements in various parts of the country; their subculture has always had a strong ethic of workmanship, industry, frugality and conservative utilitarianism. These values, combined with the social processes of upward mobility and social political and economic dominance, have given birth to a cultural milieu which is more self-centred and antipathic to values of accommodation and social justice. Their relationship with the agricultural working classes, the lower castes and Harijans is increasingly that of aggressiveness and antipathy. This is being reciprocated by the lower castes working classes as well, leading to a sharp decline in the cultural ethos of the rural society. A situation is emerging in which the dominant classes do not take kindly to policies of protective discrimination and the weaker sections do not accept the legitimacy of such reform measures either. The result is more conflict and less consensus on social issues. This happens when more and more mobility and development is taking place.

We see in this process mixed blessings for society in general. It indicates a remarkable process of restructuration and social mobility. It reflects the rise of an economic ethic which is productive and generates surpluses and capital accumulation. It has already achieved a degree of shift of authority in favour of the younger people. I reinforces the resilience of the social system for selective absorption of technology, leading to high productivity and growth in agriculture. These changes have contributed to the upward mobility of the middle castes on the one hand, and on the other sharpened the self-awareness of the lower castes and poorer classes. They have resorted to large scale migration to towns, cities and other regions of India in search of employment and better opportunities.

These developments, however, also coincide with negative social processes. A change in the value system and ideology of people which promotes localism, casteism, and communalism has taken place. This results in a conflictual and exploitative relationship between the peasant classes and the rural poor. It also results in negative perceptions of the work, status and role of women. Its cultural outcome is that of the revival of masculinism, increase in the dowry system and cultural conservatism. Thus, social changes have also brought about conflict and maladjustment in the structure of society.

The massive investment in industry and technology which took place during the first two decades after independence has resulted in significant development in industrial activities and the rise of entrepreneurial classes in the urban areas. The size of the urban middle classes has more than doubled. The numbers of entrepreneurs of small and medium size, as also those having a broader social background, have grown in substantial measure. This has come with the rise in commercial and industrial activities. Compared to the traditional business classes, who largely had their social origin in the trading castes or communities, the new merchant class comes from a diverse and broader social background. It has contributed to the weakening of the segmentry social base of commercial and industrial capitalism in India, a process similar to that taking place in rural society. The growth in the size of the services, professions and the administrative or developmental bureaucracy reflects the social dynamism and mobility in the urban-industrial sector of life. Slowly the process of mercantile capitalism growing and maturing into industrial capitalism is taking place in India. Today, it is happening on a much larger scale that it did during British rule or the initial decades after independence.

Urbanisation and Social Change

This process should be analysed together with those of demographic transition and urbanisation. As the census figures reveal, proliferation of townships with growth in economic activities and rise in transport and market facilities has taken place. The medium sizes cities have grown into cities of a million population or into urban metropolises. The rise in urban population, mostly of an unplanned nature, has put severe pressure on urban facilities, services housing, sanitation, health and ecology. It has led to proliferation of slums, over-urbanisation increase in crime and other problems. The sheer weight of unplanned growth in urban population puts it civic culture and amenities in jeopardy. Speculative and clandestine-commercial activities get linked up with exploitation of the urban poor. It breeds cultural anomie, promotes sectarianism, communalism and regionalism.

These negative aspects of urbanisation and industrialisation go together with positive growth in entrepreneurship and industry. An urban middle class has also emerged with the rise of mercantile and industrial capitalism. The social base of the middle classes has thus broadened both in urban and rural societies. The cultural background and ethos of this middle class has not, however, been studied fully, but it is obvious that it sets the trend for the contemporary process of modernisation. What is its modernisation ideology? This question assumes significance for an analysis of the existing patterns and future directions of social change in India. The cultural values of the emergent rural middle classes show sharper contradictions between their ideology and 'national' goals of social transformation. Is the cultural ethos of the urban middle classes much different in nature. This is an important question, and calls for serious investigation by social scientists.

The historical context of the urban-industrial transformation today is different. The entrepreneurs and capitalist classes, that have arisen during the past three decades, have a different value system. The traditional business classes had interacted closely with the national movement and its political and economic ideology. The new business classes, despite being a product of the national economic and social policies, have a value structure that is more inwardly directed. It is often governed by short-run business interests rather than long-term national economic and social goals commensurate with national policies. The new capitalist class has grown under the protection of the nation's economic policies and has enjoyed political support, but its commitment to the cosmopolitan values of national development, social justice, welfare, liberalism and nationality has yet to be established. The evidence often suggest its negative or indifferent commitment to these values.

Industrial capitalism has not successfully grown in any society without a strong a strong national ethical tradition and its discipline in personal and public conduct. The ethical base of the emerging rural and urban capitalism has a complex character. While in some qualities, such as motivation or commitment, discipline of work and its technical efficiency it matches standards of high quality, its functioning in the social context deviates to a significant degree. It has yet to evolve a rational-ethical world-view in harmony with the values and ideologies of the nation state. This is especially so in regard to values of distributive justice, social responsibility and non-sectarianism.

Family System and Social Change

The process of change in the family have also responded to forces of modernisation.

The studies in this area reveal that family system in India not only has undergone changes due to pressure of economic forces, social mobility and urbanisation, but has also contributed to the process of economic modernisation as such. In the rural areas the 'green revolution' has a strong base in the joint-family mode of production. There is some evidence to suggest that the nature of family authority has also undergone changes in favour of younger sons who have some education due to the demands of interaction with new structures such as band markets, administrative and developmental bureaucracies, health centres and laboratories. The older generation has seen wisdom in accommodating the younger male members of family in decision-making roles in the family.

The same process is visible in the industrial and entrepreneurial activities. The positive relationship between joint family system and industrial entrepreneurship has been established by a series of sociological studies. It is found that in raising credit, managing family firms and ensuring efficiency, continuity and confidentiality in decision-making the family members play a significant role. This reinforces the relationship between family system and industrial entrepreneurship in India. Studies have also suggested that family culture and the values of sharing and sacrifice have strengthened the corporate values of the industrial entrepreneurial systems, and a break-down in the same leads to dysfunctions in the enterprise. Moreover, the million of the joint family and its patterns of role allocations ensure entrepreneurial innovativeness among members.

Interestingly both in the rural-agricultural and industrial sectors of our economy and society the family system is seen playing a significant adaptive role in the process of change and modernisation. It is, however, not without tensions and contradictions. The increasing strength of the joint-family values together with economic prosperity have contributed to exploitation of women, increased violence against them and their marginalisation not work and status. This growth has contributed to the rise of a sub-culture of masculinism and neo-conservativism in rural and urban areas. This has caused inter gender conflicts and led to demands of dowry and violence against women. The technological innovations following economic development also seen to displace women from work more and affect their economic and social status.

The family system in the process of changes in the society do bring out this dualistic direction of change as evidenced in most other sectors of social life. There is development but in the wake of its forces new social contradictions arise that call for remedial measures.

Changing Social Values

A process of social restructuration is thus taking place in the urban and industrial sectors of our life. It symbolises social dynamism, mobility and growth and yet, it serves as a harbinger of increasing culture disvalues and anomie. The increase in the social and ideological chasm between the urban rich and middle classes and the urban poor and the weaker sections indicates it. It is compounded by the high degree of communication exposure, mass media participation and political activism. The professional and intellectual classes, who could normally perform integrative role as catalysts of modernisation and positive social values, have a fractured moral existence. Studies of the professions of medicine, law, science and technology, humanities and social sciences reveal a schismatic character of its ideology.

Yet, there have been recently new cultural and ideological movements in India. The two important cultural sources which initiate this process are those of science and religious values. The fear of social scientists that religious values in India would hamper the growth of science and technology has been disproved. Yet, traditional values do retard the process of institutionalisation of science in our social life. The view that science would displace religion from human life too has been disproved. In India, as in many other societies, modernisation processes initiated by science and technology proceed alongwith adaptive changes in religious values and beliefs. Paradoxically in most of the contemporary world, advance in science is not able to check the rise of sectarian, racial, and other fundamentalist beliefs. The cultural transformation in our society, which has made successful adaptive synthesis between scientific-technological and traditional values, too now shows tension of rising fundamentalism.

The disvalues of religion or its narrow fundamentalist, communal and sectarian manifestations have their origin in a process of mystification. Mystification is rampant in the contemporary historical context of religion. We define mystification as a process by which values which belong to the instrumental domains, such as economic, political, racial or communitarian values, etc., are lifted from their relevant contexts and transfigurated into categorical values by an interpretive fiat or demogogy. Thus, issues which normally belong to the instrumental or rational realm, and could be sorted out as such are withdrawn from this domain and passed on to the domain of unreason. This defines the character of fundamentalist ideology. One has to investigate the social conditions under which this transfiguration takes place to strike at the root of fundamentalism and its problems in modern society. Its origin lies in exploitation of peoples, anxieties and frustrations on account, of their human conditions, existential, social and spiritual. A major part of these anxieties arise from social inequalities and exploitation, and powerful vested interests who feel threatened by the maximisation of opportunities of social mobility and freedom.

The process of social restructuration going on in our society today is full of contradictions. We witness economic growth with increasing social inequalities, political freedom with fore-closure of existential opportunities, changes in values and definition of the self without elasticity in social structure, or its power base and social mobility without corresponding evolution of an organic consciousness. The segmentary nature of traditional social structure with its inter-structural autonomy had the advantage of encapsulating the impact of changes at the selective levels of social structure. That is how the first stage of modernisation could proceed in India without major up-heavals in society.

At the resent stage of modernisation the very principles of inter-structural autonomy are breaking down. In fact, this is how it should be, in order to establish a democratic, free and just social order. But this process is relating social, cultural and emotional forces in society that render the rise in expectations so fast and intense, that the process of social restructuration cannot keep pace with this transition. It thus retards the growth of organic social and cultural consciousness. This is evident from the rise of communalism, casteism, tribalism and fundamentalism in our society during the past decade.

The accelerated pace of social restructuration which has enlarged the size of the rural and urban middle classes, encouraged entrepreneurial activities and process of urbanisation, etc., has not, however, reinforced cultural values of secularism, justice and equality. It has encouraged an ideology that is non-cosmopolitan, and neoconservative. Shammeritocracy, utilitarian opportunism and ethical fuzziness are its main features. The poorer and exploited classes perceive in this cultural profile of the middle classes a rejection of their identity. Their cultural perceptions suffer a semiotic break which leads them to 'sub-alternity' or a search for counter models of values. Insurgent ideology is a product of such subalternity. We have observed it happening in the ideology of the caste system. There has been a movement among some scheduled castes to reject the Brahmanical model of pollutionpurity for one based on class exploitation. Such alienative cultural processes have obstructed the growth of cosmopolitan cultural tradition commensurate with our national ideology.

Traditionally, the organic cultural values were sustained in India by a creative linkages between the folk art-forms, its rich oral tradition and the classical art-forms of the elite. There was a syncretic relationship between the two cultural traditions. The local and the cosmopolitan cultural traditions interacted together in their diversity and unity constituting a whole. Modernisation introduces technological and structural forces that put strains both on the folk and the elite traditions of culture. The pace of social restructuration, the emergence of new classes, and the decline of traditional cultural institutions exemplify this process. Social mobility, migration and occupational diversification break the traditional institutional bases of art and culture.

Society thus faces a dual cultural crisis, decline of the traditional forms and institutions on the one hand and on the other the feebleness of the new cultural institutions and forms. Here, the role of modern communication technology, both of the point and the electronic media, assumes immenseimportance. Not only are the institutional alternatives to be innovated to continue the process of a creative cultural evolution but also our cultural identity and heritage needs to be maintained through the autonomy of the media software. This would particularly apply to the radio and television in India, particularly television which has a great potential as a catalyser of the integrative cultural consciousness.

4

Farm Technology and Social Transformation

Introduction

Indian agriculture prior to advent of green revolution in mid-sixties was almost entirely of subsistence nature. But, it gradually experienced transformation towards the end of sixties on account of adoption of agricultural innovations. At the time of its inception in 1966 Haryana was a less developed region of the country and was deficit even in food grains. Thereafter the state made alround spectacular progress particularly in agricultural sector. The sandy fields' of Hisar district became famous for the rich varieties of Australian grapes and American cotton. The world famous Basmati rice has found a new habitant in the fields of Karnal and Kurukshetra. The Maxican wheat varieties and hybrid bajra varieties have ushered the new era of green revolution throughout the state. The power utilised in agricultural increased to 40 per cent of the total consumption. Similarly, consumption of inputs like chemical fertilisers, insecticides and pesticides have increased manifolds. Number of tractors have increased from a few hundred to hundred thousands during the span of two decades (Govt. of Haryana, 1985-86). Consequently the State of Haryana became surplus in food grains production and experienced phenominal sociocultural transformation which is the subject of discussion in the present paper.

Studies have indicated relationship between adoption of innovations and socio-cultural transformation. Adoption of innovations are also conditioned by socio-cultural conditions, Ogburn (1964) noted such a relationship between technology and socio-cultural transformation. Parthasarathy (1971) found that tractor, cultivation is growing popular thereby displacing family labour and agricultural labourers from agricultural occupation. Consequently, occupational diversification has taken place in the rural society. Lack of encouragement to village and cottage industries have intensified the process of migration from rural areas to urban. The traditional are undergoing phenominal transformation and the urban culture is emerging in the countryside. Barmoda (1974) reported that dissatisfaction among farmers was quite pronounced on account of non-availability of agricultural inputs and extension services. A new class of exploiters have emerged which provide substandard inputs at a very high price to farmers, thereby putting them in big financial losses. Pandey and Kaushal (1980) revealed that adoption of modern agricultural technology alongwith additional capital borrowing have increased net incomes to a considerable extent, This in turn brought about significant socio-cultural transformation. Waglimer and Pandit (1982) noted lack of knowledge and proper guidance about seed variety, seed treatment, method of sowing, use of chemical fertilisers have been used whereas in most other situations lesser than the recommended doses of fertilisers have been used by farmers of Punjab. Similarly, the level of socio-cultural development also varied with variations in the modern of technology. Quanfiditimi (1987) found education, farm size and compatibility of innovation as important factors affecting adoption of improved farm practices indicating relation of socio-cultural factors with technology. The aforesaid review indicates close association between modern technology and socio-economic transformation, hence, providing support to the technological theory of change.

In the present paper an attempt has been made to understand the association between agricultural technology and social transformation in the rural settings. It is divided into two parts. In the first, nature and extent of adoption of selected agricultural technology is discussed whereas in the second part only selected socio-cultural transformation resulted mainly due to adoption of agricultural technology would be attended to the primary data on which the present paper is based has been drawn from the research report of the year 1986-87 of the department of Sociology, HAU Hisar.

Methodology

The primary data on which the present is based was collected from two villages of Rohtak District of the State of Haryana. Both the villages were purposively selected keeping in view the availability and non-availability of irrigation water throughout. Village Sasrli has assured irrigation throughout the year whereas village Chharra did not possess such a facility. Second, both these villages are situated in the interior, hence, devoid of effective and direct links with urban centres. For collecting primary data 100 small farmers, 50 each from Sasroli and Chharra villages were selected randomly without replacement method and interviewed with the help of a structured interview schedule in the year 1986-87. Percentages were calculated for drawing inferences, Crosstabulation between independent and dependent variables was resorted for facilitating interpretation of data.

Results and Discussion

Agricultural technology have brought about revolutionary transformation in the rural areas allover the world. Numerous studies have indicated such a transformation. In the present paper an attempt has been made to highlight some selected dimensions of agricultural technology and socio-cultural transformation at micro level. The paper is divided into two section. In section one, elementary aspects in respect of nature and extent of adoption of adoption of agricultural technology has been discussed while in selection two, salient socio-cultural transformation resulted due to adoption of agricultural technology is elaborated.

Charge in Farming Practices

The agricultural technology which is selected for knowing the nature and extent of adoption is grouped into three categories namely, agricultural machinery including tractor; agricultural inputs such as seeds, chemical fertilisers, insecticides and pesticides; and agronomical practices. The nature of adoption of agricultural technology is mainly confined to use of tractor/machine power over bullocks/camel power in an increasing number. Similarly, use of improved varieties of seeds of crops like wheat, Bajra, Cotton and Mustard was quite common among respondents, but the use of chemical fertilisers was confined to only a few crops like wheat, cotton and sugarcane and of urea and DAP fertilisers. The use of plant protection measures did not find favour with most respondents for obvious reasons. Its use was confined mainly to cotton crop followed by bajra on rare occasions. Agronomical practices were not practised as per recommendations.

None of the respondents possessed any farm machine such as tractor, thresher, sprayer, etc. for performing agricultural operations like soil preparation, transportation, spraying of insecticides, and threshing in both the sampled villages. In Chharra, respondents mostly hired the services of aforesaid machines for performing essential farm operations while those of Sasroli a majority used camel as major source of draft power because the soil is sandy, hence, suitable for cultivation through camel instead of tractor or bullocks. Moreover, it is profitable to use camel as a source of draft power because of comparatively lesser investment per annum on it compared to tractor or bullocks. High charges for hired services resulted into decreased frequency of use of tractor for soil preparation leading to low yield. The number of farmers of different farm size groups particularly of medium and large size possessing tractors, thresers, etc. are increasing considerably in the sampled village. It is another factor which motivated small and marginal farmers to hire their services for soil preparation, sowing, threshing and transportation of farm produce.

A substantial transformation was noted in the adoption of agricultural inputs like improved varieties of seeds, chemical fertilisers, insecticides and pesticides in the sampled villages. Table 4.1 details information on adoption behaviour of respondents in respect of crop inputs.

An appraisal of Table 4.1 indicates that adoption of seed technology in respect of principal crops like wheat, bajra and mustard was quite high irrespective of literacy status of the respondents. In case of chemical fertilisers substantial variations were noted both among literate and illiterate respondents as well as among selected crops. Almost all respondents used these in wheat and Bajra crops, however, adoption of its complete dozes was restricted to 50 per cent farmers in case of wheat and only 14 per cent farmers in case of Bajra crops. Its non use among both these crops was confined mainly to illiterate respondents. Since Mustard crop is grown on unirrigated land, hence, use of chemical fertilisers was almost negligible. The use of plant protection measures was nominal in crops like. Wheat, Bajra and Mustard but in case of cotton it was almost hundred per cent irrespective of literacy status of respondents. Literacy status also influenced the use of these measures in crops like Wheat, Bajra and Mustard.

Randhawa (1985) found that the farmers have adopted innovations in an irrational manner. Somewhere excessive dozes of fertilisers have been used whereas in most other situations lesser than recommended dozes of fertilisers were used by farmers of Punjab. Quanfiditimi (1987) noted education, farm size and compatibility of innovation are important factors affecting adoption of improved farm practices. Adoption of aforesaid agricultural inputs particularly seeds have enhanced production which in turn increased their income and socio-cultural transformation. Pandey and Kaushal (1980) also observed similar transformation as result of adoption of agricultural innovations.

TABLE 4.1

Education and Extent of Adoption of Agricultural Technology

Technology	Education and extent of adoption						Total	
	Complete		Partial		Nil		Literate	Illiterate
	Literate	Illiterate	Literate	Illiterate	Literate	Illiterate		
Wheat								
Seed	24	76	—	—	—	—	24	76
Fertilisers	21	29	3	33	—	14	24	76
Plant Protection	10	5	14	12	—	59	24	76
Bajra								
Seeds	24	76	—	—	—	—	24	76
Fertilisers	13	1	11	51	—	24	24	76
Plant Protection	10	2	12	26	2	48	24	76
Mustard								
Seeds	21	61	3	15	—	—	24	75
Fertilisers	—	—	—	—	24	76	24	76
Plant Protection	8	4	16	28	—	44	24	76

Third important component of agricultural technology which helped in ushering of green revolution is agronomical practices. It includes soil and its preparation for cultivation and seed treatment. Most respondents did not follow recommendations because of their economic feasibility, compatibility and knowledge about agronomical practices, however, seed treatment in case of wheat, bajra and cotton crops was unevenly done. Waglimar and Pandit (1982) also noted lack of knowledge and proper guidance about agronomical practices as major constraints in transfer of technology. Similarly, none of the respondents ever got their soil and waler tested so as to make judicious use of chemical fertilisers for maximum output.

Impact on Socio-Cultural Transformation

The socio-cultural transformation resulted as a result of adoption of agricultural innovations are numerous and manifold. This socio-cultural transformation may be looked into two ways i.e. direct and indirect. B. Russell in his famous book entitled

"The Impact of Science on Society" observed as the effects of science and technology are of various very different kinds. There are direct intellectual effects, the dispelling of many traditional beliefs and the adoption of others suggested by the success of scientific methods. Then, chiefly as a consequence of new techniques, there are profound changes in social organisation which are gradually bringing about corresponding political changes." Some of the salient changes in social life of the respondents are discussed below in relation to mechanisation of operations and changes in farming practices.

The mechanisation of most agricultural operations such as preparation of soil for sowing, use of seed-cum-fertiliser drill for sowing, transportation of farm produce and threshing of crops like Wheat, Bajra and Mustard have transformed traditional nature of agriculture from hoeculture to tractorisation. Most farmers of Chharra are hiring services for performing aforesaid agricultural operations whereas in Sasroli village camel was commonly used for these operations. Due to adoption of aforesaid technology, a lot of time has been saved and only a single person can easily operate small holding without much difficulty. Other adult members of all such families are also spared from agricultural occupations, thereby allowing them to involve in other activities like economic, social, cultural and recreational. The children of such families also find time to attend school regularly. The traditional agricultural labour families are also relieved from earning their livelihood from agricultural. Now, all these people are migrating to urban centres and other occupations in order to earn their livelihood. Such a transformation was visible to a lesser extent in village Sasroli because of soil type. Randhawa (1985) also reported similar kind of socio cultural transformation in Punjab.

The adoption of agricultural inputs in respect of common crops of the area such as Wheat, Bajra, Mustard and Cotton are mainly responsible for increased output of these crops. It increased income of the farmers which motivated them to enhance their socio-cultural status. Table 4.2 details respondents possessions which are indicative of their enhanced socio-cultural status. Table 4.2 elaborates respondents' possessions of modern artifacts.

An appraisal of table 4.2 depicts that respondents possessed artifacts which indicate their enhanced socio-cultural and economic status. Increased income status is primarily responsible for this transformation. Adoption of agricultural technology and employment in government and semi-government organisations contributed to increase in economic status of respondents thereby enabling small farmers to acquire following items. Investment on drugs such as alcoholic, tobacco, etc. was reported by 94 per cent respondents. It shows that taking drugs has become a status symbol on prominant occasions and ceremonies. Similarly, 92 respondents reported to have indicated investment on children education of both the sexes which is indicative of their raising status. Latest technologies like radio, fodder cutter and bicycle were possessed by 91, 78 and 61 respondents respectively depicting their improved status. Similarly, urban visits, employment in non-agricultural occuaptions and increased number of bank accounts were on the increase. A few decades earlier frequencies of such activities was almost negligible as reported by respondents.

TABLE 4.2

Respondents Possessions Indicating their Socio-cultural Status

	Cultural items	Frequency of possession		Total
		Chharra	Sasroli	
1.	Investment of drugs: alcohol, tobacco, etc.			
	Yes	50	44	94
	No	—	6	6
2.	Children's Education:			
	Yes	47	46	93
	No	3	4	7
3.	House type :			
	Pucca	50	42	92
	Kachha	—	8	8
4.	Foddercutter:			
	Yes	50	41	91
	No	—	9	9
5.	Radio:			
	Yes	46	32	78
	No	4	8	22
6.	Bicycle:			
	Yes	41	20	61
	No	9	30	39
7.	Urban Visits:			
	Weekly	42	12	54
	Monthly	8	34	42
	Rarely	—	4	4
8.	Employment:			
	Yes	28	11	39
	No	22	39	61

Another development resulting from adoption of agricultural inputs pertains to discontentment among respondents towards sources of availability of inputs from the private dealers. Most respondents were not satisfied from the quality, costs and kinds of inputs supplied to them by private dealers. Whereas government and semi-government dealers in agricultural inputs did not satisfy respondents because of their partial attitude, non-availability and inadequate availability of inputs in time; and of poor quality. These situations gave rise to protests of varied kinds among farmers at different periods particularly after the introduction of modern agricultural technology in mid-sixties. It also increased their political consciousness leading to political changes in the Indian polity. At the same time, respondents expressed their dissatisfaction with the working of extension services which was responsible for inadequate adoption of agricultural innovations related to agronomical practices.

REFERENCES

Barmoda, J.N., 1974, *The Small Farmers (1967-68)*, Reserve Bank of India, Central Office, Bombay, 36-37.

Ogburn, W.F., 1964, *Culture and Social Change*, The University of Chicago Press, Chicago, 86-98.

Pandey, V.K. and Kaushal A.K. (1980), "Prospects of Increasing Farm Incomes on Small Farms of Ambala District (Haryana), *Indian Journal of Agril. Economics*, XXV (2), 77-85.

Parthsarathy, G., (1971), *Agricultural Development and Small Farmers: A Study of Andhra Pradesh*, Vikas Publications, Delhi, 90-109.

Quanfiditimi, T.C. , 1981, "Adoption of Improved Farm Practices: A Choice Under Uncertainty," *Indian Journal of Extension Education*, XVIII (1 and 2), 30-35.

Randhawa, T.S. (1985), "Adoption of N.P.K. and Nutrients in Rice Crop in Punjab, *Indian Journal of Extension Education*, XXI (1 and 2), 91-93.

Russell, B., 1964, *The Impact of Science on Society*, George Allen and Unwin Limited, London, 9-22.

Govt. of Haryana, 1987-88, *Statistical Abstract of Haryana*, Planning Department, Government of Haryana, Publication no. 369, 81-400. .

Waglimer, S.K. and Pandit, V.K. , 1982, "Constraints in Adoption of Wheat Technology by the Tribal Farmers of M.P." *Indian Journal of Extension Education*, XVIII (1 and 2), 95-98.

5

In the Wake of Improved Agricultural Practices

Introduction

The improved agricultural practices in India are gaining ground ensuring self-sufficiency in food requirement. The emphasis of the state Govt. of Rajasthan on increasing food production is obvious from several programmes. But the success depends upon simultaneous support of allied facilities needed for agricultural operations and positive response of the farmers. The purpose of this case study in this respect is not to find out economic gain or loss through new economic enterprise, rather our is aim to trace the phases through which a farmer of a traditional community comes forward to adopt new ways and means for accelerating his farm produce and, thereby improves his economic condition for total happier life. I undertook a study of a farming family with an operiori knowledge that 'there is an inherent insecurity in adopting new ways of doing a thing,' however, we wanted to know the motivation behind innovation, its process leading to gradual faith and confidence, role of extension agencies social and economic implications, barriers on the way of subsequent acceptance and the further prospect. I may precisely mention that an attempt has been made to example future potential of this programme; the data obtained relate to a single farming family. Regarding the plam of this study, we should be clear that it does not examine the outcome of two economic variables, interacting with indeginous set of social and economic variables thriving upon the generic features of the peasant society. It is also important here to note that a modified frame work for case study edited by Spicer[1] has been accepted in a farming family in the village Dongiyon-ka Guda situated near Udaipur, at a distance of about 7 miles, was selected as a case. The family is a joint one, living together 15 members. The family under reference is considered one of the top most progressive farming families—in Lakhawali Gram Panchayat. Secondly, it is the richest farming family in the village. Educationally, the family has very poor record. Not a single adult member, either male or female is educated or even literate too, except the children who are attending the school. Taking relevant criteria into account, the case has been defined as a traditional family which obviously contradicts its contrary emergence as a modern farming family. This being the crucial point in spired me to undertake an indepth study in its realm. Let us examine the process as to how a traditional family adopts modern agricultural practices.

The Problem

They were not least aware of the improved agricultural practices in the early 1950s. With the introduction of N.E.S. a comprehensive programme including new agricultural practices were launched. In short, the process of innovation at the communication level started since then. Relatively, efforts made by the N.E.S. at the initial stages were not very much appreciated. Nevertheless, a first layer for rooting the idea was laid down. But there was no substantial change in the mode of their agricultural operation. Since several other agencies approached the family for adopting improved agricultural practices, the family responded with the adoption of seeds, fertiliser in small quantity, and gradually the quantum increased after deriving economic benefits being the foremost motive. Once the Sonora-64' (wheat seed) could not give desired production, the family became indifferent with a self-devastating attitude and for fellow villagers a demoralising scene, and for sometime no extension worker from any corner could approach them. But this exigency did not last long. The family got convinced again and started a gambling with luck. The adoption of improved practices along with improved seeds, fertilisers and plant protection measures gradually increased. It is significant that except those changes in the farming practices the other traits of the family remained the same as visible in the traditional community in general. Economic changes could very little disturb the social bound uniting all of them in a traditional social setting.[2]

The Course of Events

The most important of the events was launching of N.E.S. and introduction of Panchayat Raj and Co-operative society. The family premise under study, has been a central place in this village, certainly due to wealth and other potentialities for becoming a progressive farmer. Extension officers, B.D.O., VLWS and other officials too approached the family frequently. During the initial stage all the members of the family were very slow in showing positive response to the recommendation of the block development officials. But the constant efforts of the block agencies brought about a primary transformation at the ideological level in the gestalt of the family. The Village Panchayat did contribute in general, but could not do anything concrete because, by that time it had not assumed such role to perform and the village people also had not visualised that days would come when internal as well as external agencies would do something for economic advancement of the villagers. Attitude of indifference was the result of the pre-independence period official-non-official relationship between the village community and the governmental agencies. In fact, village social system and the external agencies held no common perspective and goal for development of the farmer's lot. Such non-resolving attitude climaxed towards the pre-independence period. The gradual improvement started just after the attainment of Independence. Evidences were still there in our country's socio-economic history. Anybody else pretending to be fatemaker from within or without the community's premises was not welcome. The family under study should be taken as an eventual product of such typical social surrounding of the successive phases. In 1960s one of the extension agencies of Udaipur approached the villagers. They started to project new ideas through films, about new agricultural practices, improved agricultural, use of pesticides, home economy, cleanliness, co-operation, family planning etc. They utilised documentary films to a greater extent and full length films to some extent, which attracted the villagers. The other illustrative aids like pamphlets, charts, agricultural exhibitions and fairs also paved the ways for wider transformation of ideas. All the agencies made personal approach to convince the farmers. The family under study, as mentioned earlier, being a typical, had to be contacted by several extension agencies operating in the region. The members of the family also remained susceptible to the processes of extension. Secondly, the demonstration methods proved to be a happy event. The family revealed that one of the extension agencies of Udaipur helped as an educational channel and always maintained a link between new ideas and the people. The other agencies had the benefit of both as a supply line of the needed facilities and functioning as an educational channel. The role of Panchayat Samiti and Co-operative society was not important. At the initial stage, the family accepted improved seeds, manures and new methods of sowing. The hand under improved practices was very small. The amount of newly adopted input increased very slowly but steadily. It is to note that they were not inclined to accept improved implements in the face of the problem they suffered with the motive power being the oxen and texture of the soil and the unskilled menpower as well as the high prices of the implements. However, the family gradually emerged in the village as an innovator. During the investigation, the family owned 72 bighas of land of which 25 bighas were cultivable, 50% of the cultivable land was under improved methods of cultivation, seeds of maize, wheat and vegetables, methods of sowing, plant protection measure were popular with them. They owned one irrigational well fitted with electric pump and had a partnership in three other irrigational wells. They had 20 well nursed Cattle-cows, buffaloes, oxen and calves. The preparation of the compost pit was very old practice with them, however done on un-scientific line which took scientific shape in the recent past.

The Relevant Factors

Mainly there may be two categories of relevant factors-firstly, the institutional complex which expedited the process of acceptance and the emergence of certain factors which may be considered as the gradually acquired innovative potentiality by the members of the family which reinforced the process of acceptance or did, to some extent, obstruct the process of innovation. The family became very popular for its progressive outlook. Consequently, it was always conscious enough about subsequent loss or gain after acceptance of the package of programmes. However, the process of acceptance remained slow. The installation of oil engine water pump, thereafter for irrigation assured regular supply of water on the farms where chemical fertilisers could be used without risk. Secondly, Panchayat Samiti, Village Panchayat, Co-operative society also became radical and assumed the role of developmental agencies concretely.

Here it is relevant to mention about a havoc which occured sometime back. The family purchased 'Sonora-64' (wheat seed) from the Co-operative society, Dangiyon-ka-Guda which was supplied by the Panchayat Samiti Badgaon. The yield was below expectation. This event remained a burning one for a few months. The failure of the Sonora-64 wheat resulted into a great retrogression on the part of the farmers, particularly the family under study also had suffered a lot. They were compensated either in cash or kind but the amount was not commensurate with the loss they had suffered. For the time being, it become very difficult to approach the family for convincing them about one's competence to improve the lot of the suffering farmer. However, the family along with some other farmers visited some demonstration plots prepared by an extension agency in the nearby villages. The aggrieved farmers became very happy to visit these farms. The faith was restored and they accepted 5227 (wheat seed) from the same extension agency for a trial.

It was found that they were also convinced by the high production of hybrid maize. The event took place in the manner stated above after the failure of 'Sonora-64'. The kharif sowing was to begin. The extension agencies travelled around. The Directorate of Extension, University of Udaipur played an important role in popularising the hybrid maize. On the whole, it is evident that tempo once lost would have been lost for ever if not approached by several competent agencies to revitalise the innertia of the farmers. On the basis of the above facts it can be concluded that acceptance of new ideas and new means is a very delicate process and the success lies around the confluence of the people's desire and the positive role of the extension agencies. This would result into nothingness for both—the people and the extension agencies.

The Outcome

Although the family has emerged as an innovative one but one the best criteria of total innovative character it does not prove to be fully successful. The family does not maintain input and output records. In general, as the members of the family affirmed, that economically that are far better and their investment capacity has increased. They have understood a number of things related to farming through trial and error. They have also generated faith in a number of external extension agencies who could really help them in improving their economic conditions. They were now in a position to take up decision on the basis of their own experience. However, they were guided by external agencies but the element of insecurity is still immense in their mind. At times, an extension agency can feel surprise at the total negative response of the members of the forget family, if the former has not marked properly the aspect of the total socio-economic life of the family which could be moulded easily. Precisely every extension agency has to think what to do and what not to do as the family has also categorically defined; thing 'A' in combination with thing 'B' where interference of 'C' factor is not possible. They have practical knowledge of how to apply certain chemical fertilisers, how to sow seeds of wheat, improved variety of maize and vegetables popular with them. Similarly, amonium sulphate, super phosphate, Di-amonium have been used by them. These means and methods are now thought older; they are deriving direct benefits from co-operative society.

In terms of out-come, the above events show that in the village situation process of innovation is unilinear, rather than multilinear. They have adopted new methods to some extent with regard to farming, but still, in other areas of life, they seemed most conservative, say specially to the setting of life. For example, there is no evidence of change in family life, social and community life, customs, traditions, rituals or in "pure social type" elements constitution their total life in proportion to the changes which are occurring in their economic life. Hardly change has occurred even at the ideological level, towards education, cleanliness, food habits, health, intoxication or home decoration. The failure of `Sonora 64' and its reaction exposed their fatalism and the mode of assessing any event on traditional line. Huge expenditure on ritual ceremonies are still abidingly obligatory to them. However, it is obvious, but conclusively fentative that for innovation in farming, it is not necessary to wait for spread of modern ideas and education. Farmers, even without formal education, may adopt it, provided they visualise economic gain in a neweconomic enterprise. Of course, under the pressure of economic problems, gratifying principle of extension must be given priority, otherwise, the subsequent loss may lead to a drastic reversion into the previous stage. Any attempt to bring about improvement in such a situation becomes very difficult task. For example, in this study, the failure of 'Sonora-64' (wheat-seeds) is case in point.

Analysis

Analysis of the above course of events and the genesis of the out come reveal certain complex phenomena about the process of innovation. Let us begin with the role of the extension agencies. Several extension agencies approached the family individually, specially the Panchayat Samiti (Previously NES Block), co-operative society as a complex maintained the functions of supply lines. The Directorate of Extension, University of Udaipur served the double purposes. It is to note that all the extension agencies, as it appears from the subsequent results did not function in a co-ordinated manner from the very beginning. First of all, the NES had to tackle several problems at the initial stage, later, the other agencies had some how the ground already prepared for further programme. As a means of transmission of new ideas the mass communication, informal / personal approach and demonstration methods have been most successful. If we analyse time span of innovation, we find, it is very slow process. It goes on through piecemeal speed. The farmers are not ready to take risk very soon unless they are convinced of the results. The failure 'Sonora-64' indicates that if the people lose faith once it looms large, and such consequences may have a number of repercussions, making the farmers more reluctant. Failure of one scheme is a curse and a red signal for a long time for any new scheme.

Thirdly, innovation in agriculture is also to be supported by allied facilities, otherwise the total result can hardly be realised. Fourthly, acceptance of one new idea or a set of new ideas meant for one sector of life does not simultaneously affect other sectors of life. There are changes evident in farm practices, but hardly any change is evident of the corresponding nature in social phenomena of family under study. Hence, change in farm operation does necessarily not bring about change in social life of the family. And lastly, it is observed that though economic assets are being accumulated; but their propensity to spend money on certain modern heads like dress, style of life and recreation is not increasing. Though, this generalising hypothesis is contradictory to the principles of economic but facts stand here out that family under study spent about Rs. 10,000 on a death ceremony. The general condition of the family, however, provides certain facts that they are not of this opinion that savings could be utilised far making life more decent. They can understand the value of money very easily, but it hardly means to them that there are various uses of money. They will not boast like a richman with an apprehension that government may impose tax, but they drain out money through the drains of their rituals and useless social obligations. They need to imbibe rational use of money.

REFERENCES

1. Spicer H. Edward (ed.): *Human Problems in Technological Change.* (A case Book) Russell Sage Foundation, New York, 1952.
2. The concept of culturaltag—though not comprehensive but to some extent can be used as a theoretical model to explain the events see: Ogburn William and Nimkoff, M.F.: *A Hand-Book of Sociology,* New Delhi, E.P.H. 1966.

6

Can Science Solve Social Problems?

Although I think it is unquestionably true that the social sciences have made, during the present century, more actual progress than in all preceding history, it would be absurd to pretend that this progress is, as yet, reflected to any great extent in our management of social affairs. Scientific information of a more or less reliable character is more widely diffused than ever before, but the scientific mode of thought has obviously made very little headway. Practically no one approaches the major social problems of the day in a spirit of disinterested scientific study. The idea that these problems are to be solved, if at all, by the use of instruments of precision in hands that do not shake with fear, with anger, or even with love, does not seem to have occurred even to many people who pass for social scientists. They have joined the journalist and the soapbox crusader in the hue and cry of the mob. Their supposedly scholarly works bristle with assessments of praise and blame, personalities and verbal exorcisms which have no place whatever in the scientific universe of discourse. Not only do these angry men pass in the public eye as great social scientists of the day, but they not infrequently presume to patronise honest scientists who stay with their proper tasks of building a science and the instruments by means of which any difficult problems are to be solved.

But behind this fog, this dust storm of books about the inside of various political movements, the private life and morals of its leaders, and the treatises on democracy, substantial work is going on. Men are patiently accumulating data about human bahaviour in a form which in the fullness of time will permit a type of generalisation which has never before been possible. Some are engaged in the undramatic but fundamental work, basic to all science, of classifying the multitudes of human groups and behaviour patterns as a first step toward the formulation of generalisations regarding them. Still others are pioneering in the construction of actuarial and other tables from which may be predicted not only the prevalence of births, deaths, marriages, and divorces, but also the probable relative degrees of happiness in marriage, the probable success or failure of probation and parole, and many other equally "human" eventualities. A wealth of valuable information and generalisations have already been developed about the social characteristics and behaviour of populations, such as the distribution of wealth, occupations, mobility, intelligence, an the various conditions with which these characteristics vary. Important instruments have been invented in recent years for measuring opinion, status, social participation, and many phenomena of communication and interpersonal relations.

Indeed, the invention and perfection of instruments for the more accurate and precise observation and recording of social phenomena must be regarded as among the most important developments in the social sciences. It is easy to point to the flaws in these instruments as it was easy to point to the flaws in the early microscopes and telescopes. But, without these beginnings and the patient centuries of undramatic labour, sciences like bacteriology could not have appeared at all.

Finally, there are those, and they may be the most important of all, who are experimenting with and inventing new systems of symbolic representation of phenomena. New adaptations of mathematics by which otherwise hopeless complexities can be comprehended are quite fundamental but do not lend themselves to popular display. The work of Leibnitz, Faraday, and Hertz was not the popular science of their day. Yet it is by virtue of their strange calculations with strange symbols that men today fly and broadcast their speech around the earth. This should be remembered by "writers" and others who complain that social scientists are adopting "jargon" and "esoteric" symbols which go beyond the vocabulary of the current "best-seller."

If I deal primarily with these more obscure and undramatic labours of social scientists, it is because I regard them as more important in the long run than the conspicuous contemporary achievements which are common knowledge. I do not overlook or underestimate these more obvious and demonstrable achievements. The transition in our time to more humane treatment of children, the poor, and the unfortunate, by more enlightened education, social work, and penology must in large measure be attributed to the expanding sciences of psychology and sociology. I know, of course, that whenever a war or a depression occurs journalists and preachers point to the impotence of economists and political scientists either to predict or prevent these disasters. The fact is that the course of events following World War I, down to and including the present, was predicted with great accuracy by large numbers of social scientists. That nothing was done about it is not the special responsibility of social scientists. "Doing something about it" is the common responsibility of all members of a community, including scientists, and especially of those who specialise in mass education, mass leadership, and practical programmes.

It is not my main purpose to review the past and present achievements of the social sciences.... I am here concerned primarily with the probable future of the social sciences. Even if I should admit that social scientists are today merely chipping flint in the Stone Age of their science, I do not see that we have any choice but to follow the rough road that other sciences have traveled. The attainment of comparable success may seem remote, and the labours involved may seem staggering. But is the prospect really unreasonably remote? Suppose that someone four hundred years ago had delivered an address on the future of the physical sciences and suppose that he had envisioned only a small fraction of their present achievements. What would have been the reaction of even a sophisticated audience to predictions of men flying and speaking across oceans, seeing undreamed-of worlds, both through microscopes and telescopes, and the almost incredible feats of modern engineering and surgery? Nothing I have suggested, I think, in the way of mature social science with comparable practical application seems as improbable as would the story of our people to physicist of four hundred or even one hundred years ago....

We have hitherto lacked boldness and an adequate vision of the true task of social science. Research in this field is today for the most part a quest for superficial remedies, for commercial guidance, and for historical and contemporary "human interest" stories. Everybody recognises the importance of bookkeeping, census taking, studying the condition of the Negro population, and predicting the number of girdles that will be purchased in department stores a year from now. But there are types of research the immediate practical uses of which are not so obvious, yet which are essential to scientific development.

Shall we or shall we not assume that we can formulate laws of human behaviour which are comparable to the laws of gravity, thermodynamics and bacteriology? These latter laws do not of themselves create engineering wonders or cure disease. Nevertheless they constitute knowledge of a kind which is indispensable. The present argument is obviously handicapped in its most crucial respect, namely, its inability, in the space here available, to exhibit laws of social behaviour comparable to the physical laws mentioned. Yet we have made considerable progress in this direction.

Finally, we come to what is regarded by any people, including scientists, as the most fundamental difference of all between the physical and the social sciences. "To understand and describe a system involving values," says Huxley, "is impossible without some judgment of values." Values," he goes on to say, "are deliberately excluded from the purview of natural science."

It would be difficult to find a better example of confused thinking than that offered by current discussions of "values" and their supposed incompatibility with science. A principal cause of the confusion is a semantic error which is extremely common in the social sciences. In this case, it consists in converting the verb "valuating," meaning any discriminatory or selective behaviour, into a noun called "values." We then go hunting for the *things* denoted by this noun. But there are no such things. There are only the valuating *activities* we started with. What was said above about motives applies with equal force to values. They are clearly inferences from behaviour. That is, we say a thing *has* value or *is* a value when people behave toward it so as to retain or increase their possession of it. It may be economic goods and services, political office, a mate, graduation, prestige, a clear conscience, or anything you please. Since valuations or values are empirically observable patterns of behaviour, they may be studied as such, by the same general techniques we use to study other behaviour.

As a matter of fact, everybody is more or less regularly engaged in such study of other people's values. It is quite essential to any kind of satisfactory living in any community. We try to find out as soon as possible what the values of our neighbours are. How do we find out? We observe their behaviour, including their verbal behaviour. We listen to what other people say about them, we notice what they spend their money for, how they vote, whether they go to church, and a hundred other things. On a more formal and scientific level, opinion polls on men and issues are taken to reflect the values of large groups. Economists, of course, have been studying for years certain kinds of evaluations of men through the medium of prices.

There appears to be no reason why values should not be studied as objectively as any other phenomena, for they are an inseparable part of behaviour. The conditions under which certain values, arise, i.e., the conditions under which certain kinds of valuating behaviour take place, and the effects of "the existence of certain values" (as we say) in given situations are precisely what the social sciences must study and what they are studying. These values or valuating behaviours, like all other behaviour, are to be observed, classified, interpreted, and generalised by the accepted techniques of scientific procedure.

Why, then, is the value problem considered unique and insurmountable in the social sciences?

The main reason seems to be that social scientists, like other people, often have strong feelings about religion, art, politics and economics. That is, they have their likes and dislikes in these matters as they have in wine, women and song. As a result of these preferences, both physical and social scientists frequently join other citizens to form pressure groups to advance the things they favour, including their own economic or professional advancement, Labour, Capital, Democracy, the True Church, or what not. To do so is the right of every citizen, and there is no canon of science or of civil law which requires scientists to abjure the rights which are enjoyed by all other members of a community.

The confusion about values seems to have arisen because both scientists and the public have frequently assumed that, when scientists engage in ordinary pressure-group activity, that activity somehow becomes science or scientific activity. This is a most mischievous fallacy. It is not surprising, perhaps, that the public should be confused on this point, because it may not always be clear when a scientist is expressing a scientific conclusion and when he is expressing a personal preference. But it is unpardonable for scientists themselves to be confused about what they know and say in their capacity as scientists and what they favour in religion, morals, and public policy. To pose as disinterested scientists announcing scientific conclusions when in fact they are merely expressing personal preferences is simple fraud, no matter how laudable or socially desirable may be the scientists' "motives" and objectives.

But, is it possible for a person to play two or more distinct roles, such as scientist and citizen, without confusing the two? The answer is that it is being done every day.

It is the most obvious common-place that the actress who plays Juliet in the afternoon and Lady Macbeth at night does not allow her moral or other preference for one of these roles to influence her performance of the other. In any event, her competence is measured by her ability to play each role convincingly. During the same day she may also be expected to fulfill the roles of wife, mother, etc. Likewise, the chemist who vigorously campaigns against the use of certain gases in war obviously cannot allow that attitude to influence in the slightest degree the methods of producing or analysing these gases. Science, as such, is nonmoral. There is nothing in scientific work, as such, which dictates to what ends the products of science shall be used.

In short, it is not true that "to understand and describe a system involving values is impossible without some judgment of values." I can certainly report and understand the bald fact that a certain tribe kills its aged and eats them, without saying one word about the goodness or badness of that practice according to my own standards, or allowing these standards of mine to prevent me from giving an accurate report of the facts mentioned. The only value judgments which any properly trained scientist makes about his data are judgments regarding their relevance to his problem, the weight to be assigned to each aspect, and the general interpretation to be made of the observed events. These are problems which no scientist can escape, and they are not at all unique or insuperable in the social sciences.

Have scientists, then, no special function or obligation in determining the ends for which scientific knowledge is to be used? As scientists, *it is their business to determine reliably the immediate and remote costs and consequences of alternate possible courses of action* and to make these known to the public. Scientists may then *in their capacity as citizens* join with others in advocating one alternative rather than another, as they prefer.

To the extent that their reputation and prestige is great, and to the extent that their tastes are shared by the masses of men, scientists will, of course, be influential in causing others to accept the goals the scientists recommend. In this sense, social science will doubtless become, as physical science already is, an important influence in determining the wants of men. That is, as a result of scientific knowledge, men will not want impossible or mutually exclusive things. They will not seek to increase foreign trade and at the same time establish more comprehensive and higher tariffs. They will not seek to reduce crime but at the same time maintain a crime-promoting penal system. They will not destroy the productive power of a nation and still expect it to be peaceful, prosperous and democratic. They will not expect a world organisation to be conjured into existence by semantically deranged "statesmen," before the necessary preceding integration of the constituent units has been achieved.

The development of the social sciences and the diffusion of scientific knowledge will doubtless greatly influence in the above ways the wants, wishes, and choices of men. But there is still an important difference between a statement of fact and the dictation of conduct. It is one thing for a physician to tell a patient: "Unless you undergo this operation, which will cost so much in time, money, and pain, you will probably die in one month." It is another matter to say: "Science, for which I am an accredited spokesman, says you shall undergo this operation." Any scientist who pretends that science authorises him to make the latter statement is a fraud and a menace. Dictation of this type has not accompanied the rise of physical science and it need not result from the full maturity of the social sciences. This needs to be kept in mind especially in these days of much worry about brain trusts and whether, with the development of atomic fission, scientists must become a priestly class dictating all public policy.

The misunderstanding regarding the relation of scientists to practical affairs is so widespread and mischievous as to warrant further emphasis. The *application* of scientific knowledge obviously involves value judgments of some sort. This problem is equally present in the other sciences. After we know how to produce dynamite and what it will do, there remains the question: Shall we drop it from airplanes to destroy cathedrals and cities, or shall we use it to build roads through the mountains? After we know the effects of certain drugs and gases, the question still remains: Shall we use them to alleviate pain and prevent disease, or shall we use them to destroy helpless and harmless populations? There is certainly nothing in the well-developed sciences of chemistry or physics which answers these questions. Neither is it the business of the social sciences to answer (except *conditionally,* as we have seen) the question of what form of government we should have, what our treatment of other races should be, whether we should tolerate or persecute certain religious groups, whether and to what degree civil liberties should be maintained, and a multitude of other question which agitate us. What, then, are social scientists for and what should they be able to do?

Broadly speaking, it is the business of social scientists to be able to predict with high probability the social weather, just as meteorologists predict sunshine and storm. More specifically, social scientists should be able to say what is likely to happen socially under stated conditions. A competent economist or political scientist should be able to devise, for example, a tax programme for a given country which will yield with high probability a certain revenue and which will fall in whatever desired degrees upon each of the income groups of the area concerned. Social scientists should be able to state also what will be the effect of the application of this programme upon income, investments, consumption, production, and the outcome of the next election. Having devised such a tax programme and clearly specified what it will do, it is not the business of the social scientists any more than it is the business of any other citizens to secure the adoption or defeat of such a programme. In the same way, competent sociologists, educators, or psychologists should be able to advise a parent as to the most convenient way of converting a son into an Al Capone or into an approved citizen, according to what is desired.

My point is that no science tells us *what to do* with the knowledge that constitutes the science. Science only provides a car and a chauffeur for us. It does not directly, as science, tell us where to drive. The car and the chauffeur will take us into the ditch, over the precipice, against a stone wall, or into the highlands of age-long human aspirations with equal efficiency. If we agree as to where we want to go and tell the driver our goal, he should be able to take us there by any one of a number of possible routes the costs and conditions of each of which the scientist should be able to explain to us. When these alternatives have been made clear, it is also a proper function of the scientist to devise the quickest and most reliable instrument for detecting the wishes of his passengers. But, except in his capacity as one of the passengers, the scientist who serves as navigator and chauffeur has no scientific privilege or duty to tell the rest of the passengers what they *should* want. There is nothing in either physical or social science which answers this question. Confusion on this point is, I think, the main reason for the common delusion that the social sciences, at least, must make value judgments of this kind.

But it does follow, as we have seen, that science, by virtue of its true function, as outlined above, may be of the utmost importance in helping people to decide intelligently what they want. We shall return to this subject in the concluding chapter. In the meantime, it may be noted that the broad general wants of people are perhaps everywhere highly uniform. They want, for example, a certain amount of physical and social security and some fun. It is disagreement over the means toward these ends, as represented by fantastic ideologies, that results in conflict and chaos. I have pointed out that, in proportion as a science is well developed, it can describe with accuracy *the consequences* of a variety of widely disparate programmes of action. These consequences, if reliably predicted, are bound strongly to influence what people will want. But it remains a fact that science, in the sense of a predicter of consequences, is only *one* of the numerous influences that determine an individual's wants and his consequent behaviour. Science and scientists are still the servants, not the masters, of mankind. Accordingly, those scientists who contend that they can scientifically determine not only the means but the ends of social policy should be exposed as scientific fakers as well as would-be dictators. Yet this is the very group which professes to be concerned about the democratic implications of the position I am here defending?

Finally, this view seems to some people to do away with what they call "the moral basis of society." Obviously, it does nothing of the sort. The question is not about the moral basis of society but about the social basis of morals. We merely advocate a scientific basis for morality. Presumably, all will agree that morals exist for man, not man for morals. Morals are those rules of conduct which man thinks have been to his advantage through the ages. Why should we then not all agree that we want the most authentic possible appraisal of that subject?

There appears, then, to be no reason why the methods of science cannot solve social problems. Neither should we expect more from social than from physical science. As *science*, both physical and social sciences have a common function, namely , to answer scientific questions. These answers will always be of an impersonal, conditional type: "*If* the temperature falls to 32° F., *then* water (H_2O) will freeze." "*If* a certain type of tax is adopted, *then* certain types of industrial activity will decrease." Neither of these statements carries any implications as to whether or how the knowledge should be used. Far from being a weakness, this characteristic of scientific knowledge is its greatest strength. The wants of men will change with changing conditions through the ages. The value of scientific knowledge lies precisely in this impersonal, neutral, general validity for whatever purpose man desires to use it.

For this reason, those scientists and others who try to identify science with some particular social programme, sect, or party must be regarded as the most dangerous enemies of science. They are more dangerous than its avowed enemies, because the defenders of "democratic," "communist," "religious," or "moral" science pose as defenders of science and carry on their agitation in the name of lofty social sentiments. That this group is confused rather than malicious is evident from their proposal that scientists should take an oath not to engage in scientific activity which may be "destructive" or contrary to "toleration," "justice," etc. The absurdity of the proposal is readily apparent, if we consider any actual scientific work. No scientist can foresee all the uses to which his work may be put, and in any event it is a commonplace that the *same* drug may be used to cure or to kill people. It may be granted that preposterous proposals of this kind are a temporary hysterical phenomenon superinduced by such dramatic developments as the atomic bomb. It may be granted that the agitators are motivated by lofty social sentiments. Unfortunately, the same has been said for prominent proponents of the Inquisition.

The uses to which scientific or other knowledge is to be put have always been and will continue to be a legitimate concern of men. Science, as we have noted, can be valuable in helping men to decide that question.... Our warning here has been directed against attempts to corrupt scientific methods and results by allowing them to be influenced by the temporary, provincial, ethnocentric preferences of particular scientists or pressure groups.

7

The Sociological Theory of Totemism[1]

There has been in the past some disagreement and discussion as to the definition of totemism. I wish to avoid as far as possible entering into any such discussion. The purpose of preliminary definitions in science is to mark off a class of phenomena for special study. A term is useful if and in so far as it brings together for our attention a number of phenomena which are in reality, and not merely in appearance, closely related to one another. It will be part of my thesis in this paper that however widely or narrowly we may define totemism, we cannot reach an understanding of the phenomena we so name unless we study systematically a much wider group of phenomena, namely, the general relation between man and natural species in mythology and ritual. It may well be asked if 'totemism' as a technical term has not outlived its usefulness.

It is necessary, however, to have some definition to guide and control our discussion. I shall use the term in the wider sense to apply wherever a society is divided into groups and there is a special relation between each group and one or more classes of objects that are usually natural species of animals or plants but may occasionally be artificial objects or parts of an animal. The word is sometimes used in a narrower sense and applied only when the groups in question are clans, i.e. exogamous groups of which all the members are regarded as being closely related by descent in one line. I shall regard 'clan totemism' as only one variety of totemism, in the wider sense.[2]

Even in the narrower sense of clan totemism, and still more in the wider sense, totemism is not one thing but is a general name given to a number of diverse institutions which all have, or seem to have, something in common. Thus even in the limited region of Australia, which has a single homogeneous culture throughout, there have been recorded a number of different varieties of totemism, and new varieties are being discovered by systematic researches now in progress.

In the south-east of the continent is found sex-totemism, i.e. an association of the two sex-groups, men and women, with two animal species. In the coastal districts of New South Wales, for example, the bat is the totem or animal representative of the men and the tree-creeper *(Climacteris sp.)* is that of the women.

In many parts of Australia the tribe is divided into two exogamous moieties, patrilineal in some regions, matrilineal in others. In some instances the moieties are named after species of animals, generally birds. Amongst such names are the following pairs: crow and white cockatoo, white cockatoo and black cockatoo, eaglehawk and crow, native companion and turkey, hill kangaroo and long-legged kangaroo. In other instances the meanings of the moiety names have not been discovered, and in some of them, at any rate, it seems certain that they are not animal names.

In many of the tribes that have this dual division, independently of whether the moieties are named after animals or not, there is a classification of animals and frequently of other natural objects whereby some are regarded as belonging to one moiety and others to the other.

Such moiety totemism, if we may use that term for any such association between the moiety and one or more natural species, is found in a number of different varieties in Australia, and still other varieties are found in Melanesia and in North America.

Over a large part of Australia the tribe is divided into four groups which have often been called 'classes' but which I prefer to call 'sections'. The easiest way to understand this division into four is to regard it as constituted by the intersection of a pair of patrilineal moieties and a pair of matrilineal moieties.[3]

These sections are not as a rule named after species of animals, though there are one or two instances in which a section name is also the name of an animal. Thus Bandjur in Yukumbil is the name of a section and also of the native bear. In some tribes, however, there is a definite association between each section and one or more species of animal. Thus in the Nigena tribe of the Kimberley district of Western Australia the four sections are associated with four species of hawk. In some regions this association does not carry with it any prohibition against killing or eating the animal associated with one's own or any other section. In part of Queensland, however, each section has associated with it a number of species of animals and there is a rule that the members of a section may not eat the animals so associated with their section.

This 'section totemism' requires further investigation. We may distinguish, however, three varieties. In one each section has associated with it a single species of animal which is representative of the section in somewhat the same way as the sex-totem is the representative of the sex-group. In a second variety each section stands in a special ritual relation to a certain limited number of species which may not be eaten by the members of the section. In the third variety a great number of species of animals are classified as belonging to one or other of the four sections but there is no rule against eating the animals belonging to one's own section. The one thing that is common to these varieties is that each section is differentiated from the others and given its own individuality by being associated with one or more animal species.

In some tribes the four sections are again subdivided each into two parts, giving a division of the tribe into eight sub-sections. In some of these tribes there exist special associations between the sub-sections and certain natural species. Further investigation is needed before we can profitably discuss this subject.

If now we turn to clan-totemism we find a number of different varieties of this in Australia, too many, in fact, to be even enumerated in a short paper. Matrilineal clan totemism of different varieties occurs in three, or possibly four, separate areas in the east, north, and west of the continent. In Melville and Bathurst Islands there are three matrilineal phratries subdivided into twenty-two clans. Each clan is associated with one natural species, usually a species of animal or plant, though one or two clans have two totems and one has three. The association between the clan and its totem is apparently of very little importance in the life of the tribe. There is no prohibition against eating or using the totem, there are no totemic ceremonies, and totemism has little influence on the mythology.

The matrilineal clan totemism of some tribes of New South Wales, Victoria and South Australia seems to be of somewhat more importance. Here we find matrilineal moieties sometimes named totemically, sometimes not, and each moiety is divided into a number of clans. Each clan has one or more natural species regarded as belonging to it. Where there are several species associated with each clan, as is the case in many tribes, one of them is regarded as more important than the others and the clan is named after it. Throughout this region there is, so far as we know, no prohibition against killing or eating the totem.

Totemic ceremonial is apparently little developed nor have we any evidence of any elaborate totemic mythology connected with matrilineal totemism.

It should be noted that throughout Australia the most important group for social purposes is the horde, i.e. a small group occupying and owning a certain defined territory, and that the horde is normally strictly patrilineal. It follows that wherever there is a system of matrilineal totemic clans the clan consists of individuals scattered through a number of hordes. We thus get a double grouping of individuals. For most social purposes the individual is dependent on the local group, i.e. the horde, to which he is connected through his father, while at the same time he is also connected through his mother to a totemic group the members of which are scattered throughout the tribe.

Patrilineal totemism in Australia is more difficult to describe briefly than is matrilineal totemism. Where it exists the primary totemic group is usually the horde, i.e. the small patrilineal local group. In some regions the horde is a clan, i.e. it consists of close relatives in the male line and is therefore exogamous. But in a few regions the horde is not a clan in this sense.

As an example of one variety of patrilineal totemism we may take the tribes at the mouth of the Murray River (Yaralde, etc.). Here each horde is a local clan and each clan has one or more species of natural object associated with it. There is no prohibition against eating the totem of one's clan, but it is regarded with some respect. There is no evidence of totemic ceremonial or of any elaborate totemic mythology. The function of the totem seems to be merely to act as the representative of the group.

Perhaps the most important, and certainly the most interesting, form of totemism in Australia is that to a brief consideration of which we now pass. This consists of a four fold association between (1) the horde, i.e. the patrilineal local group, (2) a certain number of classes of objects, animals, plants, and other things such as rain, sun and hot weather, cold weather, babies, etc., (3) certain sacred spots within the territory of the horde, frequently water-holes, each one of which is specially associated with one or more of the 'totems' of the group, and (4) certain mythical beings who are supposed to have given rise to these sacred spots in the mythical period of the beginning of the world. This system of totemism is now being traced and studied in a number of variant forms over a very large part of the Australian continent. It was formerly known best from the centre of the continent, where, however, the Aranda have it in a somewhat modified or anomalous form. We now know that it exists or existed over a large part of Western Australia. Recently it has been discovered and studied in the Cape York Peninsula by Miss McConnel. At the beginning of this year I was able to demonstrate its former existence on the east coast of Australia in the north of New South Wales and in southern Queensland.

Where this type of totemism is found it is usually accompanied by a system of ceremonies for the increase of natural species. The members of the horde, or some of them, proceed to the totem centre or sacred spot connected with a natural species and perform there a ceremony which is believed to result in an increase of that species. There is also an elaborate mythology dealing with the sacred totem centres and with the mythical beings who gave rise to them.

It may be noted that this kind of totemism may coexist in the same tribe with other kinds. Thus in the Dieri tribe it exists together with a system of matrilineal clan totemism. In some part it coexists with section totemism.

Finally, we may note that in some parts of Australia there exists what a sometimes called individual or personal totemism. This is a special relation between an individual and some one or more species of animal. A good example is found in some tribes of New South Wales where every medicine-man has one or more of such personal totems. It is through his association with the animal species that he acquires his power to perform magic. Whether we call this totemism or not, it is quite evident that it is closely related to totemism and that any theory of totemism, to be satisfactory, must take it into account.

This brief and very incomplete survey of Australian institutions has shown us that special associations of groups or individuals with natural species exist in that region in a number of different forms. We find all gradations from a tribe with no form of totemism at all (such as the Bad of northern Dampier Land) through tribes such as the Melville Islanders where totemism of a simple form exists but is of comparatively little importance in the life of the tribe, to a tribe such as the Dieri Which combines in a complex system two forms of totemism, one of matrilineal clans and the other of patrilineal hordes, with a highly elaborated totemic ritual and mythology. The only thing that these totemic systems have in common is the general tendency to characterise the segments into which society is divided by an association between each segment and some natural species or some portion of nature. The association may take any one of a number of different forms.

In the past the theoretical discussion of totemism was almost entirely concerned with speculations as to its possible origin. If we use the word origin to mean the historical process by which an institution or custom or a state of culture comes into existence, then it is clear that the very diverse forms of totemism that exist all over the world must have had very diverse origins. To be able to speak of an origin of totemism we must assume that all these diverse institutions that we include under the one general term have been derived by successive modifications from a single form. There does not seem to me to be a particle of evidence to justify such an assumption. But even if we make it we can still only speculate as to what this original form of totemism may have been, as to the enormously complex series of events which could have produced from it the various existing totemic systems, and as to where, when, and how that hypothetical original form of totemism came into existence. And such speculations, being for ever incapable of inductive verification, can be nothing more than speculations and can have no value for a science of culture.

For sociology, or social anthropology, by which I understand the study of the phenomena of culture by the same inductive methods that are in use in the natural sciences, the phenomena of totemism present a problem of a different kind. The task of the inductive sciences is to discover the universal or the general in the particular. That of a science of culture is to reduce the complex data with which it deals to a limited number of general laws or principles. Approaching totemism in this way we may formulate the problem that it presents in the form of the question, 'Can we show that totemism is a special form of a observation which is universal in human society and is therefore present in different forms in all cultures?'

The most important attempt to arrive at a sociological theory of totemism is that of the late Professor Durkheim in his work *Les Formes élémentaires de la Vie religieuse*. I think that work is an important and permanent contribution to sociological theory, but that it does not provide a complete and satisfactory theory of totemism. I shall attempt to point out, in the briefest possible way, where Durkheim's theory seems to me to fail.

Durkheim speaks of the totem as being 'sacred' to the members of the group of which it is the totem. This is to use the term 'sacred' in a sense somewhat different from that which it has at the present day in English or even in French, and not even identical with, though somewhat nearer to, the meaning that *sacer* had in Latin. I prefer to use a term which is as free as possible from special connotations, and therefore, instead of saying that the totem is sacred I find it preferable to say that there is a 'ritual relation' between persons and their totem. There exists a ritual relation whenever a society imposes on its members a certain attitude towards an object, which attitude involves some measure of respect expressed in a traditional mode of behaviour with reference to that object. Thus the relation between a Christian and the first day of the week is a typical example of a ritual relation.

Every society adopts, and imposes upon its members, towards certain objects, this attitude of mind and behaviour which I am calling the ritual attitude. There are, not only in different societies but in the same society in different references, many different varieties of this attitude, but all the varieties have something in common. Moreover the ritual attitude may vary from a very indefinite one to a definite and highly organised one.

One of the important problems of sociology is therefore to discover the function of this universal element of culture and to formulate its laws. This general problem obviously includes a vast number of partial problems of which the problem of totemism is one. That problem may be stated as being that of discovering why in certain societies a ritual attitude towards a certain species of natural object is imposed upon the members of a particular social group. It is obvious that no solution of the lesser problem of totemism can be satisfactory unless it conforms with or is part of a general solution of the wider problem, i.e. a theory of ritual relations in general.

With regard to the general problem Durkheim's theory is that the primary object of the ritual attitude is the social order itself, and that any thing becomes an object of that attitude when it stands in a certain relation to the social order. This general theory, with which I agree, obviously amounts to very little until we have succeeded in defining the more important types of relation to the social order which result in the object which stands in such a relation becoming an object of ritual attitude.

If I may restate in my own terms Durkheim's theory of totemism it is as follows. A social group such as a clan can only possess solidarity and permanence if it is the object of sentiments of attachment in the minds of its members. For such sentiments to be maintained in existence they must be given occasional collective expression. By a law that can be, I think, readily verified, all regular collective expressions of social sentiments tend to take on a ritual form. And in ritual, again by a necessary law, some more or less concrete object is required which can act as the representative of the group. So that it is a normal procedure that the sentiment of attachment to a group shall be expressed in some formalised collective behaviour having reference to an object that represents the group itself.

A typical example is to be found in our own society. National solidarity depends on a sentiment of patriotism in the minds of the nation. This sentiment, in conformity with the laws stated above, tends to find some of its chief expressions in reference to such concrete objects as flags, or kings and presidents, and such objects become in this way objects of the ritual attitude.

Part of a king's sacredness, whether in Africa or in Europe, is due to the fact that he is the representative of the national solidarity and unity, and the ritual that surrounds him is the means by which patriotic sentiments are maintained. In the same way in the flag we have an object which is 'sacred' because it is the concrete material representative or emblem of a social group and its solidarity.

Durkheim compares the totem of a clan with the flag of a nation. The comparison is valid, in a very general sense, for some forms of totemism, if not for all. But putting the comparison aside, the theory is that the totem is 'sacred' as Durkheim says, or is an object of ritual attitude, as I prefer to say, because it is the concrete representative or emblem of a social group. And the function of the ritual attitude towards the totem is to express and so to maintain in existence the solidarity of the social group.

With Durkheim's theory as stated above in my own terms I am in agreement, but I do not regard it as complete. In the first place it seems to me that totemism has other functions besides the one indicated above. Secondly, the theory so far as stated above does not explain why so many peoples in America, Asia, Africa and Australasia should select as emblems or representatives of clans or other social groups species of animals or plants. It is true that Durkheim offers an answer to this question, but it is an entirely unsatisfactory one. He regards as an essential part of totemism the use of totemic emblems or designs, i.e. figured representations of the totemic animal or plant, and suggests that the reason for selecting natural objects as emblems of social groups is because they are capable of being used in this way.

This hypothesis fails as soon as we apply it to the facts. In Australia no designs are made of the sex totems or of the totems of the moieties or sections, and even for clan totemism there are many tribes that do not make any representations of their totems. Totemic designs, which for Durkheim are so important or indeed so essential a part of totemism, are characteristics of central and northern Australia but not of the continent as a whole.

Moreover, the reason suggested for the selection of natural objects as emblems of social groups is of too accidental a character to give a satisfying explanation of an institution that is so widespread as totemism. There must surely be some much more important reason why all these peoples all over the world find it appropriate to represent social groups in this way by associating each one with some animal or plant.

This, then, is where I think Durkheim's theory of totemism fails. It implies that the totem owes its sacred or ritual character solely to its position as the emblem of a group. Now there are a number of peoples who have no form of totemism amongst whom we still find that natural species such as animals and plants are objects of ritual or of the ritual attitudes expressed in mythology. And even amongst totemic people such as the Australian tribes the ritual customs relating to natural species are not all totemic. In other words the phenomena which we have agreed to denote by the term totemism are merely a part of a much larger class of phenomena which includes all sorts of ritual relations between man and natural species. No theory of totemism is satisfactory unless it conforms with a more general theory providing an explanation of many other things besides totemism. Durkheim's theory fails to do this.

In a great number, and I believe probably in all, of the societies where man depends entirely or largely on the hunting of wild animals and the collection of wild plants, whether they have any form of totemism or not, the animals and plants are made objects of the ritual attitude. This is done frequently, though perhaps not quite universally, in mythology, in which animal species are personified and regarded as ancestors of culture heroes. It is don also by a mass of customs relating to animals and plants. This system of ritual and mythological relations between man and natural species can be best studied in non-totemic peoples such as the Eskimo or the Andaman Islanders. In such societies we find that the relation between the society and the natural species is a general one, all the most important animals and plants being treated as in some way sacred (either in ritual or in mythology) and some being regarded as more sacred than other, but any single species being equally sacred to every member of the whole community. The ritual attitude of the Andaman Islanders towards the turtle, of Californian Indians to the salmon, of the peoples of North America and northern Asia to the bear, constitutes a relation between the whole society and the sacred species.

Now totemism, I would suggest, arises from or is a special development of this general ritual relation between man and natural species. Let us assume for the moment that such a general ritual relation of man to nature is universal in hunting societies, as I believe it can be shown to be. When the society becomes differentiated into segmentary groups such as clans, a process of ritual specialisation takes place by which each segment acquires a special and particular relation to some one or more of the *sacra* of the community, i.e. to some one or more natural species. The totem of the clan or group is still sacred in some sense to the whole community, but is now specially sacred, and in some special way, to the segment of which it is the totem.

The process here suggested as the active principle in the development of totemism is one which I believe to be of great importance in social development, and which can be observed in other phenomena. Thus, to take only one example, and perhaps not the best, in the Roman Church the saints are sacred to all members of the church as a whole. But the church is segmented into local congregations and a congregation is often placed in a special relation to one particular saint to whom its chapel is dedicated. This is, I think, parallel to clan or group totemism. We might also draw a significant though not quite exact analogy between the patron saint of an individual and the personal totem or guardian animal of Australian and American tribes.

There is no space in this paper to discuss this process of ritual specialisation, and indeed any adequate treatment of the subject would require us to deal with the whole process of social differentiation and segmentation. I will refer to a single example that may help to illustrate the problem. Amongst the Eskimo of part of North America one of the most important features of their adaptation to their environment is the sharp division between winter and summer, and between the winter animals and the summer animals. There is a complex system of ritual relations between the society and all the most important of these animals and in this ritual the opposition between summer and winter is strongly expressed. Thus you may not eat reindeer meat (summer food) and walrus meat (winter food) on the same day. The Eskimo have made for themselves a segmentation into two groups, one consisting of all the persons born in the summer and the other of those born in the winter, and there is some slight ritual specialisation, the summer people being regarded as specially connected with the summer animals and the winter people with the winter animals. This is not quite totemism, but it is clearly related to it, and illustrates, I think, the process by which totemism arises.

In this way, I think, we can formulate a sociological theory of totemism which incorporates a great deal of Durkheim's analysis and is not open to the criticism that can be levelled against Durkheim's own presentation. We start with the empirical generalisation that amongst hunting and collecting peoples the more important animals and plants and natural phenomena are treated, in custom and in myth, as being 'sacred', i.e. they are made, in various ways and in different degrees, objects of the ritual attitude. Primarily this ritual relation between man and nature is a general one between the society as a whole and its sacra. When the society is differentiated, i.e. divided into segments or social groups marked off from one another and each having its own solidarity and individuality, there comes into action a principle which is more widespread than totemism and is indeed an important part of the general process of social differentiation, a principle by which within the general relation of the society to its sacra there are established special relations between each group or segment and some one or more of those sacra.

This theory incorporates what I think is the most valuable part of Durkheim's analysis, in the recognition that the function of the ritual relation of the group to its totem is to express and so to maintain in existence the solidarity of the group. It gives moreover a reason, which can be shown, I think, to be grounded in the very nature of social organisation itself, for the selection of natural species as emblems or representatives of social groups.

Before leaving this part of the discussion I would like to touch on the one further point. Durkheim, in reference to clan totemism, emphasises the clan and its solidarity. The totem, for him, is primarily the means by which the clan recognises and expresses its unity. But the matter is much more complex than this. The clan is merely a segment of a larger society which also has its solidarity. By its special relation to its totem or totems the clan recognises its unity and its individuality. This is simply a special example of the universal process by which solidarity is created and maintained by uniting a number of individuals in a collective relation to the same sacred object or objects. By the fact that each clan has its own totem there is expressed the differentiation and opposition between clan and clan. The kangaroo men not only recognise the bond that unites them as kangaroo men but also recognise their difference from the emu men and the bandicoot men and so on. But also the wider unity and solidarity of the whole totemic society is expressed by the fact that the society as a whole, through its segments, stands in a ritual relation to nature as a whole. This is seeen very well in the system of increase ceremonies that is so widespread in Australia. Each group is responsible for the ritual clan of a certain number of species by which the maintenance of that species is believed to be assured. For the tribe all these species are of importance, and the ceremonies are thus a sort of co-operative effort, involving a division of (ritual) labour, by which the normal processes of nature and the supply of food are provided for. One of the results of Durkheim's theory is that it over-emphasis the clan and clan solidarity. Totemism does more than express the unity of the clan; it also expresses the unity of totemic society as a whole in the relations of the clans to one another within the wider unity.

The result of my argument, if it is valid, is to substitute for the problem of totemism another problem. The question that now demands an answer is, 'Why do the majority of what are called primitive peoples adopt in their custom and myth a ritual attitude towards animals and other natural species?' My aim in this paper has simply been to exhibit as exactly as possible in a brief space the relation of the problem of totemism to this wider problem.

It is obvious that I cannot attempt in a mere conclusion to a paper to deal with this subject of the relation in myth and ritual of man and nature. I attempted some years ago to deal with it in reference to the customs and beliefs of one non-totemic people, the Andaman Islanders. As a result of that and other investigations I was led to formulate the following law: Any object or event which has important effects upon the well-being (material or spiritual) of a society, or any thing which stands for or represents any such object or event, tends to become an object of the ritual attitude.

I have given reasons for rejecting Durkheim's theory that in totemism natural species become sacred because they are selected as representatives of social groups, and I hold, on the contrary, that natural species are selected as representatives of social groups, such as clans, because they are already objects of the ritual attitude on quite another basis, by virtue of the general law of the ritual expression of social values stated above.

In modern thought we are accustomed to draw a distinction between the social order and the natural order. We regard society as consisting of certain human beings grouped in a social structure under certain moral principles or laws, and we place over against the society its environment, consisting of geographical features, flora and fauna, climate with its seasonal changes, and so on, governed by natural law.

For certain purposes this contrast of society and environment, of man and nature, is a useful one, but we must not let it mislead us. From another and very important point of view the natural order enters into and becomes part of the social order. The seasonal changes that control the rhythm of social life, the animals and plants that are sued for food or other purposes, these enter into and become an essential part of the social life, the social order. I believe that it can be shown that it is just in so far as they thus enter into the social order that natural phenomena and natural objects become, either in themselves, or through things or beings that represent them, objects of the ritual attitude, and I have already tried to demonstrate this so far as the Andaman Islanders are concerned. Our own explicit conception of a natural order and of natural law does not exist amongst the more primitive peoples, though the germs out of which it develops do exist in the empirical control of causal processes in technical activities. For primitive man the universe as a whole is a moral or social order governed not by what we call natural law but rather by what we must call moral or ritual law. The recognition of this conception, implicit but not explicit, in ritual and in myth is, I believe, one of the most important steps towards the proper understanding not only of what is sometimes called 'primitive mentality' but also of all the phenomena that we group vaguely around the term religion.[4]

A study of primitive myth and ritual from this point of view is, I think, very illuminating. In Australia, for example, there are innumerable ways in which the natives have built up between themselves and the phenomena of nature of a system of relations which are essentially similar to the relations that they have built up in their social structure between one human being and another.

I can do no more than mention examples. One is the personification of natural phenomena and of natural species. A species of animal is personified, i.e. treated for certain purposes as if it were a human being, and in the mythology such personified species are regarded as ancestors or culture heroes. The function of this process of personification is that it permits nature to be thought of as if it were a society of persons, and so makes of it a social or moral order. Another of the processes by which, in Australia, the world of nature is brought within the social order is to be found in the systems of classification of natural species, existing in a number of diverse forms in different parts of the continent with this one thing in common to them all, that the more important natural species are so classified that each one is regarded as belonging to a certain social group, and occupying a specific position in the social structure.

The suggestion I put forward, therefore, is that totemism is part of a larger whole, and that one important way in which we can characterise this whole is that it provides a representation of the universe as a moral or social order. Durkheim, if he did not actually formulate this view, at any rate cam near to it. But his conception seems to have been that the process by which this takes place is by a projection of society into external nature. On the contrary, I hold that the process is one by which, in the fashioning of culture, external nature, so called, comes to be incorporated in the social order as an essential part of it.

Now the conception of the universe as a moral order is not confined to primitive peoples, but is an essential part of every system of religion. It is, I think, a universal element in human culture. With the question of why this should be so I cannot now attempt to deal.

I may summarise what I have tried to say as follows: A sociological theory of totemism must be able to show that totemism is simply a special form taken in certain definite conditions by an element or process of culture that is universal and necessary. Durkheim's attempt to provide such a theory fails in certain important respects. We can, however, incorporate a good deal of Durkheim's analysis in a theory which rests on the same general hypothesis of the nature and function of ritual or the 'sacred'.

Finally, my argument has brought out something of the conditions in which this universal element of culture is most likely to take the form of totemism. These are: (1) dependence wholly or in part on natural productions for subsistence, and (2) the existence of a segmentary organisation into clans and moieties or other similar social units. The Andamanese and the Eskimo have (1) but not (2), and they have no totemism though they have the material out of which totemism could easily be made. There are, of course, apparent exceptions to this generalisation, in some of the tribes of Africa, America and Melanesia. The detailed examination of these, which of course cannot be undertaken in a brief paper, really serves, I believe, to confirm the rule.

I would not be understood to maintain the view that totemism, or rather the different institutions which in different parts of the world we call by this general term, have arisen independently of one another. I think that it is very likely. But it does not matter for the sociologist, at any rate in the present state of our knowledge. If anyone wishes to believe that all the existing forms of totemism have come into existence by a process of what is rather unsatisfactorily called 'diffusion' from a single centre, I have no objection. I would point out that totemism has not spread everywhere, or evenly, and that it has not survived equally in all regions. It is sufficient for my argument if we can say that it is only where certain other features of culture are present that totemism is likely to be accepted by a people when it is brought to them from outside, or is likely to remain in active existence after it has been introduced.

REFERENCES

1. Reprinted from *Proceedings of the Fourth Pacific Science Congress*, Java, 1929.
2. It is sometimes said that totemism has two aspects, a social aspect and a religious or ritual aspect. What is referred to as the 'social aspect' of totemism is simply the clan organisation. But exogamous clans similar in all essentials to totemic clans so far as economic or juridical functions go, can as we well-know exist without totemism. The so-called 'social aspect' of clan totemism is simply the social aspect of the clan.
3. If we denote the four sections as A, B, C, and D, the matrilineal moieties are A + C and B + D; the patrilineal moieties are A + D and B + C. Since a man may not marry within his own patrilineal moiety or within his own matrilineal moiety it will follow that a man of A can only marry a woman of B and their children must belong to section D, i.e. to the patrilineal moiety of the father (A) and to the matrilineal moiety of the mother (B).
4. A more precise way of stating the view I am here suggesting is that in every human society there inevitably exist two different and in a certain sense conflicting conceptions of nature. One of them, the naturalistic, is implicit everywhere in technology, and in our twentieth century European culture, with its great development of control over natural phenomena, has become explicit and preponderant in our thought. The other, which might be called the mythological or spiritualistic conception, is implicit in myth and in religion, and often becomes explicit in philosophy.

8
Interests and Attitudes

Attitudes and Social Life

Social and the psychological. In this chapter our focus will be *psychological*. Our concern remains social relationships, but our attention will be turned from the relationships themselves to the related units. When we study the nature of the behaving individuals, the structure of the individual consciousness which expresses itself in social relationships, we are taking the psychological point of view. When we study the relationships themselves we take the sociological point of view. Both sciences are concerned with different aspects of an indivisible reality. Individuals cannot be understood apart from their relations with one another; the relations cannot be understood apart from the units (or terms) of the relationship. Thus we are *also* students of psychology when we study society; and, as the psychologists themselves are increasingly affirming, we become students of sociology when we study the psychology of the individual being. In the last resort the difference between psychology and sociology is a difference of *focus* of interest in social reality itself.

The sociologist is primarily interested in the way in which beings endowed with consciousness act in relation to one another. Beneath and beyond that consciousness lie such realms as the psychoneural conditions of behaviour, the physiology of sensation or perception, the biological processes of inheritance, the functioning of the glands. But the sociologist is concerned with these matters only in so far they throw light on his own distinctive problems—the problems of conscious behaviour. Conscious behaviour is always accompanied by neuromuscular activity, but if our focus is directed to this realm and remains there we shall not make much advance in the interpretation and understanding of the processes of consciousness. A student of music may conceivably be aided by an understanding of the physiology of ear and brain, but his focus of attention is music itself. A student of society may be aided by the understanding of, say, neurons and synapses, but his quest remains the analysis of social relationships.

We shall, of course, draw on the conclusions of psychology throughout, as occasion arises. At this early point there is one distinction of a psychological nature that is of particular use in sociological analysis, the distinction between *interests* and *attitudes*.

Interests and attitudes are correlative. Put in one list such terms as "fear," "love," "surprise," "pride," "sympathy," and "veneration"; and in another list such terms as "enemy," "friend," "discovery," "family," "victim of accident" and "God." Terms of the first group connote *attitudes;* those of the second, *interests.* The former signify *subjective* reactions, states of consciousness *within* the individual human being, with relation to *objects.* The latter signify the objects themselves. When we mention love or fear we depict an attitude; when we mention friend or enemy we indicate an interest.

Social relationships always involve *both* attitudes and the interests to which they are related; complete definitions of social relationships must include both attitudes and interests. If we say, for example, that a person is "afraid" we must further identify the situation to which his fear is a response. He may be afraid of snakes or the police or publicity or ill-health or even his own "inner desires." Or, conversely, if we say that a person "is interested in" law or religion or women we must further identify the attitude that attends the interest. The burglar, the policeman, the jurist all have an interest in the law; clearly enough their attitudes are diverse. Religion gains the intense interest of both atheist and worshiper, and women that of both those who offer them devotion and those who profess to be "women-haters." Understanding of actual behaviour situations, then, requires knowledge of both *objective* interest and *subjective* attitude.

Our explanation of interest as the objects of subjective attitudes does not mean, of course, that "objects" are necessarily material or external facts. Man's interests are those items to which he devotes his attention. They range from such material phenomena as tools and soil and climate to immaterial beliefs, mythologies, and scientific theories. Take, for example, the authors' immediate interest at this point. It is the definition of concepts needed for the analysis of social reality. Social reality always includes the material and immaterial.

The development of attitudes. The role of attitudes in social life is clarified when we consider the process by which they develop in the life of the individual. The human infant acts as though he were the center of the tiny universe in which he lives and feels, and as he comes to appraise things he does so at first solely in terms of their quality of bringing pleasures or pains to himself. He does not conceive of other as persons, nor relate himself to others as persons. The mother's breast and the bottle, the hands that tend him and the crib he rests in, the nurse, the carriage, the words spoken by adults, noises, light and darkness—these are all alike construed in terms of their impact on his own being. In short, his attitude is entirely egocentric.[1]

But in the process of mental growth the young child learns to distinguish between persons and things. Only then does he become capable of *social* relationships. For he comes to conceive of himself as bound up with other *persons.* He distinguishes his own folks from other folks, establishing various degrees of nearness or intimacy, with parents and siblings, with playmates and schoolmates, reaching gradually into wider circles. He is distinguished from certain other animals of simpler species who, like the cat, appear to remain egocentric throughout life, by learning to say "we" instead of merely "I." He begins to become socialised.

But generally he invests with a halo of superiority the near circles to which he belongs. His mother is the most wonderful of women, his father the wisest of men, his school the best. Thus arise those attitudes that, directed to still larger circles, support his devotion to clan or tribe, to race or nation or class. That is why the social prejudices of men are so deeply rooted and why they offer such stubborn resistance to change: they have been nurtured and molded in the slow process of socialisation characteristic of man alone. The intolerance and prejudice that mark so many of men's relationships with one another are traceable to the same processes of socialisation that produce their opposites — tolerance and understanding.

Attitudes and Social relations. For sociological purposes a fundamental distinction between classes of attitudes centres about the question whether they tend to *unite* or tend to *separate* those affected by them. In the sociological lens, "the colourful confusion of interhuman life falls into patterns of avoidance and approach."[2] Certain attitudes are in themselves tendencies to approach those toward whom they are directed, while others express tendencies to avoidance. Love seeks to approach, fear or disgust to avoid. Hate separates, socially if not physically, and sympathy unites. Distrust and envy may unite those who share such attitudes, but only in common resistance of those toward whom they are distrustful or envious.

[1] *Attitudes and personal relationships:* Every social relationship involves in fact, an adjustment of attitudes on the part of those who enter the relationship. And the varieties of adjustment are as numerous as the varieties of processes that relate men to one another. Friendliness, for example, may be met by friendliness or by indifference or by enmity. Aggressiveness and submissiveness form a pair of complementary attitudes that often appear in social relations, like "masochism" and "sadism," in the psychological parlance. Even when we employ the same term for the attitudes exhibited by each of the related persons, these may have a complementary rather than a like quality. The love of a parent for a child, for example, is very different from and is complementary to the love of the child for the parent. Such terms as "love" and "hate" and "fear," in fact, refer to many different kinds of attitudinal complexes involved in both personal relationships and those between groups.

[2] *Attitudes and group relationships:* Attitudinal adjustments are constantly being made in the relations between *individuals*. There is a tendency, however, in every social *group* to develop like attitudes toward interests relevant to the group as a whole. Attitudes are very responsive to the large apparatus of suggestion that is part of the formal and informal educational system of all groups. Consider, for example, the extraordinary changes which were induced in the national attitudes of Italians and Germans by the Fascist and Nazi regimes, or the great alteration of American attitudes toward German and Japanese peoples during the late war. Masses of people quickly came to venerate or to execrate symbols which were formerly largely a matter of indifference, such as the swastika, the lictor's rods or fasces, the hammer and sickle, the

rising sun, the "Atlantic Charter." Everywhere we find groups—tribal, local, racial, national, kin, class—displaying characteristic attitudes and attaching then to symbols. In part, these attitudes arise out of common social situations. And in part they depend on the indoctrination the group controls bring to bear on the members. They are sustained and perpetuated within the mores of each group.[3] They are, of course, of vital concern to the student of social reality.

Associative and Dissociative Attitudes

Some difficulties in classifying attitudes. Before suggesting a classification of attitudes for use in sociological study, we must note certain difficulties. I actual experience attitudes are subtle, complex, and changeful modes of consciousness. They are constantly being modified by our training, our reflection, our health, our circumstances of every sort. When we attribute an attitude to a person, we can judge its character only by certain external signs—looks, gestures, words. These signs suggest to us fear or love or pity, but in so naming the attitude we do not fully describe the conscious fact. We are merely judging that the attitude-factor so named is dominant or at least recognisable in the subject. As psychiatry warns, our amateur judgments are frequently in error.

The terms we apply to states of consciousness, to attitudes, shade into one another. Consider, for example, the difference between "respect," "esteem" and "admiration." And the mental realities such terms denote shade still more subtly into one another. The inadequacies of our terms for psychological facts are known to every novelist, and should be realised by every sociologist.

Take, for example, attitudes which seem poles apart, like love and hate. It is an age-old observation that these two may be combined in one perplexing attitude toward a single person or object, and in recent times this observation has been elaborated in the Freudian psychology in terms of the principle of *ombivalence.* Love and hate, deep sorrow and exuberant emotional passion, intense loyalty and repugnance—these and other seemingly contradictory attitudes are frequently interwoven. This creates a complex and often frustrating problem for both the individual who is internally perplexed by such ambivalence and the student of individual psychology.

A further difficulty in classification lies in the fact that the attitude we seek to fix down by a name is itself often variable and inconstant, like a colour seen in a changeful light. An attitude is not a static possession of the individual. It is always a *changing valuation:* a way of regarding persons or things, a way of assessing them in relation to ourselves and ourselves in relation to them.

A classification of attitudes. Attitudes, as we have seen, are so complex, so blended, so variant, so individualised that any classification must be, as the logicians say, "artificial," and no classification can be complete. In other words, our classification must depend on our purpose in making it. In Chart II we are considering attitudes from a sociological, rather than a psychological view-point. That is to say, our interest is focused upon these classes of attitudes that are of frequently decisive importance in the *relationships* between man and man.

CHART II

A Classification of Attitudes

(Attitudes of persons exhibited in relations with other persons)

I. *Attitudes implying some personal sense of inferiority in the subject with respect to the object of the attitude*

Dissociative	*Restrictive*	*Associative*
Dread	Awe	Gratitude
Fear	Veneration	Emulation
Terror	Worship	Imitativeness[a]
Envy	Devotion	Hero-worship
Bashfulness	Humility	
	Submissiveness[a]	
	Subservience	
	Modesty	
	Snobbishness[b]	

II. *Attitudes implying some personal sense of superiority in the subject*

Disgust	Pride	Pity[d]
Abhorrence	Patronage	Protectiveness
Repugnance	Tolerance[c]	
Scom	Forbearance	
Contempt		
Disdain		
Superciliousness		
Intolerance		
Arrogance		

III. *Attitudes not necessarily implying a difference of plans or status (neutrality)*

Hate	Rivalry	Sympathy
Dislike	Competitiveness	Affection
Aversion	Jealousy[e]	Trust
Distrust		Tenderness
Suspicion		Love
Spitefulness		Friendliness
Malice		Kindliness
Cruelty		Courtesy
		Helpfulness

---

[a] Imitativeness and submissiveness rather than imitation and submission, since the former are attitudes and the latter processes. But often there is only one term to describe both the attitude and the process.

[b] Snobbishness, looking downward, discourages social relationship; looking upward, seeks to extend it. This attitude is placed in Class I on the assumption that while it involves a sense both of inferiority and of superiority, the former is the stronger element in the complex.

[c] Tolerance not in the sense of open-mindedness, but as the attitude corresponding to the process of toleration.

[d] Pity might seem to fall more appropriately in the restrictive class, but that is because it is so frequently associated with such attitudes as patronage. Pity as such, as for a friend fallen in misfortune, has no such implication.

[e] Jealousy might seem to fall in Class I, since it is so closely associated with a sense of inferiority. But though a sense of inferiority may underlie jealousy, it is not necessarily present in the attitude of the jealous person toward the person for whom he has a jealous regard.

Thus we place attitudes in three main columns according as they tend to prevent, to limit, or to promote social relationships. We name these attitudes *dissociative, restrictive,* and *associative.* And we divide the columns horizontally into three groups, according as the attitudes imply, in the relationships of the persons affected by them, *inferiority* feeling or *superiority* feeling or have no such implication.

The classification is merely illustrative and in no sense exhaustive. However, the student will find that if he brings to his study of social relations the distinction between attitudes of *association* and *dissociation* and between those of *superiority* and *inferiority* his task will be simplified. For the attitudes which separate us or bring us together, and those which endow a consciousness of superiority or inferiority are of primary significance in the relationships between individuals and between groups.

The Statistical Study of Attitudes

"Measuring" attitudes. A considerable part of the sociological literature on attitudes is devoted to the question whether attitudes can be "measured," and if so, how.[4] Many writers, in fact, have in recent years drawn up attitude measurement scales designed to be able to measure by certain techniques the attitudes of different people toward the church, the Negro, birth control, the United Nations, and so forth. Since these attempts illustrate very clearly the problem of the *quantitative* treatment of psychical phenomena, we shall comment on them briefly, as a way of bringing this controversial issue to the attention of the student.

We have already pointed out that attitudes are complex and variable modes of consciousness. They are expressions or aspects of the whole personality of the social being. It is therefore no easy matter for the observer to apprehend their quality from the external signs. As every sensitive student knows, a teacher's "friendliness," for example, may indicate any one of several deeper feelings. This suggests the need for a careful study of attitudes *before* we attempt to apply techniques of measurement.

The attitude-measurers face another *preliminary* task. For they must ask, what *in the attitude* is it that we are undertaking to measure? We do not measure *things,* but only certain *quantitative aspects* of things. We do not measure a table, but its length or height or weight. We do not measure the sun, but its radiation, its apparent motion, its size. What *aspects,* then, of an attitude do we set out to measure? Usually the attitude-measurers are thinking of the degree of favour or disfavour with which the individual regards some object (or interest). He is thinking of the *intensity* of the *attitude.*[5]

We seriously doubt the possibility of *measuring,* in any mathematical sense, degrees of favour and disfavour, of linking or disliking.[6] To be sure, the attitude-measurers are generally concerned with attitudes not in their full significance, as reverence and admiration and respect, and so forth, but in a simplified form as *merely* expressing favour or disfavour of some object. However, we must ask: Has the object itself precisely the same *significance* for the various persons who exhibit attitudes toward it? Does "democracy" or "religion" or "birth control" or "government regulation" *mean* the same thing to them? If not, a measuring scale cannot yield exactly comparable results when applied to the attitudes of different persons.

However, attitude scales do permit us to sort out the favourings and disfavourings, likings and dislikings, of a group of people as exhibited at any one time toward some particular interest, in a series of *grades* or *rates*.[7] (The thing so rated is the degree of approval or disapproval, not the total complex attitude.) Such scales, when carefully constructed and expertly used, often provide us with very useful information about social situations. Thus the attitudes of purchasers in the consumers' market toward various products, of radio listeners toward different ratio programmes, of collage students toward pubic and local issues of current moment, and the like, are given meaningful ranking through the use of attitude scales and similar statistical devices.[8] The interest in and use made of such devices by the manufacturer of consumers' goods, the radio advertiser, and others suggest the practical utility of grading or ranking the verbal or written responses of individuals. However, we cannot agree with those sociologists and psychologists who equate these controlled responses with the complex changing attitude itself.

Both the utility and the limitations of attitude "measurement" are illustrated by World War II. The United States. Army found that its problems of military policy and administration were greatly aided by employing the services of social scientists trained in statistical research methods. These specialists could, by securing verbal responses to carefully constructed questions administered to samples of soldiers, obtain fairly rapidly levels of reactions to such things as new types of equipment, military clothing issues, and civilians living in occupied territories. The immediate utility of such information to the high command can hardly be questioned—though we do not know the extent to which it was in fact used. On the one hand, we realise the usefulness of learning, say, that 80 per cent of a given army "strongly disapproves" of a new type of weapon or that 70 per cent "mildly dislikes" a standard winter overshoe or that 40 per cent regard German women as "more desirable" than French women.[9] But on the other hand, we must emphasise that such data do not tell us the whole story, by any means, of the reactions of soldiers toward the objects of these attitudes. Attitude scales are never adequate substitutes for the kind of *understanding* of attitude complexities that is revealed, for example, in a psychiatrist's office, in the pages of a sensitive journalist, or even in some of the cartoons of a Bill Mauldin.[10]

Polling Public opinion. The use of statistical techniques in the study of levels of attitude intensity is perhaps best illustrated by the numerous polls of public opinion.[11] Newspapers and magazines, politicians themselves, political prognosticators of every king avail themselves of the sampling of the American public's attitudes undertaken by Gallup, Roper, and many others. These investigators provide us with pictures of the "public's" view on this or that matter by obtaining verbal responses from selected representative samples of the population. The political polls, on a number of occasions, have been able to predict political behaviour, particularly election returns, within quite small margins of error. But they are still far from being infallible. While better methods have been developed since the failure of the *Literary Digest* poll of the presidential election of 1936, the complete wrongness of the predictions of practically all the "pollsters" concerning the election of 1948 revealed in a striking manner the inadequacy of current sampling techniques.

In the case of voting expectancies the polls represent, as it were, simply unofficial elections. Individuals are questioned in one way or another as to how they expect to vote. They are asked to predict their own behaviour with respect to a definite and anticipated event. Thus the polls seek to register the relative volume of approval and disapproval of parties and their candidates—as indicated by rating expectancies. So much is clear. But what is by no means clear from the poll returns is the precise nature, the constituent elements, or the genuine intensity of political attitudes. These problems require analysis of a kind that may be greatly aided by polls, to be sure, but it must be an analysis that probes social reality more deeply than polling itself can.

The public is polled on many issues other than elections. Thus Americans are asked with what "class" they identify themselves, whether or not they prefer to be employed by government or private business, the extent to which they consider their chances of economic advance good or poor, how they view their children's life chances as compared with their own, and so on.[12] We learn that our "average" fellow citizen regards himself as "middle class," that he calculates his own chances of advancement as "good," that he believes employers' and employees' interests are "essentially the same," and so on.

This kind of polling of attitudes takes us a step, perhaps a large step, along the road of understanding the general pattern—the peaks and depressions of certain attitude complexes. However, when we face such a knotty complex problem as the "class" attitudes of Americans—a problem we must face later in this book—we cannot rest content with the verbal responses made by individuals to questionnaires. For attitudes are expressions of complete human personalities—evaluations of the total social being—and, like personality itself, must be understood as part of the pattern of *relationships* among human beings.

Types of Interest in Social Life

Earlier in this chapter we stated that all social relationships involve both subjective attitudes and objective interests. Every *social* experience may be viewed as a relation, an interaction, between the experiencing person, the subject, and an experienced object, the interest. (The interest itself, of course, is often a person or persons). If, then, social experiences always involve an adjustment between the attitudes and interests of two or more persons, it is important that we consider those types of interest that are of basic significance in social life.

Like and common interests. In our discussion of attitudes we took as the fundamental ground of sociological classification the distinction between associative and dissociative attitudes. No less fundamental is the distinction between *like* and *common* interests. It is distinction subject to much confusion, partly because of the ambiguity of the words

We say, for example, that people have common capacities or common habits when we really mean that they have like capacities or like habits. The *like* is what we have distributively, privately, each to himself. The *common* is what we have collectively, what we share *without dividing up*. The credits we receive at college represent like interests; the college life in which we participate we share in common. To be sure, the like is often a *source* of common interest, as, for example, in the case of two businessmen whose like interests in profit may lead to the formation of a partnership that becomes a common possession and a common source of pride. One of the great processes of society, as we shall see later, is that whereby the common is built out of the like. Today many of us hope that the like interests of the great nations in maintaining peace may be a source for the development of true common international interests.

The concept of common interest brings into sharper focus a fundamental difference between interests and attitudes. Attitudes, as we have seen, can be harmonious. But they cannot be common in the sense in which we are applying that term to interests. Different people cannot have a common attitude any more than they can feel a common pain. They can have only *like* pains and *like* attitudes, because the subjective element is always individualised. But they can have common interests, just as they can have common possessions. There are two principal forms of common or shared interest that require special mention.

[1] *Attachment to a social group:* The first form is exemplified by loyalty to an "in-group." When men identify themselves with some inclusive indivisible unity of their fellows, common interest reveals itself. When men think of themselves as really *belonging* to a family, to a city, to a nation, to a team, to a friendly clique, they are sharing a common interest with other men. This sense of attachment to a personal unity is found in varying degrees and is manifested in different ways in social groups of many kinds—in communities, in associations, in social classes and castes, in both primary and secondary groups. It is an ingredient of group life that will concern us frequently throughout the volume.

Here we can explain more fully what was said early in the chapter, that intolerance and prejudice are traceable to the same processes of socialisation that evoke their opposites—tolerance and understanding. Man becomes socialised as the member of a group, first a very near group, the family or the kinsfolk, and then of a wider group, the local community, the social class, the ethnic group, the nation. He learns to belong, but in learning to belong he learns also to exclude. He divides people into the "we" and the "they," the "in-group" and the "out-group."[13] His devotion to the "we" easily becomes dislike or hostility to the "they." His pride in the "we" is fostered by his contempt for the "they." Thus groups prejudice is developed on every scale of belonging, from the family to the nation and perhaps to the "race"—the "race" *we* belong to.

Here is one of the greatest problems of modern civilisation. This civilisation has become very inclusive, and the parts of it—the groups within the nation, the nations themselves over the narrowing world—have become in vital respects interdependent.

Yet within the nation the various groups—ethnic groups, culture groups, interest groups—often gravely damage, through their tensions and their conflicts, the unity and the well-being of the whole. And within the world the inability of nations to set their common interest above their separate interests and their mutual jealousies has been a most formidable danger to the continued existence of our civilisation itself. What is clearly needed is a new orientation of our socialisation, in such a way that our devotion to group and even to nation will cease to be antagonistic to our membership in a more inclusive community.

[2] *Attachment to an impersonal goal or endeavour:* The interest that men show in science, in art, in religion, in tradition, in philosophy, in sport, exemplifies the second form of common interest. When the curiosity, the enthusiasm, the devotion of men is excited we see this form at work. "Causes" of all kinds, from the spread of a religious doctrine or a political creed to an intense interest in, say, antivivisection or prohibition, reveal men seeking ends beyond themselves—*common* ends.

Thus his science is a common interest of the scientist *in so far as* he thinks of it as a worth-while goal, *in so far as* he pursues it not merely for a living or purposes of prestige. As the lives of Roger Bacon, Galileo, and the Curies so vividly illustrate, common interest in the search of truth does in fact motivate much scientific endeavour.[14] Of course, scientists are usually breadwinners and persons seeking recognition in society. But when an individual's *whole* interest in science is determined by the dollars he earns or the kudos it brings him, he is an unsatisfactory scientist. In such a case, and examples may be found without difficulty, he lacks the *common interest* which makes science a value in itself and is often the spur of the most unstinted service.

The omnipresence of self-limited interest in social life. In nearly all human activity *both* common and like or self-limited interests are combined. It is inevitable that men should seek after their private interests. It is equally inevitable that they should find and feel an intrinsic worth-whileness in the groups to which they belong and in the impersonal goals and endeavours for which they strive. Examination of social behaviour itself reveals both types of interest operating—in varying degrees and arrangements.

If *all* our interests were self-limited, society could not endure. If other people were merely means to our satisfactions, we would not belong together as social beings. Love and friendship and family affection and group devotion would not sustain us as socialised individuals. We would maintain to relationship with others any longer or any further than it satisfied our egoism. Community, indeed group life of every form, would be rendered impossible.

We have already pointed out in this chapter that the earliest *attitudes* of the human infant appear to be altogether egocentric. But it should not be assumed that in the historical development of social man himself egocentricity of *interests* appears prior to or underlies the common interests. It is sometimes said that the original driving forces of man are those of self-preservation and self-expression. But social man as he appears in every generation is at once egocentric *and* sociocentric. Both elements are inextricably fused in all man, is and does. He lives for himself *and* he lives for his group. He lives for himself *and* he lives for the causes that are dear to him. And however far we pierce back to the earlier stage of human life we find the same ingredients of self-regarding and self-transcending interest.[15] The study of both and of the interaction between them is essential in the analysis of social reality.

Attitudes and Interests as Motivations

The quest for motivations. We are always seeking to discover the motives behind the overt behaviour of our fellows. Particularly when someone we know acts in an unexpected manner, we hunt for the explanatory motive. The detective seeks among the potential suspects those with motives for committing the crime, and the judge and jury must inquire concerning the motive for the deed since the same external act, say murder, is legally one or another kind of crime, or even no crime at all, according to the motive which prompted it. On a larger scale, the historian and the biographer are engaged in unearthing the motives behind the doings they record. And the novelist and the playwright make great use of their inside knowledge concerning the motives of the characters they depict.

What is the significance of this endless search for motives? In the first place, our own external behaviour is an expression of our own attitudes and interests, and consequently we endeavour to probe to the inner determinants of the behaviour of others. Secondly, we generally assume, though this assumption may frequently involve an undue simplification of the truth, that in the complex of an individual's attitudes and interests there is some dominant factor or factors which explain his behaviour in a particular situation. Such a dominant factor we call his motive. Sometimes we lay stress on the attitude aspect, as when we attribute an act to envy or jealousy or fear; sometimes on the interest aspect, as when we say the motive of an act was money or prestige. All social behaviour, as we have seen, involves *both* attitude and interest.

Motives, then are the effective incitements to action that lie behind our acts, behind the show of things. And in seeking for motives we may descend, as it were, to various levels of the conscious, subconscious or "unconscious" life. We may look for the immediate motive behind the overt behaviour, as when we attribute an activity, say churchgoing, to the desire to be thought respectable or to considerations of "society" or business connections or to religious devotion. Or we may look for motives behind the mentality associated with the external act, as when we attribute, say, an attitude of respect to a recognition of personal worth or achievement or to an acceptance of authority or to a desire to stand in well with the respected person. Or we may venture still more deeply and undertake the hazardous attempt to discover hidden subconscious urges or tendencies which find their expression in conscious activity under various disguises. Explanations referring to these different levels of motivation are illustrated in a variety of types of investigation.

Types of theories of human motivation. In the following examples we make no attempt to present the details of the elaborate formulations of the writers mentioned. Our concern is rather that the student may recognise certain views to which reference will be made from time to time throughout this book, and that he realise the difficulty of the problem of human motivation and the various avenues which have been followed by those in search of its solution.

[1] *Underlying economic motives:* The historical rise of capitalistic enterprise and the new arrangements of social organisation accompanying it have pushed to the forefront of men's thought the significance of the economic factor in human affairs. A century and a half ago Adam Smith and others pictured an "economic man" primarily motivated by a rational calculation of interests in terms of maximum economic gain. Considering the gigantic role played by economic changes in the ensuing period, it is not surprising that many writers have singled out the economic as the underlying and basically important motive of individual behaviour as well as the principal motive force of historical change itself. This view of motivation characterises, for example, the writings of Alexander Hamilton in the famous *Federalist* series, and is no less apparent in the contributions of such modern historians as Charles A. Beard.[16]

The most complex and energetic attempts to discover underlying economic motives have been stimulated by the writings of Karl Marx and his followers. Marx himself was not primarily concerned with the problem of individual motivation, but his analysis of class conflict portrays the individual members of both the owning bourgeoisie and the labouring proletriat as ultimately motivated by their conflicting economic interests. In this view, political, religious, and other "noneconomic" social forms become a "superstructural" complex to be explained in the final analysis by the objective material interests underlying them. This analytical approach, as we shall emphasise later, is, according to its proponents, essentially a device with which to interpret the historical process, not individual behaviour. However, the Marxian emphasis upon the basic function of economic interests has prompted various writers to explain attitudes that are inconsistent with Marxian-defined economic interests as "false rationalisations" or "mistaken viewpoints."[17] Such writers seek the key to human conduct in the economic structure itself.

[2] *Constant elements of human nature as motives:* For centuries men have explained the behaviour of men by attributing it to "human nature"—to that curiously nonchanging complexity that is assumed to remain a constant in a universe in which all else changes. Such an explanatory device has been a convenient technique for many who have sought the underlying motives of human action. And it remains a convenient, though scarcely revealing, technique for those modern writers, such as McDougall,[18] who postulate four or six or twenty "instincts" as the fundamental forces accounting for man's varied activities. While the instinct approach has fallen into disrepute in recent years largely because of the enormous plasticity of the social being revealed by modern psychology and sociology, constant conditions of human nature continue to be hypothesised as basic needs or drives. These needs range from the physiological necessities of the organism, such as food and oxygen intake and the elimination of waste matter, to

the demands for love and affection created by social life itself. Psychologists, sociologists, and anthropologists have recently constructed detailed theories which purport to spell out the motivating needs or "cravings" of individuals as they are shaped by and in turn shape social life.[19] Certain of these theories will concern us in the following chapter.

Perhaps the most famous attempt by a sociologist to deal with the problem of human motivation is that of Vilfredo Pareto.[20] Pareto views human conduct as essentially ins pired by certain constant ingredients of human nature which he terms "residues." He classifies the residues under six main groups: residues of combinations (the faculty of associating things or thinking them together), of group persistence (the conservative tendency), of self-expression, of sociability, of individual integrity, and of sex.[21] These, according to Pareto, are the actual motivations of human conduct but are obscured by all sorts of unsound reasonings and misleading explanations which he names "derivations." The derivations are manifestations of the human being's hunger for thinking, constituting a veil of pseudo logic between him and the realities of his nature.

It is not in place here to examine the elaborate argument by which Pareto seeks to establish his case. But we may point out his implicit and unwarranted assumption that certain types of motivation (residues) are genuine of fundamental while others (derivations), including the more idealistic motivations, are shallow and protentious. His thousands of illustrations are often suggestive and revealing. It is often the case, for example, that when a politician appeals to the electors on the grounds of his patriotic services to the glorious nation to which they belong, he is not expressing his real sentiments but is using these arguments to further his own ends. But there is another side to the story. Why does the politician appeal in these terms at all? Because he knows that his audience responds to such sentiments—unless his audience is stirred by the idealistic motivations, it is useless for him to use such devices. One might multiply illustrations *ad infinitum* to show that man is motivated thus and so—and as many illustrations would remain over to show that he is motivated otherwise.

[3] *The psychoanalytical quest for motives:* The psychoanalytical explanation of motivation, in its original formulation by Freud and his followers,[22] is essentially a version of the type of analysis we have just considered. For Freud, a physician and psychologist intent upon probing the innermost depths of the human personality, conceived of constant elements of human nature as the principal motivating forces. He named these unconscious forces the "instincts" of Eros and Death—of sex and self-destruction—and saw them in conflict with each other and as standing as the basis of personality formation and human behaviour.

The exponent of the psychoanalytic view thus regards the individual's own belief that he is animated by this or that motive as often merely a delusion masking the real determinants of his action. Psychoanalysts and evidences of "complexes" and "fixations" developing very early in the life history of the individual, and likewise find them substantiated by the ritual and taboo practices of primitive peoples. These complexes they regard as active below the conscious level and as symbolically emerging in dreams, daytime reveries, and the forgetfulnesses and "slips" of everyday existence.

This brief statement does little justice to the voluminous theoretical literature and the mass of clinical findings of the Freudian school, but it indicates the direction of its quest. The psychoanalysts attempt to discover the "unconscious motives" standing behind our actions: their search ends with the innermost workings of the human organism. Their interpretations of dreams, of primitive customs, and of adult life histories contain precarious inferences and have been attacked by psychologists and anthropologists, though few would deny the element of truth of their findings. But this element is only a segment of the interrelated totality of social behaviour which includes the human organism, to be sure, but involves as well the society itself. Men are motivated by many things. Their sex impulses and even their "death-urge" may explain some aspects of their behaviour, but, as we shall see in the succeeding chapter, any adequate theory of man's complex activities must be grounded in an understanding of the society of which he is a part.

The complexity of motivation. The theories we have sketched reveal the human tendency to "rationalise"—or perhaps we might say to "socialise"—motives. As social beings, we are disposed to select socially esteemed reasons for our conduct and present them to others, and also to ourselves, as grounds for our action. We form habits of concealing petty and self-seeking motives under high names, like duty and honour and principle and patriotism. We want to stand well in the sight of others and in our own eyes. Thus we "rationalise" our conduct, and this is the more easy and the more convincing—to ourselves at least—because it is always difficult to disentangle the many factors determining our behaviour. Historians like Beard and Robinson,[23] political thinkers of the school of Machiavelli, sociologists like Pareto, and psychoanalysts like Freud have done signal service in seeking to penetrate the facade of rationalisation which often hides the moving forces of history and the inner springs of conduct. And the same mission is zestfully popularised by novelists, biographers, and today certain movie and radio script writers who expose for us the underlying motives of their characters.

Yet such interpretations may be liable to an opposite simplification to that which their authors assail. For there is always the danger that we simplify the motives of behaviour, whether the particular motives we attribute be lofty or petty, altruistic or self-limited. The motives of conduct are indeed as complex as the human personality itself. Medical science each year discovers more of the amazing complexity of our organic structure—it has moved far from Hippocrates' belief that the organism consists of merely blood, phlegm, and the biles. So with personality—as science learns more of its structure and functions its greater complexity is revealed. To be sure, many common and erroneous assumptions are corrected by the "debunkers" of superficial rationalisations, but they, in turn, risk the superficial position of assigning an unwarranted simplicity to motivation. "A history of philosophy and theology," says Robinson, "could be written in terms of grouches, wounded pride, and aversions, and it would be far more instructive than the usual treatment of these themes."[24] Perhaps more instructive, but perhaps also not less one-sided or misleading.

Of all quests, none is more complex than the adequate understanding of motivation. The latter demands that we untangle and reveal human nature itself—human nature conditioned in each variant human being by the unique series of experiences which are the history of the individual life, and yet exhibiting in us all the universal traits of humanity. In this respect, however, the task of the sociologist is not so overwhelming as that of the historian who seeks to explain particular events or as that of the psychiatrist in search of the motivations of behaviour of this person or that. For the sociologist's interest is primarily in group phenomena where numbers of human beings act in like ways or maintain common institutions. When the same gestures or external signs are employed by many or repeated on many occasions, we can with greater assurance infer their meaning. The hazard of interpretation is somewhat less in reading the motives of a crowd of "public" than in reading those of an individual. This is a theme to which we will return, but is one which must be preceded by the examination of the fundamental relationship in sociological study—the relationship between individual man and society.

REFERENCES

1.   On the egocentric character of the child's attitude see Jean Piaget, "Intellectual Evolution," in *Science and Man* (Ruth N. Anshen, ed., New York, 1942), pp. 409-422 and *The Moral Judgment of the Child* (Eng. tr., New York, 1932).

2.   L. von Wiese, *Systematic Sociology* (H. Becker, ed., New York, 1932), p. 39.

3.   For an interesting analysis of symbols and attitudes, see H.D. Lasswell, *Politics Who Gets What, When, How* (New York, 1936), Chaps, II and IX; for an excellent discussion of racial beliefs in America, G. Myrdal, *An Americna Dilemma* (New York, 1944), Vol. I, Chap. 4; and for a lively and sound popular discussion of the subject, M. Halsey, *Colour Blind* (New York, 1946); for extensive illustrative material, *One America* (F.J. Brown and J.S. Roucek, eds., New York, 1946).

4.   For a positive answer to this question, see, for example, L.L. Thurstone and F.J. Chave, *The Measurement of Attitudes* (Chicago, 1929); Read Bain, "Theory and Measurement of Attitudes and Opinions," *Psychological Bulletin*, XXVII (1930), 357-379; G.A. Landberg, *Social Research* (New York, 1942), Chap. VIII. For balanced and not unsympathetic critiques, see Clifford Kirkpatrick, "Assumptions and Methods in Attitude Measurements," *American Sociological Review*, I (1936), 75-88; R.T. La Piere, "The Sociological Significance of Measurable Attitudes," *ibid.*, III (1938), 175-182. For a digest of the extensive literature on this question, see Deniel Day, "Methods in Attitude Research," *ibid.*, V (1940), 395-410.

5.   Two researchers have devised atttudes scales which are cleverly designed to indicate levels of intensity as measured from a zero point." See Louis Guttman and E.A. Suchman, "Intensity and a Zero Point for Attitude Analysis," *American Sociological Review*, XII (1947), 56-67.

6.   See, for example, R.M. MacIver, *Society: A Textbook of Sociology* (New York, 1937), pp. 26-27.

7.   For an excellent discussion of the logic of measurement and rating see M.R. Cohen and E. Nagel, *An Introduction to Logic and Scientific Method* (New York, 1934), Chap XV.

8.   See, for example, P.F. Lazarsfeld, *The Technique of Marketing Research* (New York, 1937) and *Radio and the Printed Page* (New York, 1940); G. Murphy and R. Likert, *Public Opinion and the Individual* (New York, 1938).

9.   Thse are fictitious examples, but are illustrative of the kinds of information obtained.

10.   *Up Front* (Cleveland and New York, 1945).

11. For a thorough discussion by a well-known veteran in this field, see G. Gallup and S.F. Roe, *The Pulse of Democracy* (New York, 1940).

12. See "The People of the U.S.A. —A Self-Portrait," *Fortune* (Feb., 1940); for a more detailed consideration of such problems, see A.W. Kornhauser, "Analysis of `Class' Structure of Contemporary American Society—Psychological Bases of Class Divisions," in *Industrial Conflict: A Psychological Interpretation* (G.W. Hartmann and T. Newcomb, eds., New York, 1939), pp. 199-264.

13. See, for example, W.G. Sumner, *Folkways* (Boston, 1907), pp. 11-16.

14. In his book entitled *Investors and Money-Makers* (New York, 1915), F.W. Taussig showed that inventors, like workers in pure science, are not actuated simply by the prospect of profit but are often dominated by the interest of discovery itself, as revealed by the happiness they derive from inventing, by their devotion to useless or unprofitable devices, and by the difficulties they have in managing the business and of their inventions. Even the financially successful Edison engaged his whole fortune in a New Jersey ore venture which resulted in remarkable engineering achievements but level disastrously. When he heard that his losses amounted to four million dollars he said "Well they gone, but we had a hell of a good time spending it."

15. Some contemporary psychoanalysts declare that the full realisation of "self," generally not possible in our modern society, necessarily would mean at the same time a *harmonious* relationship between the individual and group interests. See, for example, Erich Fromm, *Escape from Freedom* (New York, 1941).

16. See, for example, Charles, A. Beard, *The Economic Basis of Politics* (New York, 1934).

17. See, for exmaple, B. Freedman, "Stimulus and Response in Ecnomic Behaviour," in *industrial Conflict: A Psychological Interpretation*, pp. 265-279. For an interesting criticism of what he calls this "pseudo-Marxian" viewpoint see Fromm, *op. cit.*, p. 296.

18. See, for example, W. McDougall, *An Introduction to Social Psychology* (Boston, 1918), Chaps. II and III.

19. Thus, for example, in psychology; A.H. Maslow, "A Theory of Human Motivation," in *Twentieth Century Psychology* (P. L. Harriman, ed., New York, 1946), pp. 22-48; in sociology: R.S. Lynd, *Knowledge for What?* (Princeton, 1939), pp. 193-197; in anthropology: B. Malinowski, *A Scientific Theory of Culture and Other Essays* (Chapel Hill, 1944), pp. 75-131.

20. *The Mind and Society (Trattato di Sociologia Generale,* A. Livingston, ed., New York, 1935). For critical estimates of Pareto, see *Journal of Social Philosophy*, I (1935), Nos. 1 and 3; E. Faris, *The Nature of Human Nature* (New York, 1937), pp. 190-201.

21. *The Mind and Society,* II, 888 ff.

22. *The Basic Writings of Sigmund Freud* (A.A. Brill, trans. and ed., New York, 1938). For a short descriptive article see H.M. Kallen, "Psychoanalysis," *Encyclopaedia of the Social Sciences* (New York, 1935), XII, 580-588.

23. J.H. Robinson, *The Mind in the Making* (New York, 1921).

24. *Ibid.*, p. 45.

9
Individual and Society

In What Sense Man Is a Social Animal

The fundamental question of sociology. In the first chapter, in which the primary terms of sociological analysis were presented, we noted that man's *social nature* is his fundamental attribute. Before proceeding to deal with the various elements and aspects of society we must seek a proper orientation to this largest and most difficult problem that sociology offers. In what sense is man a social animal? In what sense do we belong to society? In what sense does society belong to us? What is the nature of our dependence upon it? How shall we interpret the unity of the whole to which our individual lives are bound? These questions are aspects of one fundamental question—the relation of the unit, the individual, to the group and to the social system. This question is the starting point and the focus of all *sociological* investigation, and, to a great extent, the fruitfulness of any sociological study is measured by its contribution to the problem of the relationship of individual and society.

It is not surprising, then, that men sought answers to this problem long before the term "sociology" was coined. Two misleading and opposing answers have been particularly influential in the history of Western social thought, the "social contract" theory and the "social organism" theory. A brief consideration of these may serve to remove certain false assumptions concerning individual man and the social totality of which he is a part.

Two one-sided approaches. Both of the following theories of the relationship of man and society have been expressed by many writers over many centuries. And both are frequently found today in the folk-thought—the "amateur sociology" — of our fellow citizens. The student of social science, therefore, should be able to recognise expressions of these theories and be prepared to expose their inadequacies.

We should remember that customs grow up spontaneously, gradually coming into being, whereas laws are created, emerging at the moment of legislation or of judicial recognition. Thus around law itself customs gather. Laws which are generally approved initiate attitudes as well as procedures out of which new customs evolve, and these in turn become a support of the laws. In fact, unless such customs are in being or arise to strengthen laws, the latter retain a precarious hold on the community.

[1] *Customs as a supplement to law: Custom* not only, under normal conditions, becomes a support of law but also supplements law and prepares the way for its development. Thus business customs, gathering around law, are in time in many cases incorporated within it, as for example the provision of three days of grace on bills of exchange[1] or, more generally, the introduction of standardisation or "fair price" usages into the legal code. On the other hand, law establishes conditions which bring new customs into being. Thus industrial legislation, such as acts regulating hours of labour or requiring hygienic conditions or defining the processes of collective bargaining, undermines old customs and prepares the way for new ones. Laws establishing military training induce the customs associated with military life and outlook—as we have witnessed in this country in recent years—while laws abolishing such training destroy the conditions on which these customs rest.[2] To take our earlier example of nondiscriminatory employment legislation, we can surmise that the widespread passage of such laws and their continued enforcement might affect the customs of group discrimination. However, it is *indirectly,* by creating an external order in which the old customs no longer correspond to our desires, that law is most effective in influencing custom, rather than by a frontal attack upon it.

[2] *Constitutional law and custom:* The fundamental or constitutional law is even more intimately related to custom than the type we have so far discussed. Constitutional law, though in part formulated in special documents, lives by usage, and around it a further body of usage grows up which amplifies or modifies or even annuls portions of the written formula. Thus the custom that the President shall not seek a third term of office amplified the American Constitution—a precedent upset by the last two elections of Franklin D. Roosevelt which have been a factor in bringing about a legislative attempt to codify the older custom; the custom by which the Electoral College acts on party lines modifies the Constitution; and the custom of some states of differentiating between the political rights of white and coloured in effect annuls some of its provisions. The study of American government, in fact, has become to a considerable extent today the study of the role of customary procedures that supplement the basic law of the land.

Still more apparent is the part played by custom under an "unwritten constitution" such as England possesses, where the old forms are subject at every point to the growth of customary procedures. Formally, the king can refuse his assent to a bill passed by both houses of Parliament, the cabinet can retain office after it has lost support of the Commons, and so forth. But this formal "can" is through custom supplanted by an actual "cannot." One difference between constitutional and ordinary or "municipal" law is that in the former sphere custom is not simply a source and support of the law but is an integral part of the system.[3] This is also true of the developing body of rules which we call international law, where customary practice in international relations and the formal regulations are closely interdependent.

Fashion and Custom

How fashion differs from custom. Various sociologists have contrasted fashion and custom. Herbert Spencer regarded fashion as a leveler of custom and especially of customary distinctions between social classes.[4] He thought of fashion as gaining ground when custom declines, and associated both tendencies with the growth of industrialisation. Gabriel Tarde defined fashion as the "imitation of contemporaries" and set it in contrast to custom, which was the "imitation of ancestors."[5] But neither of these views is wholly satisfactory as revealing the relation of custom to fashion, a relationship of significance in the study of both social structure and social change.

[1] *The meaning of fashion:* By fashion we mean *the socially approved sequence of variation on a customary theme.* The variations of fashion occur in a more or less regular sequence—the "cycle of fashion" as it is sometimes called; and fashion specially affects those aspects of the cultural factor which are regarded by the group as being in themselves relatively indifferent to basic values. Fashion applies to such matters as opinion, belief, recreation, dress, adornment of all sorts, house decoration and furniture, manner of speech, popular music, literature and art. In these areas fashion does not wholly supersede custom, but rather supplements it. Thus, there is in every period a *customary* type of dress, such as trousers for men, or of fiction, such as the novel, or of song writing, such as the ballad, on which fashion rings its changes.

This distinction also enables us to understand the significance of fashion as applied to artistic and other cultural changes. For every true artist his style in his own, but when any such style is followed widely by others, then the element of fashion enters in. Thus in one cultural field the host of "little Hemingways"; in jazz music the many emulators of, say, Louis Armstrong; in movie direction the wide adoption of the Hitchcock techniques. Among the followers the style is culturally a matter of indifference. The range of fashion is, in short, the limit of variation made possible by *cultural indifference.* It should be remembered that fashion is not the cultural current of a period—not the more deeply rooted tendencies of any age—but only the more detachable manifestations and mannerisms which are capable of easy imitation. A fashion is not to be explained by imitation, for reasons that will presently appear, but part of the nature of fashion is that it is an external form of observance capable of being easily imitated.

The social role of fashion: Though fashion plays from moment to moment on the surface of social life, behind its seemingly inconsequent changes there are often deeper forces at work. Fashion deals with the externals and superfluities of social life which can be changed without affecting the more basic procedures and values which we cherish. Fashion promises no utility; it makes no direct appeal to our reason. Yet it exercises a strong tyranny over us. Why is this the case?

[1] *The need for conformity and for novelty:* Fashion regulates those aspects of life concerning which we are, on the whole, individually indifferent and therefore socially susceptible. Within this region it harmonises the satisfaction of two strong demands of social man which in other areas often come into conflict—the demand for novelty and

the demand for conformity. Psychologically these logically opposite needs go hand in hand, and fashion meets the demands of both.[6] For fashion turns the desire for novelty into social practices it makes novelty the right and proper thing for the group. "The slight changes from the established in dress or other forms of behaviour seem for the moment to give the victory to the individual, while the fact that one's fellows revolt in the same directions gives one a feeling of adventurous safety:"[7]

Fashion may limit the range of innovation at any one time but it compensate for this by accelerating the tempo of innovation for the group. With the desire for novelty there is associated also the desire for distinction, and fashion also succeeds in accommodating this desire to the rule of conformity. Moreover fashion prescribes a style, not a uniform. Within it there is room for minor but for the purpose of individual distinction, important variations. People can still conform to fashion "with a difference."[8]

[2] *Fashion and social class:* Fashion generally, though not always, radiates from the elite, the prestige-owning groups. The "leisure class" especially, having both the time and the material means, tends to set the style in dress, the niceties within etiquette, styles in sport and recreation in general, and so forth. Even when a specific fashion originates within other groups, as in the case of modern jazz music, which first appeared among the Negroes of New Orleans, or the "work-shirt" type of sport garment which was first used for manual work itself, it is "taken up" by the elite before the fashion is more widely diffused throughout the population. In modern society, fashion spreads rapidly from class to class so that the Paris-designed gown, for example, is soon the model for almost all pocketbooks, differing from price to price only in quality of workmanship and material. Thorstein Veblen, in his well-known and caustic analysis of the leisure class[9] noting the role of that group in providing the models of fashion for general emulation, even goes so far as to claim that the two criteria of fashion are expensiveness and "ineptitude" or ugliness. Veblen was stressing the conspicuous expenditure of leisure and of "valuable goods" as a device by which upper classes and those imitating them, in such primitive groups as the Kwakiutl as well as in our own society, maintain and enhance their prestige. In Chapter XIV we shall examine Veblen's claims more carefully, including the question of the relation of class and fashion.

Although fashion tends to affect all groups within a community, it is always an item in the cost of living. Some forms of fashion, such as polo playing or frequenting certain night clubs or visiting "fashionable" resorts, are limited to those who can afford their expense. Few, in fact, can actually "keep up with the Joneses," though many in their striving to do so engage in expenditures unwarranted by their means, and all can "enjoy" the vicarious experience of reading and gossiping about the fashionable activities of the more affluent. This situation is especially characteristic of large-scale democratic societies, which are marked by a wide prevalence of the same fashion types, the differences within the type expressing standards of income and of taste. Long-established aristrocratic societies, on the other hand, tend to develop distinctive types of fashion for different social classes.

The spread of fashion in modern times. The area over which the same rule of fashion extends and the speed with which it makes and abrogates its laws have both greatly increase within our modern civilisation. We may consider briefly the conditions of our age that have given a freer play to fashion than it ever possessed before.

[1] *Economic and class factors:* One important consideration is the change in the character of our class structure. The development of greater mobility of people from class to class which, as we shall see later, accompanied the growth of capitalism, has broken down an important social barrier of fashion. Spencer was probably right in correlating the growth of fashion with the transition from a "military" to an "industrial" society.[10] The former is bound up with the insistence on rank, ceremonial, and status, with an inflexible order of subordination which checks the democratising reign of fashion. Another factor which has increased the range of fashion has been the increase of prosperity and leisure. This is not only due to the fact that a larger group is able to emulate the style of living of the aristocracy, but also because, as we have indicated, fashion is chiefly concerned with the superfluities of life or which the superfluous decoration of life's necessities. We do not think of fashion in overalls until they are adopted as a playsuit or as a "smart" mode of garb. There is more of fashion in the body of an automobile than in its chassis; there are changes but no fashions in steam shovels or other devices that are strictly tools. The higher the standard of living—the more playsuits and automobiles and the like—the more material there is for fashion to operate upon.

[2] *Factors of communication and invention:* The modern spread of fashion is also in part the result of the enormous development of the means of communication, which has broken down the barriers of time and distance, and the related acceleration of invention. In the numerous and complex contacts which our civilisation produces, especially in the more populous centres, the area assigned to custom has diminished. For custom is always most powerful and far reaching in the regions remote from communications. Contacts bring alien customs together and diminish the sanctity of many of the established ways. Moreover, the cumulative inventions of the industrial age, as applied both to modes of work and to modes of living, are inimical to the older customs and introduce continuous process of change which limits the formation of new ones. Thus, there is an increase in that area of moral indifference which is controlled by fashion. Where custom loses hold, fashion gains new ground. The increase of fashion's hold today, taken by certain critics of our age as a portent of social decadence, is traceable in part, then, to the civilisational accomplishment that have increased men's contacts with one another.

[3[*Fashion in diversified society:* In complex society, fashion may be view from either of two quite opposite sides. On the one hand, among frivolous or very sophisticated groups, fashion may become the main guide of life. In decadent civilisations it may usurp the place of morals. Thus Tacitus, in deploring the decline of moral standards in the Rome of his day, declared that "to corrupt and to be corrupt is called the fashion."[11] And in many subsequent ages, not least so our own, devotion to the whims of fashion and indifference to more fundamental aspects of life, whether on the part of the Italian aristocracy of the late Renaissance or the disappearing "bobby-soxers" of recent years, have bene hailed as certain evidence of social decay. We may note that many such transitory and superficial developments are not significant "evidence" whatsoever, but that when any individual or group is exclusively concerned with the code of fashion he or it, however temporarily, is in a decadent stage.

On the other hand, within its sphere fashion serves a useful social function. It introduces a common pattern into the area of indifference, an appearance or sense of likeness which enables people of very diverse interests and dispositions to meet on common ground and which makes it easier for them to retain, in harmony with one another, their essential individual and group characters. Fashion has on that account a special significance in the extensive range of a diversified democratic civilisation. But when its control passes beyond the superficialities of life, so that it becomes "fashionable" to frequently change one's wives or political affiliations or friends, it offers a poor substitute for the more established sanctions. For its rule is shallow and inconsequent, concerned with the form and no with the substance of living, devoid of conviction and of stability.

How fashion is prescribed. We have suggested some reasons why fashion holds such sway over the minds of men. What is perhaps less obvious is whence its commands proceed, who the leaders are, and why they should be so authoritative. The explanation that fashion is the "imitation of contemporaries" does not suffice. For the fashion must exist and be recognised before it is "imitated." It is followed because it is the fashion. It has leaders as well as followers, and the leaders, as we have seen, are those who have prestige in their particular field. They also must have a flair for the prevailing mood or temper of the time, whether in matters of dress or of art, of language or of thought. Even the most reputed leaders may fail at times to divine this mood and lose prestige for the moment, as the Paris fashion experts have done more than once. Nor can fashion be explained in simple terms of economic interests. It is quite capable of dealing ruthlessly with any particular economic interests which do not serve its purposes, as the woolen and other textile industries have known to their cost. It is true that important economic agencies are at work to stimulate the growth of fashion and above all to accelerate the change of fashion. When once the new mode is sensed, vast publicity is applied by these to persuade the community that a fashion has arrived and to urge its adoption. The claim that a book is a "best seller" or that a new song is the "rage" or a new play the "hit of the season" or that some particular colour or material is being worn in the "best circles," provided it has a modicum of truth, helps to substantiate itself. But economic interests do not create the appeal of fashion: they merely reinforce it.

However, fashion is not purely wayward, equally ready to move in any direction that the leaders choose. Fashion in the long run may be allied with profounder forms of social control, adapting its prescriptions to moral, religious, or economic changes. While from season to season it seems to move forward and backward, in the larger perspective, fashion exhibits distinct trends.[12] These trends are sometimes indications of more important changes within the community. It is no accident, as we have seen, that with the change in the economic and social status of women there should have gradually come about certain permanent modifications of feminine dress. (In fact, the somewhat longer skirts called for by 1947 styles induced protest demonstrations, for example, in Dallas, Texas, on the basis of modern women's "emancipation.") It is no accident that in war and postwar periods the dress of women more closely approximates that of men.

Fashion, playing at the surface where resistance is least, responding to the social whim of the moment, discovers on this level a compensation for the restraints of custom and habit and the routine of life. Through its passing conformities it helps to bridge the greater transitions of the process of social change. It often creates a series of seemingly inconsequent steps leading from one custom to another, thereby playing a part in both the maintenance and the alterations of the social structure.

We have in this chapter depicted the principal types of social codes by contrasting religion and morals, custom and law, and custom and fashion. We have discussed each of these with special reference to their functions, significance, and limitations in modern complex society. Throughout Part Two of Book Two, in considering the various kinds of groups in the social structure, and also throughout Book Three, in the analysis of social change, we shall have frequent occasion to recall this discussion of the social codes. One final task remains before us, however: to view the codes with relation to the life of the individual person, a task we face in the following chapter.

REFERENCES

1. J.C. Gray, *Nature and Sources of the Law* (New York, 1927), p. 282.
2. For a good analysis of the relation of law and custom *within* military organisation, see the articles by Morroe Berger, "Law and Custom in the Army," *Social Forces, XXV* (1946), 82-87; and "Cultural Enforcement in the American Army," *Journal of Legal and Political Sociology, IV* (1946), 96-103.
3. For the difference between constitutional and municipal law, sec MacIver, The *Modern State,* Chap. VIII, Sec. I.
4. Spencer, *op. cit.,* II, 205 ff.
5. *Laws of Imitation* (E.C. Parsons, tr., New York, 1903) Chap. VII.
6. See R.S. Lynd, *Knowledge for What?* (Princeton, 1939), pp. 195-197, for a discussion of the needs for conformity and for novelty.
7. Sapir, *loc. cit.*
8. For the social psychology of fashion, see K. Young, *Social Psychology* (New York, 1944), Chap. XVII; R.T. LaPiere, *Collective Behaviour* (New York, 1938), Chap. IX.
9. The *Theory of the Leisure Class* (New York, 1922), Chap. I. For Veblen's comments on fashion, see also Chaps. III, IV and VII of this volume.
10. Spencer, *op. cit.,* II, 213-214.
11. Tacitus, *Germania,* p. 19.
12. See A.L. Kroeber, "On the Principle of Order in Civilisation as Exemplified by Changes of Fashion," *American Anthropologist, N.S.,* XXI, No. 3 (1919), 235-263.

10

Social Codes and the Individual Life

Custom and Habit

The problem before us. Our study of the social codes arises again the fundamental question as well as in various passages elsewhere, of the relation of the individual to his society. In this chapter, we shall discuss it from the standpoint of the individual as he faces the demands and the sanctions of the variant and sometimes conflicting codes which bear upon his conduct. The nature of this problem will appear more clearly if we first consider how the social principle of custom is related to the individual principle of habit.

Custom and the nature of habit. Few distinctions throw more light on the character of society than that of custom and habit, a distinction which is often clouded by ambiguities. It is true that custom is a *social* and habit is an *individual* phenomenon, but this distinction requires interpretation. It is not enough to regard customs as the habit of the group or as "widespread uniformities of habit."[1] Of course, any particular habit that, growing out of a common situation, characterises many of the members of a group is likely to become a custom. A custom is then formed on the basis of habit, gaining the sanction and the influence, and therefore the social significance, which is peculiar to custom. Wherever, there is a widespread habit there is probably a corresponding custom *as well.* Habits create customs and customs create habits. But the two, though intricately related, are distinct. Customs could not exist unless the corresponding habits were inculcated into the rising generations, but habits can exist without the support of custom. Feral beings, such as Kaspar Hauser or the "Wolf Children," must live without customs but they cannot live without habits.

Habits are behaviour modes which through repetition have grown canalised. Man's tendency to respond in a similar way to a similar situation is confirmed and defined—grooved, as it were—by physical and psychical modifications. The acquisition of habit renders a specific action, brushing the teeth or feeding the baby or going to church, easy and familiar, relatively effortless and congenial. Habit means an *acquired* facility to act in a certain manner without resort to deliberation or thought.

When we form a habit we make it easier for ourselves, both *psychologically* and *physiologically,* to act in a certain way, and more difficult to act in ways alternative to that which has become habitual. In this sense habit is "second nature," or, more strictly, our realised nature, the established, rooted, and often almost indelible more of response for which we have exchanged the unformed potentialities of our heredity. Since human nature is so adaptable, so rich in potentialities, so accommodating, since the young life can be trained in any of so many diverse ways, indoctrinated in any of so many diverse skills and capacities, the formation of habits is of supreme importance in the process of education. For habit realises one alternative by shutting out many others. Habit closes countless avenues of life in order that a few may be more easy for us to tread. Without habits we could not achieve anything, but *which* habits we form and perhaps still more *how* we form them is of decisive moment.

Automatic habit and controlled habit. How we form habits determines whether habit shall be a tyrant or an instrument of our lives. In this determination is varying limitations of heredity play a part, but particularly important is the manner of our education.

[1] *Learning and automatic habit:* All learning, no matter what it is we learn, involves to some extent the acquisition of habits. We may learn to do things by the authoritative imposition of a routine, in which the process of learning is denuded of immediate meaning and only the mechanical result is counted. This method of learning characterises many of the routines inculcated in the very young of all societies, involved in such basic activities as nursing, weaning, elimination, sleeping and walking. Cultural variability in these matters is very great, and in each society the particular training techniques used to induce automatic habits play a role in determining broad personality types—a situation of considerable interest to many anthropologists and psychologists.

This type of habit formation is not confined to the training of infants. An extreme example is the average Army sergeant or Navy "boot school" method of drilling recruits, based upon the questionable learning theory that the inculcation of automatic obedience in one activity will carry over into others. "Theirs not to reason why" unfortunately also finds frequent illustrations in the classroom when teaching becomes dictation, and knowledge, instead of being the exploration of a world of endless interest, becomes a task of memory.

Another type of automatic habit is that imposed by the technology and urbanisation of modern society. The machine, for example, with its endless cycle of unvarying repetitions, calls for a similar routine in those who feed and tend it—a favourite subject of cartoons and one brilliantly portrayed by Chaplin's *Modern Times.* But this imposed routine is so limited and specialised that, unless it is accompanied by other conditions which rob life of interest and dignity, it does not bite so deeply into character as the enslavement of habits which impose themselves primarily in the name of authority. Nor is this authoritarian element present in those automatic habits induced by the congestion and facilities of city life, the habit of pushing to make the subway door, of walking on the right of the sidewalk, of depending for lunch on the same corner drugstore, and so forth. These are mostly habits of necessity, routinizing much of our behaviour, to be sure, but essential if we are to adjust to the conditions of modern life.

[2] *The positive function of controlled habit:* Habit as the instrument of life economises energy, reduces drudgery, and saves the needless expenditure of thought. Wherever, there are purely repetitive acts to be performed, such as shaving in the morning or walking to one's work or typing letters or punching holes in steel, it is a vast gain to be able to entrust the *process* to the semiconscious operations of habit. We could never learn to do things easily or well if we had to think afresh each step of the process. This applies not only to mechanical tasks but to the finest and most creative arts. In the mechanical tasks, thought, liberated from the conscious superintendence of the process, must divorce itself from an activity which offers no scope for its free play. In the creative arts the artist seeks to express himself through the habit-controlled technique, subordinates it to the thing he is seeking to express, and thereby prevents it from hardening into mere mechanism. His satisfaction, his achievement, is not merely an end result of the process but also a concomitant of it. When, for example, the musician is able to relegate to habit the technique underlying his art he is then free to devote himself to the interpretation of the music, so that he can both enjoy it himself and communicate to others what it means to him.

This illustration from the arts permits us to view another important aspect of habit. Where an operation is performed solely for the end result, where there is no interest sustained and developed within the process which leads to it, habit is *mechanical* and becomes drudgery or tyranny. Mechanical habit is most frequently the result of economic necessity and was as characteristic of most preindustrial toil as of our own forms of labour. Men ordinarily seek relief from the burden of mechanical habit in sport or excitement or hobby or creative employment of leisure or perhaps in alcohol or drugs or daydreams. But we should not for this reason regard such devitalised habit as revealing the inherent nature of a phenomenon the essential function of which is to save and thus to liberate our energies.

Habit as a conservative agent in social life. Most of us at one time or another have condemned the habits of others or of ourselves on the ground that they have prevented new or alternative ways of doing this or that. In other words, we have complained about the role of habit in maintaining the status quo of some situation, about habit as a conservative force in social life. This function of habit has various aspects.

[1] *The "power" of habit and its limitations:* We often speak of the "power" of habit. In an eloquent and famous passage William James described it thus:

> Habit is thus the enormous fly-wheel of society, its most precious conservative agent. It alone is what keeps us all within the bounds of ordinance, and saves the children of fortune from the envious uprisings of the poor. It alone prevents the hardest and most repulsive walks of life from being deserted by those brought up to tread therein. It keeps the fisherman and the deck-hand at sea

through the winter; it holds the miner in his darkness, and nails the countryman to his logcabin and his lonely farm through all the months of snow; it protects us from invasion by the natives of the desert and the frozen zone. It dooms us all to fight out the battle of life upon the lines of our nurture or our early choice, and to make the best of a pursuit that disagrees, because there is no other for which we are fitted, and it is too late to begin again. It keeps different social strata from mixing. Already at the age of twenty-five you see the professional mannerism settling down on the young commercial traveller, on the young doctor, on the young minister, on the young counsellor-at-law. You see the little lines of cleavage running through the character, the tricks of thought, the prejudices, the ways of the "shop," in a word, from which the man can by-and-by no more escape than his coat-sleeve can suddenly fall into a new set of folds. On the whole, it is best he should not escape. It is well for the world that in most of us, by the age of thirty, the character has set like plaster, and will never soften again.[2]

Whether this hardening of character is "well for the world" is questionable. In the instances here presented habit should be thought of as making money easy and tolerable, rather than as dictating, the persistent activities of men. Habit makes necessity tolerable, but it does not make the necessity. Habit accommodates us to the necessity, so that it seems so no longer, so that once we are habituated it may shut out even from our imaginations the alternative experiences and goals which once seemed more appealing.

The conservative quality of this accommodating function of habit is sharply illustrated in those people who for years have dreamed of new homes surroundings or a new way of life only to discover upon its acquisition a longing for the old habitual surroundings or ways—a situation often depicted in novels and movies. What from one viewpoint may seem the dreariest type of existence, through the force of habituation, takes on a value of its own to which men often cling when confronted with the opportunity for change. In time even the prisoner may come to love his chains.

But there is another side to this picture. The energies economised by habit, if they find no outlet in or beyond the activity, the potentialities unutilised or obstructed by it, may break the dams and channels of habit, seeking in new ways a hitherto denied satisfaction. This is the phenomenon which in a particular religious manifestation is named "conversion." Another form of it is seen in the conquest of addictions, such as those created by drugs. It is often thought of as the revulsion from "bad habits", but it also occurs as the sudden rejection of "good habits," imposed by past authority or by social pressure. These sudden revolts from conventional habituations are frequently portrayed in cartoon and fiction, for example by the violent explosions of a "Dagwood" or the "secret vices" of an otherwise model of propriety. This abrupt habit-defying change of the personal life is like the social phenomenon of revolution, the sudden rejection of custom and institution which have grown repressive beyond endurance, though this parallel is not complete since the custom against which we rebel is felt to be external and alien while the habit has become incorporated in our personalities.

When therefore we speak of the power or the "slavery" of habit we should remember the habit is not some all-powerful master ruling as against our will. This conception has, to be sure, a limited application to the abnormal group of drug-induced habits with their peculiar psychological character, though even here we should remember that the addict wants both the drug and freedom from it. But, in general, habit is the accommodation of the individual life to the conditions under which it must carry on its existence. Man can live in the snows or in the tropics, in the city or in the country, under the conditions of almost any social and physical environment; he can enter on anyone of a thousand occupations, and there are a multitude of interests and diversions which many claim his leisure. From these a choice has to be made, and it is made under the influences of the nearer environment, of education and training, of temperament and capacity, of economic opportunity. Once made, habits begin to confirm the choice, to counter its disadvantages and disappointments, to close the alternatives. In the earlier stages they are more subject to revision and readaptation, but once fully established, especially as we grow older, they weave themselves into our personalities, habit joining with habit to form the pattern of our lives. Then only the strongest eruptive influences, such as the shift from civilian to military life or from a free community to the life of a prison or a concentration camp, can prevail against them, and only with profound disturbance to the human personality.[3]

[2] *The case of emotionally rooted habits:* Habit's function, its advantage, its sacrifice of alternatives are seen with peculiar clearness in the case of those habits which, unlike more technical aptitudes, become closely associated with our basic emotions. Such are pre-eminently our moral and religious habits, and include also our ways of thinking and acting on those political and economic issues which closely affect our interests. The endless diversity of moral codes and practices exhibited by different peoples or groups, while each nevertheless regards with strong revulsion the divergent practices of others, has been the subject of wondering comment since ancient times. And the hotly defended habituations in morals, sex behaviour, religion, politics, and business practice are a constant source of modern speculation.

Consider sex relations. It is an obvious anthropological fact that even in this vital area different peoples can successfully accommodate themselves to a great variety of different systems. The universally shared drive of sex can adapt itself to various forms of expression so much so that "perversions" are a matter of cultural definition. However, the various possible alternatives of sex behaviour do into all remain open in any society. Some dominant system is evolved under the prevailing circumstances of each group, suited to the modes of living resulting from its geographical and economic environment, to the fixations arising from its gradual translation not law of the accidents and inevitabilities of experience, and to the whole complex of customs of which the sex code is a part. Under each system custom becomes the ground of habit, and through their combined influence the deep emotions of sex convey a profound moral import to the accepted ways. The strong deviational tendencies of an urge so imperative as sex means that there is always present the possibility of its breaking loose from the prescribed channel of custom and habit, and this no doubt helps to generate the strength of sex taboos and prohibitions. Again we may note that the habits imposed by the latter are not complete masters of our inclinations, as evidenced by the presence of sexual deviation from the prescribed norms in almost all societies.[4]

Similar considerations apply to the other habits of work and industry in our own society that have become linked with religious and moral values, with habits of political behaviour that have been built into the traditions of families and other groups, even with habits of everyday convention, departure from which sometimes causes intense personal or group disturbance. With respect to them all, the danger is that the very necessity which imposes them tends to wrap them in a shroud of blind emotion, thus precluding the possibility of growth, of flexibility, and of intelligent redirection. Here as well as elsewhere, here perhaps more than elsewhere, the only assurance against needless limitation, against stagnation, or against equally blind revolt, lies in the constant association of habit and reflection. When either habit or custom grows sacrosanct, beyond the range of scrutiny and critical evaluation, the welfare of both individual and group is threatened.

Social organisation and the relation of custom and habit. We can now draw certain conclusions concerning the distinction between habit and custom that was suggested at the outset of our discussion. If we are content to identify customs, as is commonly done, with "the habits of the group," then there is either no distinction at all, or a merely quantitative one, between the two concepts. The psychiatrist's interest in the habits of an individual would be identical with the sociologist's concern with the ways of a society. The two interests are necessarily related, are even interdependent, as we shall see, but they are not the same.

[1] *The social character of custom:* The identification of custom and habit ignores the social quality, the social sanction, of custom, a quality which is in no sense part of the meaning of habit. Habits formed in isolation, as by the hermit, or through personal idiosyncrasy, are just as truly habits as those formed under the influence of and in conformity with the conduct of the group. A custom, on the contrary, exists only as a *social relationship.* If, for example, I go to church because it is the thing to do, because it is the practice of the group to which I belong, because if I fail to do so I am subject to some degree of social disapprobation, or because by doing so I establish some useful business or social connections, then I am conforming to a custom. If when I am away from my group I have no prompting to attend church, then my former conduct, even if habitual, is to be attributed to custom rather than to habit.

Custom has for the individual an *external sanction.* It is a mode of conduct of the group itself, as a group, and every custom is in consequence adjusted to the others which the group observes. It is part of a complex of determinate relationships sustained and guarded by the group. Each individual sustains it, even though it gains also the support of habit, in the consciousness of his membership in the group. We would not give the name of custom to those habits of technical aptitude which we acquire in learning a trade or a profession. It is true that we owe these also to our social heritage, but they need no social sanction because they are direct objective means to the ends we seek. Thus the professional skill of the surgeon is habit, not custom, but his professional etiquette is custom though it may also be habit.

The peculiar social character of custom is revealed by the one great class of customs which cannot be practiced except collectively. Nearly all celebrations, rituals, and ceremonies fall within this class. They derive their significance from the fact that people come together and by participating in a common occasion stimulate the social consciousness of one another. There are many emotions for whose full satisfaction a social setting and the participation of others are requisite, and a whole range of customs, the ritual of worship, the dance, the reunion, social games, and so forth, arises to meet this need. Such customs are in no sense merely uniformities of habit, and many of them in fact involve a diversity of role on the part of the various performers.

[2] *The causal relation of habit and custom:* If custom and habit are distinct, they are at the same time causally related in social life. The customs of the group, impressed on the plastic natures of the young, shape and direct, focus and limit, their native potentialities. Undirected potentiality is also sprawling helplessness. Education is rendered both possible and necessary by the pressure of alternatives. The customs of the group are translated through education, in the broadest sense, into the habits of each generation, and the habits thus formed perpetuate the customs. In this educative process customs may be thought of as preceding habits, but if this were the whole story the weight of the past would repress all innovation, all readjustment, all development. Man is assertive as well as plastic; he refuses to take on the perfect mold of the past.

One aspect of this truth is that *habits also precede customs.* Our habits are a more intimate part of our personality than are our customs, and they arise not only from social education but also as our personal response to the immediate conditions of our lives. Thus they exhibit a greater variability, and as they impinge on customs they make these in turn more flexible and subject to modification. When personal habits are sufficiently similar, such as those induced by the discovery of new techniques, they are apt not only to modify old customs but also to stimulate new ones. Thus new habits induced by the telephone and automobile and radio have undermined old customs and have helped to bring about others. Many of the customs of our industrial age, such as the recreational custom of attending "mass spectacles" like movies and sports events or the custom of eating tinned or frozen foods or that of frequently changing one's automobile model, may be attributed in part to the habits necessitated by machinecraft and urbanisation or the opportunities released by invention.[5]

The process we have been describing — custom determining the general direction of habituations, and habits in turn sustaining and sometimes altering customs—is a significant aspect of all social organisation. As we go on to explore in later chapters the features of the social structure we should keep in mind a lesson that the understanding of habit and custom and their interrelationship teaches, namely that all social phenomena ultimately involve the strivings and dispositions and attitudes of individual human beings as well as the customs and institutions and other characteristic ways of human groups.

The Individual Confronting the Mores

Opposing aspects of the mores and the individual. From the standpoint of the individual the mores have two aspects. In the first place, as we have seen, through indocrination and habituation, they are incorporated into his very nature. Secondly, they confront him as socially sanctioned demands, bringing pressure to bear on his native inclinations, on his personal desires and personal calculations. Thus they arouse resistance and create conflict within him.

[1] *The intensification of the problem in modern society:* The conflict between the individual's desires and the mores is more apparent in complex society than in the simpler types. In all societies, as the growing child is indoctrinate in the mores, he tends, under their prompting, to rationalise his first unreasoning acceptance. The mores appear to him as the eternal, the sacred, the adult-given, the God-given. But when the child or the adolescent comes into contact with new groups and new situations, when he enters a world in which the authority of the family or the discipline of the school or the tradition of the local group no longer holds, this attitude of acceptance is subject to challenge. The presence of new mores raises questions regarding the basis of acceptance of the old. The conflict of mores and codes may shake the sense of the inevitable rightness of the hitherto established, may disturb, the psychological security of the narrower social world of the young child.[6]

This challenge and this kind of disturbance are more frequent and more formidable in modern complex society. In primitive society, generally, adolescence means initiation into the old tribal ways. In modern society it often means initiation into new ways, frequently incomprehensible to the elders, and into some degree of liberation from former indoctrinations. The consequent widespread uncertainty and conflict represent a phenomenon characteristic of modern life which is found to a much less extent in primitive life. This situation is intensified by the very complexity of modern social organisation, with its numerous and often conflicting codes.

[2] *The individual's problem of selecting a code:* The number and variety of codes in modern society confront the individual as a great social pressure, often as an overbearing but inconsistent demand for conformity. The individual is faced with the problem of charting his way through the claims of family tradition, of business practices, of political loyalties, of sex standards, of religious prescriptions, of humanitarian considerations, for example, and ultimately of his own conscience. This situation, imposed by the complexities and inconsistencies of contemporary life, has increasingly in recent years occupied the attention of psychoanalysts and psychiatrists. For many of the problems of personality maladjustment, the neuroses and some psychoses, and various physical maladies as well, according to "psychosomatic" medicine, cannot be understood without reference to this sociological characteristic of our era.[7] This is a problem to which we shall return.

However, the majority conform to the codes. Although at times everyone feels an inner resistance to some of their aspects, most of us accept them most of the time and nearly all of the time approve the conformity of others. The individual, faced by the necessity of selecting from among the number and variety of the codes, acquires a code of his own. This personal code is compounded of many elements, selective within the limits imposed by the sanctions of law and custom, deeply responsive to the influences of education and of the social environment, but nevertheless expressive of the whole of the particular personality.

There are important implications of the individual's selection of his own code. On the one hand, this liberty of choice is an essential mark of adult selfhood in our culture. The process necessarily requires the mitigation of such drastic external sanctions as those of a compulsory fear-inspired religion, typical of an earlier period in Western society, and cannot take place in a "totalitarian" environment in which the ruling authority seeks to close all avenues of choice but one. On the other hand, the freedom of the individual to select his own code may take place within social conditions that provide no guarantees of life's material requirements and few or no strong group values that are essential for psychological security. This situation, according to some writers, characterised much of Western society during the period preceding the recent European dictatorships, themselves attributable in part to the modern individual's longing, albeit unconscious, to "escape from freedom."[8] In any event, if the individual is to retain this highest mark of cultural development, the ability and desire to select his own standards, he must at the same time strive to maintain a kind of social order in which choice itself is protected and guaranteed.

[3] *Contrast of the social and individual codes:* The *social codes* are standards, but they are not, in the full sense, ideals of conduct. They are essentially workaday rules, deriving in part from tradition and in part from the necessities of group life. As we shall see in a later chapter, the social codes reveal also the dominant interests of the power holders in all societies. They constitute at best a rough translation into formulas or norms of the limited experience and reflection of the average mentality of the group.

In contrast, the *selective code of the individual* expresses, in proportion to the strength of his character and the clarity of his intelligence, a more definite and vivid and intimate set of valuations. These individual codes could not exist without the support of the social codes, but they exceed the latter in substance, vitality and detail. The mainspring of the individual's life is in fact the inner set of valuations he cherishes. Within these valuations there are often conflict and contradiction, involving in normal cases a sometimes painful adjustment to new experiences, but in extreme cases going so far as to disrupt the personality. At the same time, there is also a degree of conflict between the individual code and some dominant social code, a conflict that is most apt to show itself in relation to the sex code, to the economic code, and in many communities to the religious code of the group to which the individual belongs.

Two general types of conflict between the individual and the code. There are, then, two main types of conflict: (1) that in which personal interest or personal valuation is opposed to a prevailing code, and (2) that in which the individual is pulled opposite ways by the prescriptions of different codes, when two or more are applicable within the same situation. In the individual life the two types are sometimes found in combination. The most significant variety of the first type is that where the individual conscience denies the rightness or validity of the code, as when, for example, the citizen who abhors war is called by the state to military training or service.[9] At times closely related to this variety of conflict is an example of the second type, the situation, once so frequent and still by no means obsolete, in which the religion of the citizen prescribes a course of conduct contrary to that which is commanded by the state.

[1] *An illustration from drama:* These two types of conflict provide, because of their intrinsic interest and their consequences, the supreme subjects of literature, especially of the novel and of the drama. One of the famous dramatic presentations of the clash between two social codes is Sophocles' *Antigone,* where the heroine has to choose between the prescriptions of her religion, involving her sacred duty to her dead brother, and the edict of the king. The drama, as life itself, frequently combines the two types of conflict, as in *Hamlet.* In drama's whole range from the Orestean trilogy to the plays of more modern authors like Ibsen, Shaw, Galsworthy, O'Neill, Anderson, and Odets, its main theme has been the predicament of the "hero," incarnating some social or personal code and beset by the sanctions of an opposing social code. It is of sociological significance that when, as in *Agamemnon, Macbeth, Hamlet, Ghosts, The Emperor Jones,* the social sanctions triumphed over the "hero," the drama takes the form of tragedy; but often when, as in the Falstaff plays, *Peer Gynt, Arms and the Man,* and many others with a "happy ending" including such farces as *Arsenic and Old Lace,* the "hero" outwits, triumphs over, or achieves some form of reconciliation with the social code, the result is technically a comedy. The keen dramatist recognises and exploits the high value we generally place on the individual's selective code.

[2] *The conflict in contemporary life:* Consider the problems that face us in everyday life. Shall I vote for the candidate who seems best qualified for office or shall I follow the party of my family, my employer, my closest associates? Shall I take a position with the type of business firm in the family tradition or shall I seek one more suited to my own nature? Shall I obey the legal code and employ workers on the basis of their qualifications to do the job or shall I follow the code of custom, giving preference to Whites, "Anglos," "Gentiles"? Shall I marry the person I love who happens to be Jewish or Catholic or whatever it may be or shall I marry the "nice" girl or boy whose social credentials meet the prescriptions of my own group? Shall I remain sexually faithful to my husband or wife or shall I seek affection or diversion more in keeping with my inner desires? And so on.

Such are the questions that confront each of us as we go about the business of selecting between the social codes or between the latter and our own codes. The range of pressures and the range of accommodation to them are suggested in Chart I. The

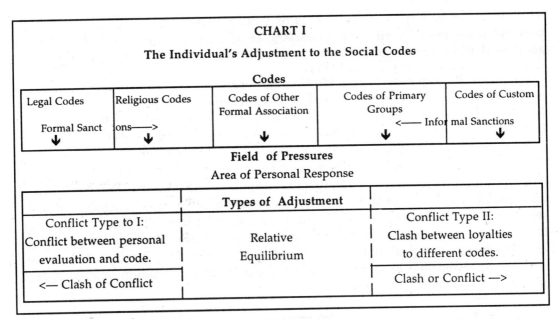

CHART I

The Individual's Adjustment to the Social Codes

Codes

Legal Codes	Religious Codes	Codes of Other Formal Association	Codes of Primary Groups	Codes of Custom
Formal Sanct ions———>			<—— Infor mal Sanctions	
↓	↓	↓	↓	↓

Field of Pressures

Area of Personal Response

Types of Adjustment		
Conflict Type to I: Conflict between personal evaluation and code.	Relative Equilibrium	Conflict Type II: Clash between loyalties to different codes.
<— Clash of Conflict		Clash or Conflict —>

accommodations, as we have seen, can take many forms, including those types our culture defines as "neurotic" and "maladjusted"— themselves manifestations of personal accommodation. If all the possible varieties of adjustment to the codes were shown in the bottom box of our chart there would be as many subdivisions as there are individual personalities themselves.

Other forms of conflict between the individual and society. It is not always easy to distinguish between the conflict of the individual with the code and his struggle with the limiting or thwarting circumstances in which his lot is cast. For he may regard these circumstances as in some sense imposed upon him by the social system. Especially is this true of the economic struggle, since the privations and restrictions against which he fights are in some measure dependent on the laws regulating property, inheritance, the accumulation and the distribution of wealth. The conditions obtaining within a society are so linked up with its codes that the latter at numerous points come into conflict with our individual desires and impulses, and especially with our strongest impulses, like those associated with property and with sex.

[1] *Three types of pressure on the individual:* The unequal conditions of power and privilege and wealth that obtain in all societies—no less, so far as the first two of these inequalities are concerned, in communistic societies than in more individualistic ones— lead to frequent situations in which the individual finds himself pitted against the code. The different types of dominance which bring about this result will be examined in greater detail in Part Two of this Book. Here three types may be distinguished.

One: The Pressure of Dominant Groups. In the first place, there are dominant groups which impose their will on other groups, bringing to bear strong social pressures under which the less dominant suffer. This is the case whatever the form of society, whether a "utopian community" such as Oneida or a huge modern nation. In one sphere the pressure takes the form of social ostracism, in another of economic exploitation, in another of arbitrary or tyrannical laws.

Two: The Pressure of Authority. Within every group, no matter how small, no matter how united by common purpose, there is the tendency of authority and prestige to seek its own ends and to express its power at the cost of the variant individualities subject to it. To secure any common end there must be common rules, but the drive of authority, fostered by lack of understanding as well as by pride of position, goes beyond the degree of regulation which the common end requires. Even in the circle of the family this tendency is displayed. The divergent viewpoints of the older and the younger lead often to bitter compulsions and revolts and sometimes to tragic sacrifices. It is the sensitive, the imaginative, the original minds on whom the pressure bears most heavily. It is these, too, who feel most bitterly the tyrannies which are often imposed by officials and bureaucrats, "clothed in a little brief authority." The resulting sense of frustration may be expressed in a bitterness against the particular organisation or even against society itself.

REFERENCES

1. So defined by John Dewey in *Human Nature and Conduct* (New York, 1922), Chapt. IV. On this point we differ from Dewey's account of custom and habit in that chapter, although it presents a penetrating and very suggestive analysis.

2. William James, *Principles of Psychology* (New York, 1890), I, 121. Reprinted by permission of the publishers, Henry Holt and Company.

3. On this point see, for example, the excellent study by two Army psychiatrists, R.R. Grinker and J.F. Spiegel, *Men under Stress* (Philadelphia, 1945), especially Chaps. XIX and XX.

4. For anthropological evidence in this field, see B. Malinowski, *Sex and Repression in Savage Society* (New York, 1927); M. Mead, *Sex and Temperament in Three Primitive Societies* (New York, 1935); and for the United States, A.C. Kinsey, W.B. Pomeroy, and C.E. Martin, *Sexual Behaviour in the Human Male* (Philadelphia, 1948).

5. For numerous illustrations, see *Recent Social Trends* (New York, 1933), Chap. III.

6. This process is admirably revealed in J. Piaget, *The Moral Judgment of the Child*, (New York, 1932). See also the analysis of G.H. Mead, *Mind, Self and Society* (Chicago, 1934), Part III.

7. See, for example, T. Burrow, *The Social Basis of Consciousness* (New York, 1927); K. Horney, *The Neurotic Personality of Our Time* (New York, 1937), especially Chap. XIV, and *New Ways in Psychoanalysis* (New York, 1939) especially Chap. X; A. Kardiner, *The Psychological Frontiers of Society* (New York, 1945), Chap. XIV; and the articles by F. Alexander, T. Burrow, E. Mayo, P. Schilder, H.S. Sullivan, and E. Sapir in *The American Journal of Sociology*, Vol. XLII, No. 6 (1937). The problem is well stated by K. Mannheim in *Diagnosis of Our Time* (London, 1943), Chaps. II and V.

8. See E. Fromm, *Escape from Freedom* (New York, 1941).

9. On the general subject, see R.M. MacIver, *Community* (New York, 1920), Book III, Chap. V. For various aspects of the problem, see K. Young, *Social Psychology* (New York, 1944), Chap. XV.

11

Rural Social Taboo[1]

The purpose of this lecture, which you have done me the honour of inviting me to deliver, is to commemorate the work of Sir James Frazer, as an example of life-long single-minded devotion to scientific investigation and as having contributed, in as large a measure as that of any man, to laying the foundations of the science of social anthropology. It therefore seems to me appropriate to select as the subject of my discourse one which Sir James was the first to investigate systematically half a century ago, when he wrote the article on 'Taboo' for the ninth edition of the *Encyclopaedia Britannica*, and to the elucidation of which he has made many successive contributions in his writings since that time.

The English word 'taboo' is derived from the Polynesian word 'tabu' (with the accent on the first syllable). In the languages of Polynesia the word means simply 'to forbid', 'forbidden', and can be applied to any sort of prohibition. A rule of etiquette, an order issued by a chief, an injunction to children not to meddle with the possessions of their elders, may all be expressed by the use of the word tabu.

The early voyagers in Polynesia adopted the word to refer to prohibitions of special kind, which may be illustrated by an example. Certain things such as a newly-born infant, a corpse or the person of a chief are said to be tabu. This means that one should, as far as possible, avoid touching them. A man who does touch one of these tabu objects immediately becomes tabu himself. The means two things. In the first place a man who is tabu in this sense must observe a number of special restrictions on his behaviour; for example, he may not use his hands to feed himself. He is regarded as being in a state of danger, and this is generally stated by saying that if he fails to observe the customary precautions he will be ill and perhaps die. In the second place he is also dangerous to other persons—he is tabu in the same sense as the thing he has touched. If he should come in contact with utensils in which, or the fire at which, food is cooked, the dangerous influence would be communicated to the food and so injure anyone who partook of it. A person who is tabu in this way, as by touching a corpse, can be restored to his normal condition by rites of purification or desacralisation. He is then said to be *noa* again, this term being the contrary of tabu.

Sir James Frazer has told us that when he took up the study of taboo in 1886 the current view of anthropologists at the time was that the institution in question was confined to the brown and black races of the Pacific, but that as a result of his investigations he came to the conclusion that the Polynesian body of practices and beliefs 'is only one of a number of similar systems of superstition which among many' perhaps all the races of men have contributed in large measure, under many different names and with many variations of detail, to build up the complex fabric of society in all the various sides or elements of it which we describe as religious, social, political, moral and economic.'

The use of the word taboo in anthropology for customs all over the world which resemble in essentials the example given from Polynesia seems to me undesirable and inconvenient. There is the fact already mentioned that in the Polynesian language the word tabu has a much wider meaning, equivalent to our own word 'forbidden'. This has produced a good deal of confusion in the literature relating to Polynesia owing to the ambiguity resulting from two different uses of the same word. You will have noticed that I have used the word taboo (with the English spelling and pronunciation) in the meaning that it has for anthropologists, and tabu (with the Polynesian spelling and pronunciation) in special reference to Polynesia and in the Polynesian sense. But this is not entirely satisfactory.

I propose to refer to the customs we are considering as 'ritual avoidances' or 'ritual prohibitions' and to define them by reference to two fundamental concepts for which I have been in the habit of using the terms 'ritual status' and 'ritual value'. I am not suggesting that these are the best terms to be found; they are merely the best that I have been able to find up to the present. In such a science as ours words are the instruments of analysis and we should always be prepared to discard inferior tools for superior when opportunity arises.

A ritual prohibition is a rule of behaviour which is associated with a belief that an infraction will result in an undesirable change in the ritual status of the person who fails to keep to the rule. This change of ritual status is conceived in many different ways in different societies, but everywhere there is the idea that it involves the likelihood of some minor or major misfortune which will befall the person concerned.

We have already considered one example. The Polynesian who touches a corpse has according to Polynesian belief, undergone what I am calling an undesirable change of ritual status. The misfortune of which he is considered to be in danger is illness, and he therefore takes precautions and goes through a ritual in order that he may escape the danger and be restored to his former ritual status.

Let us consider two examples of different kinds from contemporary England. There are some people who think that one should avoid spilling salt. The person who spills salt will have bad luck. But he can avoid this by throwing a pinch of the spilled salt over his shoulder. Putting this in my terminology it can be said that spilling salt produces an undesirable change in the ritual status of the person who does so, and that he is restored to his normal or previous ritual status by the positive rite of throwing salt over his shoulder.

A member of the Roman Catholic Church, unless granted a dispensation, is required by his religion to abstain from eating meat on Fridays and during Lent. If he fails to observe the rule he sins, and must proceed, as in any other sin, to confess and obtain absolution. Different as this is in important ways from the rule about spilling salt, it can and must for scientific purposes be regarded as belonging to the same general class. Eating meat on Friday produces in the person who does so an undesirable change of ritual status which requires to be remedied by fixed appropriate means.

We may add to these examples two others from other societies. If you turn to the fifth chapter of Leviticus you will find that amongst the Hebrews if a 'soul' touch the carcase of an unclean beast or of unclean cattle, or of unclean creeping things, even if he is unaware that he does so, then he is unclean and guilty and has sinned. When he becomes aware of his sin he must confess that he has sinned and must take a trespass offering—a female from the flock, a lamb or a kid of the goats—which the priest shall sacrifice to make an atonement for the sin so that it shall be forgiven him. Here the change in ritual status through touching an unclean carcase is described by the terms 'sin', 'unclean' and 'guilty'.

In the Kikuyu tribe of East Africa the word *thahu* denotes the undesirable ritual status that results from failure to observe rules of ritual avoidance. It is believed that a person who is *thahu* will be ill and will probably die unless he removes the *thahu* by the appropriate ritual remedies, which in all serious cases require the services of a priest or medicine man. Actions which produce this condition are touching or carrying a corpse, stepping over a corpse, eating food from a cracked pot, coming in contact with a woman's menstrual discharge and many others. Just as among the Hebrews a soul may unwittingly be guilty of sin by touching in ignorance the carcase of an unclean animal, so amongst the Kikuyu a man may become *thahu* without any voluntary act on his part. If an elder or a woman when coming out of the hut slips and falls down on the ground, he or she is *thahu* and lies there until some of the elders of the neighbourhood come and sacrifice a sheep. If the side-pole of a bedstead breaks, the person lying on it is *thahu* and must be purified. If the droppings of a kite or crow fall on a person he is *thahu*, and if a hyaena defaecates in a village, or a jackal barks therein, the village and its inhabitants are *thahu*.

I have purposely chosen from our society two examples of ritual avoidances which are of very different kinds. The rule against eating meat on Friday or in Lent is a rule of religion, as is the rule, where it is recognised, against playing golf or tennis on Sunday. The rule against spilling salt, I suppose it will be agreed, is non-religious. Our language permits us to make this distinction very clearly, for infractions of the rules of religion are sins, while the non-religious avoidances are concerned with good and bad luck. Since this distinction is so obvious to us it might be thought that we should find it in other societies. My own experience is that in some of the societies with which I am acquainted this distinction between sinful acts and acts that bring bad luck cannot be made. Several anthropologists, however, have attempted to classify rites into two classes, religious rites and magical rites.

For Emile Durkheim the essential distinction is that religious rites are obligatory within a religious society or church, while magical rites are optional. A person who fails in religious observances is guilty of wrong-doing, whereas one who does not observe the precautions of magic or those relating to luck is simply acting foolishly. This distinction is of considerable theoretical importance. It is difficult to apply in the study of the rites of simple societies.

Sir James Frazer defines religion as 'a propitiation or conciliation of superhuman powers which are believed to control nature and man', and regards magic as the erroneous application of the notion of causality. If we apply this to ritual prohibitions, we may regard as belonging to religion those rules the infraction of which produces a change of ritual status in the individual by offending the superhuman powers, whereas the infraction of a rule of magic would be regarded as resulting immediately in a change of ritual status, or in the misfortune that follows, by a process of hidden causation. Spilling salt, by Sir James Frazer's definition, is a question of magic, while eating meat on Friday is a question of religion.

An attempt to apply this distinction systematically meets with certain difficulties. Thus with regard to the Maori Sir James Frazer states that 'the ultimate sanction of the taboo, in other words, that which engaged the people to observe its commandments, was a firm persuasion that any breach of those commandments would surely and speedily be punished by an *atua* or ghost, who would afflict the sinner with a painful malady till he died'. This would seem to make the Polynesian taboo a matter of religion, not of magic. But my own observation of the Polynesians suggests to me that in general the native conceives of the change in his ritual status as taking place as the immediate result of such an act as touching a corpse, and that it is only when he proceeds to rationalise the whole system of taboos that he thinks of the gods and spirits—the *atua*—as being concerned. Incidentally it should not be assumed that the Polynesian word *atua* or *otua* always refers to a personal spiritual being.

Of the various ways of distinguishing magic and religion I will mention only one more. For Professor Malinowski a rite is magical when 'it has a definite practical purpose which is known to all who practise it and can be easily elicited from any native informant', while a rite is religious if it is simply expressive and has no purpose, being not a means to an end but an end in itself. A difficulty in applying this criterion is due to uncertainty as to what is meant by 'definite practical purpose.' To avoid the bad luck which results from spilling salt is, I suppose, a practical purpose though not very definite. The desire to please God in all our actions and thus escape some period of Purgatory is perhaps definite enough, but Professor Malinowski may regard it as not practical. What shall we say of the desire of the Polynesian to avoid sickness and possible death which he gives as his reason for not touching chiefs, corpses and newly-born babies?

Seeing that there is this absence of agreement as to the definitions of magic and religion and the nature of the distinction between them, and seeing that in many instances whether we call a particular rite magical or religious depends on which of the various proposed definitions we accept, the only sound procedure, at any rate in the present state of anthropological knowledge, is to avoid as far as possible the use of the terms in question until there is some general agreement about them. Certainly the distinctions made by Durkheim and Frazer and Malinowski may be theoretically significant, even though they are difficult to apply universally. Certainly, also, there is need for a systematic classification of rites, but a satisfactory classification will be fairly complex and a simple dichotomy between magic and religion does not carry us very far towards it.

Another distinction which we make in our own society within the field of ritual avoidances is between the holy and the unclean. Certain things must be treated with respect because they are holy, others because they are unclean. But, as Robertson Smith and Sir James Frazer have shown, there are many societies in which this distinction is entirely unrecognised. The Polynesian, for example, does not think of a chief or a temple as holy and a corpse as unclean. He thinks of them all as things dangerous. An example from Hawaii will illustrate this fundamental identity of holiness and uncleanness. There, in former times, if a commoner committed incest with his sister he became *kapu* (the Hawaiian form of tabu). His presence was dangerous in the extreme for the whole community, and since he could not be purified he was put to death. But if a chief of high rank, who, by reason of his rank was, of course, sacred (*kapu*), married his sister he became still more so. An extreme sanctity or untouchability attached to a chief born of a brother and sister who were themselves the children of a brother and sister. The sanctity of such a chief and the uncleanness of the person put to death for incest have the same source and are the same thing. They are both denoted by saying that the person is *kapu*. In studying the simpler societies it is essential that we should carefully avoid thinking of their behaviour and ideas in terms of our own ideas of holiness and uncleanness. Since most people find this difficult it is desirable to have terms which we can use that do not convey this connotation. Durkheim and others have used the word 'sacred' as an inclusive term for the holy and the unclean together. This is easier to do in French than in English, and has some justification in the fact that the Latin *sacer* did apply to holy things such as the gods and also to accursed things such as persons guilty of certain crimes. But there is certainly a tendency in English to identify sacred with holy. I think that it will greatly aid clear thinking if we adopt some wide inclusive term which does not have any undesirable connotation. I venture to propose the term 'ritual value'.

Anything—a person, a material thing, a place, a word or name, an occasion or event, a day of the week or a period of the year—which is the object of a ritual avoidance or taboo can be said to have ritual value. Thus in Polynesia chiefs, corpses and newly-born babies have ritual value. For some people in England salt has ritual value. For Christians all Sundays and Good Friday have ritual value, and for Jews all Saturdays and the Day of Atonement. The ritual value is exhibited in the bahaviour adopted towards the object or occasion in question. Ritual values are exhibited not only in negative ritual but also in positive ritual, being possessed by the objects towards which positive rites are directed and also by objects, words or places used in the rites. A large class of positive rites, those of consecration or sacralisation, have for their purpose to endow objects with ritual value. It may be noted that in general anything that has value in positive ritual is also the object of some sort of ritual avoidance or at the very least of ritual respect.

The word 'value', as I am using it, always refers to a relation between a subject and an object. The relation can be stated in two ways by saying either that the object has a value for the subject, or that the subject has an interest in the object. We can use the terms in this way to refer to any act of behaviour towards an object. The relation is exhibited in and defined by the behaviour. The words 'interest' and 'value' provide a convenient shorthand by which we can describe the reality, which consists of acts of behaviour and the actual relations between subjects and objects which those acts of behaviour reveal. If Jack loves Jill, then Jill has the value of a loved object for Jack, and Jack has a recognisable interest in Jill. When I am hungry I have an interest in food, and a good meal has an immediate value for me that it does not have at other times. My toothache has a value to me as something that I am interested in getting rid of as quickly as possible.

A social system can be conceived and studied as a system of values. A society consists of a number of individuals bound together in a network of social relations. A social relation exists between two or more persons when there is some harmonisation of their individual interests, by some convergence of interest and by limitation or adjustment of divergent interests. An interest is always the interest of an individual. Two individuals may have similar interests. Similar interests do not in themselves constitute a social relation; two dogs may have a similar interest in the same bone and the result may be a dog-fight. But a society cannot exist except on the basis of a certain measure of similarity in the interests of its members. Putting this in terms of value, the first necessary condition of the existence of a society is that the individual members shall agree in some measure in the values that they recognise.

Any particular society is characterised by a certain set of values—moral, aesthetic, economic, etc. In a simple society there is a fair amount of agreement amongst the members in their evaluations, though of course the agreement is never absolute. In a complex modern society we find much more disagreement if we consider the society as a whole, but we may find a closer measure of agreement amongst the members of a group or class within the society.

While some measure of agreement about values, some similarity of interests, is a prerequisite of a social system, social relations involve more than this. They require the existence of common interests and of social values. When two or more persons have a common interest in the same object and are aware of their community of interest a social relation is established. They form, whether for a moment or for a long period, an association, and the object may be said to have a social value. For a man and his wife the birth of a child, the child itself and its well-being and happiness or its death, are objects of a common interest which binds them together and they thus have, for the association formed by the two persons, social value. By this definition an object can only have a social value for an association of persons. In the simplest possible instance we have a triadic relation; Subject 1 and Subject 2 are both interested in the same way in the Object and each of the Subject has an interest in the other, or at any rate in certain items of the behaviour of the other, namely those directed towards the object. To avoid cumbersome circumlocutions it is convenient to speak of the object as having a social value for any one subject involved in such a relation, but it must be remembered that this is a loose way of speaking.

It is perhaps necessary for the avoidance of misunderstanding to add that a social system also requires that persons should be objects of interest to other persons. In relations of friendship or love each of two persons has a value for the other. In certain kinds of groups each member is an object of interest for all the others, and each member therefore has a social value for the group as a whole. Further, since there are negative values as well as positive, persons may be united or associated by their antagonism to other persons. For the members of an anti-Comintern pact the Comintern has a specific social value.

Amongst the members of a society we find a certain measure of agreement as to the ritual value they attribute to objects of different kinds. We also find that most of these ritual values are social values as defined above. Thus for a local totemic clan in Australia the totem-centres, the natural species associated with them, i.e. the totems, and the myths and rites that relate thereto, have a specific social value for the clan; the common interest in them binds the individuals together into a firm and lasting association.

Ritual values exist in every known society, and show an immense diversity as we pass from one society to another. The problem of a natural science of society (and it is as such that I regard social anthropology) is to discover the deeper, not immediately perceptible, uniformities beneath the superficial differences. This is, of course, a highly complex problem which will require the studies begun by Sir James Frazer and others to be continued by many investigators over many years. The ultimate aim should be, I think, to find some relatively adequate answer to the question—*What is the relation of ritual and ritual values to the essential constitution of human society?* I have chosen a particular approach to this study which I believe to be promising—to investigate in a few societies studied as thoroughly as possible the relations of ritual values to other values including moral and aesthetic values. In the present lecture, however, it is only one small part of this study in which I seek to interest you—the question of a relation between ritual values and social values.

One way of approaching the study of ritual is by the consideration of the purposes or reasons for the rites. If one examines the literature of anthropology one finds this approach very frequently adopted. It is by far the least profitable, though the one that appeals most to common sense. Sometimes the purpose of a rite is obvious, or a reason may be volunteered by those who practise it. Sometimes the anthropologist has to ask the reason, and in such circumstances it may happen that different reasons are given by different informants. What is fundamentally the same rite in two different societies may have different purposes or reasons in the one and in the other. The reasons given by the members of a community for any custom they observe are important data for the anthropologist. But it is to fall into grievous error to suppose that they give a valid explanation of the custom. What is entirely inexcusable is for the anthropologist, when he cannot get from the people themselves a reason for their behaviour which seems to him satisfactory, to attribute to them some purpose or reason on the basis of his own preconceptions about human motives. I could adduce many instances of this from the literature of ethnography, but I prefer to illustrate what I mean by an anecdote.

A Queenslander met a Chinese who was taking a bowl of cooked rice to place on his brother's grave. The Australian in jocular tones asked if he supposed that his brother would come and eat the rice. The reply was 'No! We offer rice to people as an expression of friendship and affection. But since you speak as you do I suppose that you in this country place flowers on the graves of your dead in the belief that they will enjoy looking at them and smelling their sweet perfume.'

So far as ritual avoidances are concerned the reasons for them may vary from a very vague idea that some sort of misfortune of ill-luck, not defined as to its kind, is likely to befall anyone who fails to observe the taboo, to a belief that non-observance will produce some quite specific and undesirable result. Thus an Australian aborigine told me that if he spoke to any woman who stood in the relation of mother-in-law to him his hair would turn grey.[2]

A second approach to the study of ritual is therefore by a consideration not of their purpose or reason but of their meaning. I am here using the words symbol and meaning as coincident. Whatever has a meaning is a symbol and the meaning is whatever is expressed by the symbol.

But how are we to discover meanings? They do not lie on the surface. There is a sense in which people always know the meaning of their own symbols, but they do so intuitively and can rarely express their understanding in words. Shall we therefor be reduced to guessing at meanings as some anthropologists have guessed at reasons and purposes? I think not. For as long as we admit guess-work of any kind social anthropology cannot be a science. There are, I believe, methods of determining, with some fair degree of probability, the meanings of rites and other symbols.

There is still a third approach to the study of rites. We can consider the effects of the rite—not the effects that it is supposed to produce by the people who practise it but the effects that it does actually produce. A rite has immediate or direct effects on the persons who are in any way directly concerned in it, which we may call, for lack of a better term, the psychological effects. But there are also secondary effects upon the social structure, i.e. the network of social relations binding individuals together in an ordered life. These we may call the social effects. But considering the psychological effects of a rite we may succeed in defining its psychological function; by considering the social effects we may discover its social function. Clearly it is impossible to discover the social function of a rite without taking into account its usual or average psychological effects. But it is possible to discuss the psychological effects while more or less completely ignoring the more remote sociological effects, and this is often done. in what is called 'functional anthropology.'

Let us suppose that we wish to investigate in Australian tribes the totemic rites of a kind widely distributed over a large part of the continent. The ostensible purpose of these rites, as stated by the natives themselves, is to renew or maintain some part of nature, such as a species of animal or plant, or rain, or hot or cold weather. With reference to this purpose we have to say that from our point of view the natives are mistaken, that the rites do not actually do what they are believed to do. The rain-making ceremony does not, we think, actually bring rain. In so far as the rites are performed for a purpose they are futile, based on erroneous belief. I do not believe that there is any scientific value in attempts to conjecture processes of reasoning which might be supposed to have led to these errors.

The rites are easily perceived to be symbolic, and we may therefore investigate their meaning. To do this we have to examine a considerable number of them and we then discover that there is a certain body of ritual idiom extending from the west coast of the continent to the east coast with some local variations. Since each rite has a myth associated with it we have similarly to investigate the meanings of the myths. As a result we find that the meaning of any single rite becomes clear in the light of a cosmology, a body of ideas and beliefs about nature and human society, which, so far as its most general features are concerned, is current in all Australian tribes.

The immediate psychological effects of the rites can be to some extent observed by watching and talking to the performers. The ostensible purpose of the rite is certainly present in their minds, but so also is that complex set of cosmological beliefs by reference to which the rite has a meaning. Certainly a person performing the rite, even if, as sometimes happens, he performs it alone, derives therefrom a definite feeling of satisfaction, but it would be entirely false to imagine that this is simply because he believes that he has helped to provide a more abundant supply of food for himself and his fellow-tribesmen. His satisfaction is in having performed a ritual duty, we might say a religious duty. Putting in my own words what I judge, from my own observations, to express what the native feels, I would say that in the performance of the rite he has made that small contribution, which it is both his privilege and his duty to do, to the maintenance of that order of the universe of which man and nature are interdependent parts. The satisfaction which he thus receives gives the rite a special value for him. In some instances with which I am acquainted of the last survivor of a totemic group who still continues to perform the totemic rites by himself, it is this satisfaction that constitutes apparently the sole motive for his action.

To discover the social function of the totemic rites we have to consider the whole body of cosmological ideas of which each rite is a partial expression. I believe that it is possible to show that the social structure of an Australian tribe is connected in a very special way with these cosmological ideas and that the maintenance of its continuity depends on keeping them alive, by their regular expression in myth and rite.

Thus any satisfactory study of the totemic rites of Australia must be based not simply on the consideration of their ostensible purpose and their psychological function, or on an analysis of the motives of the individuals who perform the rites, but on the discovery of their meanings and of their social function.

It may be that some rites have no social function. This may be the case with such taboos as that against spilling salt in our own society. Nevertheless, the method of investigating rites and ritual values that I have found most profitable during work extending over more than thirty years is to study rites as symbolic expressions and to seek to discover their social functions. This method is not new except in so far as it is applied to the comparative study of many societies of diverse types. It was applied by Chinese thinkers to their own ritual more than twenty centuries ago.

In China, in the fifth and sixth centuries B.C., Confucius and his followers insisted on the great importance of the proper performance of ritual, such as funeral and mourning rites and sacrifices. After Confucius there came the reformer Mo Ti who taught a combination of altruism—love for all men—and utilitarianism. He held that funeral and mourning rites were useless and interfered with useful activities and should therefore be abolished or reduced to a minimum. In the third and second centuries B.C., the Confucians, Hsun Tze and the compilers of the *Li Chi* (Book of Rites), replied to Mo Ti to the effect that though these rites might have no utilitarian purpose they none the less had a very important social function. Briefly the theory is that the rites are the orderly (the *Li Chi* says the beautified) expression of feelings appropriate to a social situation. They thus serve to regulate and refine human emotions. We may say that partaking in the performance of rites serves to cultivate in the individual sentiments on whose existence the social order itself depends.

Let us consider the meaning and social function of an extremely simple example of ritual. In the Andaman Islands when a woman is expecting a baby a name is given to it while it is still in the womb. From that time until some weeks after the baby is born nobody is allowed to use the personal name of either the father or the mother; they can be referred to by teknonymy, i.e. in terms of their relation to the child. During this period both the parents are required to abstain from eating certain foods which they may freely eat at other times.

I did not obtain from the Andamanese any statement of the purpose or reason for this avoidance of names. Assuming that the act is symbolic, what method, other than that of guessing, is there of arriving at the meaning? I suggest that we may start with a general working hypothesis that when, in a single society, the same symbol is used in different contexts or on different kinds of occasions there is some common element of meaning, and that by comparing together the various uses of the symbol we may be able to discover what the common element is. This is precisely the method that we adopt in studying an unrecorded spoken language in order to discover the meanings of words and morphemes.

In the Andamans the name of a dead person is avoided from the occurrence of the death to the conclusion of mourning; the name of a person mourning for a dead relative is not used; there is avoidance of the name of a youth or girl who is passing through the ceremonies that take place at adolescence; a bride or bridegroom is not spoken of or to by his or her own name for a short time after the marriage. For the Andamanese the personal name is a symbol of the social personality, i.e. of the position that an individual occupies in the social structure and the social life. The avoidance of a personal name is a symbolic recognition of the fact that at the time the person is not occupying a normal position in the social life. It may be added that a person whose name is thus temporarily out of use is regarded as having for the time an abnormal ritual status.

Turning now to the rule as to avoiding certain foods, if the Andaman Islanders are asked what would happen if the father or mother broke his taboo the usual answer is that he or she would be ill, though one or two of my informants thought it might perhaps also affect the child. This is simply one instance of a standard formula which applies to a number of ritual prohibitions. Thus persons is mourning for a relative may not eat pork and turtle, the most important flesh foods, and the reason given is that if they did they would be ill.

To discover the meaning of this avoidance of foods by the parents we can apply the same method as in reference to the avoidance of their names. There are similar rules for mourners, for women during menstruation, and for youths and girls during the period of adolescence. But for a full demonstration we have to consider the place of foods in Andamanese ritual as a whole, and for an examination of this I must refer to what I have already written on the subject.

I should like to draw your attention to another point in the method by which it is possible to test our hypotheses as to the meanings of rites. We take the different occasions on which two rites are associated together, for example, the association of the avoidance of a person's name with the avoidance by that person of certain foods, which we find in the instance of mourners on the one hand and the expectant mother and father on the other. We must assume that for the Andamanese there is some important similarity between these two kinds of occasions—birth and death—by virtue of which they have similar ritual values. We cannot rest content with any interpretation of the taboos at childbirth unless there is a parallel interpretation of those relating to mourners. In the terms I am using here we can say that in the Andamans the relatives of a recently dead person, and the father and mother of a child that is about to be, or has recently been, born, are in an abnormal ritual status. This is recognised or indicated by the avoidance of their names. They are regarded as likely to suffer some misfortune, some bad luck, if you will, unless they observe certain prescribed ritual precautions of which the avoidance of certain foods is one. In the Andaman Islands the danger in such instances is thought of as the danger of illness. This is the case also with the Polynesian belief about the ritual status of anyone who has touched a corpse or a newly-born baby.

The interpretation of the taboos at childbirth at which we arrive by studying it in relation to the whole system of ritual values of the Andamanese is too complex to be stated here in full. Clearly, however, they express, in accordance with Andamanese ritual idiom, a common concern in the event. The parents show their concern by avoiding certain foods; their friends show theirs by avoiding the parents' personal names. By virtue of these taboos the occasion acquires a certain social value, as that term has been defined above.

There is one theory that might seem to be applicable to our example. It is based on a hypothesis as to the psychological function of a class of rites. The theory is that in certain circumstances the individual human being is anxious about the outcome of some event or activity because it depends to some extent on conditions that he cannot control by any technical means. He therefore observes some rite which, since he believes it will ensure good luck, serves to reassure him. Thus an aeronaut takes with him in a plane a mascot which he believes will protect him from accident and thus carries out his flight with confidence.

The theory has a respectable antiquity. It was perhaps implied in the *Primus in orbe does fecit timor* of Petronius and Statius. It has taken various forms from Hume's explanation of religion to Malinowski's explanation of Trobriand magic. It can be made so plausible by a suitable selection of illustrations that it is necessary to examine it with particular care and treat it with reasonable scepticism. For there is always the danger that we may be taken in by the plausibility of a theory that ultimately proves to be unsound.

I think that for certain rites it would be easy to maintain with equal plausibility an exactly contrary theory, namely, that if it were not for the existence of the rite and the beliefs associated with it the individual would feel no anxiety, and that the psychological effect of the rite is to create in him a sense of insecurity or danger. It seems very unlikely that an Andaman Islander would think that it is dangerous to eat dugong or pork or turtle meat if it were not for the existence of a specific body of ritual the ostensible purpose of which is to protect him from those dangers. Many hundreds of similar instances could be mentioned from all over the world.

Thus, while one anthropological theory is that magic and religion give men confidence, comfort and a sense of security,[3] is count equally well in arranged from which they would otherwise be free—the fear of black magic or of spirits, fear of God, of the Devil, of Hell.

Actually in our fears or anxieties as well as in our hopes we are conditioned (as the phrase goes) by the community in which we live. And it is largely by the sharing of hopes and fears, by what I have called common concern in events or eventualities, that human beings are linked together in temporary or permanent associations.

To return to the Andamanese taboos at childbirth, there are difficulties in supposing that they are means by which parents reassure themselves against the accidents that may interfere with a successful delivery. If the prospective father fails to observe the food taboo it is he who will be sick, according to the general Andamanese opinion. Moreover, he must continue to observe the taboos after the child is safely delivered. Further, how are we to provide a parallel explanation of the similar taboos observed by a person mourning for a dead relative?

The taboos associated with pregnancy and parturition are often explained in terms of the hypothesis I have mentioned. A father, naturally anxious at the outcome of an event over which he does not have a technical control and which is subject to hazard, reassures himself by observing some taboo or carrying out some magical action. He may avoid certain foods. He may avoid making nets or trying knots, or he may go round the house untying all knots and opening any locked or closed boxes or containers.

I wish to arouse in your minds, if it is not already there, a suspicion that both the general theory and this special application of it do not give the whole truth and indeed may not be true at all. Scepticism of plausible but unproved hypotheses is essential in every science. There is at least good ground for suspicion in the fact that the theory has so far been considered in reference to facts that seem to fit it, and no systematic attempts has been made, so far as I am aware, to look for facts that do not fit. That there are many such I am satisfied from my own studies.

The alternative hypothesis which I am presenting for consideration is as follows. In a given community it is appropriate that an expectant father should feel concern or at least should make an appearance of doing so. Some suitable symbolic expression of his concern is found in terms of the general ritual or symbolic idiom of the society, and it is felt generally that a man in that situation ought to carry out the symbolic or ritual actions or abstentions. For every rule that *ought* to be observed there must be some sort of sanction or reason. For acts that patently affect other persons the moral and legal sanctions provide a generally sufficient controlling force upon the individual. For ritual obligations conformity and rationalisation are provided by the ritual sanctions. The simplest form of ritual sanction is an accepted belief that if rules of ritual are not observed some undefined misfortune is likely to occur. In many societies the expected danger is somewhat more definitely conceived as a danger of sickness or, in extreme cases, death. In the more specialised forms of ritual sanction the good results to be hoped for or the bad results to be feared are more specifically defined in reference to the occasion or meaning of the ritual.

The theory is not concerned with the historical origin of ritual, nor is it another attempt to explain ritual in terms of human psychology; it is a hypothesis as to the relation of ritual and ritual values to the essential constitution of human society, i.e. to those invariant general characters which belong to all human societies, past, present and future. It rests on the recognition of the fact that while in animal societies social coaptation depends on instinct, in human societies it depends upon the efficacy of symbols of many different kinds. The theory I am advancing must therefore, for a just estimation of its value, be considered in its place in a general theory of symbols and their social efficacy.

By this theory the Andamanese taboos relating to childbirth are the obligatory recognition in a standardised symbolic form of the significance and importance of the event to the parents and to the community at large. They thus serve to fix the social value of occasions of this kind. Similarly I have argued in another place the Andamanese taboos relating to the animals and plants used for food are means of affixing a definite social value to food, based on its social importance. The *social* importance of food is not that it satisfies hunger, but that in such a community as an Andamanese camp or village an enormously large proportion of the activities are concerned with the getting and consuming of food, and that in these activities, with their daily instances of collaboration and mutual aid, there continuously occur those inter-relations of interests which bind the individual men, women and children into a society.

I believe that this theory can be generalised and with suitable modifications will be found to apply to a vast number of the taboos of different societies. My theory would go further for I would hold as a reasonable working hypothesis, that we have here the primary basis of all ritual and therefore of religion and magic, however those may be distinguished. The primary basis of ritual, so the formulation would run, is the attribution of ritual value to objects and occasions which are either themselves objects of important common interests linking together the persons of a community or are symbolically representative of such objects. To illustrate what is meant by the last part of this statement two illustrations may be offered. In the Andamans ritual value is attributed to the cicada, not because it has any social importance itself but because it symbolically represents the seasons of the year which do have importance. In some tribes of Eastern Australia the god Baiame is the personification, i.e. the symbolical representative, of the moral law of the tribe, and the rainbow-serpent (the Australian equivalent of the Chinese dragon) is a symbol representing growth and fertility in nature. Baiame and the rainbow-serpent in their turn are represented by the figures of earth which are made on the sacred ceremonial ground of the initiation ceremonies and at which rites are performed. The reverence that the Australian shows to the image of Baiame or towards his name is the symbolic method of fixing the social value of the moral law, particularly the laws relating to marriage.

In conclusion let me return once more to the work of the anthropologist whom we are here to honour. Sir James Frazer, in his *Psyche's Task* and in his other works, set himself to show how, in his own words, taboos have contributed to build up the complex fabric of society. He thus initiated that functional study of ritual to which I have in this lecture and elsewhere attempted to make some contribution. But there has been a shift of emphasis. Sir James accounted for the taboos of savage tribes as the application in practice of beliefs arrived at by erroneous processes of reasoning, and he seems to have thought of the effects of these beliefs in creating or maintaining a stable orderly society as being accidental. My own view is that the negative and positive rites of savages exist and persist because they are part of the mechanism by which an orderly society maintains itself in existence, serving as they do to establish certain fundamental social values. The beliefs by which the rites themselves are justified and given some sort of consistency are the rationalisations of symbolic actions and of the sentiments associated with them. I would suggest that what Sir James Frazer seems to regard as the accidental results of magical and religious beliefs really constitute their essential function and the ultimate reason for their existence.

Note

The theory of ritual outlined in this lecture was first worked out in 1908 in a thesis on the Andaman Islanders. It was written out again in a revised and extended form in 1913 and appeared in print in 1922. Unfortunately the exposition contained in *The Andaman Islanders* is evidently not clear, since some of my critics have failed to understand what the theory is. For example, it has been assumed that by 'social value' I mean 'utility'.

The best treatment of the subject of value with which I am acquainted is Ralph Barton Perry's *General Theory of Value*, 1926. For the Chinese theory of ritual the most easily accessible account is in chapter xiv of Fung Yu-lan's *History of Chinese Philosophy*, 1937. The third chapter, on the uses of symbolism, of Whitehead's *Symbolism, its Meaning and Effect*, is an admirable brief introduction to the sociological theory of symbolism.

One very important point that could not be dealt with in the lecture is that indicated by Whitehead in the following sentence—'No account of the uses of symbolism is complete without the recognition that the symbolic elements in life have a tendency to run wild, like the vegetation in a tropical forest.'

REFERENCES

1. The Frazer Lecture, 1939.
2. In case it may be thought that this is an inadequate supernatural punishment for a serious breach of rules of proper behaviour a few words of explanation are necessary. Grey hair comes with old age and is thought to be usually associated with loss of sexual potency. It is thus premature old age with its disadvantages but without the advantages that usually accompany seniority that threatens the man who fails to observe the rules of avoidance. On the other hand, when a man's hair is grey and his wife's mother has passed the age of child-bearing the taboo is relaxed so that the relatives may talk together if they wish.
3. This theory has been formulated by Loisy, and for magic has been adopted by Malinowski.

12

Freedom of Speech How Free is "Free"?

The Problem of Formulations

The recent hostilities in Iraq have provoked complaints on the reporting by the military authorities, restrictions placed, on the one hand, from journalists and, on the other, from politicians and members of the public, at what is claimed to be bias in reporting.

In an article in the Times, Professor Dworkin has argued in favour of the absolute necessity in a modern democratic state of the virtually unrestricted liberty to report everything and anything which may seem to be of interest to the reading public, save only those matters which immediately impinge upon the tactical conduct of military operations. As against this, it is pointed out that reporting, contrary to the express request of the military, of the loss of an aircraft on the first day of operations resulted, as the authorities had feared, in the crew being taken prisoner before they could be rescued and in their being subjected to physical harm and indignity. Protagonist of both points of view complain, in the one case, of restriction and, in the other, of abuse of what all describe as the "right to freedom of speech."

At the same time, the final round has been played (at any rate, so far as the courts of the United Kingdom are concerned) of the "*Spycatcher*" affair. On April 11, 1991 the House of Lords dismissed the appeal of the Sunday Times against a judgement of the Court of Appeal holding that paper to be in contempt of court in publishing excerpts from Spycatcher at a time when it was known to all that an injunction against the publication of that material had been granted on the ground that the publication constituted a breach of confidence against two other newspapers. Again, the editor of the Sunday Times trumpets his intention is appeal in the European Court of Human Rights against what he loudly proclaims to be the unwarranted and unconstitutional infringement of his "right of free speech."

It may not, in these circumstances, be altogether inappropriate to take a little time to consider just what is embraced in this so-called "right": whether it is, in fact, being restricted; whether any or any further constitutional safeguards are required for its preservation; and even the sacrilegious thought whether some further restriction may not be required to prevent its irresponsible exercise.

The right of free expression, Freedom of Speech, The Liberty of the Press and the like are heady slogans. They have a strong emotive appeal. They serve as the rallying cry for a thousand demonstrations by enthusiastic, and frequently mindless crowds. But what do they actually mean? The recent months have witnessed yet another outbreak of journalistic excesses, ranging from the tasteless and intrusive exploitation of the private weakness of a harmless individual to the abuse of individual judges, as ill-mannered as it has been ill-informed, for failing to detect the falsity of fabricated evidence adduced before them. Indeed, it is one of the ironies of our times that the outstanding feature of the tolerance which underlies the "right of free speech" has been the intolerance of its exercise. One is left asking is it an unhappy chance or is it inherent that the mirror image of freedom of the press is tyranny by the press? One man's freedom can only too easily become another man's prison.

'The Right of Free Speech" is spoken of by politicians and political journalists as if it were some sacrosanct and inalienable characteristic of the individual in society which the law will or should protect and preserve. But if we are to look for a "right' in the sense in which the word is used in a Hohfeldian analysis and as importing some correlative duty (the duty to listen, perhaps?) we look in vain. The expression, as a tool of legal analysis, is, in fact, as meaningless as that other popular shibboleth, the "right to work" which, by a curious irony, is most frequently heard from the mouths of those committed to the exercise of a collective claim to prevent other individuals from working. Indeed, Lenin is said to have observed that he would gladly recognise the "right" of others to say exactly what they liked so long as it was recognised that he had the "right" to shoot them for saying it.

The truth is that there is no such thing as a "right" of free speech, nor does the law do anything to protect the individual's ability to express whatever opinion he chooses, except in the most oblique and indirect way. The last three decades have witnessed only too many examples of those who seek to express views, not universally popular, being shouted down and reduced to impotent silence, sometimes by no more than a vociferous minority, without any possibility of legal redress or interference. The "right" is no more than the liberty which arises from a legal vacuum and which every individual enjoys, whether in the realm of speech, thought, movement or other activity to do that which the law does not forbid. It is no more than a convenient, if misleading, descriptive term to signify the ability to move without hindrance within the circumscribed area within which the law has not yet sought to intrude. And when we speak of freedom of speech or liberty of the press as "fundamental rights" or as "basic" liberties preserved by the constitution, we say no more than that the constitution of the relevant society has conferred upon its courts the power to negate and to decline to enforce legislative or administrative measures which purport or attempt to encroach further upon the boundaries of the existing vacuum.

The Human Rights Convention

The United Kingdom is a party to the Convention for the Protection of Human Rights and Fundamental Freedoms of 1953 and it is, perhaps, symptomatic of the confusion of thought engendered by the use of the inaccurate language that it has led to a strongly held and frequently expressed view that the terms of Article 10 of the Convention ought to be expressly incorporated into the Law of England. Had this been done, it is said, neither the Sunday Times nor any other newspaper would have been inhibited from publishing the material in Spycatcher. Much less could such publication have resulted in successful proceedings for the contempt of court. The proposition is not one which, at any rate, in the opinion of this writer, bears any close examination; nor is it readily perceivable what possible advantage, either to the press or to the public, would accrue from the express enactment of provisions which, in any event, largely reflect the existing state of the law. There may be, though few English lawyers would agree, advantages to be had from the superimposition of a written Constitution, but it is difficult to see what possible benefit could be found from the piecemeal introduction by a statute of quasi-constitutional "rights" which do no more than reflect the existing boundaries of permissible activity and which would in any event be freely alterable by subsequent legislation.

Article 10 begins with the same confusing reference to "right". It provides:

1. "Everyone has the right to freedom of expression. This right shall include freedom to hold opinions and to receive and impart information and ideas without interference by public authority and regardless of frontiers¼"

2. "The exercise of these freedoms, since it carries with it duties and responsibilities, may be subject to such formalities, conditions, restrictions or penalties as are prescribed by law and are necessary in a democratic society, in the interests of national security, territorial integrity or public safety, for the prevention of disorder or crime, for the protection of health or morals, for the protection of the reputation or rights of others, for preventing the disclosure of information received in confidence, or for maintaining the authority and impartiality of the judiciary."

One has only to consider for a moment the terms of this Article in order to see that its incorporation, lock, stock and barrel, into the domestic statutory law of the United Kingdom would present the courts with some formidable problems in relation to the existing statute law. If the incorporating statute did not go on to provide that any statute imposing restrictions on the imparting of information was henceforth to be construed so as to conform with the terms of the Article, it would result in an insoluble conflict in any case where the existing statutory restriction could not be justified within the four corners of the Article. If, however, it did so provide, the courts would find themselves involved either in the essentially legislative function of determining whether, in imposing the restriction, the Parliament had been properly exercising its function in enacting that which it had thought fit to provide and upholding it or striking it down according to the court's and not Parliament's view of what was "necessary in a democratic society", or in what is essentially an executive function of determining in any given case whether the enforcement of an *ex facie* unequivocal statutory prohibition was similarly "necessary". There is, in any event, an initial difficulty in determining the degree of necessity and whether the reference to restrictions being "necessary in a democratic society" has any greater significance than as a mere ritual genuflexion to the perceived desirability of a democratic form of government, for it is not readily discernible why any restrictions should be more or less "necessary" in a democratic society than, for instance, in a society whose governmental structure is oligarchic, aristocratic or even dictatorial. But this apart, the terms of the Article confer, on any analysis, a considerable degree of flexibility in construction.

It has been said above that the restrictions envisaged by the Article as permissible are already largely reflected in the domestic law of the United Kingdom. It has also to be acknowledged at the outset that the extent of what is permissible is necessarily a matter of interpretation and there is a natural tendency to construe the limits of each of the enumerated heads either widely or narrowly according to the predelictions of the individual protagonist asserting or contesting the liberty in any particular case. The devotees of unilateral disarmament, for instance, would argue that restrictions upon the liberty of the subject to disseminate freely information regarding the defence secrets of the realm are not only unnecessary but positively injurious, a view unlikely to be shared by the majority of Her Majesty's subjects. It seems, to say the least, improbable that a domestic court would take the same view about what restrictions are "necessary" for the security of the United Kingdom as either the governing council of the Campaign for Nuclear Disarmament or, probably, the European Court of Human Rights in Strasbourg; nor can one readily envisage any responsible government, democratic or otherwise, delegating to an external court or agency the task of determining what national security requires. So straight away and, in this sphere at least, what is necessary for national security is likely to be what the government of the day thinks is so necessary.

If, then, one goes on to consider what existing restrictions on freedom of speech and communication actually exist in the Law of England, it becomes apparent, or it is certainly arguable, according to how the terms fall to be construed, that not only do they go, in some respects at least, beyond the limits prescribed by the Article as permissible derogations from the "right" asserted in Paragraph 1, but also that to tailor them so as to conform with what might be thought to be the ordinary construction of the language used would result in the necessary repeal of legislation which is regarded as both necessary and desirable by some of the most vociferous exponents of the "right".

The Adequacy of the Existing Law

The ability freely to express sentiments and opinions or to convey information without restriction or penalty is circumscribed at common law by the law of defamation, by the law relating to the protection of confidential information, by the criminal offences of uttering words with seditious intent, of incitement and of blasphemy, and by the law relating to contempt of court. All these with the exception of blasphemy (which is considered below) are compatible with the terms of Article 10 (2) of the Convention, though many would argue that the law of contempt, as recently developed, goes further than is necessary for maintaining the authority and impartiality of the judiciary, while it is certainly necessary for the protection of the right of a litigant to a fair and impartial trial.

There are, in addition, numerous statutory restrictions, the most obvious of which are those imposed by the Official Secrets Act, 1989. Although the major emphasis of the restrictions imposed on public servants is upon national security and the preservation of the confidentiality of communications made in the course of government service and, indeed, Sections 1 and 2 relate to security and intelligence and defence, it is at least open to doubt whether the entirety of the restrictions imposed upon the disclosure of information can be fitted comfortably within the persmissible limits of the enumerated derogations in the Article. It is, for instance, an offence for a Crown servant or a Government contractor to disclose any information (whether or not confidential information) obtained by him by virtue of his position and relating to international relations if such disclosure *(inter alia)* "seriously obstructs.....the promotion" of the interests of the United Kingdom. Now the promotion of the interests of the United Kingdom in, for instance, the sphere of international trade or commerce has no necessary connection with national security, with territorial integrity or with public safety; and it is difficult to see, therefore, how this restriction could be said to go no further than the Article permits.

It is equally difficult to see how, for instance, restrictions on advertising of gaming places or lotteries (Gaming Act, 1968, s. 42), inciting others to bet (Betting, Gaming and Lotteries Act, 1963) inviting minors to borrow money (Consumer Credit Act, 1974, s. 50 (1) or advertising arrangements for adoption (Adoption Act, 1967 s. 58) could be justified within the terms of the Convention. Few continentals would agree that there is anything harmful to morals in a government lottery or in inviting friends to bet at the local casino and although there are very good social reasons for discouraging people, whether or not of full age, from getting into debt and for channelling the adoption of children through properly regulated adoption agencies, the restrictions can hardly be said to be "necessary" either for the protection of public morals or for the prevention of crime.

Perhaps, more importantly and strikingly, one of the most notable and most frequently invoked restrictions on free expression is that imposed by the Race Relations Act, 1976. Yet if those who claim that the "right of free speech" is of such overwhelming importance in a democratic society as to outweigh all other considerations are to be consistent, it would follow that they must also advocate the repeal of at least a part of what is generally considered to be both beneficent and necessary legislation in a multi-racial community. If an individual, for whatever reason, nurtures a strong dislike for the adherents of a particular religion or a particular political party, he is perfectly at liberty to express it in terms calculated to cause them to be subjected to hatred or abuse so long at least as he does not overstep the bounds set by the crime of blasphemy.

One has only to recollect the late Aneurin Bevan's castigation of his political opponents as "lower than vermin". On what basis, it may be asked, if he entertains an equally strong dislike for persons of a particular nationality or pigmentation, should he not equally be free to express his views, however hurtful or insulting they may be, so long as the expression does not cause or threaten a breach of the peace and so impinge upon considerations of public safety? Obviously, there is a public safety aspect to the legislation, for incitement to racial hatred can and frequently does lead to violence although there is no inherent reason why it should be more likely to do so than, for instance, incitement to political hatred. However, the restrictions in the Act go further than this. A person commits an offence if he publicly utters words which are abusive or even merely insulting if, in the circumstances "hatred is likely to be stirred up against a racial group" (Section 70, amending the Public Order Act, 1936). This provision can arguably be justified on the ground that it is, in the final analysis, "necessary in the interest of public safety" or possibly that it is for the protection of the "reputation" of others. But it has to be noted that the offence is committed simply by stirring up hatred, quite regardless of whether any breach of the peace is threatened or even likely. But nobody has a "right" not to be disliked.

Certainly no aspect either of public safety or of reputation can possibly be involved in the provisions of Section 29, which make it unlawful to publish an advertisement which "might reasonably" be understood as indicating an intention to discriminate on racial grounds, or Section 31, which subjects to a criminal penalty one who induces or attempts to induce another person to do any act of discrimination contravening Parts II or III of the Act. Those acts, though declared "unlawful", are not criminal, so that these provisions cannot be justified on the ground that they are necessary for the prevention of crime. Nor can they reasonably be said to be in the interest of public safety or to protect public health or morals. Moreover, similar provisions appear in the Sex Discrimination Act, 1975 (Sections 39 and 40) and it is really quite impossible to fit them, in this context, into the framework of the derogations in Article 10, the more so since the Court of Human Rights itself has indicated that these derogations are to be narrowly construed [Sunday Times v. United Kingdom (1979) 2. E.H.R.R. 245].

Morality and Law

Now no one suggests, and it is certainly not this writer's purpose to urge, that these are not entirely desirable provisions for furthering the purposes of the Acts any more than it is suggested that it is not a desirable social purpose that minors should not be encouraged to borrow or that people should not be encouraged to jeopardise their own and their families' security by gambling. But these desirable purposes have little or nothing to do with public safety, health, morals or any other of the purposes for which the Article provides that restrictions upon free expression shall be permissible and before advocating the wholesale incorporation of these provisions into the law as if inscribed on tablets of stone. It is important that their import should be fully grasped and the consequences appreciated.

Another egregious example of legal restraint upon free expression which is quite irreconcilable with the provisions of Article 10 (2) is to be found in the law of blasphemy—a particularly interesting case because it incidentally reveals some of the confused thinking behind demands for the incorporation of the Convention provisions into domestic law. The offence of blasphemy is both ancient and openly discriminatory. In its original form it consisted simply of a denial of the truth of Christianity. In its more modern form, however, as expounded by the House of Lords in Whitehouse v. Gay News Ltd. and Lemon (1979 A.C. 617), it consists of the publication of matter which vilifies the Christian (but no other) religion in such indecent or offensive terms as are likely to shock and outrage the feelings of the general body of Christian believers in the community. It does not depend upon an intent to cause outrage nor does it involve any tendency to endanger peace. To many it will seem an anachronistic and irrational survival and it may well be thought that if the adoption of the Convention as a part of our domestic law were to result in its necessary statutory abolition—a course which, in any event, has been proposed by the Law Commission—that would be no great sacrifice.

It is, however, one of the ironies of life that the complaint of some of the most stalwart champions of free speech is not that the existence of the offence is too restrictive of free expression but that it is not restrictive enough. Their solution to an offence which discriminates invidiously in favour of Christians is not to abolish the offence altogether but to extend it to all religions. The recent attempts, by both lawful and unlawful means, to procure the banning and destruction of Mr. Salman Rushdie's "Satanic Verses", which was considered deeply offensive to the overwhelming majority of the Moslem community in Great Britain, included an unsuccessful attempt to review judicially the refusal of the Chief Metropolitan Magistrate to issue a summons for blasphemous libel against both Mr. Rushdie and his publishers (see R.V. Chief Metropolitan Magistrate, ex p. Choudhury, 1990, 3 W.L.R. 986). That refusal, far from being applauded as a triumphant vindication of Mr. Rushdie's "right" freely to express unpopular views, is now criticised as an infringement of another "right"—that conferred by Article 9 of the Convention on freedom of religion—apparently on the footing that a citizen of the Moslem (or any other) persuasion is not "free" to profess and practise his faith in the community unless he can do so without being outraged by others who deny it in terms which he finds offensive or insulting. This is a view which has been solemnly propounded in an article in a recent legal publication where the Choudhury decision was described as "flagrant breach" of Article 9 of the Convention (see 54 M.L.R. March 1991). What, then, one asks, is to happen if both Articles 9 and 10 are incorporated into English law?

Conflict of Freedoms

It is, therefore, suggested, that it is a mistake to think that the Convention could be easily accommodated into our domestic statutory law without the making of a number of substantive alterations, some of which would not be welcomed by the body of so-called "liberal" opinion which demands that the change be made.

Nor ought it to be thought that the United Kingdom is alone among European countries in preserving restrictions or individual rights of action which are not readily compatible with a narrow interpretation of Article 10. It is, of course, possible to widen the area of the permissible derogations. Since they embrace measures necessary for the "protection of the rights of others", a restriction on free expression can strictly be brought within the terms of the derogation simply by conferring on an individual a legal right to have the restriction enforced. German law, for instance, confers the right of privacy which entitles an individual to prohibit the making or reproduction of a record or tape of a conversation in which he has been engaged; to prohibit the publication of personal letters or of misleading reports about his personal or professional affairs (subject to an exception where the publication is held to be in public interest), and to recover compensation for wounded feelings if his name is used without his consent in furtherance of the economic interests of the user.

Similarly, the Swedish legislation on the freedom of the press imposes criminal penalties for, *inter alia*, publications bringing into contempt, racial, ethnic or religious minorities, and the wilful publication of any public document which, under the Official Secrets Act, is not available to everyone. Again, the Italian *Dichiarazione Universale*, although providing that everyone has the right of free expression, including the right to see and publish information through every means, nevertheless also confers on the citizen a right to be protected by law from being subjected to interference in his private life or that of his family or in his correspondence. It is, indeed, interesting to note that the right to personal privacy, which some European systems provide and which necessarily qualifies total freedom of the press and cannot easily be fitted into the enumerated permissible derogations in Article 10, is signally lacking in English law except to the extent to which it can be brought under the umbrella of confidential communication.

But to say that the incorporation of Article 10 without modification as a substantive part of the our statute law might be embarrassing and would serve little useful purpose—at any rate so long as the theory of the sovereignty of Parliament permits its repeal—does not, of itself, answer a basic question: does the preservation of what are widely and rightly regarded as essential democratic values not demand the adoption of some legally unalterable safeguards against any further encroachment upon the area within which untrammelled expression of opinion is permitted. In countries which enjoy the benefit of written constitutions this would probably present no difficulty, although events in, for instance, Malaysia and Fiji during the past few years have demonstrated the fragility of constitutional safeguards for the independence of the judiciary. In the United Kingdom, where the only check on parliamentary sovereignty rests in the last analysis on the observance of well-established but legally unenforceable conventions, it is not easy to see how further protection against future incursions upon the liberty of expression could be practically conferred. Proponents of a new Bill of Rights would argue that the statutory enshrinement of basis freedoms in solemn form will achieve the result since public opinion and convention provide a practical safeguard against repeal or alteration. But in the ultimate analysis the responsibility for maintaining and upholding the values which the statute would seek to express and preserve would come to rest where it is at the moment in the courts whose task it is to construe and enforce the statutes. So, one asks, what changes?

Freedom to Licence

The complaint so often made, and so often made in the most intemperate terms, is that the courts are not vigilant enough to satisfy a press hungry for an unrestricted licence to operate without any inhibitions at all; that, they are executive minded, and indeed, on occasions, that they are malevolently resolved upon suppressing the subject's freedom to express his views. In the Times of April 29, 1991, for instance, a prominent journalist, whose admiration either for the law or the judiciary is seldom more than lukewarm, wrote: "If there is one thing that unites all our higher judges.......it is that free speech is to be regarded as certainly suspect and in all likelihood pernicious, so it is their duty as well as their pleasure to ensure that the less there is of it the better". This, not an untypical gem of journalistic hyperbole was a predictable reaction to a decision which did not accord with the writer's frequently idiosyncratic opinion of what the law ought to be. It goes far to justify the conclusion, which it is sometimes difficult to resist, that the journalistic view of freedom of speech is simply that whatever inhibitions may apply to *Her Majesty's* subjects in general, none of them, whether imposed by law, by civic responsibility, by the rights of others or by good taste, can have any application to what has come to be described as "the media". Now that is, of course, a perfectly permissible, though possibly not a very rational view and one which journalists in general and that writer in particular must be at liberty to express. Even the Royal Commission on the Press, however, did not go this far and were content in their report in 1977 to define the freedom of the press as "that degree of freedom from restraint which is essential to enable proprietors, editors and journalists to advance the public interest by publishing the facts and opinions without which a democratic electorate cannot make responsible judgements."

Nor must it escape our attention that Article 10 itself stresses that liberty carries responsibility. Nevertheless, there is still current a view socandidly expressed by W.P. Hamilton of the Wall Street Journal: "A newspaper is a private enterprise owing nothing whatever to the public, which grants it no franchise. It is, therefore, affected with no public interest. It is emphatically the property of the owner, who is selling a manufactured product at his own risk". The sentiment is one which merely reflects what has to be acknowledged as a fact of life, that the liberty which the law permits imparts necessarily the freedom to exercise it irresponsible and abusively. In the end, it has to be faced that the business of a newspaper proprietor is selling newspapers and the purpose in life of journalists and editors is to assist him in doing so. To dress up the daily coverage of the sexual peccadilloes of film stars as making any contribution to the making of responsible judgments by the democratic electorate is simply humbug. Such coverage is the inevitable corollary of the lack of restraint that is essential to permit the free interchange of ideas that do make such a contribution. Lack of responsibility and the sort of preposterous overstatement quoted above from the Times newspaper are certainly no new phenomena—indeed, it is a good many years since one exasperated rhymester proclaimed that

> "You cannot hope to bribe or twist,
> Thank God, the British journalist;
> But seeing what the man will do
> Unbribed there's no occasion to."

But the natural and instinctive reaction of demanding that the law should intervene in order to control abuse and irresponsibility is one which leads down a very dangerous road, for once it is sought to control that which is written or published, at least beyond the point of the necessary protection of the substantive legal rights of others, it can only too easily be found that there is no logical stopping place short of a centrally imposed censorship enforced by criminal sanction. Irresponsibility, ignorance, prejudice, lack of taste, malevolence and, sometimes, downright deliberate misrepresentation are the price which a free society has to be prepared to pay if it is to remain free. As Professor Munro has written in a recent article in the Modern Law Review (54 MLR 104) "the danger is that instances of abuse and bad taste, because they are conspicuous, come to mind, while the continuous benefits derived by having a free press is liable to be taken for granted in a country which has enjoyed it for so long".

The prospect of press censorship is one from which there is an instinctive and, it is to be hoped, universal revulsion. Nevertheless, a totally unrestricted right to abuse, and if so disposed to misrepresent, which is what some of our more extravagant journalists appear to demand, even where this overrides or destroys those private rights of individuals, which the law is otherwise concerned to protect, does raise serious questions about the role of the courts in seeking to uphold private law rights and to preserve a sensible balance between the freedom of the press and its arrogant abuse to the point where it becomes a tyranny. The individual who is brought into hatred, ridicule or contempt is in all truth helpless enough, for no legal aid is available to him in seeking to re-establish his reputation. But there is at least a remedy open to him and few would assert—although there are some who do—that the freedom of the journalist to publish ought to import also a freedom from civil liability to pay compensation for the damage done by a false and unjustified assault upon another's reputation. But it is widely asserted that no similar inhibition should affect the freedom to publish material wrongfully disclosed or obtained in breach of an obligation of confidence or which will have the effect of depriving the individual of his rights before the court in pending litigation or, indeed, in some cases of his reputation and even his liberty in a pending prosecution. No one can deny the importance of a free press; but equally no one should deny the importance of the ability of the individual to assert and prosecute his rights under the law before a court of justice without having that process interfered with or prejudiced from outside.

The Spycatcher case, which was what prompted the attack upon the judiciary already referred to, was an application to sequester the assets of the Sunday Times for contempt of court and there should be no misunderstanding about what the newspaper's claim was however much it may be sought to conceal it behind the clarion call of freedom of the press. The claim was to be entitled to public material with the deliberate intention of prejudicing the fair trial of civil proceedings before the court. That was and is asserted as a general right quite regardless of the nature of the litigation and of the parties to it and it proclaims as its basis not only that the court is, but that it must, in the name of liberty, be powerless to protect its own process or to protect the litigants who, in the legitimate exercise of their rights, have sought to invoke it. The fact that the litigant in the particular case was the Attorney General was irrelevant, for an officer of the Crown, asserting a private law right of the Crown, whilst entitled to no more protection or consideration than a private individual, is certainly entitled to no less.

The newspaper's claim was accordingly to an absolute entitlement to exercise its liberty of communication for the express, sole and mischievous purpose of interfering with the fair trial of a pending action. That is not an overstatement for the argument advanced before the House of Lords was, advisedly and deliberately, framed in that form. No court of justice could accept such a claim and it can be no cause for surprise that it was rejected.

Similarly, extravagant claims are made with regard to the disclosure of sources of information in the course of legal proceedings. The media claim that any disclosure must jeopardise their ability to collect, and thus to disseminate, information and that this admittedly important function is so vital to the survival of a democratic community that any limits upon a privilege of non-disclosure which the law denies to every other witness is unacceptable by a witness claiming to be a journalist. Now, to a degree, that claim has been recognised by Parliament in Section 10 of the Contempt of Court Act, 1981, but subject to the important qualification that disclosure may be ordered where it is "necessary in the interests of justice or national security or for the prevention of crime". And it is, of course and inevitably, the journalist's complaint that his views and the views of the courts about what the interests of justice or of public security require not only do not coincide but do not even overlap.

But unless society is going to be prepared to accord to the media the privilege of total immunity from any of the restrictions accepted by other members of the community, no matter what the damage to the public, to individual rights or to the fair administration of justice, whether civil or criminal, the dilemma inevitably remains that someone, somehow, has to be entrusted with the task of deciding where a line which, in its nature, cannot be the subject of precise definition, is to be drawn. That task clearly cannot be left to the media themselves, who are *parti pris* even before the inquiry begins. So that, in the end, it inevitably falls upon those whose function it is to interpret and administer the law the unpopular burden of determining and holding the delicate balance between the interests of the public in the unfettered dissemination of information, be it momentous, trivial or even frivolous, and the interests of the public in the fair and impartial administration of justice both between society and subject and between subject and subject.

That balance is a great deal more delicate and more difficult to determine than the media would have use believe. It is not the purpose of this paper to suggest that the courts necessarily always get it right nor to engage in polemics with the media with regard to the political desirability of the Crown's attempt to hold against Mr. Wright the right which it undoubtedly possessed in law to preserve the confidentiality of the Spycatcher material. There are, indeed, respectable arguments for saying that the interlocutory processes of the law are too cumbersome and too lengthy and even that the House of Lords could have imposed a more stringent requirement than a mere probability for demonstrating that damage to the public interest which they held to be essential to the grant of injunctive relief.

It is interesting to note, for instance, that a somewhat similar problem confronted the Supreme Court of Israel in 1988 when it was called upon to review a ruling by the military censor. The case was dealt with within a matter of some three months from start to finish, as compared with the two years required for the completion of the Spycatcher case, and the Supreme Court declined to accept that disclosure would damage the public interest in the absence of a degree of probability amounting to virtual certainty [see Schnitzer *v.* Chief Military Censor (1988) 42 (iv) P.D. 617]. It is, however, the writer's purpose to suggest that whatever shortcomings may be perceived in the performance by our courts of the difficult tasks that are necessarily cast upon them, the remedy is not to be found either in an emotive appeal to demotic slogans or in the uncritical adoption into domestic law of the terms of the Convention.

It is, and it must remain, the privilege of the media, in common with every other citizen, to criticise the judiciary and, if they feel it right, to employ extreme terms in doing so. But this is a two-way traffic and the judges must equally be free to criticise the media and to prevent the misuse of the media's privileges for the purpose of interfering with the judges' function of administering justice between citizen and citizen.

In a recent letter to the Times newspaper a distinguished German jurist has pointed out that one of the first steps towards the seizure of power by the National Socialist Party in the 1930s was a concerted propaganda campaign to undermine confidence in the judicial system. But so to state is not to advocate further attenuation of the legal vacuum in which the vital privilege of freedom of expression is exercisable, although it is an unfortunate fact that the behaviour of some representatives of the media has not been such as to leave it immune from calls for the imposition of further restrictions. For instance, an attempt has been made to introduce a private member's bill conferring a "right to privacy" somewhat along the lines of that conferred by the said German law. Another suggestion has been that there should be conferred on every person who is subjected to unwelcome public criticism or comment a "right of reply" which would impose on the proprietor of a newspaper the obligation of making, at his own expense, space and newsprint available for the aggrieved person to publicise his own comments. Now however much sympathy one may feel for anyone subjected against his will to a blaze of unwelcome publicity with regard to his private and personal affairs, neither of these suggestions is capable of practical implementation. The problem remains and can, it is suggested, be met only by self-regulation, although it has to be said that the press's own attempt to regulate itself through the medium of the Press Council has signally failed to meet it or to command public respect and confidence.

Freedom of Speech and the Free Media

Another problem which English law has—perhaps fortunately—not yet been called upon to meet is that of media bias—although, in all truth, there has been, in recent months at least, a chorus of public complaint, both in the press and in Parliament. Whether or to what extent it is justified depends no doubt upon the political views of the hearer, but the fact that the complaint is made poses a number of serious questions which ought, perhaps, to be debated a good deal more than they have been. We live in an age where the control of the most influential mass media—radio broadcasting and television—lies in a very few hands. *The "right" of free speech entitles the individual, within the limits prescribed by law, to say what the likes, where he likes, to whom he likes and by any means that he likes. But what about the corollary? Is he also free to deny to others the opportunity to say what they like?*

Now plainly a newspaper is not bound to print anything that anyone wants printed but, equally, there is—at least in theory—nothing to prevent an individual from creating his own platform by founding his own newspaper. But what of the case where there is not only a practical but a legal monopoly of a particular means of dissemination? To what extent is the body having such a monopoly to be at liberty to arrange for A's views to be represented and for B's not to be heard at all? The question has not yet arisen in an acute from before the courts of the United Kingdom. Under the Broadcasting Act of 1981 the Independent Broadcasting Authority is obliged by statute to satisfy itself, so far as possible, that "due impartiality" is preserved on the part of the persons providing the programmes as respects "matters of political or industrial controversy or relating to current public policy." [Section 4 (1) (1)]. There is a similar requirement for the Satellite Broadcasting Board under the Cable and Broadcasting Act, 1984. The British Broadcasting Corporation, on the other hand, is under no similar restriction, having only, under its charter, the obligation to provide a proper service to the public. In all three cases, the Secretary of State has power to require the BBC, the Authority or the Board to refrain from broadcasting a particular matter, a power recently exercised in order to ban the showing on television of live interviews with terrorist organisations in Northern Ireland. But how, in practice, can the "slanting" of programmes be prevented and how can those with views not immediately popular be given a fair opportunity of presenting them?

"In the era of mass communication, the words of the solitary speaker or the lonely writer, however brave or imaginative, have little impact unless they are broadcast through the great engines of public opinion—radio, television and the press." (Barron, Freedom of the Press, 1972).

If a position were ever to arise in which the government of the day directly controlled the most important media for the dissemination of news and views, there would be and rightly so an immediate and vigorous outcry if it exercised its control to propagate its own views and to suppress those of its opponents; for freedom of speech is as much denied by inequality of access to the means of expression as it is by direct prohibition. But whilst freedom from direct governmental interference may be guaranteed by placing the control, ownership and management of the means of communication in the hands of independent statutory corporations or private entrepreneurs, controlled perhaps by statutory bodies with supervisory powers, a body, however, whether supervisory or managerial, is only as good as the people who compose it. The censorship of views which the management consider "deviant" is just as effective when it is privately imposed as it is when it is imposed by government decree or by the superimposition of government appointees.

The problem is one which has been directly tackled by the Courts in other jurisdictions but has received very little attention in the United Kingdom, possibly because of the establishment of extrajudicial machinery which is designed to prevent it arising, or to cure it if it does arise, although it is questionable whether it does so effectively or, indeed, at all. The BBC and the IBA have what is essentially a voluntary code of conduct as regards avowedly political propaganda—established in the case of the BBC by Aide-Memoires in 1947 and 1969—by which they are pledged to allow proportionate air time for ministerial broadcasts and for broadcasts by the principal political parties and a Press Council (now the Press Complaints Commission) and a Broadcasting Complaints Commission have been established to entertain and investigate complaints from the public, the former by the newspaper proprietors and the latter by statute. But the functions of these bodies are limited to the consideration of complaints and the publication of their findings neither has any effective power of regulation. In the end, what is and what is not broadcast, what views are and what are not represented, is left to the discretion of the programme makers and the idiosyncratic opinions of those who supervise them. No doubt in theory a decision by the Broadcasting Complaints Commission that a particular complaint is or is not justified might be made, the subject matter of judicial review, just as the decision of the Secretary of State under the Broadcasting Act of 1981 to prohibit the broadcasting of particular material may be reviewed (see Reg. *v.* Home Secretary, *ex parte* Brind, 1990, 2 W.L.R. 787). But the grounds for judicial review render the scope of this extremely limited and in any event the final decision would be months after the event complained of and would almost certainly be of academic significance only. This is an area from which, effectively, the courts are excluded and if one asks "what remedy has the citizen who complains about misrepresentation or the denial of an opportunity to air his views," the practical answer is, quite simply, "none".

But should there be one? Perhaps, more pertinently one should ask *can* there be one? The public is subjected daily to seemingly endless doses of bad language, offensive dialogue, obscenity and what is known as "factional" reporting slanted to propagate a particular political viewpoint. A recent survey by the National Viewers and Listeners Association, for example, disclosed that in the past two years examples of the use of objectionable swear words in television programmes projected after 9 p.m. have risen from 861 to some 2000. Members of the public can and do protest against the systematic debasement of public taste, the degradation of language and the exposure of children to mindless violence, but they have, in the end, to accept it as perhaps an unwelcome but nevertheless inevitable corollary of the privilege of free expression.

But ought we not, perhaps, to be turning our attention to what is *not* broadcast, to the platform that is denied, to the views which, because not coincident with the opinions of the programme makers, are never permitted to reach the public ear at all? Ought we not to be considering whether adherence to the principle of freedom of expression does not demand a greater power, not necessarily in the courts but at least in some independent regulating body, not to prohibit the free propagation of opinion but to compel it by the practical observance of an obligation of impartiality?

The problem is one which has been faced directly by the courts of the United States. In *Columbia Broadcasting System Inc. v. Democratic National Committee 412 US 84 (1973)*, Justice Brennan observed: "In light of the unique nature of the electronic media, the public has strong First Amendment interests in the reception of a full spectrum of views—presented in a vigorous and uninhibited manner-on controversial issues of public importance…"Nor are these cases concerned solely with the adequacy of coverage of those views and issues which generally are recognised as `newsworthy'. For also at stake is the right of the public to receive suitable access to new and generally unperceived ideas and opinions." (See also *Red Lion Broadcasting Co. v. Federal Communications Commission, 395 U.S. 367, 1973*).

Now this is not merely paying lip-service to the value of the general concept of freedom of expression. The subjection of the public to permanently slanted coverage dulls the mind and is as dangerous to democracy (or perhaps, even more dangerous) as, then active repression itself, which at least has the merit of stimulating covert revolt. In a stirring passage in his judgement in *Whitney v. California* (274 U.S. 357, 375, 1927) Justice Brandeis observed that *"those who won our independence believed.....that the greatest menace to freedom of speech is an inert people"*. And, as Justice White said in the *Red Lion Broadcasting case (supra) "it is the right of the viewers and listeners, not the right of the broadcasters, which is paramount.......it is the right of the public to receive suitable access to the social, political, aesthetic, moral and other ideas and experiences which is crucial here."*

It is difficult to overrate the importance of this dimension. To confer on every citizen who desires it the right to be heard would not only be impractical, it would almost certainly be anti-social. But the real question is rather whether those who control the media of communication should have an *uncontrolled* privilege of denying an opportunity to be heard. "In the light of the current dominance of the electronic media as the most effective means of reaching the public, any policy that *absolutely* denies citizens access to the airways necessarily renders even the concept of `full and free discussion' practically meaningless… The issue in this case is not whether there is an *absolute* right of access, but rather whether there may be an absolute denial of such access. The difference is, of course, crucial" (*Columbia Broadcasting Co.*, supra, Per Justice Brennan).

Perhaps, one of the most striking recent examples of the intervention of the courts for the protection of minority views is that of the Supreme Court of Israel in *Kahane v. The Broadcasting Authority* (HC 399/85) where the Court, by injunction, compelled the state-controlled Broadcasting Authority to make air time available for a small extremist political party espousing frankly racist views. In a masterly judgement, Barak J. reviewed the doctrine of fairness which governed the exercise of the Authority's discretion. "By basic principles of administrative law..........a public authority operating by law must act equitably and fairly towards views and opinions, and therefore the B.A. must allow a political party whose views have been criticised in the media a chance to reply. Fairness does not require the B.A. to allow drug pushers to reply to a broadcast criticising drug use. But I cannot accept that when a political party represented in the Knesset has been criticised, it is not allowed to respond". "The views and opinions of Petitioners make me shudder, but I insist upon their right to express them.......Democracy is tested according to the speaker's freedom of speech, not by the value of his words".

This was a bold decision which points the way to judicial control of a state enterprise through the mechanism of judicial review. In the context of the United Kingdom, however, where the communication media are in the hands either of an independent statutory corporation or of privately funded corporations, subject only to the supervision of statutory or extra-statutory bodies which themselves are without effective powers of enforcement, this weapon is of little or no value. As matters stand, the only ultimate sanction would be the withdrawal by the Secretary of State of the broadcasting licence under the Wireless Telegraphy Act 1949, where no doubt the Secretary of State's decision could and would be reviewed in an appropriate case if matters ever reached that stage. But this is a fragile consolation for the aggrieved subject and it could, in any event, scarcely be applied outside a clear case of discriminatory allocation of air time to or against an organised political party.

The real worry lies much deeper than this, for we are not only concerned with the dissemination of news or of views openly expressed from a political platform. The dulling of the public mind and the consequent creation of public inertia is a much more subtle process and the problems which arise are the direct result of the growth over the past fourty—odd years of television as the universal vehicle not only of public instruction but of public entertainment. In truth, there has never in our previous history been a generation so consistently and so relentlessly entertained. Indeed, it is no exaggeration to say that, outside the house when they are at work, the great majority of the population of all ages are being subjected to a continuous process of being "entertained" in their own homes. And the propagation—and the suppression—of views can be and is achieved through the medium of "entertainment" just as effectively as it can be through the medium of news coverage and avowedly political broadcasting. The author of a play written to advance a political tenet is as much denied free expression by the rejection of his work on political, as opposed to artistic, grounds as a politician is by the refusal of a slot for a party's political broadcast. In the world of conventional publishing this does not matter, for he can always find another publisher. In an area in which there is legal monopoly of the means of communication, it matters a great deal and particularly where the suppression of unpopular or unconventional views is so easily excused on grounds of taste or artistic evaluation and thus is not easily susceptible of articulate complaint.

Broadcasting, whether on radio or television, must be "free" but the fact remains that this universal medium of communication is a potentially destructive monster capable of swallowing the very liberty that it proclaims. The problem of selective media bias—only very ineffectively met at present by the toothless watchdogs of supervisory agencies without means of enforcement—is one which, sooner or later, society is going to have to face. It is not a problem conventional processes of law and certainly not one in which the courts would wish to become involved. Perhaps, an answer could be found by broadening the composition of the Broadcasting Complaints Commission, and the independent Television Commission strengthening these by investing them with powers of intervention which could be enforced by the application of conventional legal remedies, and conferring upon them very much wider powers of investigation and review than they possess at the moment. The problem is a delicate one and one inevitably ends with the question *"quis custodiet ipsos custodes?"* However that may be, it is the writer's view that the guardians of our liberties might be better employed in this inquiry than in exploring the theoretical advantages of the statutory adoption of the terms of a Convention that does little to solve the real problems that surround the necessary preservation of our liberty of speech.

13

The Concept of Secularism: A New Interpretation

Classical Secularism

The classical concept of secularism, which India adopted soon after India attained freedom has been subject to immense pressure and seems to be rapidly disintegrating. There are three main reasons for it.

Firstly, the western concept of 'secularism' originated Europe several centuries ago when the question separation of the Church and the State had become a major concern and a subject of fierce political controversy. India has never had an organised *church*. The European concept of secularism was not really relevant to India's requirements. The term *Sarva-Dharma Samabhava,* which is sometimes used in place of secularism, is a far more meaningful formulation and certainly much closer to the views of the Father of the Nation, Mahatma Gandhi, who was deeply imbued with the Vedantic concept of the essential unity of all religions.

Secondly, India's new secularism was based upon the assumption, which has proved to be erroneous, that religion is a purely private affair and with which the State is not concerned. This may be true as far as individual prayer and spiritual practices are concerned, but quite clearly the collective impact of religion upon society and the State is something which is far from personal. That millions of Indian citizens should flock regularly to the *Kumbha Melas* and numerous places of worship, whether Hindu, Muslim or any other, is itself an indication that the State has necessarily to take cognizance religion as a social force. When we add the conflicts within and between religious groups, which create serious security and law and order problems, it becomes quite clear that the myth of religion being a purely personal matter can no longer be sustained. Indeed, that view is often put forward by a section of the intelligentsia who, for all practical purposes, are not believers and who, therefore, tend to look upon all religions as being *equally irrelevant* hangovers from the past. It is obvious that such a view is shared only by a miniscule percentage of India's vast population.

The third assumption upon which classical secularism is based revolves around the belief that as education increases, and living standards improve, religion will steadily lose its hold over the minds of people and become increasingly peripheral in its impact upon the human psyche. This assumption too has been repeatedly disproved in our own lifetimes. Not only in India but in other developing countries as well it has become clear that there is little relation between economic progress and the decline of religion. On the contrary, there is evidence to show that with increasing affluence in hitherto poor nations the interest in religion shows a marked upsurge. One has only to travel in the more affluent parts of India to see the tremendous burgeoning of new temples and gurdwaras, mosques and churches, and a survey of rural India will show that a place of worship is one of the first demands of a new affluent area. The upsurge of Islam in the oil-rich countries of West Asia proves the case convincingly.

New Directions

If these premises are accepted, it is quite clear that we have to move on to an entirely new concept of secularism if it is to have relevance in the years and decades to come. In the Indian context, secularism cannot mean an anti-religious attitude, or even an attitude of indifference towards religion on the part of the State. What is should mean is that while there is no State religion, all religions are given respect and freedom of activity, provided they do not impinge upon each other and, that foreign funds are not allowed to be channelled through ostensibly religious organisations for political purposes.

It is also essential that we overcome the religion-phobia in our educational system. At present we are getting the worst of both worlds. On the one hand, we refuse to take the positive attitude of presenting our rich, multi-religious heritage to our students, thus depriving them of contact with much that is noble and great in our civilisation; on the other, we leave religious education entirely in the hands of bodies which are seldom adequately equipped to undertake the task and usually offer narrow and obscurantist interpretations of the living truths that permeate religious traditions. The new education policy talks only of "value education". Without and understanding of our religious heritage, it will be extremely difficult to develop a coherent and widely accepted value system.

Negative Viewpoint

The multi-religious situation in India is a reality which will not go away. Instead of approaching the whole problem from a negative viewpoint, it would be far better to take the bull buy the horns and convert what is sometimes looked upon as a major "problem" into a positive asset for the new India that is struggling to be born. This can only be done if our educational system gladly accepts the multiplicity of our religious tradition. I have before me an admirable textbook brought out in London entitled "Worlds of Difference", which presents a variety of cultural traditions in a simple, positive and appreciative manner. Sponsored by the World Wildlife Fund, and with a foreword by His Holiness the Dalai Lama, the book published by Blackie has separate chapters on the Chinese world, the Humanist world, the Jewish world and the Muslim world. Attractively illustrated with photographs from the various religious traditions, it is accompanied by a guide which provides the teacher with an interpretative framework for the classroom. The book is designed mainly for the age-group 9-13, but much of the information can be used for older children.

I doubt if the Indian educational system, whether at the primary, secondary of higher levels, has a single book which presents the rich diversity of the Indian cultural tradition in this manner. Even at the post-graduate level there is hardly any significant work being done in the field of religious studies and comparative religion, which is so popular an area in the West, while the inter-religious dialogue is also virtually non-existent. All this is a reflection of the fact that among the "elite", religion seems to have become unfashionable. This is a sad commentary upon our intellectual capabilities. India is by far the richest area for multi-religious studies anywhere in the world and should attract some of our best scholars. Hinduism itself, the religion of over four-fifths of Indians, is a vast treasure-house of philosophy and mythology, sociology and worldly wisdom. Yet, in the last four decades, more work on Hinduism has been done by foreign scholars than by our own. Evidently their "secularism" is not compromised by working on one of mankind's oldest religious traditions.

If we are really serious in our efforts to build a strong and integrated India, it is incumbent upon us to ensure that the younger generation understand and appreciate not only its own religious traditions but also that of the other traditions in the country. How many Muslims in India are able even remotely to appreciate the depth of feeling among the Hindus regarding the sanctity of Lord Rama's birth place? Conversely, how many Hindus understand the emotional trauma among Muslims when they see idols being worshipped in what they consider to be a mosque? I am not here commenting upon this deeply divisive issue, which is still *sub judice*, except to say that in Kashmir we do have places of worship which are common both to the Hindus and the Muslims where *'aarti'* and *'namaz'* are done at the same time. But my point is that the gulf of incomprehension between the Hindus and the Muslims on this issue is fraught with grave danger for the nation, and is a reflection of our failure over the last fourty years to tackle religious issues adequately.

No nation can continue to grow if its central concepts become fossilized, and it loses the capacity for creative re-interpretation of its philosophical roots. The great secret of the Indian civilisation, which has persisted down the long and tourtuous corridors of time from the very dawn of civilisation, lies precisely in its capacity for such periodic reformulations. It is no longer good enough for us to try and hide behind an outmoded concept of secularism. What is needed is a deeper understanding of the importance of religion in the life of our people, and the formulation of a new and dynamic interpretation of secularism which would ensure the creative coexistence of our many religions, all making a positive contribution to the rich and varied mosaic that is India.

The entire cosmos, whatever is still or moving, is pervaded by the Divine.

— Ishavasya Upanishad

14
Elements of Communalism

P.C. Joshi (1980: 168) observes that ' the study of communalism from a macro-sociological or political-economic standpoint has not yet emerged as an important field of enquiry in social science research', and goes on to say that 'very rarely does one come across an attempt to evolve a comprehensive and integrated approach to the problem'. While sharing this judgment in the main, I have come to believe that the phenomenon of communalism can be understood only through an analytic field which acknowledges its multiple levels and whose terms can cope with situations as diverse as, say, the pressure upon Muslims in a village in Mysore (Epstein 1962: 32f) as well as what the historians of medieval India recognise as the Naqshbandi reaction: a movement away from Akbar's search of bridges, doctrinal and political, between Hindus and Muslims (A. Ahmad 1964: Ch. 7; Friedmann 1971). Consequently, when Professor Joshi states that the paucity of work on communalism 'has originated both from a lack of adequate theoretical perspective and of poverty of authentic empirical material,' I am rather uneasy; for 'authentic empirical material', often in its wide-ranging context, is strewn through virtually every monograph on Indian society and history, waiting merely for an 'adequate theoretical perspective' to draw it together.

This essay seeks such a perspective. It begins with a synoptic review of the work of sociologists and historians and asks why we have not been able to sustain an interest in communalism. Later it sketches the terms proposed for the analytic field. Material interests are part of this field, and these are especially important in explaining the phenomenon at local, and sometimes regional, levels. These enter the wider processes too, but here one may have to acknowledge greater weight for beliefs and attitudes and traditions. Still later it considers the nature of religious traditions from several angles, dilating on the issue largely because it has been so sadly neglected over the decades. This review will clear the way for sketching, in conclusion, the context wherein communalism grew during the colonial period.

Another introductory note: it is the conflict, the adversary relations, phrased in terms of 'Hindu' and 'Muslim', which will be discussed here. This is not to deny that most Muslims and Hindus, most of the time, have lived with each other cordially, though in my judgment, reflected in the following analysis, intimate relations and confident understanding across this boundary have not been common; and behind the cordiality of public encounters, there has often been antagonism in private.[1] To acknowledge the last element is neither to justify it nor to accuse anyone for it; but to deny its scale and depth would amount to foreclosing any serious attempt at understanding communalism.

The Literature

Questions of power and of economic interests are inevitably implicated in communalism, but these will enter our discussion principally through the disciplines of sociology and history with which I have some familiarity.

Numerous studies of local communities, the staple of sociological research in India over the past generation, provide more or less detail about the nature of relations between Hindus and Muslims in their localities. The localities tended to be rural in the earlier years, as in the work by S.C. Dube (1955: 85, 111, 115, 187, 226 in Telengana), T.S. Epstein (1962: 32f in Karnataka), T.N. Madan (1972, In Kashmir), Partap Aggarwal (1971, in Rajasthan), and Marc Gaborieau (1972, in Nepal); and later work has often been on urban areas, as by Harold Gould (1974, in Faizabad, U.P.), Mattison Mines (1972, in Tamil Nadu), Christine Dobbin (1972, in Bombay in late nineteenth century), S.P. Jain (1975, in U.P.), and Lina Fruzzetti-Ostor (1972, in West Bengal). Principally anthropological in inspiration, this literature is certainly useful; yet there has been a singularly puzzling inability on our part to draw creatively upon the sociological tradition which arose with the nineteenth century attempt to interpret the social crisis in Europe, one whose dimensions approach those of our own.[2]

Specially, Indian sociologists have been wary of questions which would have had to be asked of the published, secondary literature. Communal relations, ranging over time and space, are one such question. At this wider level we have Ramakrishna Mukherjee (1973) on developments in Eastern Bengal, and D.N. Dhanagare (1977) on the Moplahs; and, for both the dimension of communal conflict is incidental to other interests. Beyond that, Yogendra Singh (1973) has a chapter on 'the impact of Islam and modernisation'—marginal to our theme, but also much too uncertain about its authorities as well as its own analytic stance.[3]

One must note, finally, Louis Dumont's long, complex, and insightful paper, 'Nationalism and Communalism', an inquiry away from his central interests. The essay is built around critiques of the earlier writings of A.R. Desai, W.C. Smith and Beni Prasad, and finds the last most congenial. A widespread tendency to assume the pre-eminence of economic factors in all situations strikes Dumont as the principal obstacle frustrating many earlier discussions of the question. Both the communities, says Dumont, had during the medieval period edged towards 'a compromise which depended for its maintenance on the continuance of Muslim Power' (1964: 55). They lived together for centuries, generally peacefully, yet there was little fusion of their values; together they did not come to 'constitute a society'. During the nineteenth century flux which attended the ongoing change of scale, political mobilisation which appealed to sacred symbols, as Tilak's did, was necessarily separative in its effects; and because the Congress was unable to accommodate this great cleavage in its political vision and style, it could not secure Muslim support generally. Though long neglected as an aberration by both sociologists and historians, Dumont's analysis is a necessary beginning for further work on the issue.[4]

Questions of communalism have a remarkably different cast in the historians' literature. At least some of a group of scholars writing in the 1960s appear to see communal antagonisms as a consequence substantially of tendentious historiography which has sought to put allegedly 'Hindu' or 'Muslim' constructions upon medieval and later events (I. Habib, 1961; Thapar *el al.* 1961).[5] The erring scholars are not named, but may be guessed; and to an outsider it appears that they should be seen as *victims*— perhaps willing, perhaps unwitting—of a society which is rent by antagonistic communal attitudes, as scholars who understand social process too little to shed the prejudices they share with their neighbours; and not as *culprits* responsible for the fact of communalism: its cultural roots are very much older than the corpus of modern historiography, though the latter undoubtedly is an element in the milieu.

This critique of communal historiography was Marxian in inspiration, and it has certainly been influential in the social sciences in India over the past generation; yet its analytic logic has virtually no place for such categories as 'Hindu' and 'Muslim', or for the associated cultural traditions and needs, conscious and unconscious, that these meet.

In relation to this historiography, Mushirul Hasan's *Nationalism and Communal Politics in India* (1979) is poised uneasily. Marxian in conviction, in epigraph, and in occasional interpretation, Hasan is not shy of the categories Hindu and Muslim and offers perhaps the most satisfactory analysis yet of communal politics, focussing on developments before, during, and after the Khilafat and Non-Cooperation, and outlining the road to 1947. The Muslims were a category, divided internally by region, sect, and class; and it was the acceptance of the principle of communal representation, by the government in 1909 and by the Congress in 1916, and the subsequent enlargement of franchise in 1919 and 1935, that Professor Hasan sees as spurring on the communal and separatist politics. He is exceptional in his acute awareness of the power of religious symbols and ideas, yet implicitly equates communalism with communal *politics*. The focus set thus, the explanation covers the period examined; but the sense of communal identity and the associated antagonisms, here manifest, there latent, have survived the end of separate electorates, and undoubtedly antedated their introduction.

The spur to communalism is located by Professor Bipan Chandra a generation or two earlier in the nineteenth-century competition for jobs, in the colonial universe of small opportunities in a potentially expansionary social scale, so that if claims to one's 'community's backwardness' and the like could confer additional leverage, these were eagerly brought into play (1984: 39-43 and *passim*). The attempt here is to locate the *'causes or factors in Indian society* responsible for [the growth of communalism] and for the stage-by-stage enlargement of its social base' (ibid.: 29; emphasis his); but while the various religious traditions and social experiences are noticed, the possible contribution of their mutual abrasiveness to communalism is virtually defined out of the analytic field.

It seems to me, however, that this competition for government jobs and the separation of electorates are causes too minor to account for the effects to be explained. A certain matching of magnitudes between causes and effects seems to be warranted. If the historian's fine sense of causation takes him to the spark that lights the tinder, the sociologist's gross sense draws him to the tinder instead; both are necessary for the fire to start.

I happen to be a sociologist; but before proceeding further, we should note that the social sciences in India in recent decades have been rather reluctant to take serious account of religious beliefs and institutions in any context, with the limited exception of some followers of Dumont. This reluctance, especially in India, demands analysis in its own right; and its implications for understanding communalism are sufficiently serious for it to be examined itself now. In the earlier pages we have reviewed some *academic* inhibitions to such interest; but wider influences have also been active, and these are considered in the Appendix (pp. 76 ff)..

Interests and Traditions

I started out by suggesting that communal relations between Hindus and Muslims have to be seen at several levels, ranging from a village to a ruling class. Such a phenomenon cannot be unitary or homogeneous, yet any of its specific expressions may be analysable over common conceptual ground, provided its categories have strategic fit. Here, as elsewhere, it is useful to consider the framework of *interests* separately from, as well as in relation to, the realm of *ideas*, which appear in this case as religious *traditions*.[6]

Both these realms, of interests and of ideas and traditions, are of course part of every social situation; and each has its own distinctive logic—of meaning, of coercsiveness, and of the resources available for renewal; yet their separation is an analytic artifact. On the ground, all these usually constitute unseparated experience. In that experience, the religious traditions are transmitted and renewed in processes, social and cultural, which are both conscious and unconscious; and the latter is especially important for such societies (and persons) as do not habitually bring their own unconscious to the inquiring gaze of consciousness.

Framework of Interests

Let us begin with the central Marxian recognition of the sociological reality—call it coerciveness—of the context in which human beings labour and of the mechanisms whereby the product of their labour is appropriated. For reasons that will become clear, however, we have to keep in mind not merely the work situation, agrarian or industrial, but the broader question of access to a mode of making a living, and of the defence of one's hold on that living; and for these one uses certain relationships which may thereby separate one's social universe into allies and adversaries and neutrals. This separation may be done in terms other than those of material interests alone, as we shall see.

Interests may come to be defined in several ways. During the early twentieth century, the cultivators in certain parts of Malabar and in eastern Bengal were Muslim, their landlords Hindu; and the conflict of *class* interests between them tended, or could be made, to look like communal conflict (On Malabar: Dhanagare 1977, Panikkar 1979; on Bengal: R. Mukherjee 1973, Sarkar 1973: 443 *et seq.*) In certain parts of late nineteenth-century Punjab, differences of economic interests tended to coincide with differences of caste and also sometimes of religion (van den Dungen 1972, R. Smith 1971). More generally for the nineteenth century, P.C. Joshi (1980: 172-5) speaks of Muslim landowners steadily losing out to Hindu merchants and moneylenders; and this interface was not unknown during the medieval period. Situations of this kind express variously the common historical tendency in India for occupation to correspond with caste or ethnicity, with the provisio that in any particular case the link could have begun from the end either of occupation or of ethnicity. That is to say, *either* persons entering a particular occupation may constitute themselves into a caste—as in the historic cases of Rajputs and Kayasthas—*or* persons of a particular caste may move into the same occupation, as in a Punjabi town during the 1960s— the erstwhile leather-workers moving into lathework (Saberwal, 1976: Ch. 5).

Change of religion has usually been not an individual but a collective matter, tending to associate caste with religion in any locality. Consequently, the internal social cement for occupational groups in adversary economic relations often consists indistinguishably of caste and religious ties. Where the two identities, say of Hindus and Muslims, are separated by the coincident boundaries of occupation, caste and religion, the religious symbols may come to the fore by virtue merely of their mobilisational potential; but, as in the Moplah conflicts, men of religion may also be catalytic, or more active, in channelling what may otherwise seem to be 'purely' class interests.

Communal identities may however be implicated not only in *class* conflict but also in what, for want of an established term, may be called the *competitive* conflict of interests within a 'class.' It arises over access to a given array of opportunities; and we have noted that Bipan Chandra sees the competition of government jobs in late 1800s as pivotal to the later emergence of communalism in colonial politics. The boundary seen to be activated here is the religious one (and similar anxiety is reported for the late 1500s and early 1600s among certain elements of the Mughal nobility).[7] However, to attribute this to 'false consciousness' (Chandra 1984: 18-22 and *passim*) seems to me to be an evaluation, not an explanation. A search for explanation merely turns the attribution into a further question: namely, what were the historical antecedents that made the 'false consciousness' emerge along this particular boundary much more than along others associated with such criteria as caste, region, rural/urban differences and so forth?

Religious Traditions

Religious identities, I have suggested, tend to get implicated in conflicts of interest, whether of the class or the competitive sorts; but why should religion be implicated in identities at all, and why should these identities engage each other so often in antagonistic terms? With this question our inquiry has to go on a long but unavoidable detour. The length of this detour is deliberate. It demarcates a limited, strategic domain to which we must attend, however strong our aversion to doing so may hitherto have been.

I see religion in the following pages as part of culture, viewed anthropologically. While a religious tradition can be integrative, of a social group as well as of the individual psyche, its symbolic order sometimes persuades its believers in various ways to set themselves apart from the followers of other traditions, laying the basis for communal identities. The transmission of religious traditions is associated with religious experience which is commonly not verbalised or even conscious. And where the religious identities have come to adversary arrays, their antagonisms are stored in the unconscious, in addition to their presence in individual consciousness and enactment in more or less public settings. The run of my analysis will thus force me to point towards the importance of the unconscious, however distant the latter be from my limited competence.

Culture and Religion

Culture here refers to the totality of more or less changing conceptions concerning nature and society, self and others, past, present and future, which any functioning human group possesses, renews and lives by. All cultural conceptions are ultimately man-made but most are inherited from one's own or others' ancestors, substantially organised into complexes of ideas and social relations; except in acutely disrupted societies, these complexes of ideas and relationships are received by the next generation carrying the marks of 'transcendental law-like necessity' (Bauman, 1973: 76f);[8] much of the scepticism of our time is itself a cultural complex of ideas and relationships.

The human perception of whatever is observed is almost invariably mediated by culturally given conceptions.[9] What is culturally organised may be deliberately so by consciously acting human beings, resorting to culturally derived preferences and routines; but central to the modern understanding of society is the recognition that a great deal of this organisation at any time may in fact be *unconscious*. Cultural conceptions are subject to continuous patterning and selecting, part of an often unconscious process of cultural integration.

The principles underlying the integration of culture are too varied to be considered here; I need only make a few simple points. Modern societies organise road traffic, *inter alia*, by specifying the side that the traffic should keep, but these rules are neutral to the travelers' states of ritual purity. [10] The Hindu tradition employed ideas of ritual purity and pollution to organise a great deal of the social traffic, but it tended to be neutral to a vast range of social observances, leaving the caste group largely free to manage its own affairs. Islam came to stress the importance of the *sunnah*, the beaten path of Islamic tradition, and expected its observance by every Muslim, by the entire *umma*, the entire community; but there is no Islamic law for organising road traffic.[11] Through time and cumulative experience a culture comes to be centred upon certain key ideas which have served recurrently in meeting a wide range of contingencies; these key ideas together may be said to constitute a culture's integrative core.

Until the secularist growth of the last two or three centuries, this integrative core in complex premodern societies invariably claimed transcendental origins, and the sanctions behind this core were widely believed to have transcendental legitimacy. Modern historiography is beginning to show that, at the time of the initial promulgation, the early ideas of some of the great religious traditions arose in sharp intuitive insight into the prophet's own social milieu, showing for example how to re-order the framework of social relations so as to accommodate the changing structures of interests more adequately.[12] In the prevailing struggle between competing sets of ideas, the evidence of a prophet's extraordinary experiences, possibly of the supernatural, would give his message an edge, sometimes decisively.

Later generations would amplify and systematise the prophet's message, but certain core symbols would run through and recognisably unify the inevitably vast diversities of the community of believers. Thus in Islam we have the Prophet as the Messenger of God; his sayings and actions as the roots of Islamic law; the sacred core in the Meccan shrines; the unity of the *umma*, the religious community, guided by the *ulema*, the religious scholars. When, say, the Haj brought together Muslims from Djakarta and Rabat, or from Calicut and Agra, they would recognise in each other a certain sharing of religious sensibilities, a bond that made them brothers in faith. This bond would be sensed by their neighbours at home, too, who only heard about the pilgrimage, and could not themselves make it.

This bond, we have to concede is *not* commonly subjected to empirical judgments as to whether or not the mutual commonalities outweigh the mutual differences. It arises, rather, in faith, in the implicit acceptance of the symbolic order, which acts much of the time at more or less unconscious levels of experience: such elements as purity and pollution, the sanctity of the cow or the power of the Mother, the importance of conserving one's semen...these elements are suffused through and are expressed in numerous seemingly unconnected areas of belief and experience.[13] Each element in the symbolic order acquires its meaning within a psychological universe, which is also an experienced universe; and this meaning is created by the ceremonial, by recurrent experiences, and by its confirmation by others during and outside these ceremonies and experiences. In a phrase, this experienced universe is also a moral order. Its meanings are not available immediately outside such a universe; but for the believer these are often critical in intra-psychic integration, and their effectiveness is the greater for their being unconscious.[14]

Religion and Communal Identity

In premodern societies the sense of community fostered in the religious traditions would give direction to much of the prevailing life-style. Imprinted on the child's mind is the sanctity of worship, its place, words, gestures, sounds, smells and personnel. Religious acts and functionaries attend many of the critical episodes in life: birth, illness, marriage, death. There are dietary injunctions: be a vegetarian, eat only *halal* meat, beef may or may not be prohibited. Key complexes of religious belief, with their organising symbols, are thus implanted during the *pre*-reflective years of childhood, when one has little option but to accept one's elders' ideas without question.[15] It would not have happened equally for everyone; but it did happen in enough families to set the temper in their social group. To one born into and surrounded by a faith, its *shared* experiences, meanings, and gestures have the taken-for-granted quality which underlies social ease; and therefore nearly all marriages would have been made within the faith. It would have also been an important basis for *separation* from the followers of another faith—in worship, in religious education, in residence—within the local community and, when the need arose, for a set of potential supra-local links for those who reached out.

A religious tradition, put otherwise, is or used to be like a compass, helping one chart a course through life. It used to be a sanctified manual, listing the do's and dont's for coping with the universe.[16] Members of a multireligious society, however, would work with different manuals, listing divergent codes for life. Where people lived by different manuals, one way to anticipate the other's behaviour, attitudes, and intentions would have been to reckon with the other's manual, the other's religion. Social unease could furthermore be obviated by signalling one's own manual, through various diacritical marks: clothing, hairstyle, facial marks, perhaps one's language and manners. Religiously rooted social identities would thus be established and be mutually acknowledged.

Awareness of the socio-religious identities, then, would help one constitute useful social maps in one's mind, demarcating the social territory into sacred, friendly, neutral, hostile, etc. These social maps are sometimes expressed in, and validated by, myths and legends. Marc Gaborieau (1972: 92f) reports the transformation of a seventh-century event in central Iraq into a religious myth in the hills of Nepal:

> ...in the central hills, the martyrs Hasan and Husain are venerated during the ten first days of the lunar month of *Muharram;* further west the fair of Ghazi Miyan is held in the beginning of the solar month *of Jesth....* In actual history, Hasan and Husain were killed by Muslims, Ghazi Miyan by Hindus; but in the mind of the hill Muslims, the two legends blend curiously, and the story of the former is shaped on the same pattern as that of the latter: it runs briefly as follows.

> The heroes are Muslims: their marriage is going to take place and the rejoicing has begun to the sound of auspicious music. Suddenly there is news that the enemies, who are Hindus, are coming attack; the auspicious music is changed into a martial music and the heroes, mounting their horses, rush to fight the enemies. They are finally killed and the story ends in lamentation and the funeral music.

...during *Muharram* and Ghazi Miyan fair [they] can express successively joy in evoking he marriage, aggression when they commemorate the battle in a sham fight, finally grief when they sing lamentations, for this legend tells of the greatest sorrow: death on the day of marriage. And one should emphasise that the main theme of those festivities, where Muslims express themselves without restraint, is an irreducible enmity between Hindus and Muslims.

A traditional account undergoes transformation in the course of meeting the conscious and unconscious needs of those who recite it and thus comes to reflect their social maps of their universe. A traditional recital defining a group as hostile thus renews its status as an adversary, and such definitions persist when the corresponding expectations are confirmed episodically in experience (e.g., ibid: 93).

These social maps remain much in use even when the latter-day secular understandings of nature and society, or life and death, and of one's inner world make one sceptical of the received religious manual and its transcendental aura.

Religious Traditions and the Unconscious

Religious grounding used to be, and often continues to be, important for identities which constitute the social maps for regulating *public* social relations; and it so happens that similarly grounded devices also provide the means for coping with and for organising the *inner* worlds.[17] I proceed now to sketch the connections in the latter direction.

While the exigencies of life are infinitely variable, some of the key themes in any society arise as its cultural resources and constraints are used for canalising instinctual impulses—including those of sexuality—and for coping with the trauma left over from childhood. The enormous importance of these devices for the individual psyche is being attested by the slowly growing psychoanalytic work on Indian cultural materials (Kakar 1978, Masson 1980). These historically created devices—austerities, devotions, pilgrimages—are options available *within* a tradition; and just as many of the traumas and instinctual difficulties arise in the ongoing functions and malfunctions of society, so too their bearers take to these devices selectively, recurrently. The point to note here is that a great many of these devices for creating order within one's private self appear to be embedded intimately in the meanings and symbols associated *contrastively* with the several religious traditions. These core psychological and cultural devices also would sustain the social separation.

The use of communal identities by the unconscious at another level was called to my attention by Sudhir Kakar, the psychoanalyst, drawing upon his own fieldwork at Balaji's temple, off Bharatpur in Rajasthan. From various parts of North India—Bihar, Punjab, Rajasthan and elsewhere—persons with mental disturbance, usually considered to be possessed by a spirit, a *bhuta* come to the temple for its curative rituals. During these rituals, the spirit, 'speaking' through the patient, is persuaded to reveal its own identity and attributes. In the culture surrounding the temple, 'Muslim *bhutas* are considered to be the strongest and the most malignant of evil spirits, indicating perhaps the psychological depths of the antipathy between Hindus and Muslims' (Kakar 1982: 63). In the categories of this social context, the Muslim belongs with the untouchable: [18]

> *bhangiwara*...specialises in dealing with the Muslim *bhuta* and [spirits from] the untouchable castes. When a patient comes out of the *bhangiwara* enclosure after having exorcised one of these *bhutas*, it is imperative that he take a ritual bath to rid himself of the pollution. Otherwise it is held that if the patient touches someone else after his *bhangiwara* sojourn, it is almost certain that his *bhuta* will be transferred to the other person (1982: 60).

Translating the healing, exorcising routines at the temple into modern psychotherapeutic terms, Kakar sees these as strengthening:

> attempts to transform the patient's belief into a conviction that his bad traits and impulses are not within but without; that they are not his own but belong to the *bhuta*. The fact that fifteen out of twenty-eight patients were possessed by a Muslim spirit indicates the extent of this projection in the sense that the Muslim seems to be *the* symbolic representation of the alien in the Hindu unconscious. Possession by a Muslim *bhuta* reflects the patient's desperate efforts to convince himself and others that his hungers for forbidden foods, tumultuous sexuality, and uncontrollable rage belong to the Muslim destroyer of taboos and are farthest away from his 'good' Hindu self (1982: 87).

Interpreting the unconscious is a highly specialised field, one for which I have no credentials; yet nearly a century after Freud the sociologist must willy-nilly come to terms with this domain. He has to reckon with the interconnectedness of the social, the conscious, and the unconscious; and this applies to the phenomenon of communal separativeness too. The analysis continues with the social organisation of religious traditions and communal identities.

Social Organisation of Tradition

It is not merely beliefs and symbols and myths but also, as Red-field (1956) and Singer (1964) pointed out, a social organisation that makes a tradition: religious specialists, temples, traditional schools, ceremonies and recitations, sacred centres, networks, pilgrimages and the like. Important for us are the links between localities which arise in this social organisation. In a world of small, often defensive communities, the religious specialist, intinerant or resident, with his literacy and wider connexions and awareness of the sacred and sometimes secular literature, has been the man interpreting new situations, appealing to prior categories and symbols, and sometimes re-sacralising hitherto dormant ones. My illustrations of these inter-local connexions, actual and potential, come from the colonial period.[19] Mushirul Hasan has reviewed how the *ulema* helped to get the Khilafat Movement going:

> They took the lead in voicing Muslim concern over Turkey and Holy Places and, after 1918, they seized the initiative from the Muslim League leaders,

thus unleashing forces of vast political consequence. Fired by religion and buoyed up by their romantic sympathy for the Turkish *Khalifa* they carried pan-Islamic ideology to town and countryside where in mosque and *maktab*, Muslim artisans, weavers, and peasants were susceptible to their religious exhortations. They used the Quran and the *Hadith* as powerful weapons to gain adherence of the faithful who accepted them as infallible. They also forged an alliance with Muslim professional men and utilised their experience in agitational politics to further the cause of Pan-Islamism (1979: 307).

Or consider the late nineteenth-century campaigns in Lahore and Allahabad in support of reviving the Vedas, encouraging *shuddhi,* protecting the cow, and propagating Hindi (K. Jones 1976; Bayly 1975). Meanings and symbols—Quran and *Hadith*, Vedas and the cow—emotionally charged and exclusively bounded. Such potent, symbolic elements lie across the psychic, the social, and the cultural, and, for many, at the core of social identities and religious traditions. We have noted earlier that these traditions are maintained and renewed in complexes of specialists, institutions, pilgrimages, literature and so forth. These socio-religious webs have vast inter-local spreads, but few inter-connexions *across* the religious boundaries. Altogether, these tend to be separative.

The Rise of Communalism

Let us take stock of my argument. I have outlined the experiential bases of religious belief and identity, the use of religious identities to organise one's social space, the play of religiously embedded mechanisms in the run of one's inner life, and finally the separativeness of the inter-local networks within what have been called the Great Traditions of the historic civilisations. In settings where the religious symbolic order pervades the daily round, there would seem to be a widespread tendency for religious traditions to try to insulate these symbolic orders from each other by way of both residential separation and careful social routines. This tendency would be expressed categorically at the core of religious experiences and activities and more or less ambiguously in the more secular pursuits.

I move now to the milieu of the 1700s and the 1800s and consider the rise of communalism during this period, trying merely to indicate the major processes which appear to have fostered this growth.

I begin with everyday social relations. To the general tendency to religious separativeness, noted earlier, medieval India appears to have added:

1. the inter-cultural social distance between non-Indian immigrants and the natives, until time and circumstance combined to induce a measure of intimacy, at least in the ruling circles; and

2. the stigma of untouchability carried by the lower castes, whose conversion to Islam would scarcely remove that stigma, especially in their localities of origin. On the contrary, it seems that for Hindus both the general tendency to religious separativeness and the specific antagonisms, consequent to loss

of power, came to be set in the idiom and the routines of this untouchability.

From the medieval encounter there seems to have been inherited a social separation, sometimes hardened into patterns of residence, commensality, dress, and other acts of daily living. Yet the village community or the small town had relatively stable populations, and the marks of separation would have been taken for granted in an easy, daily round of life, where the caste order accommodated other sorts of separation too. This situation prevailed until, as we shall see, the setting began to shift in the 1800s.

Secondly, it is important to remember that Hindus, in numbers which grew with time, had high places in the ranks of the later medieval nobility (M. Habib 1958: 229f; Athar Ali 1968). In this political structure there were numerous relationships between Muslims and Hindus wherein the differences of their religious affiliations were in some measure set apart from the secular, political and administrative tasks at hand. The sense of religious affiliation, which has commonly been central to the sense of one's identity, is ordinarily acquired during childhood, in the course of *primary* socialisation, as we saw earlier. Affiliation in political, administrative, economic and similar contexts, in contrast, is ordinarily learned much later, during adolescence or adulthood in the course of *secondary* socialisation. During the 1700s, the Mughal politico-administrative structure got dismantled, and its constitutive relationships tended to lapse; and in so far as these had previously acted in counterpoint to the separative religious and social relationships, rooted in primary socialisation which continued relatively undisturbed, henceforth the separative relationships would come into play without this secondary set of moderating influences.

Thirdly, as we have noted in earlier chapters, during the 1800s, *the social framework was beginning to grow in scale*. This process was embodied in part in the expanding metropolitan centres. In the older localities—villages and small towns—the social separation of various caste-like groups was cross-cut by the necessity for cooperation in agriculture, commerce, and so forth, and a corresponding involvement in mutual ceremonials (Aggarwal 1971: Ch. 9; Mines 1972: 102f); but migrants into the metropolitan centres have commonly travelled along the social corridors of kinship, caste, etc. (Rowe 1973; Timberg 1978: Sec. C). The metropolis of the 1800s and early 1900s appears to have been organised so that rather large areas were relatively homogeneous as to religious community. The prior sense of social separation carried by the migrants with them tended to be confirmed as they settled into these larger, relatively homogeneous areas.[20] This pattern of metropolitan residences is important not only for the consciousness of religious community fostered in them, but also for the long-run, fitful influence of metropolitan models and messages on the lesser communities over the next century and more.

To sum up, I am suggesting that the rise of communalism during the colonial period should perhaps be seen in relation to the long-standing separativeness of religious networks, the acute social distance expressing a high level of social antagonism between Muslims and Hindus, the lapse of formerly functioning, integrative political and administrative ties, and the growth of communally homogeneous neighbourhoods in the new metropolitan centres.

It is in this historic context that we notice the conflicts of interests—class or competitive—which have in numerous localities often pitted, or been seen to have pitted, groups of different religious affiliations one against the other.[21] When, during the 1800s, with expanding scales of some social relations, the inter-local linkages of a *secular* sort began to expand vastly, this process built upon the pre-existing social matrices, realigning these for their resources and their influence in the changing milieu (Saberwal 1979). This process did not often violate the boundaries of exclusion which had been associated with the religious identities, and had been built into vast regions of the prevailing styles of life. In ever changing manifestations, it was this combination of interests with inherited, antagonistic, social separation which became the basis for the *social organisation of communal identities*. This social organisation includes such elements as educational institutions, social service organisations, political and quasi-political formations, journals, ceremonies, and so forth. Somewhat detached from religious belief, yet religiously rooted, these 'communal' identities gathered strength as the wider social and political arenas came into being.

With older restraints weakening, and newer linkages forming separately in an era of unprecedented economic shifts, what had once been relatively stable, largely local interfaces between Hindus and Muslims tended to become much wider and more active oppositions. Of this situation, the colonial regime was at times more than willing to take advantage (e.g., Sarkar 1973: 8-20).[22]

APPENDIX

Religion and the Social Sciences

Despite their varied persuasions, the social sciences in India, for a generation now, have tended to be dismissive of religious matters but, unfortunately, such an attitude has helped neither to improve our understanding, nor to reduce the power, of the phenomena so dismissed. This attitude has not been problematical—one takes it for granted.

In retrospect, this attitude seems to have been associated with a scientific, secular world-view noticeable in at least some areas in Indian society. For one who takes this latter world-view seriously, it can mean something of a break with the ancestral faith, which can be seen to be threatening by one's kin—and it may add up to a struggle in the family. Yet decay in ancestral religious observances has, in recent decades, come to be tolerated relatively well, and one settles for an easy agnosticism, taking on a rather passive identity as one or another sort of Muslim or Hindu or Christian, without an active search for rigorous belief, religious or secular. In reducing one's uncertainty levels, the prevailing routines seem to spur us into intensified social relations rather than critically won beliefs and impersonal strategies. Above all, the operative premise seems to be that 'religion' is not to be taken seriously. The word connotes communal riots, meaningless ritual, and a surrender to blind faith by those unable to cope with a crisis. Robust minds, we presume, need no religious beliefs. To take serious interest in these would be to admit one's own weakness—to others and to oneself.[23]

There are even greater difficulties in relation to religious traditions other than one's ancestral one. The medieval tradition of the relations between Hindus and Muslims was a mixed bag, and it has left its mark on the tenor of communal relations. Religious encounters during the 1800s, however, came to be charged with anxieties of another sort. Whereas Europe in the 1700s had sustained the inquisitiveness of the Renaissance about things alien, the 1800s opened with a lowering of the cultural shutters, as Europe's industrial sinews grew to guarantee her political dominance over Asia (e.g Dumont 1976: last section). The evangelicals became more aggressive in Europe (Thompson 1963: Ch. II) and in India (Stokes 1959: 27ff). As the nineteenth century grew, the din of religious competitiveness became more raucous in India (Kopf 1969: Chs. 14-15; K. Jones 1976). The struggle for souls led by Christian missionaries put the other religious traditions very much on the defensive.

Christian Missionary institutions were, however, often rated high for their educational calibre, and Hindu or Muslim parents sent their children to them; yet they sought to guard them against alien religious influence (Webster 1976: 150ff).[24] Any serious interest in a religious tradition other than the familial would be perceived to be threatening by one's group of origin; for should it lead to a change of faith, it would mean a virtually total breach in the convert's relations with the group of origin.[25] The coexistence of numerous religious traditions in India has by and large meant not mutual interest and curiosity but insulation and indifference. These latter attitudes few of us have been able to outgrow; and without the will to understand in a relaxed manner the inner logic of the different religious traditions, how can one grasp the dynamic of their mutual relations?

REFERENCES

1. My failure in this essay to take note of the countless syncretic beliefs, practices, and sects arises in the judgment that, during and after the colonial period, these syncretisms have proved to be rather weak in the face of resurgent Islamic and Hindu traditions and identities, Why this should have been so is a question for another occasion.

2. See Nisbet (1966). Our difficulty has been due partly to the burial of much of this nineteenth-century sociological tradition under the rather dreary sands of formalized, quantified, scale-building survey research in the United States. The plain lesson is that we cannot escape the task of constructing our own sociology, and I suspect that we will find its materials in nineteenth-century sociology, in twentieth-century anthropology, and in a comparative study of the long-run Indian and Western historical experience.

3. Illustratively, on authorities, consider n. 17a, on p. 65, for its adequacy to the context. On the analytic stance, Chs. 1 and 3 leave me wondering how Yogendra Singh sees Islam: a modernising element in India owing to its 'heterogenetic' status, or a traditional one owing to an allegedly hierarchical spirit? Or are these not the right questions?

4. Ratna Naidu's monograph (1980) appeared after the initial writing of this essay; I have reviewed it at length elsewhere (1981).

5. Their project included the writing of the well-known NCERT textbooks, reflecting the new historiography.

6. Cohen (1974) similarly places the interactions between relations of power and symbolic order at the centre of the social process. I thank Josef Gugler for giving me a copy of this book.

7. This is the 'Naqshbandi reaction': A Ahmad (1964): Ch. 7); Friedmann (1971).

8. Bauman (1973: 76f) presents something of the complex patterning in cultural phenomena and the complex formulations of the concept which prevail today.

9. For the underlying theoretical tradition, see Rose (1962), especially the papers by Rose and Blumer. Admittedly, numerous situations are shaped by a logic so coercive as to permit one to simplify analysis by eliminating the interpretative mediation, e.g., the economic consequences of colonialism. In the case of *communalism*, however, interpretative mediation happens to be the heart of the matter.

10. My choice of traffic rules to illustrate the cultural integration of modern societies is deliberate. It is characteristic of 'rationality' in these societies to devise rather simple rules to regulate various sorts of dense traffic—on rails, on radio waves, in the mails, in the air, and so forth. Cp. Hannerz (1980: 102).

11. I owe my limited understanding of Islam to von Grunebaum (1955), Watt (1961), Rodinson (1971,1974), Geertz (1968).

12. For the rise of Islam, both Rodinson (1971) and Watt (1961) write in these terms. For Buddha, likewise, D.D. Kosambi (1965: 104-13).

13. At this point one has to read the psychoanalysts: Erikson (1970), Kakar (1978), Masson (1980). Cp: 'The more meanings a symbol signifies, the more ambiguous and flexible it becomes, the more intense the feelings it evokes, the greater its potency, and the more functions it achieves.' This is from the anthropologist Cohen (1974: 32). See also Berger and Luckmann (1966: 110ff).

14. My comments draw upon personal experience of the Arya Samaj and Quakers in India and in North America. Fieldwork among the Embu of Central Kenya (1963-4) covered their beliefs concerning the supernatural too; but my interest in the anthropological understanding of religion was aroused only recently as I turned to the literature on Islam.

15. This situation has concomitants: see pp. 70, 74 below.

16. This is a deliberately utilitarian stance on religion. For a modern, anthropological attempt to comprehend the ineffable in religion, see Geertz (1966, 1968).

17. There is also the tiny minority able to live largely by the modern, secular understanding of these matters.

18. Apparently connected with the logic of purity and pollution, this equation is rather widespread: e.g., Khare (1976: p. 249 and *passim*). See discussion later.

19. For medieval analogues of these relatively insulated inter-local connections, see Rizvi (1977: 24-30), Sarma (1966).

20. On Calcutta, Siddiqui (1973), Bose (1968); on Bombay, M. Kosambi (1980: 121-36). On Allahabad, a *much older* city, Bayly (1975: 39-46) suggests for the late 1800s a considerable admixture of Hindus and Muslims.

21. *Within* the social organisation of a religious tradition or of a communal identity, too, there are interests to defend: those of the specialists in the organisation, or of outsiders able to influence or control them, or, more likely, of both. In defence of these more limited interests too, the specialists may try, covertly if necessary, to mobilise the believers. It would be wholly wrong, however, to dismiss such organisations simply as groups of self-servers. It is characteristic of any enduring complex tradition, and of the associated identities, that these can generate individuals and groups committed to defending the integrity of the tradition, and of identity, regardless of personal cost: that is very much the stuff of martyrdom—a prolific source for fresh symbols!

22. The wedge would look, of course, for whatever cleavages happened to be there in a region: thus the Brahmin/Non-Brahmin divide in Madras.

23. This is not a necessary position. Clifford Geertz, an atheist, has worked on religious beliefs, and so have E.E. Evans-Pritchard and Victor Turner, both practising Roman Catholics. Observation of one's own private search for meaning—if it abides by the elementary rules of accurate observation—can enrich one's public accounts of the nature of religious experience.

24. Much of the guarding would have been via the attitudes instilled during the child's earlier socialisation.

25. Illustratively, Conlon (1977: 79-84) documents the turmoil among Saraswat Brahmans in Mangalore following several such conversions in 1843 and 1862.

15
Networks in Indian Social Structure

Much has been written on the concept of social structure since Radclifee-Brown first started making systematic use of it more than thirty years ago. Apart from writing about it in abstract and general terms, most British anthropologists have used it as a central concept in presenting their field material.

Evans-Pritchard's use of the concept in *The Nuer* remains as a model of its kind. There the concept was used to mean 'relations between groups of persons within a system of groups,' such groups, further, having 'a high degree of consistency and constancy.' This way of viewing social structure has enabled the fieldworker to present his data in an economical manner. The concept is also relatively easy to handle. One begins by locating the enduring groups in a society, then proceeds to define their boundaries, and finally one specifies their mutual positions, or their inter-relations in terms of a series of rights, duties and obligations.

The approach outlined above has been widely used by social anthropologists (particularly British anthropologists or those trained in Britain) in the study of Indian village communities. The papers by Srinivas and Kathleen Gough in Marriott's collection may be taken as illustrations. The village is viewed there principally in terms of a set of enduring groups and categories such as castes, sub-castes and economic classes.

A model of society which is conceived in terms of enduring groups and categories has also to deal with the problem of interpersonal relations. It has, in addition, to devise ways of depicting the relations between groups and categories which form parts of different systems, e.g. between lineages, territorial segments and age sets, or between castes, classes and power blocks.

The distinction between a system of groups and a system of interpersonal relations has been nicely posed by Evans-Pritchard. This distinction, it appears, is a part of Nuer kinship terminology. The Nuer used the word *buth* to refer to relations between lineages viewed as groups. The word *mar* is, by contrast, used to refer to kinship relations between persons belonging either to the same agnatic lineage or to different ones.

It should be recognised in this connection that, when one talks of the 'relations between groups in a system of groups', one is representing things at a certain level of abstraction. Representation of the relations between castes in a system of castes involves one level of abstraction. On the other hand, a representation of the relations between the system of castes and the system of classes involves an abstraction at a higher level. Evans-Pritchard shows a clear awareness of the problem which this raises, and its difficulties.

> Not only can we speak of the relations between territorial groups as a political system, the relations between lineages as a lineage system, the relations between age-sets as an age-set system and so forth, but also in a society there is always some relationship between these systems in the whole social structure, *though it is not easy to determine what this relationship is.*

It may be pointed out that the abstract relations between groups and systems of groups can be better understood by mapping out the concrete relations between individuals in their diverse roles. This may be achieved by making a shift from a study of groups within a system of groups to a study of social networks. What are the concrete relations which an individual has in his capacity as Brahmin, landowner and *panchayat* member with other individuals? The concept of social network paves the way to an understanding of the linkage existing between different institutional spheres and between different systems of groups and categories.

It is necessary to point out that the model of social structure which bases itself on enduring groups and categories, and their interrelations has been developed largely by social anthropologists engaged in the study of primitive societies. Such a model does, indeed, take one a long way in the description and analysis of societies which are small, homogeneous and relatively static. In the study of large, complex and changing societies, however, this approach is faced with certain limitations.

In a complex society such as India the number of enduring groups, classes and categories is very large, and they present a bewildering variety of types. It may be difficult within the compass of a single study even to enumerate such units, not to speak of providing a coherent account of their complex interrelations. Evans-Pritchard has been able to provide a fairly comprehensive account of Nuer social structure while confining himself almost wholly to three systems of groups. Clearly, it is impossible to analyse in such an economical manner the social structure of even a single district in India.

There is another factor which imposes limitations on the approach which confines itself to the study of enduring groups and systems of groups. In traditional India groups such as village communities, sub-castes and lineages had sharply defined outlines. It was relatively easy to delimit their boundaries. Today the situation is somewhat different. Boundaries between groups tend to be blurred or broken down, there is greater circulation of personnel, and an increasing degree of interpenetration between different systems of groups, classes and categories. This process makes it increasingly difficult to locate and define the boundaries of groups, and hence to talk meaningfully of groups of persons within a system of groups.

In India this partial dissolution of a rigid, segmental and hierarchical social structure is associated with increasing social mobility, both horizontal and vertical. It is also associated with the transition from a status-bound ascriptive social order to one which gives greater scope to contractual relations based on personal choice. The allegiance of the individual to his village, his sub-caste and his lineage has, to some extent, loosened. Along with this, the individual is being progressively drawn into networks of interpersonal relations which cut right across the boundaries of village, sub-caste and lineage.

The process outlined above may be illustrated with a concrete example. Let us consider the case of Sripuram, a multi-case village in Tanjore district which has been exposed to the forces of change since the end of the nineteenth century. Sixty years ago one's social position in Sripuram was defined largely in terms of one's membership of the village, of a particular territorial segment of it, of a sub-caste, a lineage and a household. Much of the social life of the villagers could be understood in terms of the relations between these diverse groups, each of which had fairly easily determinable boundaries. Today the social contours of the village are becoming blurred, its population has acquired a shifting character, and lineages and families have become greatly dispersed.

Many of the former residents of Sripuram have left the village and gone to Tanjore, Madras, Delhi, Bombay and Calcutta. In each of these centres they have developed new relations, while retaining many old ones with people who still live in the village. Many of those who have left the village continue to influence its social life in a number of ways. Often they return at harvest time to receive rents, and renew leases with their tenants. Several of them send remittances to relatives in the village every month. On occasions of birth, marriage and death they revisit the village.

The concept of social network makes for an effective representation of the links radiating from the village to the outside world. These links sometimes stretch across wide territorial gaps, and often they are made up of strands of diverse kinds. One of the Brahmin landowners of Sripuram wanted to get a seat for his son in an engineering college at Madras. He approached an influential non-Brahmin friend at Tanjore who was also his father's client, the father of the Brahmin landowner being a lawyer in a nearby town. The non-Brahmin friend, who is chairman of a transport undertaking at Tanjore, had influential business associates at Madras. Some of these persons were able to put the landowner from Sripuram into touch with a member of the committee of the college to which he was seeking admission for his son. In the contemporary world of Sripuram the individual finds it increasingly necessary to become a part of the kind of network described above. Sixty years ago, when the social horizons were narrower, this necessity was far less keen.

Having sketched the conditions under which networks emerge and become increasingly important in social life, let us consider the distinctive features of networks as opposed to groups, class and categories. The distinction between groups and networks is primarily one of boundaries. A group is a bounded unit. A network, on the other hand, ramifies in every direction, and, for all practical purposes, stretches out indefinitely. Further, a group such as a lineage or a sub-caste has an 'objective' existence: its boundaries are the same for the 'insider' as well as the 'outsider'. The character of a network, on the other hand, varies from one individual to another.

This distinction between groups and networks, which was first elaborated by Barnes, should not, however, be pressed too far. Networks can be either close-knit or loose-knit. In other words, the chain of relations emanating from a person may either lead back to him, or it may not. In traditional India, particularly in the South, the network of kinship and affinal relations was a close-knit one. In fact, this network had, inevitably , to stop short at the boundary of the sub-caste and therefore to form a closed circuit. Mrs. Karve has shown how, in many cases, an entire sub-caste can be placed on a single genealogy. Here we have an instance where the kinship network is, in reality, coterminous with a bounded group, namely, the sub-caste. Thus, in the limiting case, a close-knit network becomes a group (or a category).

A social network can be viewed as a set of concrete interpersonal relations linking the individual to other individuals who are members of diverse systems of enduring groups and categories. Here we represent the network from the viewpoint of the actor, and there are as many networks as there are actors in a social system. Before we pass on to a consideration of the network from the viewpoint of the 'observer' (i.e. the anthropologist), let us examine a little further the implications of the subjective definition of a network.

The anthropologist as fieldworker begins to learn about the way in which a society works precisely by following concrete networks of interpersonal relations with the individual actor as his point of departure. He sees how individuals cut through the boundaries of household, lineage, sub-caste, village district, party and class so as to form interpersonal relations in the pursuit of interests of diverse kinds. He learns to differentiate one individual from another in terms of the range and variety of interpersonal relations, and tries to relate these differences to factors such as generation, education, occupation and so on.

A network, even when viewed from the standpoint of a single individual, has a dynamic character. New relations are forged, and old ones are discarded or modified. This is particularly true of rapidly changing societies in which individual choice plays an important role. However, extensions of the individual's social network may also be studied in relatively static societies. Thus, in the field of kinship we may observe how the individual's network of effective interpersonal relations is extended as he passes from birth through initiation and marriage to death.

Although the anthropologist may begin by mapping out the concrete networks of interpersonal relations of individual actors, this mapping, in itself, does not fully meet the needs of his analysis. At best it can provide him with a broad idea of the linkage between the groups and systems of groups in a society. For a deeper understanding it is necessary not only to chart the concrete networks of different individuals, but to relate these different networks to one another, to draw up, so to say, a master chart, in a coherent and systematic manner. This involves abstraction and synthesis.

It is easy to see what one means by an individual's network of interpersonal relations, for this has a concrete character. But can one speak, for instance, of the social network of a village? What would such a statement mean? The village comprises diversity of individuals, each with his own network of concrete interpersonal relations. These partly overlap, and partly cut across, and are, in fact, related to one another in very complex ways. In some spheres, the separation of one individual's network from that of another is quite clear. Thus, the network of kinship and affinal relations of a Brahmin will not at any point meet that of a non-Brahmin, even though they be of the same village. In the economic sphere, on the other hand, these networks are likely to meet at a number of points. Can one distinguish in systematic way between different institutional areas in which networks are relatively close-knit or loose-knit?

It seems evident that the kinship network in India is relatively close-knit as compared, let us say, to the economic or political network. It may be that the same forces which lead to the extension and loosening of the economic and political networks also lead to the shrinkage and tightening of kinship networks in contemporary India. Territorial dispersal and mobility lead to the extension of economic and political ties; they often also lead to a shrinkage of the network of *effective* kinship relations based upon reciprocal obligations.

We have now been led to a point a which it is necessary to talk in somewhat more abstract terms. From viewing the concrete networks of interpersonal relations of a number of individual actors we have been led to talk about networks pertaining to different institutional areas. We can now speak about economic networks, political networks, ritual networks, and so on. It is evident that when we speak, say, of an economic network, we are making an abstraction. A concrete network of interpersonal relations cannot be wholly economic in its constitution, except in the limiting case. Generally such relations have economic components which have to be abstracted from concrete matrix, and then put together.

The economic system may be viewed as a network of relations regulating the flow of goods and services. The political system may, likewise, be viewed as a network of relations regulating the flow of command and decision. It must be pointed out that the links in networks of this kind are unitary in character, as opposed to concrete networks of interpersonal relations where the links are usually composite or multi-bonded.

Economic, political and ritual networks of the kind described above would correspond to what Marion Levy characterizes as 'analytic', as opposed to 'concrete' structures. Thus, a network of economic relations provides an understanding of the organisation of production in a society, and a network of political relations provides an understanding of the distribution of power. Such networks in a complex society cut across the boundaries of communities and corporate groups and, in fact, serve to articulate them to wide social systems. And, once we shift from the individual actor and his network of concrete interpersonal relations to the productive system and its corresponding network, we move from the 'subjective' network of the actor to the 'objective' one of the observer.

We have seen earlier that a crucial distinction in the study of networks is that between close-knit and loose-knit networks. It may be urged that one way of understanding social change in India would be to analyse the manner in which close-knit networks are being transformed into loose-knit ones. Traditionally the villager lived in narrow world where the ties of locality, caste, kinship and hereditary service led back and forth between the same sets of persons. Relations were multiplex in character, and the circuit of relations had a tendency to become closed.

The situation is changing in contemporary India. New interests tend to create relationships which cut right across the boundaries of the old established groups. Increased mobility has led to the physical dispersal of castes, lineages and families. The individual cannot any longer afford to confine his relations within a village, a caste or a kin group. He has to develop relations with people who are spread far and wide and who have diverse social, economic and political positions and interests. The network of social relations emanating from the individual does not as easily lead back to him. The closed circuit tends to become more and more open.

The phenomenon sketched above can perhaps be best illustrated from the field of politics. To take once again the instance of Sripuram, one can get only an imperfect understanding of its political life by confining oneself to groups such as the *panchayat*, the party or the sub-caste. What appear to be of greater importance are the networks which link the village leaders to politicians and influential people outside, and which cut right across the boundaries of parties, *panchayats* and sub-castes. Bailey has spoken of 'brokerage networks' in the context of Orissa. Such networks are of great importance to the working of the political process throughout the country. In and around Sripuram they link the village leader with the district leader, the patron with the client, the MLA with the 'vote-bank', the party boss with the financier, and the *panchayat* president with the contractor.

It is evident that some of the most radical changes taking place in Indian society today are in the field of politics. A rigidly hierarchical and segmental social structure is being transformed into one which seeks to bring about political articulation between people at all levels of society. The peasant in a Tanjore village is linked directly with the Member of Parliament at Delhi. To what extent can such a linkage be effective or successful? It is in this context that he problem of communication acquires central importance to both the politician and the political sociologist in India. How does the system of political communication actually operate? How does it affect the existing systems of groups and categories in Indian society, and how is it, in turn, affected by them? A study of the concrete links between villagers, local leaders, party bosses, MLAs, and MPs is indispensable to an understanding of the channels along which communications flow, and the barriers at which they are blocked.

In a recent paper Ithiel Pool has emphasised the importance of informal social channels of communication in providing necessary support to the mass media in traditional societies. Political events in the state capital are interpreted and transmitted along social networks of various kinds whose nature requires to be investigated. There is little doubt that such networks today link individuals not simply on the basis of caste or occupation or locality, but on the basis of a complex combination of these and numerous other factors.

India has embarked on a course of planned social change and economic development. This involves, among other things, the transmission of certain key ideas, principles and values from the highest to the lowest levels of society. What are the social networks along which such ideas are transmitted? What kind of refraction do they undergo as they pass from one level to another? How is this refraction conditioned by the nature of the social network along which the ideas flow?

The entire process of political mobilisation in a country such as India highlights the importance of networks of interpersonal relations. How does the politician reach down to the voter, and how does the latter, in turn, articulate with the former? In a country where literacy is low and where the mass media are new and limited in scope, networks of interpersonal relations are of primary importance to the mobilisation process.

The process of political modernisation has many immediate and far-reaching consequences for the structure of traditional society. It breaks down the barriers between groups which had crystallised over centuries. It gives a new amplitude to individual choice in severing old relations and forging new ones. All this lead to the development of networks on the basis of new interests which criss-cross the entire social fabric.

In conclusion, we have to consider briefly the existence of social networks and the part played by them in traditional Indian society. It would, of course, be far from correct to say that networks had no existence in traditional society, or that the social life of the individual was completely contained within systems of enduring groups. Even in the past the village was never entirely a closed or self-sufficient unit. Links of various kinds radiated from it, connecting its individual members to other individuals outside. Such links, however, played a far less important part in the past than they do today. Even the extra-village ties of the individual often articulated him with other groups such as lineages or sub-castes which were themselves closed in character.

A village community which forms part of a wider civilisation can never be entirely a closed unit. In fact, articulation of a particular kind is a basic characteristic of a civilisation as distinguished from a primitive society. The manner in which little and great traditions are articulated through social networks in a primary civilisation has been discussed by Redfield, Singer and others. But it cannot be denied that the nature of articulation in a relatively static and compartmentalised social order is different from one which is fluid and changing in character.

16

Sanskritisation and Westernisation

Caste and Status Mobility

The concepts of 'Sanskritisation' and 'Westernisation' were developed by M.N. Srinivas in 1952 in the analysis of the social and religious life of the Coorgs of South India. Up to the middle of the twentieth century, caste was studied either in terms of the *varna* model or in terms of status based on notions of heredity and pollution and purity. Srinivas analysed the caste system in terms of upward mobility. He maintained that the caste system is not a rigid system in which the position of each caste is fixed for all time. Movement has always been possible. A low caste was able to rise, in a generation or two, to a higher position in the hierarchy by adopting vegetarianism and teetotalism. It took over rituals, customs, rites and beliefs of the Brahmins and gave up some of their own considered to be impure. The adoption of the Brahmanic way of life by a low caste seems to have been possible, though theoretically forbidden (1985: 42).

The occupations practised by castes, their diet, and the customs they observe determine their status in the hierarchy. Thus, practising an occupation such as tanning, butchery, or handling toddy puts a caste in a low position. Eating beef, fish and mutton is considered defiling. Offering animal sacrifices to deities is viewed a low practice than offering fruit and flowers. As such, castes following these customs, diet habits, etc. adopt the life of the Brahmins to achieve a higher status in the caste hierarchy. This is moving of a low caste upwards in the social structure. Srinivas termed this process as 'Sanskritisation'.

The Concept of Sanskritisation

Srinivas has defined 'Sanskritisation' as a process by which the low castes take over the beliefs, rituals, style of life and other cultural traits from those of the upper castes, specially the Brahmins. In fact, Srinivas has been broadening his definition of Sanskritisation from time to time. Initially, he described it as 'the process of mobility of lower castes by adopting vegetarianism and teetotalism to move in the caste hierarchy in a generation or two (1962: 42). Later on, he redefined it as "a process by which a low caste or a tribe or other group changes its customs, rituals, ideology, and way of life in the direction of a high twice-born caste" (1966: 6). The second connotation of Sanskritisation is thus much broader because first Srinivas talked of imitation of mere food habits, rituals and religious practices but later on he talked of imitation of ideologies too (which include ideas of *karma, dharma, pap, punya, moksha,* etc.)

In the process of imitation of customs and habits of high castes or Brahmins by the low castes, sometimes even when the low castes followed some such practices which according to the present rational standards are considered to be good and functional, they discard such customs and in their place adopt those ideas and values of Brahmins which according to the present standards are considered degrading and dysfunctional. Srinivas has given some such examples from his study in Mysore. Low castes are liberal in the spheres of marriage, sex, and attitudes towards women. They permit divorce, widow remarriage, and post-puberty marriage. But Brahmins practise pre-puberty marriage, regard marriage indissoluble, restrict widow from remarrying and expect her to shave her head and shed all jewellery and ostentation in clothes. They prefer virginity in brides, chastity in wives, and continence and self-restraint in widows. But as a low caste rises in the hierarchy and its ways become more sanskritised, it adopts the sex and marriage code of the Brahmins. Sanskritisation results in harshness towards women. Another example of taking up irrational practice is that a Brahmin and a high caste Hindu wife is enjoined to treat her husband as a deity. A wife is expected to take her meal after the husband had perform a number of *vratas* (religious fasts) to secure a long life for husband, regard the importance of having sons a religious necessity, and so forth. Sanskritisation involved taking up all such beliefs and practices by the lower castes. These examples thus point out that Sanskritisation is nothing but a blind and irrational imitation of the customs, practices, habits, and values of higher castes, specially Brahmins.

Could it be said that the process of de-Sanskritisation is also possible? Srinivas has conferred that "it is not inconceivable that occasionally the de-Sanskritisation of the imitating castes may take place" (1985: 62).

Sanskritisation and Brahmanisation

Srinivas (1985: 42-43) preferred the term 'Sanskritisation' to 'Brahmanisation' because of several reasons: (1) Sanskritisation is a broader term while Brahmanisation is a narrower term. In fact, Brahmanisation is subsumed in the wider process of Sanskritisation. For instance, the Brahmins of the Vedic period consumed alcohol (*Soma*), ate beef, and offered animal sacrifices. But these practices were given up by them in the post-Vedic times, perhaps under the influence of Jainism and Buddhism. Today, by and large, Brahmins are vegetarians and teetotalers; only the Kashmiri, Bangali and Saraswat Brahmins eat non-vegetarian food. Had the term 'Brahmanisation' been used, it would have been necessary to specify which particular Brahmin group was meant. (2) The reference group or the agents of Sanskritisation are not always Brahmins. In fact, it were Brahmins who, entrusted with the authority to declare laws, had prohibited members of other casts in following the customs and rites of Brahmins. But such prohibitions did not prevent the lower castes in sanskritising their customs and rites. Srinivas has given the example of low castes in Mysore (South India) who adopted the way of life of

Lingayats; who are not Brahmins but who claim equality with Brahmins. The smiths of South India, call themselves Vishwakarma Brahmins, wear the sacred thread and have Sanskritised their rituals. However, some of them still eat meat and take alcohol because of which many castes, including some untouchable castes, do not accept food or water from their hands (1985: 43). Thus, since the low castes imitated Kshatriyas, Vaisyas, Jats, etc., in different regions of the country, the term 'Brahmanisation' was not considered adequate enough for explaining the process of cultural and social mobility.

Features of Sanskritisation

A few facts are worth nothing in the process of Sanskritisation:

(1) The concept of Sanskritisation has been integrated with economic and political domination, that is, the role of local 'dominant caste' in the process of cultural transmission has been stressed. Though for sometime, the lower castes imitated Brahmins but soon the local dominant caste came to be imitated. And the locally dominant caste was often a non-Brahmin caste.

(2) Sanskritisation occurred sooner or later in those castes which enjoyed political and economic power but were not rated high in ritual ranking, that is, there was a gap between their ritual and politico-economic positions. This was because without Sanskritisation, claim to high position was not fully effective. The three main axes of power in the caste system are the ritual, the economic and the political ones. The possession of power in any one sphere usually leads to the acquisition of power in the other two. But Srinivas mentions that inconsistencies do occur.

(3) Economic betterment is not a necessary pre-condition to Sanskritisation, nor economic development must necessarily lead to Sanskritisation. However, sometimes a group (caste, tribe) may start by acquiring political power and this may lead to economic betterment and Sanskritisation. Srinivas (1985: 57) has given the example untouchables of Rampura Village in Mysore who have got increasingly sanskritised though their economic condition has remained almost unchanged. Economic betterment, the acquisition of political power, education, leadership, and a desire move up in the hierarchy, are all relevant factors in Sanskritisation, and each case of Sanskritisation may show all or some of these factors mixed up in different measures.

(4) Sanskritisation is a two-way process. Not only a caste 'took' from the caste higher to it but in turn it 'gave' something to the caste. We find Brahmins worshipping local deities which preside over epidemics, cattle, children's lives, and crops, besides the great gods of all India Hinduism. It is not unknown for a Brahmin to make a blood-sacrifice to one of these deities through the medium of a non-Brahmin friend (Srinivas, 1985: 60). Though local cultures seem to 'receive' more than they 'give', yet sanskritic Hinduism has also absorbed local and folk elements. The absorption is done in such a way that there is a continuity between the folk or little tradition and the great tradition.

(5)   Unit of mobility is group and not individual or family.

(6)   The British rule provided impetus to the process of Sanskritisation but political independence has weakened the trend towards this change. The emphasis is now on the vertical mobility and not on the horizontal mobility.

(7)   Describing social change in India in terms of Sanskritisation and Westernisation is to describe it primarily in cultural and not in structural terms. Srinivas himself has conceded (1989: 55) that Sanskritisation involves 'positional change' in the caste system without any structural change.

(8)   Sanskritisation does not automatically result in the achievement of a higher status for the group. The group must be content to wait an indefinite period and during this period it must maintain a continuous pressure regarding its claim. A generation or two must pass usually before a claim begins to be accepted. In many cases, the claim of the caste may not be accepted even after a long time. Further, it is likely that a claim which may not succeed in a particular area or period of time way succeed in another.

The fact that Sanskritisation may not help a lower caste to move up does not prevent it to discard the consumption of beef, change polluting occupation, stop drinking alcohol, and adopt some sanskritic customs, beliefs and deities. Thus, the process of Sanskritisation may remain popular without achieving the goal of mobility.

Factors Promoting Sanskritisation

Factors that have made Sanskritisation possible are industrialisation, occupational mobility, developed communication, spread of literacy, and western technology. No wonder, the spread of Sanskrit theological ideas immersed under the British rule. The development of communications carried Sanskritisation to areas previously inaccessible and the spread of literacy carried it to groups very low in the caste hierarchy. M.N. Srinivas has specifically referred to one factor which has helped the spread of Sanskritisation among the low castes. It is the separation of ritual acts from the accompanying *mantras* (citations) which facilitated the spread of Brahmanical rituals among all Hindu castes, including the untouchables. The restrictions imposed by the Brahmins on the non-twice-born castes banned only the chanting of *mantras* from the Vedas. Thus, the low caste people could adopt the social practices of the Brahmins. This made Sanskritisation feasible.

The political institution of parliamentary democracy has also contributed to the increased Sanskritisation, according to Srinivas (1985: 49). Prohibition, a sanskritic value, has been mentioned in the Constitution of India. Some states have introduced it wholly or partially.

The Concept of Westernisation

This concept refers to "the changes in technology, institutions, ideology and values of a non-western society as a result of cultural contact with the western society for a long period" (Srinivas, 1962: 55). Giving an example of Indian society, the technological changes, establishment of educational institutions, rise of nationalism and new political culture etc., may all be described as the bye-products of Westernisation or of the British rule of two hundred years in India. Thus, by Westernisation, Srinivas primarily meant the British impact.

The important features of Westernisation are: (1) Emphasis on technology and rationalism. (2) This process (of Westernisation) is not retarded by the process of Sanskritisation, but to some extent it is accelerated by it. Srinivas had earlier maintained that Sanskritisation is a prelude to Westernisation. However, later on, he changed his view and maintained that it is not necessary for Sanskritisation occurring prior to Westernisation (1985: 60). But the two processes are linked with each other. It may not be possible to understand one without the other. Harold Gould has also said that for Brahmins and other higher castes, sanskritising is an attempt to maintain the distance between them and the lower castes who are sanskritising. Thus, the Brahmins are, in a sense, running away from the lower groups who are trying to catch up with them.

The form and pace of Westernisation of India varied from region to region and from one section of population to another (Srinivas, 1985: 51). For instance one group of people became westernised in their dress, diet, manners, speech, sports and in the gadgets they used while another absorbed western science, knowledge and literature, remaining relatively free from Westernisation in externals. For example, Brahmins accepted the dress and appearance (tuff giving way to cropped hair), sending their children to westernised schools, using gadgets like radio, car, etc., but they did not accept the British diet, dancing, hunting, and freedom from pollution. This distinction is, however, only of relative emphasis. It is not a clear-cut distinction.

Srinivas prefers the term 'Westernisation' to 'Modernisation' (whereas Daniel Lerner, Harold Gould, Milton Singer, and Yogendra Singh prefer 'Modernisation' in place of 'Westernisation.' He considers the later term as subjective and the former term as more objective (*Seminar*, 88, 1986: 2). The so-called 'rationality of goals' in modernisation could not be taken for granted because human goals are based on value preferences. As such, rationality could only be predicted of the means and not of the ends of social action.

Scholar's Support to the Concepts

Scholars like Bernard Cohn and Milton Singer have supported the validity of the concept of Sanskritisation on the basis of their empirical studies. Cohn had studied a village in eastern Uttar Pradesh in 1950s. This village consisted of two main castes—a dominant caste of Thakurs and a large untouchable caste of Chamars. The landless Chamars had tended to become sanskritised by adopting their landlord's (Thakur's) rituals at times of marriage and birth through education obtained in the local schools and through a rise in their income. On the other hand, many Thakurs had migrated to cities and became industrial workers, clerks and teachers, taking on in their dress and manner and in their religious outlook, what may be called a more westernised form of Hinduism. Thus, while upper caste was westernising its style of life and religious beliefs, the lower caste was sanskritising and assuming more traditional forms of ritual, practice and belief.

Singer (1967: 66) on the basis of his study of leading industrialists in the city of Madras found a different process of change (what he calls 'compartmentalisation') in the style of life and religious beliefs of lower and upper castes (as different from Srinivas's process of Sanskritisation and Westernisation). He found that there was a decline of fear of ritual pollution both in the office and factory. For example, different castes mixed freely in the factories, they ate at the same cafeterias, travelled in the same buses, and attended political rallies freely with one another. Brahmins and upper castes had even taken to work considered highly polluting, for example, the tanning of skins and hides. Singer called it the process of 'compartmentalisation'. There was no conflict in the work of upper castes in industry and their obligations as good Hindus. The two (factory situation and home situation) were separate spheres and had different standards of conduct and behaviour. For example, they used western dress, spoke English, and followed western customs in the factory, while at home they used Indian dress, spoke the local language and conducted themselves as good Hindus. This is what Singer called 'compartmentalisation'.

But Singer's view does not give any new explanation. Individual's behaviour varies from situation to situation is a known fact. This does not mean that there is compartmentalisation. In fact, there is a continuity. Even Cohn feels that compartmentalisation in Indian society is not different from continuity in the society. However, it can be accepted that in this continuity, there is conservative persistence of tradition. It is an active, dynamic continuity. And Singer accepts this fact (1967: 68). People adapt to new conditions.

Perception of the Concepts

The process of Sanskritisation indicates:

(a) a process of change;
(b) upward mobility of aspirations of lower castes to move upward in hierarchy; and
(c) attack on hierarchy and levelling of culture.

As regards attack on hierarchy, it is not only the lower castes but even the tribes and castes in the middle regions of the hierarchy which try to take over the customs and way of life of the higher castes. Thus, Brahmanical customs and way of life spread among all Hindus. Could this be called attack on hierarchy and levelling of culture? Harold Gould (1961: 965) has described it not as a process of cultural imitation *per se* but an expression of challenge and revolt against the socio-economic deprivations. Some scholars hold that it was an attack on hierarchy but it did not succeed in levelling of culture.

As regards the upward mobility, Yogendra Singh calls it 'contextual specific' connotation of Sanskritisation. This is because it explains the process of cultural imitation by lower castes of upper castes, which could be Rajputs, Jats, Brahmins, Baniyas, etc. In some places, tribes are reported to imitate the customs of the caste Hindus.

Lastly, as regards merely 'the process of change', Yogendra Singh calls it the 'historical specific' connotation of Sanskritisation. In this sense, it refers to the process in the Indian history which led to changes in the status of various castes or its cultural patterns in different periods of history. It is also indicative of an endogenous source of social change.

Usefulness of the Concepts in Understanding Social Change

The usefulness of the concept of Sanskritisation as a tool in the analysis of Indian society has been described by Srinivas himself as "greatly limited because of the complexity of the concept as well as its looseness" (*ibid*, 1985: 44). We may also point out certain deficiencies in the concept:

(1) Since the reference group is not always a Brahmin caste but in many cases it is the local 'dominant caste' (which could be a Rajput, Bania, Jat, etc.), the context of Sanskritisation varies not only in each model (that is Brahmin model, Rajput model, Bania model, etc.) but also within the same model from region to region. According to Yogendra Singh (1973: 8), this introduces contradictions in various 'contextual specific' connotations of Sanskritisation.

(2) Power and dominance have been integrated by Srinivas with the process of Sanskritisation. This introduces the structural element in the Sanskritisation model of social change. Srinivas has not made this explicit. He has maintained that many lower castes in the past ascended to higher positions and became dominant castes either through royal decrees or through usurping the power. This means that without going through the process of Sanskritisation too, lower castes can rise in the social scale through structural changes, that is, through conflicts and war, through rise and fall of power, or through political stratagems.

(3) The concepts of Sanskritisation and Westernisation primarily analyse social change in cultural and not in structural terms. Sanskritisation involves 'positional change' in the caste system without any structural modification.

(4) Zetterberg (1965: 40) is of the opinion that Srinivas's two concepts are 'truth asserting' concepts. This connotation is often vague. Srinivas himself has said that Sanskritisation is an extremely complex and heterogeneous concept. It would be more profitable to treat it as a bundle of concepts than as a single concept. It is only name for a widespread cultural process.

(5) Srinivas's model explains the process of social change only in India which is based on the caste system. It is not useful for other societies.

(6) These concepts do not lead to a consistent theory of cultural change. Even their nominal definitions are devoid of theory. Zetterberg (1965: 40) has said that these two concepts can be appropriate of inappropriate, effective or worthless, but never false or true.

(7) Harper treats this concept as a *functional* concept distinct from a *historical* concept of change.

(8) Yogendra Singh maintains (1973: 11) that Sanskritisation fails to account for many aspects of cultural changes in the past an contemporary India as it neglects the non-sanskritic traditions, which often are a localised form of the sanskritic tradition. McKim Marriott (1955: 196-97) also found such phenomenon in his study of a village community in India.

(9) In some parts of the country (like Punjab and former Sind), what was imitated by castes was not sanskritic tradition but the Islamic tradition. In Punjab, Sikkhism emerged as synthesis of the Hindu tradition with the Islamic movements of Sufism and mysticism.

All this points out that the two concepts developed by Srinivas indicate only the limited and not the complete change in India.

REFERENCES

Aiyappan, A. and Balratnum, L.K. *Society in India*, S.S.A. Publications, Madras, 1956.

Chanana, Dev Raj, "Sanskritisation and Westernisation in India's North West", *Economic Weekly*, Vol. 8 No. 9, March 4, 1961, pp. 409-414.

Cohn, Bernard S., "The Changing Status of a Depressed Caste" In McKim Marriott (Ed.), *Village India*, University of Chicago Press, Chicago, 1955.

Gould, Harold, "Sanskritisation and Westernisation: A Dynamic View", *Economic Weekly*, Vol. 13, June 24, 1961, pp. 945-50.

Ishwaran, K., *Change and Continuity in India's villages*, Columbia University Press, New York, 1970.

Srinivas, M.N., *Religion and Society Among the Coorgs of South India*, Clarendon Press, Oxford, 1952.

Srinivas, M.N., *Social Change in Modern India*, California Press, Los Angles, 1966.

Srinivas, M.N., *Caste in Modern India and Other Essays*, Media Promoters and Publishers, Bombay, 1962.

Srinivas, M.N., "A Note on Sanskritisation and Westernisation" in *Far Eastern Quarterly*, 15, pp. 481-496.

Singer, Milton, *Traditional India: Structure and Change*, Philadelphia, 1959.

Singh, Yogendra, *Modernisation of Indian Tradition*, Rawat Publications, Jaipur, 1983.

Weiner, Myron, *Modernisation: The Dynamics of Growth*, Higginbothans Ltd., Madras, 1967.

Zetterberg, Hans, *On Theory and Verification in Sociology*, Bedminster Press, New York, 1965.

17

Perspective for Rural Development

Introduction

Rural India is real India. Seventy-six per cent of the population lives in rural India. It produces about 165-170 million tonnes of food as well as agricultural raw materials like sugarcane, cotton, tobacco, groundnut etc., to feed the agro-industries. The contribution of village industries, too, is equally significant. Above all, rural India offers a vast domestic market for the goods produced in urban India. However, over the years, the quality of village life has deteriorated and poverty in all spheres has afflicted over 35 crores of people.

Development as a concept, when applied in the specific context of rural India, acquires a new meaning. Fundamentally, rural development signifies not only the aggregate development of the area but the development of the people living there. The objectives of development include sustained increases in per capita output and incomes, expansion of productive employment, greater equity in the distribution of the benefits of growth, and adequate provision of infrastructure and other amenities which promote socio-economic growth. It also includes the upgradation of the cultural level as well as value systems of the people living in rural areas.

Rural Development

Over the years, rural development has emerged as "a strategy designed to improve the economic, social and cultural life of a specific group of people living in rural areas." The objectives of rural development are multi-directional as well as multi-dimensional. It aims at increased employment, higher productivity, higher income, minimum acceptable levels of food, clothing, shelter, education, health, as well as a sound value system which is in keeping with the high cultural heritage of the country. In other words, the term "rural development" refers to all aspects of human development. It is a major part of the development strategy which is designed to serve the rural population.

Over the years, the village socio-economic fabric has undergone a profound change. More than 31 crores of rural people do not have an adequate income. Employment opportunities fall short of demand. Illiteracy and ignorance are rampant. Under-cultivation of land and its fragmentation have created new problems. Ecology has been degraded, and infrastructural facilities have not kept pace with the growth of the rural population which, moreover, is unorganised. A large number of marginal farmers and agricultural labourers are without any skill. More than 75 per cent are illiterate; 80 per cent live in unhygenic houses; nearly 30 per cent go hungry everyday; many villages do not have all-weather roads or safe drinking water. Rural India is divided into the rich and the poor. Only 22 lakh rich families in rural India have grabed all wealth and rule over 60 crores of rural people. The apathy of the villagers has been accentuated by the prevalence of social and deep-rooted caste hierarchy. Village politics has deteriorated following the dilution of the spiritual value system. To lift the people from this near-stagnant milieu of life, integrated rural development has acquired a new urgency. It is now the crore of development, and is a continuous process.

In order to alleviate the lot of the rural poor—the small and marginal farmers, landless labourers, rural artisans, women, tribals, etc.—the governments at the Centre and in the States have implemented a variety of programmes. Broadly speaking, these programmes are either beneficiary-oriented or promote the development of infrastructure. The former directly benefit individuals and their families, while the latter are directed at strengthening those infrastructural activities which have an indirect long-term impact on the socio-economic milieu of the rural population. There are, moreover, some time-bound programmes which are limited to small geographical areas. In a way, these programmes are economic-oriented, and touch only one aspect of rural development—improvement in the income generation of the beneficiaries. But the dilemma is still there: how to make life better for the rural poor without encouraging their migration to urban areas and, at the same time, enlarge their opportunities for work and for a better standard of life.

Rural development has assumed greater significance, particularly since the beginning of the Fifth Five-Year Plan. During the last 40 years, the Government has done more to alleviate rural poverty than to promote rural development. New programmes were introduced as and when the older ones lost their appeal or validity.

Numerous evaluation studies have referred to identical areas of weaknesses and shortcomings in the sphere of implementation. It has been stated that "the comprehensive strategy of rural development not only dovetails the schemes for provision of minimum needs (food, clothing, house) but....envisages a far-reaching transformation of the socio-economic structure including redistributive land reforms and the promotion of Panchayati Raj institutions."

The Seventh Plan document identified the weaknesses in the implementation of the poverty-alleviation programmes so far and outlined the strategy that would be followed in the Seventh Plan to make the anti-poverty programmes more effective and useful to the rural people.

Poverty Alleviation Programme

Poverty alleviation programmes have to be viewed in the wider perspective of socio-economic transformation in the country. While the present strategy of direct attack on poverty through specific poverty alleviation programmes is justified on account of insufficient percolation of benefits to the poor from overall economic growth, it should be appreciated that the strategy of direct attack on poverty cannot be sustained and would not yield the desired results, if the overall growth of the economy itself is slow and the benefits of such growth are inequitably distributed. For one thing, the resources and the capabilities needed for running such programmes cannot be generated in the system unless the economy itself is buoyant and there is a sustained increase in output. Secondly, the demand for gods and services produced by the poorer household enterprises rises significantly in response to the overall increase in incomes in the country so that the viability of these household enterprises depends critically on the sustained increase in national income. Further, it is necessary to ensure that the pattern of overall economic growth itself is such as to generate adequate incomes for the poorer sections through its greater impact on employment generation and on the development of the less developed regions. The programmes for poverty-alleviation should thus be regarded as supplementing the basic plan for overall economic growth, in terms of generating productive assets and skills as well as incomes for the poor.

The economic betterment of the poorer sections cannot be achieved without social transformation involving structural changes, educational development, growth in awareness and change in outlook, motivation and attitudes. The social framework should be such as to provide opportunities for the poorer sections to display initiative and to stand on their legs. Moreover, such a framework can ensure that the benefits of poverty alleviation programmes really reach the poor and are not frittered away through various leakages. Strict enforcement of land reforms and revamping of credit institutions can provide the necessary access to assets and resources for the poor as well as promote a more equitable social structure. Greater participation of the poor through the elected institutions at the grassroots level as well as through their own organisations is another means to achieve social change. Improvement of literacy and education, both through formal and non-formal means, and the imaginative use of various mass media for communicating useful information and knowledge as well as for changing the outlook of the people by instilling in them the egalitarian spirit, the urge for and confidence in achieving self-betterment through co-operative endeavour, are essential for spending up the process of socio-economic transformation.

Beneficiaries

Admittedly, there have been various deficiencies in the implementation of the poverty-alleviation programmes. However, there has been a distinct improvement in the actual implementation of these programmes over the Sixth Plan. The approach to the Seventh Plan reiterates the goal of bringing down the percentage of population below the poverty line to less than 10 by 1994-95. Therefore, the special programmes for income generation for the poor through assets endowment and wage employment for them will be continued at an accelerated pace during the Seventh Five Year Plan.

In view of the deficiencies noticed in the implementation of the Integrated Rural Development Programme (IRDP), it has been suggested that greater priority should be assigned to rural employment programmes by shifting resources away from IRDP. The argument is two fold. First, the household enterprises of the type visualised are inherently uneconomic and are in any case handicapped for lack of necessary infrastructure. Secondly, owing to the illiteracy and weak economic position of the beneficiaries and the existence of a chain of intermediaries, only a small portion of the intended outlay reaches the actual beneficiaries. Employment programmes on the other hand, it is argued, can provide/secure wage-income to the poor, through the creation of durable community assets.

However, the experience of the working of the poverty-alleviation programmes is by no means uniform in the country. In general, the performance of IRDP has been better in the relatively developed regions which are well provided with infrastructure and where level of awareness among the beneficiaries is high. Even in the less developed areas, performance has been satisfactory wherever special efforts have been made for undertaking the necessary follow-up measures and for greater involvement of people through their representatives.

As to the economic viability of the household enterprises, it should be noted that such enterprises are already in existence on a wide scale in the developed as well as the less developed regions. In fact, they are a major source of employment and income for the poor in rural areas—next only to land. But they suffer from various handicaps in regard to the supply of raw materials, access to credit, facilities for marketing etc. As a result, there is considerable exploitation of these households by the middlemen. Public intervention to provide the necessary services to these already existing enterprises would contribute to a substantial increase in their income. Government—sponsored programmes for the poor, such as dairy and poultry, account for only a small proportion of the total market for such products now, sometimes even less than one per cent.

The demand for such products, and for a number of other rural crafts, is highly responsive to increase in income and, therefore, there is no reason for pessimism about the prospects for income generation for the poor from such activities so long as overall economic growth is satisfactory. Besides, the possession of productive assets and skills confers other advantages such as economic security, social status and credit worthiness. Such activities are labour-intensive and not land-intensive and, therefore, typically suit the marginal holdings and the landless. Even though the capital-output ratios (investment per unit of output) for some of these activities are higher than that for crop production, they are still very much lower than for many of the small-scale industrial enterprises. In many cases, where traditional skills are available and remain underutilised for want of resources, the capital-output ratio turns out to be much lower than even for crop production. These activities, in general, required government support for resources, training in skills and marketing.

IRDP and employment programmes are not mutually exclusive. As it is, most of the IRDP beneficiaries supplement their incomes through wage earnings in agriculture as well as from projects under National Rural Employment Programme (NREP) and Rural Landless Employment Guarantee Programme (RLEGP). These activities supplement one another and together ensure a more stable flow of incomes to the poor throughout the year. The problem of ensuring maximum benefits to the target groups by minimising leakages is common for all the poverty-alleviation programmes and indeed for the rural development programmes in general. Apart from the necessary restructuring of the administrative set-up, there is no alternative to raising the awareness of the rural poor and involving representative institutions from below in the formulation as well as implementation of such programmes.

Cost Effectiveness

Cost-effectiveness of the programmes and minimisation of leakages should be the two guiding principles in the implementation of poverty-alleviation programmes. Economic viability should be understood primarily in terms of cost effectiveness, i.e., maximum income generation per unit of total expenditure incurred. This is to be distinguished from economic viability defined as level of investment sufficient to enable a family to cross the poverty line. The ability of a poorer household to cross the poverty line depends on its overall income, i.e., income from the poverty-alleviation programmes and other wage and non-wage incomes accruing to them.

Cost-effectiveness or efficiency of programmes depends to a considerable extent, on the nature of activities chosen. In view of the significant regional diversities in the country in regard to resource endowments, availability of infrastructure, administrative arrangement, etc. there needs to be sufficient flexibility in the choice of activities in different regions in keeping with the specific circumstances of the area concerned. One should thus expect considerable diversity in the mix of activities from region to region.

The total impact of the programme depends on the degree to which the different poverty-alleviation programmes, including the Minimum Needs Programme (MNP), are integrated with one another and with the overall development of the area. For example, endowment of land under land reform measures can enable a family to grow fodder for the animal given under the IRDP; development of house sites under MNP can be integrated with the construction of houses under NREP or RLEGP and *vice versa*, and both in turn integrated with the IRDP by developing worksheds and production estates around the housing complex. NREP and RLEGP can also be used extensively for raising productivity in agriculture through construction of fields channels for irrigation and for drainage.

To achieve the above objectives of cost-effectiveness and minimisation of leakages by imparting the necessary flexibility in the choice of activities and by achieving integration in the programmes, a three-pronged strategy is envisaged in the Seventh Plan.

(a) Poverty-alleviation programmes would be formulated and implemented in a decentralised manner with the participation of people at the grassroots level through village panchayats, panchayat samitis, zilla parishads, etc. Such an approach will contribute to the selection of projects suited to local conditions, and to the integration of poverty-alleviation programmes with area development. This framework will also help in the timely provision of services in their appropriate sequence and in ensuring that the benefits of such programmes really reach those for whom they are intended. The Working Group on District Planning constituted by the Planning Commission had recommended a gradual approach towards decentralisation for achieving the objectives of effective implementation of poverty-alleviation programmes and balanced regional development. During the Seventh Plan, decentralisation of the planning process and full public participation in development will be pursued on the lines suggested by the Working Group.

(b) The launching of a large number of programmes both through the normal sectoral efforts and other steps designed to cater to target-group household has resulted in multiplicity of organisations, leading to duplication of management efforts. Further, the delivery system at various levels has proved to be inadequate. The effective implementation of poverty-alleviation programmes would call for better planning at the district level involving various disciplines or department, tighter organisational set-up to ensure optimal use of resources and closer monitoring. A High-level Committee has been set up by the Planning Commission to review the existing administrative arrangements for rural development and poverty-alleviation programmes and to recommend an appropriate structural mechanism to ensure that they are planned in an integrated manner and effectively implemented. Measures will be taken during the Seventh Plan for strengthening, proper training and orientation of the local administrative machinery within the framework of an integrated administrative organisation.

(c) Keeping in view the limited absorptive capacity of the poorest households, the approach to the Seventh Plan has also emphasised the need for taking up group oriented activities for beneficiaries to the extent possible, through the promotion of co-operatives, registered societies, informal groups, etc., so that the economies of scale, inherent in some of these activities, especially in the provision of services, are fully realised while, at the same time, group initiative and effort of the poor are promoted. This is necessary to protect the beneficiaries from the adverse operation of market forces whether on supply of inputs or on the sale of their produce. The mass media will have to be geared for increasing awareness among the rural poor and for disseminating information, non-formal education and functional skills and knowledge required by them. For purpose of bringing about a greater degree of awareness among, and participation of beneficiaries, a central scheme is proposed to be launched for the organisation of the beneficiaries, both in terms of group-oriented economic activities and increased conscientisation. Further, voluntary agencies would be increasingly involved in the formulation as well as implementation of poverty-alleviation programmes during the Seventh Plan, especially for ensuring greater participation of the people.

Given proper project planning for the development of local infrastructure, the Panchayat make a positive contribution to increased agricultural productivity and improving the quality of rural living. Wage employment can create an effective demand for the wage goods produced in rural areas. An integrated agricultural and rural development strategy can lead to the avowed goal of higher employment, increased production alleviation of poverty, and rural development.

Some Observations

The experience of rural development programmes and projects initiated and implemented by the Central and State Governments, voluntary agencies, industrial houses and individuals, both at the macro and micro levels over the years, appears to confirm that:

(i) It is possible to develop rural areas under local leadership with a dedicated approach by awakening the rural people, by the exploitation of environmental resources and the development of infrastructural facilities, and by removing the cultural barriers to rural development, which is best achieved through education. A package of programmes aimed at the all round development of the target groups with enforced discipline and value systems would go a long way in sustaining development in rural areas.

(ii) Rural development is a continuous process, and a dedicated local worker or leader can bring about drastic changes in the living conditions of the rural poor.

(iii) Whenever the strident Kulak lobby develops some political clout, it uses it largely to garner benefits for the Kulaks in the form of cheaper credit, subsidised power, cheaper fertilisers and pesticides, high prices for their products, and so on. So, in the name of justice to rural India, the top 10 per cent of the rural rich grab the maximum benefits. In the process, rural India continues to suffer. Rural development programmes should guard against the strident Kulak lobby in rural areas.

(iv) It is possible to reach a large number of rural poor as well as target groups at a moderate cost and with reasonable expectations of acceptable economic returns. Towards this end, stress should be on the rapid development of agriculture and allied activities in the tertiary sector.

(v) If this is done, it would involve political commitment to a strategy for rural development and to the general policies necessary to support such a dynamic strategy. Political commitment is to be translated into reality by the target groups with the co-operation of others, particularly the well-to-do people in rural areas.

(vi) Low cost delivery systems for the supply of inputs on credit terms, for providing extension and marketing services, and for organising communal activities are of crucial importance if large number of the rural poor are to be reached. A greater use of special financial intermediaries, co-operatives, community groups and farmers' associations should be explored. In particular, regional rural banks, supported by other commercial banks, should play a catalytic role in the development of rural areas.

(vii) It is important to balance overall central control with decentralised regional and sectoral project planning. Rural development programmes require a degree of flexibility in design and in responding to the lessons of experience; but the flexibility must be within the limits of minimum national, regional or village standards and financial resources. Though village level, sector-wise and target group-wise planning is essential, block level planning should be given a good trial by improving the techniques of local planning.

(viii) Greater efforts should be made to integrate project management into existing and, if necessary, reformed central and local government organisations and procedures for providing the necessary momentum to rural development.

(ix) It is important to involve the rural poor and particularly the target groups in the planning and implementation of rural programmes. With their active co-operation, various productive and economically viable programmes can be successfully started and implemented in rural areas. This will go a long way in creating tangible assets as well in improving the living conditions of rural people.

(x) Increased training is necessary at the local level, particularly for development managers, regional and project planners, branch managers and the staff of bank branches, co-operative societies and extension agents. These people should lead the rural people and, in particular, the target groups, and motivate them for a united effort at rural development.

(xi) An equitable and adequate provision should be made for the recovery of costs so that funds for additional rural development programmes may flow back into the villages. This will provide the necessary momentum to rural development.

(xii) Technical packages have to be devised which are appropriate to the requirements of small farmers, rural artisans and tiny industries based on adaptive national research. Adaptive technology is a forerunner of development.

(xiii) It is necessary to improve knowledge of local natural resources and provide an improved flow of information as a basis for a realistic national, regional, district and village planning.

(xiv) Although increases in output can be achieved with existing technology, increases in productivity will require new technology which is suitable for use by small farmers, tiny entrepreneurs and rural artisans. In particular, educated rural youth need appropriate guidance in channelling their energy productively for the betterment of the rural community, in this way they would contribute to national development. Educated rural youth will provide the necessary leadership for rural development.

(xv)   The pricing of agricultural and other rural products has always been biased in favour of the urban consumer. In pricing agricultural and other rural products, the same considerations as are prevalent in industry should be made applicable. The prices of agricultural products should not only cover the cost and margin but serve as a cushion for possible crop failures, which are quite frequent in the rural setting in India.

(xvi)   The principle of treating agricultural labourers on par with industrial workers in the matter of reasonable wages and social security benefits must be accepted.

(xvii)   A crash programme of adult literacy must be mounted to educate agricultural labourers, so that they may organise themselves to protect their own interests.

(xviii)   An integrated approach to rural development has proved very beneficial in uplifting the rural areas from the existing apathy and at the same time, improving the living conditions of the rural poor. In this effort, the co-operation of the rural rich and upper castes is most essential. The target groups should be educated so that they may adhere to the principle of a small family norm and realise the importance of development.

The major premise of the anti-poverty programmes or rural development programmes is that benefits will flow to the weaker sections or the target groups. In the absence of comprehensive studies of the impact of the varied programmes on the weaker sections, it is rather difficult to judge whether the intended beneficiaries have, in fact, gained from these significant public interventions across the country. Partial studies present a mixed picture. The weaker sections did benefit under some of the programmes and not under others.

The progress of rural development in India is marked by instances of achievements on one side and marred by disturbing shortcomings on the other. While blooming fields and highly productive livestock reflect the prosperity of the farmers in some areas, the scenes of conspicuously low-productive farms, ill-fed animals and farmers struggling hard to make both ends meet are not rare either. The instability of output and income and the disparities in sharing the benefits of growth may still be broadly described as the chronic maladies of the Indian rural scene. The frequent incidents of drought and scarcity are still accepted as a part of life in most rural areas. Disparities exist between different geographical areas and even within areas between different economic classes of people. While the success of the green revolution and the strategies of dairy development have raised the productivity of farms and have reduced the intensity of instability in some, they have widened disparities both among regions and within region among different segments of the rural society.

It has been found that funds are sometimes allocated on considerations other than the prescribed ones. Worse still, funds are not released on time, which makes it impossible to spend the allotted money, besides promoting spending in a hurry, leading to waste and infructuous expenditure. Above all, the bureaucracy is still dominated by the upper caste and the relatively well off members of society, brought up in urban environment and with urban orientation, who are unmoved by, and are indifferent to, rural poverty. And they seldom feel the urgency of the need for fighting the abysmal poverty of the rural poor, who include most members of the scheduled castes and tribes. More importantly, it is difficult to have the right type of men who are in sympathy with the poor in the villages and who recognise the imperative necessity of fighting the scourge of poverty. The anti-poverty programmes are not, to be sure, exercises in gratuitous benevolence. They are generally connected with productive work. Even when they are not and are in the nature of welfare work, they make for social peace, without which no orderly progress is possible, particularly in developing countries which require social peace for faster growth and where, paradoxically enough, social peace is hard to maintain. The anti-poverty programmes have to be continued with a clear-cut reorientation and stress on production and productivity to create a suitable climate for development in rural areas.

In Perspective

A pragmatic approach to rural development can be made only if the Central Government and State Governments concentrate on strengthening the rural infrastructure, on regulating land laws, providing marketing avenues for goods, fixing fair prices for both inputs and outputs, and creating a proper climate for the growth of labour-intensive works in rural areas. The main responsibility for rural development—mobilising resources, supplying inputs, opening up marketing avenues, deployment of funds—should be entrusted to rural regional banks, rural branches of commercial banks and co-operatives. Voluntary organisations, industrial houses and others should take the responsibility of education, health care, motivation, training and other disciplines. All funds have to be channalised through banks/co-operatives, and they should be given the necessary support by other institutions. The government should discontinue all welfare fringe benefits for the people. The same money should be utilised to create productive as well as protective tangible assets. Though rural development is a continuous process, the initial development effort may be phased and planned. During the first phase, the most backward villages should be taken for micro-level development. In the second phase, medium level villages should be taken up for development. Finally, the well-to-do villages. In this way, rural development will gather momentum. Once it reaches the take-off stage, the strategy of development has to be suitably modified to fit it into the requirements that may then emerge.

This programme of rural development will open up increasing employment opportunities in rural areas rather than create a hierarchy of employment opportunities in urban areas. Second, villager's participation will be forthcoming in a large measure. Third, new marketing opportunities will be created for consumer goods. Fourth, the awareness so generated would be conducive to rapid growth. Finally, this will reduce non-development expenditure considerably.

To-day, rural development has been done more by urban and middle class people with the concurrence of rural vested interests. Trickle down scheme has failed, failed miserably. As such, rural India, paradoxically became poorer, while a small segments amassed wealth. In the result, the rank and file of rural poor swelled to well over 41 crores, there is an exponential growth of unemployment, prices are soaring and poverty is growing, matched by growth of corruption in the administration, criminalisation of politics and debasing of value systems. Over the years, terrorism, corruption, communalism are spreading with ease. The growth achieved in some segments has pushed the country into a debt trap.

In such a grim situation, the administration, design and strategy of rural development should be entrusted to village panchayats. Let the Gram Sabha raise the resources and with the co-operation of the people and the state achieve rural development on an ongoing basis. Panchayats, co-operatives, banks and schools should be the corner stones of rural development.

Each sector should give top priority to growth, productivity, stability, awareness, motivation, participation and population reduction. This should be followed by education, health care, character building, value system, consolidation and unity. The third priority would be the eradication of social evils such as drinking, smoking, drugs, etc., which are now constraints on growth and are injurious to health. At the socio-cultural levels, the right type of education will be effective in giving the necessary push to the rural development movement. But much depends upon organisational resources and political and entrepreneur skills.

A national debate has been initiated on the question of strengthening the Panchayati Raj Institutions to enable them to function as vibrant instruments of democracy and local self-government at the villages. Necessary legislative measures are under consideration for the purpose.

The present strategy of direct attack on rural poverty through the existing major programmes of self-employment and wage-employment will be continued and diversified.

NREP and RLEGP will be merged into the new Jawahar Rojgar Yojana to make a single programme. The implementation will be decentralised on the basis of revised guidelines. Government of India will fund 75 per cent of the cost of the scheme and the states will contribute 25 per cent from their resources.

The new Rojgar Yojana introduced for the first time and named after Jawaharlal Nehru is to be launched in 120 backward districts. The guidelines for the selection of the district have been worked out. This will allow fuller employment opportunities to at least one member of each family living below the poverty line in these districts. A special provision of Rs. 2,100 crores has been made in the Budget of this scheme in addition to allocation under the existing employment programmes.

Efforts are being made to strengthen the professional competence of DRDAs. Young professionals from reputed management institutions are being deputed to selected DRDAs on a pilot basis to prepare resource survey of the area and take readily implementable projects. At the state level, Planning Cells are being strengthened to effectively co-ordinate activities of various departments with programmes of IRDP. Special programmes like development of sericulture, fisheries, fruit and vegetable growing, garment making, assembly of electrical and electronic goods etc. are being promoted on project basis.

Rural industrialisation will be the key to greater diversification of IRDP. With the shift in emphasis to the secondary sector, the major concern under the programme has to be on marketing the products of the IRDP beneficiaries. State governments have been advised to review and strengthen the infrastructure for marketing. A Marketing Cells has also been set up in CAPART and it will be taking up the constancy and advisory functions not only for voluntary organisations but also to various other IRDP groups set up through DRDAs.

In order to strengthen the Computerised Rural Information System Programme (CRISP) which has become operational during the year, it is proposed to develop a technical support organisation at the state level. The main functions of this support system will be to take over on-going process of software enhancement, training of staff and general technical support to DRDAs. States have been advised to identify a state level electronic corporation or a computer directorate which can be the nodal agency for this purpose.

In the field of land reforms, one of the major tasks in the coming years will be to concentrate on speeding up disposal of pending litigation cases on ceiling surplus lands by setting up special tribunals and complete the distribution of all available surplus lands to the rural poor. The other items of work relate to ensuring possession of land to the allottees of surplus land, restoration of alienated tribal lands to the tribals and updating of land records.

The Technology Mission on Drinking Water is expected to complete its task by March, 1990. It is expected that all the major goals of the mission will be largely achieved by that time.

Concurrent Evaluation

Besides monitoring the performance of the various programmes through periodical returns and field visits by senior officers, concurrent evaluation studies in respect of the major programmes are being undertaken by the department with the help of reputed research institutions. The aim is to ascertain the areas of concern and to improve/streamline implementation of the programme.

- Two rounds of concurrent evaluation of IRDP have already been taken up during September 1985—October 1986 and January 1987—December 1987. Reports on the main findings of these concurrent evaluation studies have been published. Corrective measures were taken on the basis of the finding of the survey.

- The third round of the concurrent evaluation of IRDP is proposed to be undertaken from January 1989—December 1989 with a revised and enlarged sampling frame and household schedules.
- Concurrent Evaluation of Rural Water Supply Programme was taken up during October 1986—September 1987. Report on the findings of the survey for this period is in the pipeline. The quarterly and half-yearly reports on the findings of the survey have already been published. The second round of the Concurrent evaluation is proposed to be undertaken soon.
- Concurrent Evaluation of NREP was taken up from November, 1987 to October, 1988. Quarterly and half yearly reports on the main findings of the survey have been published. On the basis of the findings, necessary corrective measures are being introduced.
- Similar studies in respect of DPAP and DDP and other rural development programmes are also proposed to be taken up.

Eighth Plan Policy Perspectives

The developmental strategies in the Eighth Five Year Plan are still to emerge but some ideas of the Planning Commission's thinking are available from its paper on 'Eighth Plan: Perspectives and Issues'. From this document, it appears that the Plan will place emphasis on creation of productive work on a large scale in agriculture and related activities and in villages and small industries, through massive efforts at skill formation and technological upgradation on farms and industries. In the field of agriculture, more diversification in terms of activities and regions will be aimed at and with the help of scientific research, efforts will be made to cross the humps in crops where significant productivity gains have already been achieved.

Inter-regional productivity differentials will be sought to be overcome, with emphasis on improved land and water management strategies and formulation of regional agriculture plans, on the basis of agro-climatic regions. Emphasis on agro-climatic, regional planning will also entail detailed attention to non-crop-based agriculture, including dairying, horticulture, poultry, fishery and forestry. Rural development programmes will have to be more closely integrated with related sectors on an area-wise basis. Agro-climatic regional programmes will have to organise land-use as between crop-production and other agriculture activities, on the basis of regional specialisation of agricultural crops. Agro-climatic regional projects will provide planning back-up but the details will have to be integrated with the district and state level plans.

Looking Ahead

The experiences of government programmes, voluntary agencies, industry and the financial intermediaries, particularly banks, in the task of rural development bring important issues and problems into focus. In fact, these hurdles have been responsible for none-too-impressive performance of rural development. Many explanations are offered for the failure of special programmes for the weaker sections—IRDP, NREP, 20-Point Programme, etc.—to make any significant impact on the magnitude of poverty and unemployment. The failure is attributed to the technocratic approach, administrative inefficiency, lack of motivation and urban bias of political leadership and bureaucracy, organisational weakness, non-application of refined management techniques and faulty delivery system. Hesitant approach to decentralisation of planning and decision-making and the consequent absence of people's participation, *ad hoc* and piece meal approach, inadequate attention to forward and backward linkages and lack of co-ordination amongst implementing agencies at the local (district) level are also emphasised as being responsible for poor results. Several case studies have established the validity of one or all of the above explanations. Although, some programmes have resulted into significant progress but resulted into inequality and gave birth to a neorich culture on the basis of western culture in Indian ways. As a result, poor in rural India continue to multiply and remain poor. Even though rural development has failed, it must succeed and rural development programmes should be taken up with enthusiasm, there should be no illusions about the inherent difficulties and complexities of rural development. The need of the hour is to implement policies effectively with courage and sincerity.

Economic Outlook

The Indian economy is in shambles. To rejuvenate it, a careful planning of imports is necessary so as to contain the trade deficit. Liberalisation policy has to be reversed, determined action is required to check prices. The continuous current account deficits over years have added to India's external indebtedness. However, India's external liabilities and debt service payments in relation to Gross Domestic Product have remained so far at reasonable levels. They call for drastic actions to keep them in manageable proportion. While estimating the net inflow of resources from abroad for the Eighth Plan, which aims at a higher rate of growth than was envisaged in the previous Plans, the policy of keeping external liabilities within the prudent limits should be maintained. With a contemplated target of 6 per cent rate of growth in GDP, it seems appropriate to plan for not more than 1.5 to 1.6 per cent of GDP as net inflow of resources from abroad during the next plan.

Broadly, the three major objectives of economic policy are growth, social justice which implies a more equitable distribution of income, and price stability. While all of these objectives are relevant for development policy, price stability has to be its chief focus. This does not, however, mean that it cannot contribute to the attainment of other major objectives. Credit and banking policy, particularly during the past two decades, through the various schemes of direct credit allocation and interest rate changes, has helped to promote such objectives as the promotion of the weaker sections of society and balanced regional development. Nevertheless, monetary policy is able to make a more effective contribution towards the objective of price stability than to the other objectives. The importance of price stability as an objective of economic and monetary policy is not, always, well-appreciated. In some situations there is perhaps a trade-off between growth and inflation in the very short run. Over a longer time period growth cannot however be bought with the aid of higher prices and there is no evidence to show that a higher growth rate is associated with a higher inflation rate. In India, quite the contrary is the case. In fact, it is price stability which provides the appropriate environment in which healthy and sustainable growth can occur. In an economy where a predominant proportion of the population operates in the unorganised sector with little protection against inflation, maintenance of price stability is intimately linked with social justice.

Population

Rapid population growth shows down development. It restricts investment in development. It also slow down the continued effort in raising the quality of life of the rural population. It not only enlarges unemployment, underemployment, but also affects productivity and ultimately production. During the eight decades, rural population rose by 315 million from 210 million in 1901 to 525 million in 1981. The growth was highest at 87 million in 1971-81 decade as against 78 million in the previous decade. At this rate, the level of population is likely to be around 620 million in 1991 an 725 million in 2001. As a result, the land resources available for agriculture and allied activities will be shrinking during the next two decades. Two serious consequences will be rapid for deforestation of land under forests. It means that about 200 million more people within the age group of 20 will be added during the next two decades. On the present reckoning, the population below poverty line in rural areas is expected to be around 410 million in 1989 as against 271 million in 1984-85. Growth of rural population will, therefore, have to be checked drastically so that the impact of rural development becomes meaningful and effective. The growing pressure of population on land will indeed lead to a deterioration in the rural employment situation. Increase in population during the next two decades makes additional demand for about 65-70 million tonnes of food, 180-200 lakh tonnes of milk, 8,500 million eggs, 16-20 lakh tonnes of fish, 250-300 lakh tonnes of tea as well as social demands like health—6,800-7,500 additional hospitals, doctors health, visitors, and lakhs of health centres, particularly in rural areas and 15 lakhs of educational institutions with particular stress on technical education in rural areas over, 60,000-75,000 bank offices and additional recreational and cultural facilities, additional open space for play grounds, gardens and zoos etc., and more employment opportunities have also to be created to the teeming millions, who are likely to be thrown out of land or surplus labour. The net increase of 192 million in rural areas during the next decades means more divisions in land, the main supporter of rural living. The pressure on land is going to be quite tremendous. Efforts should be made to slow down the population growth by all religions, castes and the poor. The country has to adopt one child policy for survival.

Structure

The causes of rural poverty are structural in nature. Between 1964-65 and 1974-75, the number of rural households has increased by 11.7 million or 17 per cent, from 70.4 million to 82.1 million, and further to 90.87 million in 1981. On this reckoning, it is likely to increase to over 120 million by 1990. They do not stem from what its people have done or not done, but from the social and economic relations that prevail in rural India. The National Commission on Agriculture (1976) has pinpointed the need for reordering of the agricultural structure for the establishment of a prosperous and egalitarian rural society. On the one hand, only 11.5 per cent of farmers own over 52.5 per cent of land, another 32 per cent cultivators own 35.7 per cent of land, and 56.5 per cent own only 12 per cent of cultivated land. Small and medium cultivators account for over 84.5 per cent of total cultivators. A far more important structural hurdle is the excessive and growing fragmentation of land holdings. Consolidation operation should be given high priority in irrigated areas and in the command areas of irrigation projects.

According to the 1981 census, there were 5.55 crores agriculture labourers constituting 24.9 per cent of total working force and 37.5 per cent of total agriculture workers. There were 10.48 crores of scheduled castes and 5.16 crores of scheduled tribes in India. They formed 23.6 per cent of the population. Class and caste barriers have suppressed the people from improving their living conditions. This can be interpreted as growing proletarianisation within the rural economy. The need of the hour is rural integration.

Land

The most valuable assets in the rural economy is land. However, land is limited. The total land area is 328.8 million hectares, of which, 55.4 per cent available for cultivation. It is estimated that the land available for cultivation may increase by 7.1 million hectares to 158.0 million hectares by 2000 A.D. Of which, 78 per cent is likely to be under foodgrains and 22 per cent under non-foodgrains. On account of soil erosion, waterlogging and salinisation at least two-third of the cultivated land is in poor health. Further one-third has become unproductive. While, soil erosion is caused by deforestation, waterlogging and salinisation is due to the absence of adequate drainage. With the steady erosion in the land not available for cultivation, the pressure on land for human settlement will increase in coming decades pushing the land prices higher and higher. Additional demand for land will be forthcoming for strengthening rural infrastructure, building additional houses, recreational centres, locating new agro-based industries and for schools, storehouses, dispensaries, etc.

Land Holdings

With the increase in rural population during the next two decades, it is estimated that the marginal and small holders are expected to increase by 24.70 million households from 62.13 million households (74.4 per cent of total farm households) to 86.83 million household (80.4 per cent). With further division in land holdings, there will be a sharp increase in the population group of agricultural labourers. The average holding is likely to decline to less than 0.5 hectare as against 1.7 hectares in 1982. With a view to check this from further deterioration, inheritance laws have to be suitably amended so that there is no further sub-division in land holding in particular at its earliest and at the same time, fragmented holdings be consolidated into economically viable units for better farming and increased production of food as well as non-food, particularly cash crops.

Agricultural Census—Operational Holdings Distributions

Sl. No.	States/UTs	Operational holdings less than 2 hectares and operated area as % of total						Operational holdings over 10 hectares and operated area as % of total					
		1970-71		1976-77		1980-81		1970-71		1976-77		1980-81	
		No.	Area	No.	Area	No.	Area	No.	Area	No.	Area	No.	Area
1	2	3	4	5	6	7	8	9	10	11	12	13	14
States													
1.	Andhra Pradesh	65.5	19.3	66.9	22.1	72.7	29.3	4.3	30.7	3.4	24.8	2.1	18.8
2.	Assam	80.8	40.6	82.2	42.6	82.2	42.7	0.4	15.1	0.3	14.0	0.2	14.2
3.	Bihar	79.0	29.7	84.6	37.7	86.7	41.6	1.8	20.6	0.8	13.2	0.6	10.5
4.	Gujarat	42.9	9.8	44.1	11.1	45.9	12.9	.9.6	36.5	7.2	29.1	5.9	24.8
5.	Haryana	46.3	10.7	49.5	11.4	51.4	13.4	8.1	34.2	7.2	33.6	6.4	31.3
6.	Himachal Pradesh	78.5	33.5	76.7	33.6	77.2	35.3	1.1	17.1	1.2	12.8	1.1	12.7
7.	Jammu and Kashmir	88.6	56.7	86.7	52.0	87.2	53.6	0.1	2.5	0.2	6.6	0.2	4.3
8.	Karnataka	54.1	15.6	56.7	17.2	59.0	19.4	6.2	31.7	5.2	28.7	4.3	24.5
9.	Kerala	93.2	56.7	95.7	62.3	96.1	63.6	0.2	12.6	0.1	8.9	0.1	7.2
10.	Madhya Pradesh	48.6	9.6	50.7	11.4	51.9	12.4	9.3	41.2	7.5	35.9	6.8	34.0
11.	Maharashtra	42.8	8.8	45.9	11.2-	52.0	15.8	10.4	10.0	7.4	31.1	4.4	21.6
12.	Manipur	83.8	62.9	84.4	62.6	82.8	59.4	0.3	0.4	Neg.	0.3	Neg.	0.2
13.	Orissa	76.2	38.5	75.7	40.3	73.6	37.9	1.4	12.5	1.0	9.2	0.9	7.4
14.	Punjab	56.5	15.0	60.6	15.9	38.6	10.2	5.0	26.9	4.1	26.2	7.2	29.2
15.	Rajasthan	43.8	7.2	48.5	8.5	49.0	9.6	14.0	57.1	11.6	52.2	10.9	49.6
16.	Sikkim	—	—	59.5	21.0	68.7	28.2	—	—	2.9	20.9	1.6	13.1
17.	Tamil Nadu	79.7	37.6	83.0	41.9	86.0	47.1	1.1	13.0	0.8	10.4	0.5	8.7

1	2	3	4	5	6	7	8	9	10	11	12	13	14
18.	Tripura	88.3	53.7	83.2	49.2	88.6	59.1	0.2	8.7	0.2	8.2	0.1	6.4
19.	Uttar Pradesh	84.0	41.9	85.8	45.4	86.9	48.3	0.7	9.9	0.5	7.4	0.4	6.2
20.	West Bengal	82.3	47.2	87.1	55.6	89.3	60.4	0.08	4.6	0.04	4.0	0.02	3.7
	All India	69.6	20.9	72.7	23.5	74.5	26.3	3.9	30.9	30	26.2	2.4	22.8

*Notes:*1. Percentage of Marginal (below 1 ha.) and Small (1 to 2 ha.) holdings has increased between 1970-71 and 1980-81 in all states except Himachal Pradesh, Jammu and Kashmir, Manipur, Orissa and Punjab.

2. Percentage of large holdings (10 ha. and above) has increased in the states of Jammu and Kashmir and Punjab.

3. Information is given above for only those states with land ceiling legislation.

4. In regard to the change in the average size of operational holdings in different size classes between 1970-71 and 1980-81 (for Sikkim between 1976-77 and 1980-81), the position is as follows:

Land Reforms

If land reforms is to serve as an effective instrument of planned social change—i.e., eliminate constraints on growth of agricultural production and secure social justice—it is necessary to have a fresh look at its theory and practice in the country. Land in rural India has already undergone minute sub-division and fragmentation as a result of partition and population pressure. There has been an increasing struggle for living space leave alone land for cultivation. In the process, the land prices are shooting up from one year to another. With a view to create and improved and equitable system of agriculture, land reform must be followed by appropriate institutional and organisational arrangements that will help to organise the rural population for each successive stage of rural development. The economic balance can and should be shifted in favour of the small and marginal farmers mainly by helping them increase their productivity and by other concomitant measures.

Agriculture

Although, food production has gone up, it has, however, been neutralised by population growth. The average per capita availability for consumption has stagnated at 460-470 grams per day. This average consumption conceal a severe mal-distribution of available foodgrains. A large segment of rural people are not only affected by under nourishment but also by mal-nutrition. This calls for increasing food production and also augment the purchasing power of the rural poor to avail nutritious food.

Extension of minor irrigation, application of modern technology are the means to increase yields of all crops and thereby substantially increase agricultural production. Marginal and small farmers lands should be consolidated into viable agricultural units and cultivated and managed on the principle of co-operative and collective farms— irrigation land 10-15 hectares, dry land 150-200 hectares. Supplementary jobs in village crafts, forestry, animal husbandry, piggery, fisheries, etc. should be encouraged and developed. Productivity of food and non-food crops should be almost doubled with the application of scientific methods and technology in order to be self-reliant in food production and produce adequate surplus for exports. From the point of view of exports, there is a special need to step up production of plantation products by extending their area as well as improving their yield per hectare. Co-operatives or commercial banks shall guide the farmers in their production efforts, storage and marketability. Village panchayats will have to play a lead role in regard to development of agriculture, village industry, forestry, animal husbandry, horticulture, sericulture and other allied activities.

Irrigation

As at end 1987-88, 74.29 million hectares was under gross irrigation (net being 61.5 million hectares). However, a recent study by the Administrative staff college of India has estimated that around 10 million hectares of canal irrigated land has become water-logged and therefore, is no longer fit for cultivation. Another 25 million hectares is threatened with salinity. It means that 68.8 per cent of the irrigated area is in-danger. In

Size class	Constant	Marginal Decrease (Less than 10%)	Large Decrease (Over 10%)	Marginal increase (Less than 10%)	Large Increase (Over 10%)
Marginal (below 1 ha)	Uttar Pradesh	Assam, Bihar, Karnataka, Orissa, Rajasthan, Sikkim, Tamil Nadu, West Bengal	Kerala	Andhra Pradesh, Gujarat, Haryana, Himachal Pradesh, Jammu and Kashmir, Madhya Pradesh, Maharashtra, Manipur	Punjab, Tripura
Small (1 to 2 ha)	Gujarat, Himachal Pradesh, Rajasthan, Uttar Pradesh	Bihar, Jammu and Kashmir, Madhya Pradesh, Maharashtra, Punjab, Sikkim, Tamil Nadu	Orissa	Andhra Pradesh, Assam, Karnataka, Kerala, Tripura, West Bengal	Haryana, Manipur
Semi-medium (2 to 4 ha)	Karnataka	Andhra Pradesh, Assam, Bihar, Gujarat, Himachal Pradesh, Jammu and Kashmir, Kerala, Madhya Pradesh, Maharashtra, Punjab, Rajasthan, Sikkim, Tamil Nadu, Uttar Pradesh	Orissa	Haryana, Manipur, Tripura, West Bengal	
Medium (4 to 10 ha)	Jammu and Kashmir	Andhra Pradesh, Assam, Bihar, Gujarat, Karnataka, Kerala, Madhya Pradesh, Maharashtra, Orissa, Punjab, Rajasthan, Sikkim, Tamil Nadu, Uttar Pradesh	—	Haryana, Himachal Pradesh, Tripura, West Bengal	Manipur
Large (over 10 ha)	—	Andhra Pradesh, Bihar, Gujarat, Karnataka, Madhya Pradesh, Punjab, Rajasthan, Uttar Pradesh	Himachal Pradesh, Kerala, Maharashtra, Orissa, Sikkim	Haryana, Tamil Nadu	Assam, Jammu and Kashmir, Manipur, Tripura, West Bengal

view of this imminent danger, proper scientific and technical methods be applied and the managerial problems be sorted out before embarking on fresh investment in irrigation. Every efforts should be made to reclaim the water logged and saline land with the adoption of new technology. Further, irrigation should not be considered in terms of short-term gains but planned for long-term and lasting benefits. It calls for judicious water management. Plans are in operation to provide irrigation facility to 45 per cent of net sown area by 2000 AD. If available techniques of minimising the loss of water through evaporation, sewage and over watering are fully used, the irrigated area can be easily increased by 50 per cent to 100 per cent. To introduce new plastic technology to cover the village tank beds for storage of water and build small bunds at intervals of half—a kilometer on streams and rivulets to store water for irrigation purpose. These measures go a long way in managing water for productive purpose.

Modern Technology

However, mere adoption of optimum crop pattern is not enough. The key to raising productivity and production of crops lies in the technology that is applied to crop cultivation. The HYV seed-fertiliser technology, that has proved successful since its introduction in the mid-sixties, is supposed to be scale-neutral in theory, but, in practice, it favours those farms and areas which are well-endowed with irrigation resource or have assured rainfall or access to irrigation facility. The technology succeeds to the degree that this critical condition is fulfilled. This has meant that the technology, from the very start, contained seeds of causing or exacerbating inequalities among farmers and among regions. These variations in growth and development have to be corrected through appropriate area-specific strategies. Otherwise, a large segment of the country will continue to be poor. The need of the hour is to reassess the feasibility of modern technology to rural development.

Forestry

Forests have multifarious uses. They meet the basic needs of the poor people in many ways. Development of forests will accelerate the momentum of rural development. With proper linkages forests will foster development. As at end 1986-87, only 10.7 per cent of land was under forest cover. In order to ensure balance in the eco-system, the land under forest must be raised. It is envisaged that additional 65.70 million hectare is expected to be brought under forest raising its share to 28.0 per cent by 2000 A.D. Reforestration is a must. Besides extended farms and social forests to meet the increased requirements of fuel, fodder, wood and other raw materials, Panchayats should be entrusted with the task of reforestation work within rural areas. The development of protected forests should be the responsibility of forest divisions.

Long-Term Planning

In the wake of massive growth of rural development programmes and the stress on rapid development of rural areas, in the post-Independence period, certain stresses and strains have developed. It is in this context that I would like to submit the need for formulation of a well-defined long-term rural development plan. The long-term plan will cover all facets of rural activities, production and conversion of the available resources to meaningful wealth and their equitable distribution to the community, while protecting as well as enriching the eco-system. Towards this end, India would do well to borrow more and invest the funds in carefully selected projects for generation of new wealth in rural areas. Until and unless rural areas produce a surplus to sell in the urban market, their economy will not improve. Further, the long-term planning should emphasise on launching non-farming projects in rural environment to absorb the surplus labour productively. If need be a reversal of economic activities has to be enforced. The ultimate objective of long-term planning should be to identify priorities for action concerning social and economic policy interventions, appropriate investments, and institutional changes. Thus, it would be enough to take care of debt servicing burden and for providing surpluses for re-investment. What is needed is the prompt implementation of selected projects.

Integrated Development Programme

Integrated programme for rural development should be formulated so that the living standards of people in rural and urban areas are continuously improved and the eco-system is enriched. This should be also linked with industrial development. Integrated development assessments calls for an understanding of the proximate and under lying physical and economic linkages between different levels and manners of resource use, and their socio-economic consequences. The extent to which the management skills, the knowledge and know-how, the scientific and technological resources could be harnessed should ultimately be left to the choice of the local people rather than to the manipulative coterie. Gunnar Myrdal has already given a timely warning, "In the absence of more discipline—which will not appear without regulations backed by compulsions—all measures for rural uplift will be largely ineffective."

Awareness

The Khadi and Village Commission (KVC) is a potential instrument of change. It has conceived to play and it has to play a transforming role, not merely a change in economic status, but creation of a new man with a yearning for self-reliance is the inspiring ideal of the Commission. What we need today is a result oriented approach, which puts a special responsibility on the implementing agency or individual. This calls for steps like simple procedures, target maintenance, "awareness to people" and energising rural institutions.

The object cannot be fulfilled if the programmes are forced on the rural masses from above. We have to win the hearts of the people. They must be fully involved in these programmes. A comprehensive plan for the upliftment of the rural areas for enabling the members of the rural community to take full advantage of the opportunities being created in near future may be prepared after consultation with the agencies primarily concerned with rural development. The idea is to create self-confidence in the rural masses and to make the people personally interested in the programmes of development. The vast unutilised energy lying dormant in the countryside should be harnessed for the welfare of the rural poor.

Group Effort

There is a need for promoting group co-operation among families living in a village. Promoting group effort without affecting the basic structure of land ownership can be achieved by an intelligent deployment of public policy instruments, involvement of Panchayati Raj institutions and community orientation to administrative co-ordination. At the same time, through minimum productivity and soil health care guidelines, it should be made clear that the right of land ownership does not include the right to abuse it and destroy or diminish its biological potential.

A mission mode of organisation which involves mechanisms for effective co-ordination and monitoring and for adoption of a systems approach may be good for tackling a multi-dimensional problem with unidimensional administrative structures. It is a method by which the return from investment from the available resources and the existing infrastructure can be optimised.

For example, irrigation water will increasingly become the most important limiting factor in several parts of the country. Water conservation and use can be organised at the state and village levels in a mission mode. A micro-level and location-specific approach is what is needed.

At the same time, better co-operation and co-ordination among the agencies working in the field of agriculture, industry and rural development is necessary. Group efforts compelled with trusteeship will not doubt change the rural scene. In this respect, the village panchayat has to play a pivotal role.

Leadership

The need of the hour is a benevolent leader like Chandragupta Maurya aided by able administrator like Kautilya for speedy uplift of rural people. There has to be more human touch, an approach closer to the people than to the insipid institutions that have enslaved them throughout the past. The leaders should not be allowed to float trusts in the name of the rural poor but for their acquiring additional power. All such trusts must be taken over by the government in the larger interest of people. The leadership at all levels should be enlightened, self-less benevolent, concerned for the rural poor, innovative, not interested in power or position. And at the same time, firm and innovative. More important task to get dedicated, able men at helm. The leaders should be exemplary to one and all.

Political Stability

Political instability hinders economic development in various ways. In short phase, food prices shoot up, garbage clearance affects, raw materials do not reach industries, finished good do not reach consumers. In fact, working of trade and industries stand paralysed. There will be transport bottlenecks. On the other hand, not only it wipes out the infrastructure facilities built up over the years, but also the gains of economic development. Political instability increases crimes and destroys property public as well as private created over the years. It throws people of the streets who should be given the basis necessities like food, clothing and housing. Above, all, rehabilitate the affected people from scratch. In a way, political instability means burning both ends at the same time political stability depends on matured leadership, communal harmony and patriotism. The people living in India should live like Indians as a one nation. Feudalism and fanatisms should cease to exist and people should be aware of their rights and duties to the community and the country. Popple should give up their narrow mindedness and broaden their vision and attitude to mankind.

Democratic Decentralisation

Democracy means equal opportunities, discipline, tolerance and mutual regard. In a democracy changes are made by mutual discussion and persuation and not by violent and/or unfair means. It goes without saying that for a real rural development, decentralisation is a must, be it in the area of economy, structural changes, institutional network and their re-orientation, planning process, industrial strategy etc.

Decentralisation in true sense envisages a devolution of decision-making authority both at the levels of the formulation and the implementation of plan and programmes within the framework of a given political, social and economic structure. It encompasses a field wider than mere administrative devolution which is pragmatic bureaucratic in nature. In its wider sense, decentralisation has to adopt to local conditions fully and respond to the local environment, local level activities suiting the needs, resources endowments and potential of a particular région, coupled with democratic process, the process of development is made much easier.

When we say, democratic decentralisation, we admit that there is centralisation of power. We start from the wrong end. In a democracy, the distribution of power, planning, discussion and development should be from base upwards. The Gram Sabha is the fundamental unit of democracy and not the Lok Sabha as it is to-day. The very expression of democratic decentralisation carries an odour of condenscension.

The prerequisite of successful democratic decentralisation is, therefore, to create a proper environment to bring a kind of attitudinal change among the people toward democratic development; to make them conscious about their rights and duties through various audio-visual aids at the grassroot levels. Thus, the rural development covers from village to village, town to town. On the whole, democratic decentralisation for rural development would mean working for a number of basic changes in the rural society, the basic concept of democracy as well as in the approaches being adopted for its development.

The Balwant Raj Mehta Committee emphasised the importance of local bodies from the development point of view aptly observed that:

"So long as we do not discover or create a representative democratic institution which will supply the local inter-supervision and care necessary to ensure that expansion of money upon local object conforms with the needs and wishes of the locality, invest it with adequate power and assign to it appropriate finances, we will never be able to evoke local interest and excite local initiative in the field of development."

Panchayati Raj

The network of panchayati raj institutions covers the length and breadth of the country today but not in the sense and manner they were meant to. Numerically and quantitatively there are myraids of these institutions dotting the entire landscape of our country. Powers and functions have been conferred on them by legislative enactments. There is, however, a feeling that these institutions have become moribund and that they have been donated of their promise and vitality. There is a legitimate question mark against these institutions, not because the constitutional promise has been abandoned nor because self-government is no longer an article of faith with us, not because we have lost faith in ourselves; but because we have allowed these institutions to be neglected, because we have failed to nurture them with the inputs and material and human resources necessary for them and because the operational claims and quest of political power have taken a heavy toll on the fundamental concept of self-government and public service.

The panchayati raj should be entrusted with the task of village administration, community development from decision, strategy to implementation.

Striking a balance between techno-economic viability and village identity in an optimum mix of demographic and geographical size should be a policy goal and practical endeavour keeping in mind that each village must be viewed as a unit of self-government. Optimisation of economic growth and social justice is bound to follow in the wake of village panchayats operating as units of self-government and as cradles of civic culture, social ethos, public education, poverty alleviation programmes, voluntary citizen action and constructive work. It will require considerable patience but it will pay handsome dividends.

The strengthening of the panchayati raj provides an opportunity for dealing with the management of local resources and local commons in a more meaningful and sustainable manner. The panchayati raj institutions should be organised as a part of the process of democratic decentralisation for building up the institutional edifice from the grassroots upwards and not as a gift of devolutionary process. Thus, the Indian villages and the Gram Sabha becomes the base of our democratic nation.

In fact, the Gram Sabha is the embodiment of direct democracy. It is time to restructure and redefine democracy from Gram Sabha upward to Lok Sabha and not vice-verse. In the process the real representatives of the people and not the dummy's head the nation.

The implementation of the programmes has of necessity to devolve on the "associate" organisations of people. The social programmes under panchayati raj can be handled by the chain of social organisations that can be set up such as Yuvak Mandals, Mahila Mandals, Bal Mandals and other functional groups of people. Economic activity has necessarily to be conducted as part of Sahakari Samaj through different specialised co-operatives inter-acting and cross fertilising mutually. Panchayati Raj and Sahakari Samaj are twin instruments for a common consummation. They can play their part only if they blossom in freedom and achieve mutual interdependence. A working group was appointed by the Ministry a short while ago which has recommended how co-ordination should be achieved between these two vital institutions so as to avoid conflicts and overlapping in effort. These recommendations will soon be put in operation. But ultimately their implementation will depend on the wisdom of the people themselves whose organs these are, whether they function as inter-dependent institutions for promoting the larger interests of the people or as feudal organs to battle against each other at the expense of the people.

Tests of Health in Co-operative Society

The co-operative society must progress in sound health if it is to discharge the role assigned to it in the economy of the country. This calls for clear criteria. For the present these may consist broadly of whether or not there is:

(1) Broad-based membership in the villages;

(2) Linking of credit, supplies and services with concrete production plans;

(3) Development of marketing and processing services;

(4) Spontaneous spread of the movement in the direction of the other sectors of the economy, more particularly industries;

(5) Pooling of savings by the community in co-operative institutions;

(6) Evolution of the federal organisation of co-operatives to guide and regulate institutions below;

(7) Help offered by the strong in the co-operative sector to the weaker members;

(8) Inter-relationship and cross fertilisation between different sectors of the co-operative movement;

(9) Progressive growth of competence in non-official leadership in the movement;

(10) Cohesion, mutual aid and co-operative self-help in the community and participation by members in formulation of policies and review of action.

Co-operative Society and Integrated Development

The socialist pattern in India visualises a strong public sector controlling the basic means of production. There will also be a strong private sector whether or not government wills it; for the private sector depends on private initiative. In a democracy growing from a feudal and colonial base, private sector cannot but have a major pressure of its own to exert for its own survival and promotion. The public sector as has already been mentioned earlier, can tend in certain context to foster totalitarian trends of the extreme left. The private sector left to itself cannot but have feudal trends to the extreme right. The two sectors are vital as they are for national existence in the context of the fast advancing sputnik age, cannot be left free to become a menace to freedom and initiative. A growing co-operative sector as an active balancing force between the two grows thus to be an inevitable must. To play this strategic role, the co-operative sector must develop the requisite organisational strength and technical competence to provide services at economic cost. It should not grow to a monopoly at the cost of the community. Co-operation between members of a community can act like magic.

The socialist pattern demands deduction in inequality between citizens. It calls for an egalitarian economy. It demands reduction in the wide disparities that now rule. Co-operation which literally means operation by equals, grows thus to be the yardstick for the growth of our people in the democracy we have set as our goal. The essence of Community Development is the extension of the concept of the joint family till it encompasses the nation as a whole. Joint family means co-existence of the genius and the moron, the artist and the buffoon with all the ramifications in between. Joint family cannot permit starvation, physical or spiritual for any member of the family however weak or unfit. Co-operative society means mutual aid between members of the joint family. It means aid by the strong to the weak so that the latter can rise to the level of the strong as equal members of the community. Co-operative Society and panchayati raj are but the means to the building of the joint family—the community. The development of the community will depend on the development in freedom of co-operative society and panchayati raj as the twin instruments of integrated development of the rural community. The goal is co-operation, unity, discipline, dedication and hardwork.

Other Measures

The most important aspects of rural development are the education of rural people, improving the health standards, bringing in new awareness towards benefits of small family and sanitation and motivating them towards whole-hearted participation in all developmental activities.

All ameliorative and welfare measures should be abolished and the said amount of money be invested in projects generating additional employment opportunities as well as in increasing production. Maximise the output per labour, capital to meet the crisis of tomorrow. This could be done by building up character, identity, better utilisation of resources and adequacy of administration and leadership. Totally eradicate the permissive atmosphere prevailing everywhere in the society. This is an up-hill task.

Politics should be an effective tool of development rather than seat of power. This calls for various changes in the structure and organisation of rural society. The foremost aspect is rejuvenating values system governing life. Particularly, inculcating 'discipline,' 'truthfulness,' 'perseverance,' 'honesty,' 'dedication,' 'patriotism and 'service.' The dominating features of demographic development is the sharp rise in the number of persons in the working age group.

To accelerate the rate of productive employment, productive work opportunities will have to be generated on a very large scale in agriculture and related activities and in village and small industries. This will require a massive effort at skill formation, technological upgradation in rural areas and small towns, in farms, artisan households and small manufacturing units. Hence, it is now an economic necessity to promote quality improvements in education, vocationalisation, training and re-training programmes for workers and the re-orientation of the scientific and technological infrastructure to serve the needs of rural areas and the unorganised sector.

The real task is to ensure that no person anywhere in the country is held back from improving his lot because of the lack of education or appropriate technical skills. This aim must be translated into specific programmes for education, training, technology development and scientific research.

Elimination of poverty on a durable basis and rural development on ongoing basis can be achieved only by ensuring that all rural households, especially those currently below the poverty line, (Rs. 9,800 per annum per family of 5) have an entitlement to productive viable assets and skills which provide them gainful employment and adequate earnings to enable them to live above subsistence level. Hence, all the avenues which would facilitate removal of poverty or arrest the process of poverty in rural areas need to be explored. The attack on rural poverty and emphasis on rural development calls for a multi-pronged approach administered through a nodal agency which is really committed to the important task of rural development.

Results

Otherwise, more and more power will be monopolised by a select few cutting at the roots of social justice to the majority of rural poor. And, what is more, the percentage of rural poor may increase to over 60 per cent as against 50.8 per cent in 1989. In absolute terms, over 440 million rural people will continue to remain poor, in spite of huge investments. Poverty is however still the No. 1 problem. Rural people may continue to live lacking bare essentials face grim, ordeal of hunger, malnutrition, disease, illiteracy and wise noble living conditions. Rural isolation, unemployment and poverty are closely linked. If not checked, the country may disintegrate lose national identity and character, development of more and more permissive society, loss of rural heritage, spread of corruption, scarcity of food ecological imbalance and disruptions, natural calamities, spread of disease spread of violence and agitations, (as it is erupting in the various parts of the country and the world) and crisis of civilised culture and mankind, like bad money drives away good money, bad elements may drive away good things from the rural society and cultural heritage.

In the ultimate analysis, all efforts towards improving the standards of living in rural areas through varied rural development programmes may result in inequality and millions of rural poor knocking at urban centres for food, cloth and work. This may give rise to law and order problems took. What is more, all efforts of rural development and planning will be washed away. Frustration looms large and the rural India stands disintegrated.

The principle components of rural development are coined in 20 words forming I promise rural welfare which is in consonance with the process of rural development. It means as follows:

I	Increase in irrigation potential	(1)	R	Rural Electrification	(11)
P	Pulses Oilseeds Development	(2)	A	Afforestation	(12)
R	Rural Development	(3)	L	Lever for Family Welfare	(13)
O	Observe Equitable distribution		W	Wealth through Health	(14)
	of Land	(4)	E	Eradicating Malnutrition	(15)
M	Minimum Wage Payment	(5)	L	Literacy Promotion	(16)
I	Independence to Bonded		F	Fair Price Shops	(17)
	Labour	(6)	A	Accelerate rural Industrial	
S	Scheduled Castes Welfare	(7)		Growth	(18)
E	Essential Water Supply	(8)	R	Restrain Anti-Social Elements	(19)
R	Rural Housing	(9)	E	Efficiency in rural sector	(20)
U	Urban Housing	(10)			

This is as it should be, as our progress to be rapid and enduring has to be based on the development of rural resources.

If rural poverty and degradation of the environment is not tackled properly, it will push urban areas also into a poverty trap. So, a corrective step is necessary right now.

We may conclude by quoting Pandit Jawaharlal Nehru, "whatever plan we might make, the test of its success is how far it brings relief to the millions of our people who live on a bare subsistence level, that is, the good and advancement of the masses of our people," and pledging to put this test whatever development plans we make for rural upliftment.

18

Political Participation and Rural Development

I

The concepts of politicisation, political participation, and political communication are cognate or related to one another in nature. Politicisation, broadly, implies the orientation of people to political perspectives and political actions. Politicisation connotes people's acting as political actors. We find that, in an absolute sense, it is difficult to come across a society which is far from politics, whether politics is taken in the good sense or the bad sense. Politics, as capture or pursuit of power for public ends, has always characterised all human societies in one way or another, to a greater or lesser extent. The need for the politicisation of a people arises only in these societies where politics or pursuit of power for public ends does not figure prominently. In various societies, various non-political factors such as economic, religious, ethnic, cultural, may dominate the thinking and activities of the people. In such cases efforts may be made to politicise the people in the sense that politics is given sufficient importance attention and place in the affairs of the people.

Against the background of politicisation, we can now proceed to discuss the nature of political participation. Political participation implies participation by the various people in the politics of the country. Political participation may imply participation by the un-politicised people as well as the political ones. It goes without saying that the goals are as numerous as there are persons engaged in political participation. At times the goals or objectives may be more numerous than the people engaged in political participation in the sense that a person may have more than one goal or objective. The ways, the methods or means by which political participation is engaged in by the various people, may be as various or as numerous as there are people engaged in political participation. Here too the ways, the methods or means may be more than the persons engaged in political participation in the sense that one person may employ more than one person, may employ more than one method. In actual practice, this means that you can participate in politics as a president of India, as a minister, as Chairman or member of Zila Parishad, as the Mukhia of Gram Panchayat, as a Pradhan of Panchayat Samiti, as a professor, as a student, as an engineer, as a doctor, as a broker, as a dramatist, as a tamasbin—as a shoe-shiner or as just an idler.

The situations and channels through which political participation may be seen may be various and numerous. Political participation may be seen, to take some common examples, in the action of the president's ordinance, the session of a state legislature, a Zila Parishad sponsored agricultural programme, a family planning camp organised by a district officer, a democratic body of a university, an election meeting, a propaganda pamphlet, a student demonstration, a Bihar bandh or a Delhi bandh, lathi-charging or tear-gassing an unruly mob and so on.

Broadly, we may say that political participation tends to get polarised into two lines, of thinking or acting in support of or in opposition to a particular principle, a particular philosophy, a particular economic doctrine, a particular piece of legislation or a particular administrative measure. Those who are engaged in political participation generally get classified or polarised in the camps of proposition or opposition, extension of support or withdrawal of support, increase of power or decrease of power, in respect of a particular leadership, particular ideology, particular policy, laws sections or groups of people, particular problems or issues or particular troubles or evils.

The objectives of political participation for proposition or opposition, extension or withdrawal of support, increase or decrease of power may branch off into or assume the following different or related forms:

> Story inventory;
> Fabrications (making-up of stories);
> Rumour-mongering;
> Whisper campaign;
> Vilification campaign;
> Propaganda;
> Character-assassination;
> Blackmail;
> Buck-Passing;
> Blame-Shifting;
> Scapegoating;
> Conspiracies, plots;
> Uprisings, mass upsurges;
> Civil wars, Cold wars, Hot wars, etc.

When people are engaged in political participation, they generally tend to resort to the various measures, methods, techniques or means as broadly classified as follows:

1. Activating political parties and pressure-groups.
2. Personal meetings, talks, discussions, consultations, etc.

3. Press conferences.
4. Action through
   i. Newspapers;
   ii. Radio;
   iii. Television;
   iv. Telex;
   v. Telephone;
   vi. Posts and telegraphs;
   vii. Specific or special debates, seminars, symposia, colloquia, refresher courses, workshops or work projects, summer institutes, camps and on.
5. Protests and strikes of various kinds;
   i. Pen-down strike;
   ii. Chalk-down strike;
   iii. Tool-down strike;
   iv. Work-to-rule strike;
   v. Wearing or displaying of buttons badges, blazers, placards, posters, banners, etc.;
6. Processions, morchas, rallies, demonstrations;
7. Dharnas, sit-ins, etc.;
8. Gheraos;
9. Bundhs.

II

In the theoretical framework of political participation, now we turn our attention towards politics of participation in rural development in India. In course of the long struggle[1] for independence, political participation was articulated in India as the top evocative value in politics. If Tilak declared freedom as a birthright, Gandhi championed participation in the struggle for Indian freedom as the personal obligation of every Indian. His call for boycott of the institutions erected by the British Raj was responded enthusiastically by a large number of Indians throughout the country. People belonging to various walks of life, including a very large number of college students, joined the struggle for Indian freedom.

While they deserted of some kinds of institutions, many of them entered into the local government institutions, securing popular support when elections were held in the twenties. Jawaharlal Nehru and Sardar Vallabhbhai Patel, former lawyers, for example, became municipal chairmen in their respective cities, Subhas Chandra Bose, who declined a job in the ICS he had earned through a through competition, became the Executive Councillor of the Calcutta municipal corporation.

This was because the local government institutions, in accordance with a new policy of the British Raj, offered the first opportunity and freedom of decision-making to Indians. When similar scope for uninhibited decision-making and political participation at the upper layers of government, vizo, the provincial assemblies, in particular, was offered after 1935, the leaders of freedom movement joined such institutions also.

At the turn of independence, the more articulate Indian leaders moved to provincial and central assemblies, many of them leaving behind their positions and role in local government. Desire for participation in political institutions turned out to be so widespread in India after independence that the state and central stage of politics got overcrowded. Local government institutions receded to an unimportant place because of the meager power that they offered to the incumbents. But this was also because, after the acceptance of the principle of adult suffrage, which, under the republican constitution of India, was to inform all political institutions of the country, was to be implemented in the area of local government; but because of the stupendous nature of the task, a clear-cut policy was taking time to evolve. In the absence of such a well-defined policy, the newly enacted Village Panchayat Laws, in states like Bihar, took recourse to a policy of unanimous elections of Panchayat leaders. Unanimous elections kept the local squabbles subdued no doubt; but it did little to speed political participation. Almost everywhere it initially resulted in imbuing the traditional village leaders, usually the largest landholders, with statutory authority under the village Panchayat Laws. (Prasad 1971,1974).

National concern was re-focussed on Local government institutions in the wake of the centrally felt need of associating the local people in the process of implementing the centrally formulated schemes of development under the five-year plans. This occurred in 1957. Between 1946 and 1952, they were too pre-occupied with the national issues erupting in the wake of partition, with integration of Indian princely states with the Indian Union and with creating the structure of an independent state of the size of India. During the period to the first five year plan, they experimented with a centrally sponsored programme of community development. The programme, begun experimentally in 1952, made a modest headway; and, so in 1957, on the recommendation of the famous Balwantrai Mehta team of study, the National Development Council decided to create new local institutions of each Community Development Block area and to restructure and refurbish the district local council already in existence in some form since 1885. Existing local councils that covered a sub-district area of a Tehsil/Taluka/Sub-division, each was the local government system that was created for rural India after 1957.

In reality, the new rural local government system took two diverse patterns; one, in the states of Maharashtra and Gujarat, the district councils were endowed with effective power; two, in almost all other states, the block councils were given the key role in the implementation of the rural development programme. Thus, while the experiment in the system of rural local government and district development administration still keeps on, the (development) block covering around a hundred villages has emerged as the area of local government as well as of field administration of the State, national government. The village (a single village in case of a large one and a group of villages where they are small in size), the block and the district are now the three locuses of rural local government. Like local government units throughout the world, they invite for their effective functioning active participation of local men of character, vision and organisational ability. In the present Indian context in particular, on their effectiveness depends, also, the success of the rural development programmes, both those framed locally and those sponsored by the state and central government. The latter kind of programmes constitute the bulk of the items that have concerned the local government units in India since 1957.

Broadly along the lines suggested in the Indian Planning Commission study team's report (Balwantrai Mehta report)[1] rural local government laws were amended by the state throughout the country, with a view to linking up the three levels of local government at the village, the block, and the district. The central government leaders pinned much hope on this new web of institutions. During the early sixties, there was discernible a widespread activeness in these institutions who were involved in a big way in the process of implementation of the rural development activities, necessitating a diversion of the country's resources to defined needs.

While, however, the development programmes of the new local government organisations suffered a setback, the political activities gradually picked up in India's Panchayati Raj institutions over the sixties. This was for several related reasons. One, the policy of unanimous election of Village Panchayat leaders was withdrawn. Two, universal adult suffrage, which now formed the basis of elections, resulted into displacing traditional rich farmer leaders by the lower middle class and poor peasants. Three, the structural inter-linking of the various rural local government councils imparted a new significance to who got elected as chiefs of the Village Panchayats: for the chief of the village Panchayat would automatically become a member of the block council whose chairman, in turn, would be a member of the district council. Panchayat elections thus got linked to the wider arena of politics of the district. Quite naturally, then, village Panchayat elections have since the sixties been fought ferociously, often giving rise to violent clashes in course of the elections especially in the course of the efforts of the contender to usurp the ballot papers and cast them in favour of the candidate of one's choice. This is what is known as both-capturing, and it is on the increase in Panchayat elections and has of late inflicted the state assembly and parliamentary elections of the country, too (Mishra, 1980). Local elections are, however, seldom in any state conducted as regularly as stipulated by the Panchayat election rules.

On the other hand, towards the end of sixties, the macro strategy of rural development underwent a basic change. Centrally sponsored development agencies were kept delinked from the Panchayat Raj institutions. The stress was shifted from developing the institutions of Panchayati Raj to agricultural[1] development. The Ministry of Community Development was merged in the Ministry of Agriculture (Dey, 1972). Later, in early seventies a new clientele specific agencies were created: (a) Small Farmers Development Agencies; (b) Marginal Farmers and Agricultural Labourers Development Agency[2]. Both of these were later merged into a composite Small Farmer's Development Agency (SFDA).[3]

Alongside these clientele specific agencies created mainly for the development of the weaker sections in the rural areas' area development programmes were also initiated in the seventies. These were: (1) Drought Prone Areas Programme; and (2) Command Area Development Programme. Under both these programmes special care is taken to help develop the small farmers and poorer sections of people as under the SFDA.

In 1979, the strategy of rural development underwent a change under a new label: Integrated Rural Development. It is founded on the concept of local level planning and is designed to serve the goals, especially of the development of agriculture and related rural sectors, village and cottage industries and marketing and processing of rural products. It aims at integrating field programmes relating to these primary (agriculture), secondary (cottage industries, and tertiary (marketing etc.) sectors.

The role of the local government institutions of Panchayati Raj in the centrally sponsored developmental activities has been peripheral since the late sixties. The Planning Commission admitted: 'The involvement of the Panchayati Raj institutions in the development process has not been adequate in the past (India, 1978: 16). The Janata Government[4] that came to power in 1977 and was committed to freedom, decentralisation, and Panchayati Raj, appointed a committee to review the role of the Panchayati Raj institutions in the process of rural development. The committee (Ashok Mehta Committee) reported: The Panchayati Raj institutions 'have not been given a chance to serve as a vanguard of development in village India. Wherever they have been given the responsibility to whatever limited extent, as in Maharashtra and Gujarat, they have done well.' (Mehta, 1978: 8). 'The Development Programmes were not channelled through them.' (Mehta, 1978: 175).

The Panchayati Raj was an 'act of faith', as Nehru often declared. His successors did not seem to have enough faith in it.[5] So the Panchayati Raj was kept aside from the national effort in rural development since the late sixties. The Janata regime might have re-involved the Panchayati Raj institutions in the process of rural development in a significant way. But its regime ended only two years after it came to power.

III

The Indian experience does not provide the theorist of participation with clear-cut and conclusive evidence. Local government institutions of Panchayati Raj did not operate systematically and continuously over a large period. The state government did not conduct their elections regularly at periodic intervals. The state politicians always looked at the Panchayati Raj politicians as competitors. Political chiefs of the block and district councils, in particular, seemed to rival the power and patronage potential of the state legislators.

Internally, too, these local institutions suffered from apathy of the masses in the initial stage. And later, the first flush of enthusiasm of participation took mainly political (quite often violent) form.

Yet the Indian experiment is quite relevant to the theorists of participation. First, the vastness of the country provides a tremendous amount of data relating to diverse contexts over a particular point of time. Almost over the same point of time, Maharashtra and Gujarat experimented with a form of Panchayati Raj different from the rest of the country, while states like Bihar mainly carried on without a full-scale implementation of the scheme of Panchayati Raj. Second, across a period of three to four decade, it provides data on various aspects of participation in relation to development and development references to participation. A broad approximation of the situation obtaining in different parts of the country would show the following pattern of the relationship between the two variables of participation and development since independence (see Figure 18.1). In this we assume the national policy, as the independent variable and the local feed-back as the dependent one.

FIGURE 18.1

Time Phase	National Policy	Local Feed-back
1—1947-52	Participation	Development
2—1952-56	Development	Participation
3—1956-61	Participation	Development
4—1961-66	Participation	Development
5—1966-71	Development	Development
6—1971-76	Development	Participation
7—1977-79	Participation	Development
8—Since 1980	Development	Participation

Notes to Figure 18.1

1. Village Panchayat laws were in operation even before the three-tier Panchayati Raj came in operation. Village Panchayat Councils were elected on limited franchise. Little development (in macro terms) activities was however, undertaken.

2. Community development programmes were launched. Participation of local people was not required in their formulation, and little participation was required in their implementation.

3. The period of the second five-year plan of India. Although the Panchayati Raj scheme—democratic decentralisation schemes—was yet to be launched, a Block Advisory Committee, later christened Block Development Committee, comprising Village Panchayat chiefs and others, began to operate.

4. The period of the third five year plan. The Panchayati Raj Scheme was launched in many states in 1959 with some fanfare.

5. Development was largely delinked from Panchayati Raj. The invention seeds attracted the farmers. Panchayati Raj elections now began to be fought ferociously.

6. The experiment of clientele specific development agencies delinked from Panchayati Raj institutions began.

7. Involving Panchayati Raj institutions in local development was accepted as a policy. Programmes were chalked out. But they could not be pursued before the regime changed.

8. The policy of delinking development from Panchayati Raj seems to have been revived.

Figure 18.1 represents a broad perceptive summation of the reality relating to Indian experiment in the relationship between participation and development. The perception of Ashok Mehta Committee, concerning the period since Panchayati Raj came in existence, confirms the formulation presented in figure. To quote from the report (Mehta, 1978: 4):

> The story of Panchayati Raj has been a story of ups and downs. It seems to have passed through three phases: the phase of ascendancy (1959-64); the phase of stagnation (1965-69); and the phase of decline (1969-71). 5 (Mehta, 1978:4).

Local development and local participation have thus been very much connected to the national policy in this regard. Rural development (in agriculture and related activities) has since independence been a direct outcome of national concern for the development of the rural areas. This is hardly surprising. But what is to be underscored is that rural development has at times been officially envisaged to ensue from the local participation in the local institutions. Secondly, the policy of rural development is also often assumed to activate the local people to participate in its implementation even from inside the local institutions (of Panchayati Raj). In rural, in particular, participation and development are enmeshed phenomena, so enmeshed, indeed, that often times it is not easy to disentangle specific impact of each participation, what is more, is so much part of the development process that many regard participation as an indicator of development (Dayakrishna, 1979, Prasad, 1980).

Yet, it is difficult to deduce from Figure 18.1 that participation has spurred (economic, agriculture etc.) development in rural India, even though it indicates some intensity of positive connection between the two. Indeed, often times the relationship is found to be so weak that it creates the impression that political democratisation and participation are not a factor of local economic development (Prasad 1971b). Yet it has always implicitly worked out to spur economic development in the rural areas. Even during the period when participation had not been institutionalised in Bihar through the instrumentality of Panchayati Raj, the new Mukhiya (the President of Village Panchayat), by virtue of his and his lieutenant's good relations with the Block Development Officer 'succeeded in getting allotted for his village a fairly large number of development schemes of various kinds' (Prasad, 19716:239). Even now, the village Panchayat President continues to 'serve as the link-man between the villagers and the government.' (Asisrajan, 1979: 272). Local participatory factors could be translated into developmental outcome, as the Programme Evaluation Organisation's nine case studies of village Panchayat confirmed, with the help of two supportive factors:

(1) Linkages with layers of government and administration (which imply existence of the facilities of communication (road) and physical contact with people in district and state centres); (2) a kind of local leadership which can establish connections with the leadership of the block, district, and state politics.[6]

The undeniable fact is that India is quite a centralised political system: indeed its polity is more centralised than even its administrative system (Appleby 1952). Inside the state, the administrative system is more highly centralised than the political. Another notable fact is that seldom so far have the central and the state leadership of politics shown inclination to part with their constitutional and arrogated power and share with the lower units of politics and government. Not that it was never intended or attempted. But such instances had either a brief tenure or proved abortive.[7] The bureaucrat sees the local government institutions as local agencies of the State government to help implement the state and central government policies and programmes. The local to him is lower than and below the state. In such a context, then, political participation restricted to local government institutions tends to be sterile. The interest generally gets all centred on electoral participation (Prasad, 1975) unless effective linkages are built up with the upper layers of politics and administration.

However, one of the great contributions of the Panchayati Raj institutions of India which has failed to be appreciated adequately has been that it provides a forum of establishing linkages between leadership and political activists of various layers of government and various sectors of activity (Narain, 1978). We would return to this theme now.

IV

Political participation in the Panchayati Raj system, which thus emerges from the empirical evidence collected by political scientists and others, made a timid start when the statutory Panchayat system was introduced in village India. Like the general assembly in an Israelean kibutz (Kelso, 1978; Bin-Yosef 1963: 29), poor attendance continues to be a feature of the village assembly (Gaon Sabha) meetings. Even the village Panchayat executive seldom meets regularly: it was more especially true of the early years of their beginning; but the situation is hardly much improved now (Asisrajan, 1979; Dutta, 1981). The lower caste men and Harijans have, however, begun to take more interest in village Panchayat elections and they have also succeeded in acquiring positions of leadership in village Panchayats in many areas (Mishra, 1977). In the district of Aurangabad (Bihar), which has always elected a Rajput member to the Lok Sabha, while the Rajputs continue to dominate, many Harijans and Muslims and middle caste men have emerged through elections as Panchayat leaders. Across the river in the district of Rahatas, a Brahmin-Rajput dominated district, the picture is, however, more encouraging and the situation is changing for the better gradually for the downtrodden.

A survey could reveal the fact that change, thus, is more perceptible in terms of age and education, but not in terms of economic status of the Mukhiya of the Panchayats. Actually, even from among the lower caste people, it is the economically better off persons who can afford to give time to political leadership activities on a regular basis or can even think of contesting elections which demand preparedness in terms of money, men and material (including firearms and other lethal weapons now).

So the change in the pattern of leadership is not quite as fast as some radical visionaries would want. Maybe partly because of this, but mainly because of economic factors (pattern of land ownership etc.). Some groups of radical activists, who do not bother about violence either, have of late started a programme of physical extermination of these Panchayati Raj leaders. In the areas, particularly around the district towns of Aurangabad. Gaya, Bhajpur, Patna and Sasaram, all in central and west-central Bihar, this phenomenon is on the increase. It is on the increase since mid-seventies and the vanguard group of leaders of this kind of movement is generally identified as the Naxalites who through this method seek to mobilise the Harijans and other dominated sections of the local people.

Panchayat elections, though not held at regular intervals,[8] are nevertheless contested with much gusto. But interest in elections and the high percentage of participation in voting for electing Panchayat leaders is no index of public participation in decision-making about village Panchayat matters. Electoral participation is high and out of proportion to efforts to influence routine decision-making by the Panchayat leaders.[9] The people would want to make their choice of Panchayat leaders but would not worry much about the course of choice-making by Panchayat leaders. And the few of those who afford time to influencing choice-making by Panchayat leaders are oftener they who are the past or prospective seekers of these offices themselves. The number of such aspirants is on the increase, which largely explains why Panchayat elections are being increasingly fought with growing ferocity and violence.

The role of such activists is significant both for the political institution of the village Panchayat and for the development of the village. Young and educated, their interest is not confined to the village alone. Educated in the towns, and returned to the village for want of jobs in an era of growing educated unemployment, they have, unlike their uneducated elders of the previous generation, at least the confidence to deal with townsfolk as well as administrators and political activists, operating at the block, the district, and even at the state level. It is they who have come to serve as linkmen between the local people and village problems and administrators and politicians, operating at higher levels—who can bestow financial and technical help to solve the local problems. Linkages between the village and the outer world of administration, politics, and commerce are established through such local activists, many of whom occupy leadership positions in village Panchayats by turn of elections, while some of whom are the potential stuff of higher levels of politics and, maybe, of commerce but very unlikely of administration.

These local activists not only ventilate local demands, they also allow themselves to be used as the local agents of the political organisations of the district and state level. In Rajasthan, 88 per cent Panchayati Raj leaders participated in campaigning for candidates in the 1967 Lok Sabha and State Assembly elections. According to the same study, 64 per cent of them took tremendous interest in the Lok Sabha snap elections of 1971 (Narain, 1978:101-3).

What is also worth underscoring, oftener most of them work for the party in power. A study conducted in Assam in 1981 confirms this observation that Panchayat leaders were the supporters of the party in power. In all the Assembly elections till 1972, Panchayat leaders had voted for the Congress. In the 1978 Assam Assembly elections, however, the majority of the Panchayat leaders voted for the Janata Party and also changed their personal affiliation from INC to Janata (Table 18.1)

TABLE 18.1

Political Preference of Panchayat Leaders

Election	INC	Janata	Others	All
1977 Lok Sabha	70%	30%	—	100%
1978 State Assembly	36%	44%	18%	100%

Note: In 1978, INC (I) got only six per cent of votes of Panchayat leaders and thirty-two per cent was obtained by the other faction of the Congress, than led by Swaran Singh.

Source: Nikunjalata Dutta (1981, 211).

This is nothing surprising in the present Indian context: rather it is part of 'politronics' of Indian politics, more especially since 1969. Local leaders have, by and large, no rigid loyalty to particular political ideology or organisation, even though often they may seem to have some for particular individuals (maybe, the mentors or benefactors). Ideology is, indeed, largely irrelevant at the local level; for all the manner of political parties have, more or less, the same manner of approach to local activists, local controversies and local demands. On the other hand, the local activists' main concern is the fulfilment of local needs and demands. His own political survival in local government depends on his capacity to fulfil the local demands. He, therefore, cannot go against the state party in power. If he does, it is very likely that the Panchayat elections, which may be already due, or over-due, would be announced sooner rather than later. Or, the local Panchayat would be superseded. Or grants, already in pipeline as ordered by the previous party in power, could be withheld or snapped or at least diminished. This explains why and how the upper layers of government and politics despite the canopy of local autonomy and the trappings of authority of the local government institutions, political linkages, thus, militate against the administrative autonomy of the local government institutions.

V

1. Political participation in local government depends largely upon the macro-political context. The upsurge of local political participation in the early twenties was the direct outcome of the policy of the leadership of the Indian National Congress to capture the newly created local political institutions. Participatory activity in local government remained subdued for some time after independence until, in the late fifties, the Union Government, the Planning Commission and the National Development Council decided to involve the local people in a big way in a new process of development through local government (Panchayati Raj) institutions. Again, it did receive a setback when the strategy of agricultural rural development underwent a modification at the national level in the late sixties.

2. The Constitution of India provides every adult Indian with a vote in shaping governments at the local level as at the state and the national levels. Participation of all is thus guaranteed; and gradually more and more Indians feel more free and inclined to participate. But two snags stump political participation. One, the participation of the vast masses is very largely confined to the electoral process. Two, (and this is a really disturbing phenomenon in India witnessed of late at all levels of politics) even electoral participation is inhibited by the emergence of a process of surrogate participation: Some who can bully all, participate on behalf of all. This is known as booth capturing (see Prasad 1975b and Mishra, 1980b).

3. While all may, and many do, participate in the electoral process, only a few participate in implementing the course of decision-making at and through the local government institutions. They may be identified as the local political activists. They not only seek to influence the choice of decision-makers in local government, but also forge links to higher levels of government and administration to influence the course of decisions at higher levels relating to their locality.

4. Local development, whether through the local government institutions or through the local (field) organisations of the higher levels of government, is a function of a dovetailing of the efforts of local leadership (and activists) with those of the leadership (and activists) at the upper levels. Development, seen from the local level, is a function less of participation merely at the local level than of forging a linkage or linkages between the various levels of government. This is a rural development item on the agenda of the state and national government.

5. Formal legal autonomy is no index of the real autonomy of the local government institutions. Political linkages between the local and the state level activists very much negate the autonomy of the local government. In twin, the local government is saved from sinking into inactive isolation.

6. The State Government would seldom seem to tolerate non-cooperating with local government institutions controlled by activists who receive political sustenance and

support from elsewhere than through the group of men who control the State Government. The conduct of local government elections is determined more by this than by any other factor. This political factor explains the irregularity in organising the elections to the local government institutions.

In the Indian process of rural development, thus, the macro-level planning and policy formulation have so far since independence played more determinative role than any other factor. Within this macro-framework micro-level participation does speed up development to an extent especially initially. But, oftentimes the political process of participation in the institutions of local government gives rise to some negative factors and impedes the process of development.

Rural development, whatever the achievement, has so far been made due largely to the effectiveness of linkages between the local level and upper levels of governmental institutions. For, the Panchayati Raj institutions have little base to sustain themselves finally. Because of their weak financial base, the chief purpose of political participation in local government institutions of Panchayati Raj thus turns out to be the establishment of vertical linkages, however effective, with the upper world of politics, government, and commerce. This process of forging vertical linkages is perceived at the macro-level as the growing demandingness of the rural people. Indeed, this is a notable feature of the Indian political development and pervades all the various dimensions of politics in India. The functioning of political and administrative institutions has been greatly affected by this development. And it is at once the source of democratisation of public institutions and, at the same time, largely explains the malfunctioning of the public organisations and institutions in India.

REFERENCES

1.   This was under the Government of India Act passed by the British Parliament in 1935.
2.   Established under the fourth five years plan (1966-71) for a period of five years, these agencies started functioning under Societies Registration Act from 1971-72.
3.   This occurred during the fifth five years plan period. The Agency functions as the co-ordinator between identified participants, development departments, and extension organisations at the field level (Menon, nd.)
4.   In March 1977; the Janata Party came to power in the union government and in June in most North-Indian states. The Janata Party remained in power for a short period; and Mrs. Gandhi's Congress Party returned to power in January 1980 at the centre and in June 1980 in most states.
5.   In 1964 Nehru died. In 1964-66, Lal Bahadur Shastri was the Prime Minister. Mrs. Gandhi took over on the death of Lal Bahadur Shastri in 1966. But the acquired pre-eminence in politics as Prime Minister only in 1969. The Mehta report formulation takes these dates a cut-off point in the history of Panchayati Raj. This all the more illustrates how macro-level changes affect local level development in India.
6.   The P.E.O. brought out in 1960 nine case studies of Panchayats selected from various states (India, 1960). None of these nine Panchayats, however, owed their developmental performance to any special form of local sources.
7.   Short-tenured because of Chinese aggression during Nehru's time; abortive because of the collapse of the Janata Government much before its time.

8. As the Report of the High Power Committee on Panchayati Raj, 1973, of Rajasthan (called Vyas Committee) observes: 'The over-whelming majority of persons whom the committee met and interviewed was of the opinion that the postponement of elections of Panchayati Raj bodies has resulted in widespread criticism in the public and has also shaken the faith of the common man in Panchayati Raj (Rajasthan, 1973:13).

9. In the 1970-71 elections to village Panchayats in Orissa, out of a total rural population of 16 million, 500,000 people took part in voting (Roa, 1977:219). It is an incredibly high participation in voting by any standard.

19

Participation in Social Defence

I

In recent years there has been an increasing recognition of the potential of the public and possibility of its being fully involved in the social defence.[1] Consequently the need for adequate intervention by the citizen is viewed as one of the key factors for a successful implementation of programmes and politics of social defence aiming at the prevention, treatment, reclamation and rehabilitation of the people who deviate from the normative standards of approved socio-legal behaviour and invite legal sanctions implying punitive-cum-treatment of the society. It is now considered an obvious-evasion of the fundamental responsibility of the members of the community if they tend to rely entirely on the efforts of the public organisations with regard to actions taken for the sake of prevention and control of crime and delinquency.[2] As a result, immense importance is being attached to bringing the public to a closer knowledge of participation in, and collaboration with, the governmental efforts in the prevention of crime and delinquency.

We now inevitably witness a fervent search for exploring the ways and means to strengthen the existing modes of citizens' involvement in social defence endeavours. In keeping with the desire to mobilise the potential of the public in the planning of programmes for the prevention and control of crime and delinquency, and in the correction and rehabilitation of offenders within and outside the institutions of social defence, a considerable amount of research work is being done in the contemporary corrections systems.

Research studies in the field of public participation in social defence, undertaken particularly after 1950, describe and evaluate various modalities in which public participates in the administration of criminal justice and the execution of institutional and non-institutional programmes for the prevention of crime and treatment of offenders. The findings and suggestions of these researches have prompted many criminologists and correctional workers, all over the world, to publish articles, books and monographs on several fields of modern social defence programmes and policies, in which they have shown how the people, either voluntarily or under certain official inducements, are drawn closer to police, judges and correctional workers for cooperating and collaborating with the official machinery of crime prevention and correction of offenders. The Regional meetings of the social defence experts concerned by the United Nations in 1969-70 in Africa, Asia, Latin America, and in Arab States discussed the subject of public participation in social defence in terms of its needs and significance in the light of existing and anticipated prospects and possibilities.

With regard to research on public participation in social defence, India presents a peculiar case. Despite a rich tradition of research in the field of social defence in general, and public participation in particular, it continues to be minimal. The available research material on such an important subject is limited and very often sketchy and peripheral.

Very little is therefore known about the effectiveness of different modalities through which people's cooperation is solicited in the actual operation of social defence policies and measures. The time is, therefore, ripe to fill up this gap in knowledge and settle down to the task of working out the methodological details for rendering an objective account of voluntary participation performed, to discover its strength and weaknesses, and to advance scientific knowledge about the actual or anticipated problems in the field.

With the emergence of the concept of community corrections and its growing acceptance and popularity all over the world, the experts in the field of social defence, i.e., the prevention of crime and treatment of offenders, who meet at an interval of every five years under the U.N. auspices as 'conference men' are clamouring for bringing the public closer to corrections and strengthening the existing and newly found methods and modalities as a result of which a large number of social welfare-minded people in each society can associate and contribute meaningfully to the prevention of crime and treatment of offenders. The contemporary columbuses in the field of social defence have started their voyage in order to discover a 'crimeless society' with a firm belief that whatever strategy is used for the prevention of crime and delinquency, the paucity of monetary resources would call for exploring new techniques to optimise the results. The optimisation of results could be achieved through several measures, and mobilisation of social forces can surely and certainly be one such measure. The voyagers are certain that the contribution of social forces to crime prevention is a matter of great significance. The involvement of well-meaning citizens in this task can alone result in reducing the enormous cost of prevention and corrective programmes in the field of social defence.

Several such experts have spoken eloquently about the need and significance of public participation in social defence.

Thus:

'Constructive cooperation by the public in general and specific welfare-minded citizens in particular, be made a permanent part of crime prevention programme so that the harmful or passive attitude of society—which assumes the professionals alone can solve the rapidly growing problems as if by a miracle—may give way to responsible citizen action.'[3]

'Correction cannot solve the problem of crime and delinquency by itself. It needs community involvement'.[4]

'Because no governmental policy of social control of correction method (in reality defences against crime) has proven very effective in the reduction of crime, the ultimate solution for alleviation of the crime problems must rest in the hands of general citizenry. It is the citizenry that will curb crime, not the police, nor the courts and nor the prisons'.[5]

'If crime rates are to be reduced, it is not enough to rely upon the state mechanism alone. People's participation is the hall-mark of any successful plan for crime control.'[6]

'It is clear that no country can deal with its crime problems through its criminal justice system alone. There must be understanding and active involvement by the public as a whole.'[7]

'Amongst many aspects in the development of social defence programmes, there is an awakening in the forethoughts of penologists which encompasses the belief that more the participation in them by members of the community is enhanced, the more effective will be the programmes for the control of crime and delinquency. In other words, there must be a smooth flow of relationship between a country's criminal justice system and public participation with the aim of establishing sufficient rapport to achieve efficiency in the prevention and treatment of crime and delinquency and the provision of suitable social services.'[8]

'Social defence programmes in every country should involve community groups and its implementation for bitter protection of the community against the crime, and the government should support such efforts.'[9]

'A well-founded programme of social defence covering various aspects of prevention of crime and treatment of offenders heavily relies on an active cooperation of voluntary welfare resources and agencies which represent the consciousness and concern of the public towards the problems in this field.'[10]

II

After discussing need and significance of public participation in social defence, it is desirable to explain the terms, which are frequently used in this context. As such, the succeeding lines encompass the meaning and the senses of the terms in which they are generally used.

Public: Local citizens and constellation of officials and non-officials, social service organisations, associations and bodies actively involved in the operation of institutional and non-institutional programmes and activities in the field of social defence as volunteers to augment the working of such institutions in the prevention of crime and delinquency and correction and rehabilitation of the persons who have been judged guilty and exposed to institutional incarceration.

Participation: Officially sanctioned or functionally desired ways and means of identification, involvement, cooperation and collaboration of local citizenry in the operations of crime prevention programmes, law enforcement functions of the police and operation of correctional programmes through direct volunteer service or through organised action undertaken to improve the nature and quality of services provided by the social defence system.

Social Defence: Governmental and non-governmental institutional programmes and services for the prevention and control of crime, delinquency, beggary, immoral traffic and the prosecution, incarceration, correction, rehabilitation and after-care of the persons released conditionally or unconditionally from prisons and other peno-correctional institutions.

Public Participation in Social Defence

By public participation we mean the ways and means through which community groups offer support for governmental and non-governmental action in the prevention and treatment of crime and delinquency. Alternatively, such a participation refers to the ways in which the public is brought to cooperate with official social defence programmes by doing some of the work that would otherwise be done by governmental agencies, assuming duties and functions in the prevention and treatment of crime and delinquency, i.e. in work of criminal justice system, in the work of police, in the work of adult and juvenile courts and in the operation of agencies and institutions for the treatment of offenders. Such a participation might take the form of individual or collective efforts of the voluntary social workers, societies, associations and organisations engaged in social welfare work and by community's opinion leaders who press for the enactment of suitable social defence legislations, initiate appropriate reforms in the existing laws and procedures of social defence institutions and agencies and/or extend the desired assistance in solving the day-to-day problems and difficulties which agency executives and inmates face in achieving their goals.

III

After spelling out the operational definition of the terms with regard to need for public participation in social defence, following assumptions may be taken into account:

1. That people's apathy or their minimal involvement in the field of social defence, both at the policy formulation and implementation levels has resulted in poor performance of the programmes that have been undertaken for the prevention and control of crime and delinquency and for the correction and rehabilitation of those who have fallen prey to criminality.

2. That only a handful of social service-minded persons either individually or collectively participate in social defence endeavours and devote part of their time and energy in this area of social service either through their association as citizen representatives or as members of the governing bodies of the private and public welfare agencies catering to the institutional and non-institutional services for the correction and rehabilitation of the social defence clientele.

3. That for want of meaningful citizen participation, the realisation of the social defence programme is in serious jeopardy.

4. That the programme of an effective social defence system can be realised only when a large mass of people (who are resourceful, articulate and influential) are significantly involved as direct or indirect contributors and collaborators in the purposeful implementation of social defence policies and programmes in their respective communities.

5. That the only hope to activate the social defence programme lies in bringing the public closer to social defence organisations and institutions irrespective of their official or non-official character and set-up.

6. That despite the fact of decline in the number of good Samaritans, there still are many people in the communities who, if asked or persuaded, would be too willing to shoulder numerous responsibilities in the social defence system. Such people can serve as citizen auxiliaries in the police department, as voluntary probation officers, as honorary magistrates, as visitors, leaders, and counsellors in the correctional institutions, and voluntary agencies working in the field of prevention of crime and treatment of offenders.

7. That increase in public participation in social defence operations and activities is desirable and that increased participation is not an impossibility.

8. The public participation in social defence has so far been minimal, because (a) there is an in-built public resistance to crime prevention work; (b) not many people are fully conversant with the structure and mechanism of social defence programmes and services; (c) the majority of people (including local elites and community opinion leaders) do not know how best they can associate or involve themselves in the working of institutional social defence programmes and activities; (d) people in urban communities tend to be individualistic having little or no regard for the promotion and preservation of law and order situation in their community; (e) the urban people are more inclined to leave the task of prevention of crime and treatment of offenders to only those who are specially appointed and officially paid for it; people in the urban areas tend to believe that their role in the control and prevention of crime and in the reformation of offenders is only subordinate and auxiliary and therefore it must be left to the professionals who have been especially trained for the job; (g) many people in urban areas consciously avoid participation in social defence activities because it is time-consuming; (h) voluntarism is declining very fast from urban life and people tend to rely

solely on government efforts, believing that the implementation of the ideals of welfare state is the exclusive responsibility of the government and their role is secondary and does not have any real significance; (i) the personnel engaged in the implementation of social defence policies and programmes have not been able to educate people with regard to their role in social defence work; (j) for want of any definite thinking on the need and significance of enlisting public participation in social defence, the public is not represented in a formalised way at the national, state, district or community level, in policy planning, in setting goals and priorities and in developing strategies for the attainment of social defence goals; (k) the majority of governmental institutions in the field of social work in isolation under the guarded cloak of secrecy; and (l) the factors the stand in the way of meaningful participation of the public in social defence programmes and activities are complex.

9. That increased participation of the public in social defence programmes and activities can be made possible if the subject is given high priority in the developmental policy of modern social defence work and if the elites of the community are persuaded to extend their best possible cooperation and assistance. In order to ensure their meaningful participation, the government shall have to offer them a respectable place in policy formulation and programme execution.

IV

Now we come to the discussion of public participation in social defence in India. Whereas a large majority of people have a kind heart for the persons who are destitutes or are physically, mentally and socially handicapped, they hesitate to show a sufficient concern or sympathy for the clients of the social defence institutions and agencies. This tendency is so natural and widespread that it is difficult to find many people who are willing to help criminals, delinquents, prostitutes, beggars, alcoholics, drug addicts, gamblers and other varieties of social derelicts found in their neighbourhood or community. This attitude is surprising when viewed against the very significant participation of laymen in other areas of social concern.

This indifference of the citizen to the social defence system, which is designed to protect him, is due to three factors.[11] First, the states of social defence or criminal justice system cannot be shared by or delegated to, private individuals or groups. Secondly, the very complexity of the system of law enforcement, courts and corrections and its impenetrability tend to ward off any initiative from the citizen. Thirdly, the size and complexity of the crime problem makes a citizen feel helpless. To a layman the problem seems unmanageable and he has no notions of solutions.

Consequently, some people do not want to spoil their social prestige and reputation by working for the welfare of the persons who are guilty of violating law, and for whom the only reasonable treatment is deterrent punishment in the uncomfortable prisons, detention centres and coercion-based work-houses. The legal and social stigmas that these clients of social defence system carry, makes people apathetic. This situation is not new and has continued from time immemorial. The historical documents of modern criminology and penology bear testimony to people's apathy and indifference (and also open hostility) to all kinds of criminals and delinquents. People want them to be hanged, tortured, incarcerated, exiled, stigmatized, ostracised but not reformed. The general citizenry wants for them the kind of police that can deal with them sternly, the kind of prisons that punish them harshly, and the kind of judicial system that prescribes heavier doses of penalties and blood squeesing means of coercion, torture and punishment. The large mass of people still find solution to the evils of crime and delinquency in those kinds of punishment that are retributive and deterrent in character. These self-righteous groups of persons do not see eye to eye with the handful of criminologists, penologists, police officials, judges, prison workers and other corrections personnel who want to sell to them the idea of correction, reformation and rehabilitation of criminals and delinquents. People are not prepared to believe that criminals, delinquents, rowdies, hoodlums, toughs, prostitutes and gamblers have proved to respond favourably to the benevolent and humanitarian appeal of the reformist ideology. The public finds them incorrigible and unworthy of any dignified and humanitarian treatment. It is this public that clamours most for increasing the number of policemen, judges and prisons for effectively dealing with our fast multiplying throng of law-violating anti-social persons.

In a social situation of this kind, the administration of criminal justice and management of police, prisons and correctional institutions falling under the jurisdiction of social defence system has been working without any significant sympathy or cooperation of even those well-to-do citizens who have done commendable work in other areas of social concern. The few who showed willingness to cooperate found minimal support from their neighbours and friends and only felt discouraged and defeated. The net result has been that social defence programmes and policies lack public cooperation for want of people's confidence, credibility, concern and willingness to assist. The result is that social defence operations are now ineffective, its personnel diffident and its policies incredulous. The personnel engaged in social defence work functions without any significant social support like a hired group who could be fired on the flimsy accusations that they are corrupt, lethargic, inefficient and inhuman in their behaviour and style of working. The social defence functionaries, on the other hand, blame people's non-cooperation for their inefficiency, failure and corruption. Thus both the parties are unhappy.

When crime figures are escalating to frightening proportions, the realisation has dawned upon the professional criminologists in the governmental sector that they are bound to meet failures in their mission if they cannot secure public participation in their day-to-day functioning. They have also been compelled to realise that by mere exhortations, the public would not join them in the risky task of the prevention and control of crime and delinquency. In their opinion too there has arisen the need for creating more avenues, more machinery and more means for persuading people to take active part in social defence programmes. The persuasion can bear fruit if substantial incentives of both monetary and non-monetary kinds are offered. Furthermore the formal and informal agencies of crime control police, courts and corrections will have to dismantle their grandiose isolationist mechanisms and must invite the public to enter their fortresses. This new approach to social defence work might bridge the barriers that cripple people's desire to extend help to the police, judges and correctional workers around them.

Modalities of Public Participation

Right from the British days in India, several legislations relating to the criminal justice administration and other allied fields of modern social defence system, contained provisions which seek to involve community groups in the prevention and control of crime and delinquency through their association with police, courts, prisons and other correctional institutions. The provisions or modalities of public participation which have grown in India which deserve special mention in this regard can be conveniently discussed under the following heads: Public participation in the administration of criminal justice; (2) Public participation in crime detection and investigation; (3) Public participation in the treatment and rehabilitation of adult offenders; (4) Public participation in juvenile correction; (5) Public participation in the suppression of immoral traffic in women and girls; and (6) Public participation in the prevention and control of beggary. These are some of the important areas of our social life in which public participation can help a lot in improving the social condition. However, we would be confining our discussion at this place only to the public participation in the criminal justice administration.

Public Participation in Administration of Criminal Justice

The administration of criminal justice process in India makes it possible for some selected representatives of the public to associate with the adjudicatory process. Three representative are or were; (i) jury; (b) honorary Magistrates; and (c) Nyaya Panchayats.

System of Trial by Jury

The earliest reference that one has regarding the introduction of trial by jury in the provincial criminal courts in India dates back to the year 1827. Before that the system of disposal of disputes by panchayats was recognised in the regulations of Madras presidency. In that presidency besides courts of superior grades, each village had a village court presided over by the headman of the village, usually known by the designation of patel. Such a person was entrusted with the power of trying all causes or matters upto the amount of rupees ten in value and also for matters upto the amount of Rs. 100 in case both the parties chose to submit such causes for their decision. The regulations also recognised trials of causes by panchayats, their number ranging from five to nine, with none to preside over their deliberations. The decisions of the majority prevailed. The decisions were not open to appeal and it was provided that it was the duty of the Zila judge to see that the decisions were put into execution. It is thus evident that the principles of this mode of trial in civil cases were analogous to that of a trial by jury in criminal cases.

In one of the regulations passed in 1827, it was ordered that the trial by jury as a normal mode of trial in all criminal cases, be gradually introduced. The first section of this regulation provided that the government had deemed it expedient to introduce the system of trial by jury in order to expedite criminal trials and to raise the character of the people and their gradual involvement in the administration of criminal justice.

The criminal procedure code of 1861 introduced the system of trial by jury by providing that the Indian juries were to be of the nature of an examining body selected from the loyal subjects of Her Majesty and to be guided with regard to the technicalities of law by the presiding judge. They were to try only specified offences. Under the code of criminal procedure, 1898, Sections 267, 268 and 269 provided for the right to trial by jury in India.

Section 267 provided that all trials before a high court shall be by jury. The rules regarding the choosing of the jury under the code of criminal procedure, 1898 were as follows:

1. Section 276 provided that the jurors shall be chosen by lot from the persons summoned to act as such in such manner as the high court may by rule direct.

2. Section 277 laid down that each juror when chosen, his name shall be called aloud and, upon his appearance the accused shall be asked if he objects to be tried by such jurors.

3. Section 278 provided the ground of objection to the selection of the jurors: (1) presumed or actual partiality of the jurors, (2) personal ground such as alienage, deficiency in the qualifications required by law or being under 21 or above 60 years of age, (3) having relinquished care of worldly affairs, (4) holding an office in or under the courts, (5) having been convicted of an offence, (6) inability to understand the language in which evidence is given or interpreted, and (7) another circumstance which in the opinion of the court renders him improper as a juror.

4. Section 279 provided that every objection to a juror shall be decided by the court and such decision shall be recorded and be final.

The law commission of India (in its fourteenth report on Reform of Judicial Administration) opined that the jury system has had a long trial, has been a failure and should be abolished.

Accepting the law commission's recommendations the code of criminal procedure of 1973 makes no reference whatsoever to trial by jury.

Provisions regarding trial by jury which were continued in the criminal procedure code of 1898 do not find any place in the code of 1973. The commission despite its observation that the system of trial by jury has the advantage of associating the public with the administration of justice pleaded for the discontinuance of the system. The commission's observation was: 'The evils of unscrupulous professional jurors were mentioned to us by some witnesses who gave evidence before us. It is obvious that such a state of affairs must render trial by jury almost a mockery and seriously affect the administration of criminal justice.' The Commission was also of the view that 'since trial by jury system has failed to deliver the intended good, its continuance cannot be supported any further.' Several factors contributed to the decision for the abolition of trial by jury in India.[12]

(i) it proved to be time consuming process; (ii) it took much longer time than trial held by judges; (iii) it meant more expenses to the state; (iv) intelligent, capable and honest jurors were difficult to find; (v) in several places people made it almost a profession to get themselves chosen as jurors for the sake of remuneration and even for the illegal gratification they expected to receive.

There were therefore compelling reasons to believe that the transplantation of the practice of trial by jury on the Indian soil could not be successful. Its abolition, therefore, was a right step in the right direction.[13]

Honorary Magistrates

Section 14 of the criminal procedure code of 1898 contemplated the appointment of special (or honorary, as they came to be known) magistrates. It provided: (1) The State Government may confer upon any person who holds or has held any judicial post under the Union or a State or possesses such other qualifications as may, in consultation with the High Court, be specified in this behalf by the State Government by notification in the official gazette all or any of the powers conferred or conferrable by or under this code on a magistrate of the first, second or their class in respect to particular classes of cases, or in regard to cases generally, in any local area outside the presidency towns; (2) Such Magistrates shall be called special Magistrates and shall be appointed for such term as the State Government may by general or special order direct; (3) the State Government may delegate, with such limitations as it thinks fit, to any officer under its control the powers conferred by sub-section (i); (4) no powers shall be conferred under this section on any police officer below the grade of Assistant District Superintendent, and no powers shall be conferred on a police officer except so far as may be necessary for prescribing peace, preventing crime, and detecting, apprehending and detaining offenders in order to their being brought before a Magistrate and for the performance by the officer of any other duties imposed upon him by any law for the time being in force.

Speaking about the role of these honorary Magistrates, the Law Commission of India has pointed out that 'The honorary Magistrates are intended to give relief to the stipendiary Magistrates in their work. Most of the work entrusted to them is of a petty type which does not require to be dealt with by any trained judicial officer and which would necessarily dog the files of the stipendiary Magistrate. The institution of honorary Magistrates is also helpful as a method of associating the public with criminal justice administration. In practice, these magistrates are appointed where the volume of criminal work is very large and the regular magistracy feels the need for additional help. As the appointment of a sufficient number of paid magistrates in some areas would impose a heavy financial burden upon the state suitable persons are chosen and appointed in those areas to work as Honorary Magistrates.'

The system of appointing honorary magistrates has both been applauded and criticised at a great length. Some have expressed the view that the system should continue but some have said that it should be abolished.[14] The Law Commission, however, recommended the continuance of the system with the modification that the power of appointment should be with the High Court and not with the State Government.[15]

The recommendation with regard to vesting of powers of appointment in the High Court was in tune with the general approach of the Commission to separate the judiciary from the executive. The Joint Committee of Parliament was not very much disposed towards the system, but recommended its continuance with the modification that the persons to be appointed as honorary magistrates should be either persons in government service or those who have retired from government service. In the new criminal procedure code of 1973 Sections 13 and 18 contain provisions for the appointment of special Magistrates.

Nyaya Panchayats

In India village courts or Nyaya Panchayats are institutions of antiquity and their functions included the adjudication of disputes between the villagers without any elaborate or complicated machinery and procedure. These organisations continued to function during the Moghul rule but suffered during the British period because of the highly centralised system of British administration. After independence the institution of village Panchayat received due importance. The State wanted to reorganise its judicial system with a view to making legal relief easily accessible to the indigent and backward in the villages. Nyaya Panchayats can provide local machinery for the resolution of legal disputes with an eye to promoting settlements and good neighbourly relations. Also it can provide cheap and expeditious justice easily accessible to rural population in small cases arising out of their daily lives and instil among villagers a growing sense of fairness and responsibility towards their fellow citizens. Article 40 of the Indian Constitution expressly provides that 'the State shall take steps to organise village Panchayats and endow them with such powers and authority as may be necessary to enable them to function as units of self-government.'

The jurisdiction of the Panchayat Courts in criminal matters extends to a large number of offences under the Indian Penal Code. Generally the Panchayat Courts have not been given the power to sentence an accused to a term of imprisonment either substantatively or in default of payment of fine. Their powers to impose maximum fines range from Rs. 15 to Rs. 250. The procedure followed by these courts is simple and the guidance Act and similar procedural codes do not apply to them. Errors of law, miscarriage of justice and irregular exercise of jurisdiction could be corrected by appeals to the Panchayats and revisions before the Magistrates' Court.

Though the institution of Nyaya Panchayat has often been severely criticised on the grounds of undesirable politicking and sinister local influences, the Fourteenth Report of the Law Commission recognised the role of Nyaya Panchayat in the following adulatory terms; 'Panchayat Courts are capable of doing a good deal of useful work by relieving the regular courts of petty civil litigations and criminal cases of simpler types. The Panchayats are in a position to dispose of simple cases more cheaply and expeditiously and with less inconvenience to all concerned than ordinary courts. An effort should, therefore, be made to establish and popularise such courts in states where they are not firmly established.'

REFERENCES

1. Yasuyoshi Shiono, "Use of volunteers in the Non-institutional Treatment of Offenders in Japan", International Review of Criminal Policy. No. 27, 1969, United Nation, 1970, p. 25.
2. Tsuda Minoru, "Participation of the Public in the Prevention and Control of Crime and Delinquency", paper presented at the fourth United Nations Congress on the Prevention of Crime and Treatment of Offenders, August, 16-17, 1970 Kyoto. Japan, p. 1.
3. A. Gardenwitz, "The Role of Volunteers in work with Juvenile Delinquents", International Review of Criminal Policy, No. 22, 1964, p. 68.
4. Robert E. Keldgord and Robert O. Norris, "New Directions Corrections", Federal Probation, Vol. 36, March 1977, No. 1 p. 2.
5. Dac H. Chang, Supra note, 1, p. 125.
6. Mahmoodin Muhamand, "Planning and Research for Crime Prevention", Resource Material Series, No. 8 UNAFEI, Oct. 1974, p. 29.
7. F. Lovell Bixby, Introduction to "Papers presented by the participants of the 25th International Training Course," UNAFEI, Resource Material Series, No. 1, p. 39.
8. Teo Boo Lat, "Public Participation in the Asian region—Modalities, Problems and some Possible solutions", Resource Materials series, No. A, UNAFEI, Oct. 1972, p. 110.
9. Report of the Fourth United Nations Congress on the Prevention of Crime and Treatment of Offenders, p. 18.
10. Editorial, "Mobilising Voluntary Resources", Social Defence, Vol. XI, No. 41, July 1975, p. 1.
11. Milton G. Rector, "Mobilising Public Participation in Social Defence: A Blue Print for Action. International Review of Criminal Policy, No. 27, 1969, p. 32.
12. A.T. Marcose, "Structural Public participation in the criminal justice process", paper read at the Seminar on Public participation in the Criminal Justice Process held at the Tata Institute of Social Sciences, Bombay, November 4-8, 1974, p. 8.
13. Ibid.
14. See the Evidence of the witnesses before the Joint Committee of Parliament on the Code of Criminal Procedure Bill, 1970, pp. 83, 126, 155, 224, 264, (Vol. I); and pp. 104, 162, 179, 265, (Vol. II).
15. See the Fourteenth Report of the Law Commission and Report of the Code of Criminal Procedure, 1893 (Thirty-seventh Report).

20

Participation, Institution-Building and Social Development

One of the most significant challenges before India is that of achieving social, political and economic development along with social justice. With regard to active Participation, Involvement and Control (PIC) of people in the development process, an attempt is being made in this chapter to provide a theoretical framework of achieving social political development. At this stage a hypothesis may be developed that the Participation, Involvement and Control (PIC) of people can give rise to a social-political system more conducive to the attainment of economic development along with a greater degree of social justice.

An attempt is also being made to provide a conceptual framework of institution building which we believe facilitates the process of people's participation, involvement and control. It is generally felt that the existing socio-economic and political order does not provide a proper opportunity for active participation to general masses. The existing decentralised institutions also do not provide opportunity to general masses for participation due to their elitist bias. An attempt is also being made to define social development which in the last analysis should be the goal of all economic growth.

Most of the post-war nations have professed belief in a democratic system of government. Michden states that "definitions of democracy and timing are different, but the ideologies of almost all countries proclaim some sort of democratic system as the ultimate goal.'[1] Attempts of other developing nations of Asia, Africa and Latin America to achieve a parliamentary or presidential system of democracy have met with similar scant success.

The reason is that many countries after gaining their independence from the colonial power tried to introduce an electoral system based on universal adult franchise, the provision of political parties and so on. To put it differently, they tried to make provision for the formal trappings of a representative democratic system similar to that obtaining in the former colonial countries. However, it must be realised that democracy is something more than a form of government. It entails: (1) certain attitudes; (2) some degree of political loyalty and belief in the worth and dignity of all people; (3) tolerance and a genuine effort at understanding the other point of view; (4) respect for the views of the opposition and an understanding of its role in providing certain checks and balances. The manner in which the representative system of the west operates also requires an educated and well-informed electorate, a relatively free press and other media to reflect and mould public opinion. Briefly speaking, democracy, besides being a way of life, requires institutional reforms where such variables 'as the degree of popular participation in the political process, the degree of freedom of the political opposition and the press, the degree of competitiveness among political parties and the degree to which the individual citizen regards it possible to have his input on public policy, are observed and roughly measured.'[2]

Obviously in most of the developing countries these pre-requisites did not exist but those at the helm of affairs were alive of the significance of these pre-requisites and were keen to thrust on their countries a foreign system of government and alien political institutions.

If we look into the fifty to sixty years' history of developing countries, we find that in country after country, the same story is repeated and the same drama is enacted, particularly in countries that were under colonial rule; simply speaking, the drama presented in three acts are somewhat as follows, with some difference in degree, depending on the stage of development of a particular country:

I. It is a commonplace knowledge that a colonial power subjugates a country and replaces the indigenous social-political-economic system with its own which deprives the people of almost all forms of self-government. The entire nation and all activities therein are controlled either by the colonial power itself or by indigenous officers carefully prepared to play the tune of the piper. The educational system is not geared to produce people with initiative and creativity but men who can carry on the day-to-day tasks of the government in power. H. Halsrey comments as follows:

> In India before independence, 12,000 Britons administered a country of 400 million people. This necessitated the British educational policy which was stated by Macaulay in 1835 thus, 'We must do out best to form a class who may be interpreters between us and the millions we govern, a class of people, Indian in blood and colour, but English in taste, in opinion, in morals and in intellect.'[3]

Not only this, the educational system was so geared that it only provided opportunity to rich and urban few. The people living in the rural areas, and particularly the rural poor, were kept out of the system as education was an expensive commodity that they could not buy. The consequence of such a policy was that, on the one hand, the indigenous system was distorted, if not totally destroyed, and on the other hand, it was not replaced with another system capable of providing education to the population at large.

In the economic area too, the indigenous population carried out its daily activities around farming, shop-keeping, small businesses and continued paying taxes to the government in power. The colonial powers shipped the raw materials out of the country, processed and manufactured these and brought them in as finished products to an almost captive market. No efforts were made to set up industries at home to process the raw materials and thus to develop the colonial economies. The development of infra-structure, namely, roads, railways, power, and water, etc., depended on whether the foreign government needed these services to augment its revenues and to maintain law and order.

The colonial powers centered their objectives around maintenance of law and order and continued to carry away the spoils from the countries under their subjugation. Provision of education and other social services was offered at a minimum level to help provide a climate conducive to carrying out these primary activities. The motivation for any reform or services was rendered only to that extent which could help the colonial power.

II. However, the scene changed to some extent when the indigenous population under the guidance and leadership of some enlightened and educated leaders agitated and demanded a voice in the government. As a result, the violent and non-violent activities brought about certain concessions for the indigenous population and some rudimentary form of self-government. It began with local government and usually went a little further than membership in advisory council to the governor or as nominated/ elected members in state governments. Ultimately, the yoke of colonial rule was thrown away, independence was achieved and the third act began.

III. With the advent of independence, the more articulate Indian leaders moved to provisional and central assemblies, many of them leaving behind their positions and role in local government. Desire for participation in political institutions turned out to be so widespread in India after independence that the state and local government institutions receded to an unimportant place, much because of the meagre power that they offered because after the acceptance of the principle of adult suffrage, which, under the republican constitution of India, was to inform all political institutions of the country, was to be implemented in the arena of local government, but because of the stupendous nature of the task, a clear-cut policy was taking time to evolve. In the absence of such a well-defined policy, the newly-enacted village Panchayat laws, in states like Bihar took recourse to a policy of unanimous election of Panchayat leaders. Unanimous elections kept the local squabbles sub-dued, no doubt, but it did little to spur political participation. Almost everywhere, it initially resulted in imbuing the traditional village leaders usually under the village Panchayat laws.

National concern was re-focused on local government institutions in the wake of the centrally felt-need of associating the local people in the process of implementing the centrally-formulated schemes of development under the five-year plans. This occurred in 1957. Between 1946 and 1952, they were too pre-occupied with the national issues erupting in the wake of partition with integration of Indian princely States with the Indian Union, and with creating the structures of an independent state of the size of India. During the period of the first five year plan, they experimented with a centrally-sponsored programme of community development. The programme, begun experimentally in 1952, made a modest headway; and so in 1957, on the recommendation of the famous Balwantrai Mehta team of study, the National Development Council decided to create new local institutions for each community development block area and to re-structure and re-furnish the district local councils, already in existence in some form since 1885. The existing local councils that covered a sub-district area of a tehsil/taluka/sub-division, each was squeezed out of the new framework of the local government system that was created for rural India after 1957.

An analysis of the above-mentioned phenomenon leads us to five basic conclusions.

The first is that the elites of the country are making the most of the political and economic decisions and are devising a system of government on the basis of their own knowledge and preference. Second, the system chosen in the political and economic areas are those that their former colonial masters, namely, the capitalistic model in the economic area and the parliamentary model in the political system. Third, as regards the socio-political and economic development of the country, the population at large is not involved in the decision-making processes. Fourth, the models adopted by the elites are foreign and alien to the people and impose a life style and perhaps even a belief system that is in conflict with the values they hold sacred. Fifth, the pre-requisites for the successful operation of models of the west are totally missing in the developing countries or are present only in a very rudimentary way. Thus, the attempts of many developing countries to achieve political stability have met with scant success. Rather, the educational, political and economic systems introduced by the elites have aggravated the dualism present within the societies and increased the gulf between the haves and the have-nots. Even the agricultural policy aimed at achieving self-sufficiency in food, namely, the green revolution, has heralded the red revolution and led to the development of rich farmers and further impoverishment of the small land-holders.

Rural Economic Sector

Recent theories projecting the behaviour patterns of socio-economic system have distinctly identified the impact and influence of spatial rural urban dichotomy on the growth and development of the economic system of the countries. This dichotomy associates itself, rightly or wrongly, with every phase of economic development. Ordinarily, it has been observed that the developed countries comprise or command a larger urban sector than the rural. Whereas the proportionate magnitude of this twin sector is great, the opposite is the case in the developing countries. This attribute is so axiomatic that even the process of economic development has been regarded as one which should result in the expansion of the urban and simultaneous contraction of the rural segment.

Colin Clark[4] observes that the rural sector occupies a major space in the econosphere of an under-developed country. He identifies three distinct phases of economic development, which are:

(i) When agriculture is the dominant occupation and is the major source of natural income;

(ii) When the urban industrial sector grows relatively higher than rural agricultural; and

(iii) When the service sector emerges by over-riding the industrial as well as agricultural sectors in the urban and rural areas.

As a matter of fact, the transformation of rural into urban is the outcome rather than the symptom of economic development. The reason is that the economic development implies and envisages capital investment not only for the promotion and development of industries but equally also for building up the infrastructural facilities *sine qua non* for mobilising and channellising material, monetary and manual resources from one sector to another.

A portrait of the rural economy of a country generally reflects a number of sequester settlements wearing a morose and lackadaisical look. These micro-spatial settlements or constellations of different orders contribute negligibly in absence of adequate infrastructural facilities. This structure is characterised with inadequate momentum and motivation necessary for economic upliftment. As a result, the rural sector in totality appears to be a spectrum of incohesive and disjuncted block of immense but inert resources and potentialities. Low responsiveness and reactivity is the inherent behaviour pattern of the rural economic sector.

Contrastingly, the urban economy evinces relatively a higher degree of factor mobility coupled with a greater degree of modernisation due to the development of industrial as well as physical infrastructure. In this connection Sim[5] says, 'Urban sector is multiple and complex, but the rural is more limited and simple. The latter is territorially determined whereas the former is based on interest.'

A rural community is tradition-bound and somewhat apathetic to modernisation while adaptation to modernisation and change is discernible in urban community. The social possibilities, however, of these sectors do not show any conflict or exploitation despite their different characteristics. 'These personalities', says B. Ghosh[6], 'are not always complementary to each other and many confrontations have taken place'. Such confrontations arise as a result of their different economic personalities based on exploitation of the rural economy, howsoever marginal its contribution may be. Being primarily agricultural, it channellises foodgrains and non-foodgrains surplus for the subsistence of the urban economy. Although since the dawn of urban development, the cities have sheltered classes which consciously or unconsciously have sought more often than not with distinct success, to exploit the rural classes, nevertheless, without the fundamental contribution of the agricultural industry all the rest of the fabric of our civilisation would topple into rains almost overnight.'[7]

The magnitude of contribution of the rural sector in the form of the farm product in the Gross National Product (GNP) determines the character of an economy . The GNP, in fact, is the aggregate gross value of farm and non-farm products. Their relative proportions and the subsequent changes therein manifest the character of economic development.

The dichotomy of rural urban sector in the developing economy of India is perceptible. Gandhiji used to say 'India lives in her villages'. The foundations of the village economy are so deep-rooted and strong that the process of industrialisation over the period of last three decades could do little to change the spectrum. The rural sector in India occupies a prestigious place because it is economically resourceful and politically powerful.

Until recently, there had been an overemphasis on the development of heavy industries, sophisticated technologies and newer supra-structure in order to accelerate the pace of economic development of the country. But before generating the needed momentum for the development, a number of maladies came to affect the body of economic system. The benefits of development efforts could not reach and penetrate into the larger sections of the community. The rich became richer and the poor, poorer. This went against the constitutional economic policy which aimed at establishing an egalitarian society.

The concentration of development efforts in urban sector alienated the resource-rich rural sector. No doubt, some programmes were launched in the agro-rural sector but they were least commensurable with regard to its size and status. Now, the era of development of the urban industries sector is coming to a halt.

Why Participation at the Grass Roots?

In the preceding pages we have tried to narrate that the political and economic elites have not been able to introduce a viable political system nor economic growth with social justice. The models—political, economic and educational—provided by so-called elites do not reflect the people's values and aspirations as they are alien to the general masses. Brown, while commenting on political parties as media for reaching the people, makes following observation:

> The conversion of Asian, African and Latin American political parties into mass organisations (was) not simply a technical problem involving such matters as the creation of local branches and publication of party newspapers. Nor (did) it rest upon the triumph of the principle of universal suffrage. The real difficulty (was) that an enormous gap (existed) between a small, educated elite and the illiterate peasant masses. Not only (were) there few organisational links between the elite and the masses, there (was) hardly any communication.[8]

Another political scientist[9] describes this state of affairs as follows:

The juxtaposition of an elite educated in a tradition of exogenous inspiration and a mass rooted in a variety of indigenous cultures engenders problems that turn up throughout the world of the new states.

Here we are trying to make an attempt at providing a theoretical framework that the socio-political and economic development of the country (it may apply to all the countries of the Third World) could be better achieved through the participation, involvement and control of the people. As such this effort may give rise to a political system that is, at least in relative terms if not in an absolute sense, more conducive to the attainment of socio-political-economic development with greater social justice.

One of the problems of the constitutional government and democracy in India (it may apply also to other Asian countries) is the fact that in our country political changes have preceded social and economic change. [10] Providing people a climate conducive for participation, involvement and control (PIC) it is but natural to resort to the strategy of institution-building. But before discussing institution-building, it is necessary to explain what we mean by institution-building, its scope and parameters.

Since the elites have not been successful in introducing and maintaining a political system capable of developing the country and its people, it seems only logical to look for another set of people who could deliver the goods. However, expediency alone is not the reason for seeking out the 'people *per se*' to don the mantle of leadership. For participation in the decision-making that affects their lives, the people, being the citizens of a free country, have the inherent right. However, the representative democracy as pursued by elites of our country has not been able to provide the vehicle for such involvement. Another reason given for the non-involvement of the people in the political and economic decision-making is that they do not possess the requisite knowledge and expertise to participate in the complex decision of twentieth century problems. The facts, however, state very eloquently that it is the educated elites, often immersed in twentieth century scholarship, who have not been able to introduce a political system that could reflect the aspirations of the people and lead them to a better life. If the decision-making processes are brought to their level and involve issues and problems that they are concerned with, the apparent lack of education and even literacy will not prove deterrent to the involvement of the people in the decision-making process. The apparent lack of education does not mean that people do not possess intelligence and the wisdom to be able to discern programmes and activities that would help them to achieve a better life. Instead of depending on experts, local or foreign, who make the decision in the confines of the planning commission, the process of people's participation, involvement and control (PIC) will lead to the determination of what constitutes a 'better life' by the people themselves. The decisions as to what constitutes a better life would then also reflect the value system of the people rather than being at cross purposes with what people consider significant and sacred.

'It is a sound principle of human order that social tasks should be left at the simplest and most human level at which they can be adequately performed beginning with the family'.[11] By doing so it may be possible that the process of involvement of the people would lead to social development that would make the process of political development easier and less hazardous.

Social Development

Social development can be defined as a process and goal that aims at the total development of people in a manner that they deem fit and desirable. In other words, the people determine what is development, its parameters, and the trade-offs they wish to make for achievement a certain kind of development. Development is also considered as a total process, not a fragmented, piecemeal and isolated approach to issues and problems. To provide greater social justice, social development may be inter-sectoral, inter-regional and inter-disciplinary and may visualise institutional and structural reforms. Social development encompasses in its domain strategies that aim at the total enhancement of the life of all people, its conceptual base is belief in the dignity of human beings which has as its logical corollary, the equality of all people. To put it differently, the concept of exploitation of some people of some region by people who have greater power and resources is alien to the concept of social development.

Institution-Building on Decentralised Basis

After a brief description of social development, we turn our attention towards discussion of participation, involvement and control of people in these socio-political processes that affect their lives. To facilitate this process the strategy of decentralised institution-building could be adopted.

By institution-building here is meant the formation of mechanisms that afford a continuous and sustained forum for people to discuss the issues and problems that concern them to decide ways and means to meet such problems and to plan activities that reflect their needs and aspirations. Such institutions could be as simple as that of a neighbourhood committee or as complex as a cooperative bank. They could be formal or informal, though it is possible that formalisation may occur as these institutions strive to enhance and strengthen their work.

By decentralisation we mean that such institutions would operate at levels very close to the people. And the attempt should be to make participation as direct as possible. In the concept of decentralisation the implied belief is that the human activities, programmes and institutions can be so devised that it is possible to delineate their various parts and decentralise the planning and implementation of programmes. The hypothesis is this that the smaller the unit of decentralisation, the more direct the participation and the greater the involvement and control of those directly affected. This will serve yet another purpose that the process would also make the people more accountable to one another and thereby to the society at large.

However, certain programmes and activities do need to be organised on a somewhat larger scale. If institutions need to be organised at relatively higher levels the process of representation could be used but this process should not be far removed from its geographical constituency. We are alien to the fact that the small units cannot take over the multifarious work that is required to meet community needs and the needs of the larger society. To accomplish such work and to resolve issues that require the cooperation of more people and larger bodies it is possible for two or more units to join hands or engage in a more formal federation to meet their mutual needs or to tackle their multifarious problems. For example, many neighbourhood committees could form themselves into a council to set up a secondary school that could serve their neighbourhood. We can build decentralised institutions which involve the setting up of institutions at various levels to attend to tasks that require the efforts of several grass-roots organisations. However, the institutions at the various levels would be so organised that their composition would reflect as directly as possible representation of people from on school to the other.

Decentralised institutions in India, if properly organised can, over a period of time, achieve the following:

1. At a number of levels they can create more leadership of various kinds. For example, neighbourhood groups and council at higher levels would provide greater opportunities for people to participate in meeting the needs of the local population, and in utilising their skills for the general improvement at the local level.

2. They can give people a greater voice in decision-making that affects their immediate environment—social, economic and political as well as in matters that affect their surrounding communities. The participation of people would become more intense and lead to local control over decisions and resources, as the institutions at the local levels and higher echelons develop with the increase in the number of institutions. People's participation at various levels will also increase giving them greater control of their own affairs.

3. They can enlarge the centres of power and authority, people's control at the local level and the opportunities for leadership this creates would lead to the diffusion of power and authority which in India is vested in a few hands, namely that of the landlord, emerging affluent section of the society and the bureaucracy.

4. They can lead to the creation of an infrastructure such as bridges, roads, wells, etc., by the people and those at the helm of affairs, namely the people themselves would be more interested in providing such facilities.

5. They can strengthen municipal services—people's councils and committees get involved in local government which will lead to a more stable tax base and enlargement of municipal services.

6. They can reduce the hold of bureaucracy as the people get more control, the role and the power of the bureaucracy; participatory that of the petty government officials, will decline.

7. They can reduce court cases and litigation—people's participation and control will also lead to the reduction of petty cases in the courts and the lengthy litigations that go with them. As the people's councils become stronger, people can rely more on the arbitration and conciliation efforts of the members instead of taking their feuds to the courts.

8. They can lead to greater cohesiveness—activities such as those described above would lead to greater cohesiveness within the community and to lesser factions.

9. They can reflect the felt needs of people as large numbers of people would be involved in these institutions directly and indirectly, the programmes and activities they will undertake would reflect the felt needs of the people. If agriculture is their main concern, the council's activities will reflect this need. If credit is what the people want, it is possible for such institutions to form a credit cooperative or to establish liaison with the agriculture credit banks.

10. They can enable people's determination of the parameters of development—if the institutions determine their own priorities, it means that they are determining the kind of development they wish to have and the risks they wish to take and the trade-offs they are willing to make. We somehow equate the terms development and modernisation and wish that societies in the process of becoming modern shun tradition and communal mores, look at issues and problems from an economic stand-point and not from a culturally determined normative perspective. We believe that the decision to shun or retain traditional norms and behaviour should be made by people themselves rather than by professional experts, indigenous or foreign.

11. They can lead to greater social justice, it is visualised that over time such control over determination of priorities and use of resources exercised by the people would mean greater social justice as a much greater number of people would be involved in the decision-making process. In the words of Freire 'the basic elementary criterion is whether or not the society is a being for itself. If it is not, the other criteria indicate modernisation rather than development'.[12]

12. They can achieve integrated and holistic development—through decentralised institutions, development could become an integrated, holistic venture rather than a piecemeal fragmented effort of one sector of the economy or the attempt of a particular government department to promote its departmental activities. As problems faced by people do not necessarily fall within one sector or one discipline, solutions suggested through the community and efforts to solve problems may use inter-sectoral and inter-disciplinary strategies.

13. They can develop the rural sector—the major thrust of economic development in most developing countries should be in the rural areas and through the agriculture sector which employs 60 to 70 per cent of the labour force and provides 40 to 50 per cent of the GNP. The developmental model pursued by many Third World countries of

rapid industrialisation and urbanisation has not been successful and has left the rural areas through decentralised institutions that will reflect the needs of the people. Similarly, agriculture credit could also be organised through the efforts of people's institutions as community norms, values and control can play a very important part in the repayment of credit. People's institutions can also assist in the matter of collaterals. This will help farmers to borrow from established credit institutions rather than becoming a prey of the team sharks.

REFERENCES

1. Fred, R. Mchden, Von Der, Politics of the Developing Nations, Prentice Hall, Inc., 1964, p. 118.
2. W.W. Rostow, Politics and Stages of Growth, Cambridge University Press 1971, London, N.W. 1, p. 208.
3. H. Halsey, "The Education of Leaders and Political Development in New Nations", from L. Richard Merrit, and Stein Rokhan (ed.), Comparing Nations, Yale University Press, 1965, p. 207. The Educated Man in India. Dryden Press, New York, 1955, p. 14.
4. Colin Clark, Conditions of Economic Progress, London, Cambridge University Press, 1957, p. 145.
5. Sim, N.L. Elements of Rural Sociology, Routledge and Keggan Paul, USA, 1946, p. 15.
6. Ghosh, B. Planning Process, Readings on "Micro-Level Planning and Rural Growth Centres", National Institute of Community Development, Hyderabad, 1972, p. 290.
7. Wilson Gee, The Social Economics of Agriculture, 1942, p. 156.
8. Bernard E. Brown, New Direction in Comparative Politics, Agra Publishing House, 1962, p. 25.
9. Melden, *op. cit.*, p. 22.
10. Sharma Parmatma, "Thoughts on Democracy" from Political Studies by Tiwari and Sharma, Shiva Lal Agrawala, Tiwari and Co., Agra, 1966, p. 187.
11. Barbara Ward, Nationalism and Ideology, W.W. Norton and Co. Inc., New York, 1960, p. 106.
12. Panlo Frive, Pedagogy of the Oppressed, Continuum Books. Seabury Press, New York, p. 161.

21

Panchayats for Rural Development

Village is basic unit of our Indian society. Over 63 crores of people live in 5,79,132 villages. The concept of rural development emphasises on development of these villages, people living in these villages. The process of development should, therefore, originate in villages. Instead for the last three hundred years the administration has been concentrated. The cry for decentralisation appears to respond both to organisational needs within the district and the demands of emerging linkages with the dynamics of development.

The "panchayat" or the institution of the village council is as old as India's history and is a part of her tradition. The ancient panchayats, serving as units of local government, discharged most of the functions that affected the life of the village community. These institutions flourished in relative isolation and were unaffected by the social and political changes that took place in urban India up to the 18th century. Dr. Altekar gives us a detailed account of village communities in India and of the working of rural communities. He states: "Since early times, the village has been the pivot of administration in India... There is no doubt that villages were the real centres of social life and important units of country's economy. They sustained the edifice of national culture, prosperity and administration." Rural development will be more meaningful when the village agency assumes responsibility and initiative for developing the resources of the village. Only a village organisation representing the community as a whole can provide the necessary leadership.

The concept of panchayats was a part of the philosophy of *'Purna Swaraj'* and *'Gram Swaraj.'* Mahatma Gandhi and Jawaharlal Nehru breathed into those concepts and inexorable and practical patriotic impetus during the era of India's struggle for independence. Indeed, at the seed time of our Constitution, the concept of village panchayats was not a remote and hoary historical concept. It was a part of the legacy of India's struggle for freedom and its quest for its own traditions and identity.

The Constitution of India was enacted, adopted and proclaimed in the name of the people of India as an organic document of democratic self-government as a rule of law. Enshrines for democratic faith and resolve of the resurgent people of India committed to the philosophy of "Swaraj" not only in the sense of emancipation from the colonial yoke of an alien imperial power but in the sense of self-government and the protection of the fundamental rights and dignity of the individual as a way of life and social habit. The fabric of our constitutional philosophy is woven with the warp and woof of democracy and rule of law.

The Constitution of India provides for republican democracy at the national level in the form of its bicameral Parliament and by making the Council of Ministers collectively responsible to the House of the People. The same basic pattern of parliamentary institutions is replicated at the level of states which form the Union of India. The quasi federal framework of India's parliamentary democracy, the creation of Panchayati Raj institutions and their organisation was, however left to a general directive embodied in Article 40 of the Constitution in the following terms:

Organisation of Village Panchayats—"The state shall take steps to organise village panchayats and endow them with such powers and authority as may be necessary to enable them to function as units of self-government."

The true potential of Article 40 lies not merely in its directive to the Indian State at all levels as a part of constitutionally formulated principle of State Policy to organise village panchayats but in its significant concommitant mandate that panchayats should be endowed with "such powers and authority as may be necessary to enable them to function as units of self-government." "The message of that mandate is clear and clarion. It means that the task and the tryst of the founding fathers of the Constitution would remain incomplete unless village panchayats begin to function as units of self-government as a part of our democratic policy. An attempt to conceptualise the framework of panchayat institutions is to take its inspiration from the constitutional mandate to complete that unfinished task. The theological emphasis of that constitutional mandate is structural, operational and functional with its implicit ramifications for our democracy and development, for freedom and welfare, and for justice, liberty, equality, individual dignity, national unity and Indian people's fraternity as integrally correlated concepts.

Integrated Vision of Democracy

The National Parliament and the Central Government, the State Legislatures and the State Governments and the whole pyramid of our judicial system are important to the working of democracy and the maintenance of the rule of law. In their own respective spheres, these legislative infrastructure. To the common Indian villager, however, they do not represent a preoccupying part of his daily life. The revolution in communication technology does often enough lift and transport him audio-visually to the ambiance of these institutions but he cannot quite relate to them in terms of his daily needs and everyday concern. Self-government may mean to him only the spectacular occasion when he exercises his franchise; but his participation in the electoral process for the Lok Sabha and the Vidhan Sabha cannot give him a sense of full and meaningful participation in the democratic responsibility for being a citizen in the democratic republic of India. There are gaps and anomalies in the democratic experience of the

Indian citizen, particularly in the countryside. Panchayati Raj institutions in our rural areas and municipal bodies in our urban areas represent, first and foremost the possibility of a truly dependable and durable institutional assurance for overcoming those distances and gaps. Without local units of self-government, we cannot hope to establish a viable and vibrant democracy. It is in its perspective that rural and urban development are, in effect, two sides of the same coin and are parts of a composite continuum of what may be called democratic urbanisation. Self-government necessarily subsumes and supplements developments in all its ramifications in rural as well as urban contexts. It is with an integrated vision that they have to be reviewed, restructured, reclaimed, renewed and revitalised.

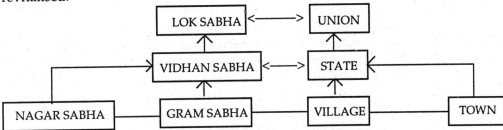

Fig. 21.1. Democratic Decentralisation.

The experience of local self-government in the urban areas and in the districts in different parts of India during the period of British rule was uneven. It is true that certain ground rules of municipal self-government were evolved in the cities and towns during that period. Some of the municipal bodies acquitted themselves so creditably that they become examples of civic self-government at its best. There were, however, other municipalities which appeared to be insufficiently imbued with the philosophy of local self-government. The District Councils were primarily administrative structures and did not quite come into their own. One of the obvious reason was that the country was dominated by colonial administration and its pre-emotive imperatives. In the countryside, panchayats were quite often caste institutions with a pivotal social role but they did not function as institutions of State and instruments of self-government and social change.

The constitutional vision of republican self-government at the village level enshrined in Article 40 came to be unfolded a few years after the commencement of our Constitution when it became increasingly self-evident that community development and socio-economic transformation could not be achieved without democratic participation. This compelling and inescapable realisation of the limitations of the bureaucratic models led to an enthusiastic interest in Panchayat Raj institutions which was enlivened by generous impulses.

The Community Development Programme launched in 1952. The blocks came to be established as units of development administration. The National Extension Service was established soon thereafter with a view to reinforce the administrative network to tackle the problems of growth and development at different local and functional levels.

At that stage there was, relatively speaking, only nominal public interest. Soon, lack of public involvement and participation began to be perceived as an impediment in the successful implementation of Community Development and National Extension Service Programmes. Based on that perception, the Second Plan document recognised the necessity for speeding up the development of democratic institutions and concluded that "unless there is a comprehensive village planning, which takes into account the needs of the entire community, weaker sections like tenant-cultivators, landless workers and artisans may not benefit sufficiently from assistance provided by the Government. "Referring to the aim of the National Extension Movement to reach every family in the village, the Second Five Year Plan reported that in order to fulfil that aim it was necessary to have "an agency in the village which represents the community as a whole and can assume responsibility and initiative for developing the resources of the village and providing the necessary leadership. Indeed, rural progress depends entirely on the existence of an active organisation of the weaker sections mentioned above into common programmes to be carried out with the assistance of the administration." The thinking underlying the Second Plan was that village panchayats along with co-operatives could play a considerable art in bringing about a more just and integrated social structure in rural areas. The thrust of the Second Five Year Plan was to establish statutory panchayats in all the villages though more as vehicles for national extension and community development projects and not so much as units of self-government. It was primarily from this angle that the number of panchayats was to be more than doubled by 1960-61.

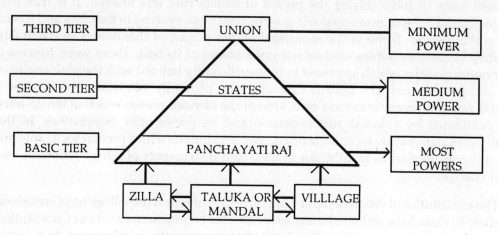

Fig. 21.2. Ties of Administration.

Ascent on Panchayati Raj Momentum

The Balwantray Mehta Team was appointed in January, 1957 to study and report on the Community Development Projects and National Extension Service with a view to "economy and efficiency" and, among others "for the assessment of the extent to which the movement has succeeded in utilising local initiative and in creating institutions to ensure continuity in the process of improving economic and social conditions in rural areas." Once again the approach was primarily to achieve economy and efficiency.

The Balwantray Mehta Team, however, found that "Development cannot progress without responsibility and power. Community development can be real only when the community understands its problems realises its responsibilities, exercises the necessary powers through its chosen representatives and maintains a constant and intelligent vigilance on local administration." It was with this objective that the team recommended on early establishment or statutory elective local bodies and devolution to them of the necessary resources, powers and authority.

The recommendations of the Balwantray Mehta Study Team came as a fresh breeze and gave a new lease to community development and extension service project. It paved the way for a new era of Panchayati Raj institutions which was inaugurated by Pandit Jawaharlal Nehru on 2nd October, 1959 at a national rally at Nagaur.

Pandit Jawaharlal Nehru described the new beginning as "the most revolutionary and historical step in the context of new India." In a sense, it was an act of faith in republican democracy and was as important an event as a establishment of the parliamentary system itself for the people of India and by the people of India. The idea rode on the crest of the new wave of public enthusiasm which had found a sense of direction and an institutional habitat. The spirited launching of Panchayati Raj institutions at Nagpur seemed to capture the public imagination. That memorable rally aroused high hopes and great expectations. The idea was not meant to be a mere counsel of convenience or as a design of an auxiliary system of development administration. Indeed, the momentum of that momentous change was lost and the Panchayati Raj institutions began to decline when their status and role as units of self-government were eclipsed by a combination of several factors of decadence and disarray. When the basic premise of Panchayati Raj institutions as units of self-government was lost, these institutions also lost their capability to fulfil the promise of development.

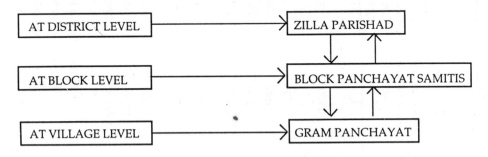

Fig. 21.3. Structure of Panchayats.

Panchayati Raj Legislation

All the states have accordingly established Panchayati Raj. The necessary legislation has been passed and implemented in the States of Andhra Pradesh, Assam, Tamil Nadu, Maharashtra, Karnataka, Orissa, Punjab, Rajasthan and Uttar Pradesh. Legislation for this purpose has also been passed in the states of Bihar, Gujarat and Madhya

TABLE 21.1

Number of Panchayati Raj Institutions at Various Levels and their Coverage of Rural Population and Villages

(As on 31.3.88)

States/UTs	Lower level i.e. Gram Panchayats (No.)	Middle level i.e. Panchayat Samities Taluka Panchayat (No.)	District Level i.e. Zilla Parishads (No.)	Rural Population Covered (In Lakhs)	Villages Covered (No.)	Remarks
(1)	(2)	(3)	(4)	(5)	(6)	(7)
1. Andhra Pradesh*	19550	330	22	409.85	29293	
2. Arunachal Pradesh*	714	—				
3. Assam*	11653	589	31$	171.83	20799	$—At sub-divisional level
4. Bihar	NA	NA	39	611.96	76488	
5. Goa*	13059	182	NA	NA	NA	
6. Gujarat	5790	102	19	234.84	18550	
7. Haryana	2597	67	Abolished	100.96	7064	
8. Himachal Pradesh	1469	—	—	42.57	18843	
9. Jammu and Kashmir*			19	47.27	6900	
10. Karnataka*	#	#		264.06	29390	Fig. relates 1981-82
11. Kerala*	1001	—	...	206.82	1219	
12. Madhya Pradesh	18801	459M	43	415.92	76603	
13. Maharashtra	24600	298Z	29Y	407.91	39345	Fig. relates 1987-88
14. Manipur*	**	**	**	5.79	667	
15. Meghalaya*	No Panchayati Raj Set up					
16. Mizoram*	No Panchayati Raj Set up					
17. Nagaland*	Refer to Annex. I					
18. Orissa*	4388	314	Abolished	232.60	51639	
19. Punjab	10953	118x	12x	121.41	12795	
20. Rajasthan	7351	237	27	270.51	37124	

	(1)	(2)	(3)	(4)	(5)	(6)	(7)
21.	Sikkim*	153	—	...	2.65	440	
22.	Tamil Nadu*	****	****	24	359.00	16696	
23.	Tripura*	704	...	...	18.27	864	
24.	Uttar Pradesh	73914	895	56	909.13	112566	
25.	West Bengal*	3242	324	15	394.78	38047	Fig. relates 1982-8
U.Ts.							
26.	A and N Islands*	43	...	...	0.97	183	
27.	Chandigarh*	21	1	1	0.29	22	
28.	D and N Haveli*	10	...	...	1.03	72	
29.	Delhi*	191	5@	...	4.52	228	@ Non-statutory body
30.	Daman and Diu*	No Panchayati Raj Set up					
31.	Lakshadweep*	No Panchayati Raj Set up					
32.	Pondicherry*	...	11	...	...	334	Only at Block Level

#—8373 Panchayats and 175 Panchayat Samities are under Administrator Control.

**—107 Panchayats and 6 Panchayat Samities Dissolved.

***—118 Panchayat Samitis and 12 Zilla Parishads are Under Super Session, Since 1978.

****—13097 Panchayats and 378 Panchayat Samitis Superseded.

x—Superseded w.e.f. Oct. 1978.

Y—19 Z.P. are in Position and 10 Z.P. are Under Administrators.

Z—255 PS in Position.

M—No Distributed 415.

Pradesh and has been implemented. In West Bengal, the West Bengal Panchayat Act, 1956, is in force, and legislation for the setting up of bodies at the block and district levels has been undertaken. In Kerala, a new and comprehensive Panchayat Act was passed in 1960, and has been implemented. Legislation for the upper tiers has also been implemented.

Origin and Coverage

Panchayati Raj was introduced in 1959 as a three-tier structure of self-government at the village, block and district levels.

There are, today more than, 2,72,658 village panchayats in the country covering over 96% of about 5.79 lakhs inhabited villages and 92% of the rural population of our country. There are about 4525 panchayat samitis of different nomenclature at the block, taluka or tahsil level; each panchayati samiti or mandal panchayat has on an average 60 village panchayats covering an average population of about 65,000. There are about 330 Zilla Parishads covering about 427 districts in the country; each Zilla Parishad has on an average 13 to 14 Panchayati Samitis and about 826 Gram Panchayats covering a population of 9.10 lakhs on an average.

Structure

A review of the present position of Panchayati Raj in the states shows a similarity in the basic institutional structure. In many States, there is the Gram Sabha, consisting of all adult residents. It discusses the annual budget of the panchayat, the administration report and the development works to be undertaken in its area. But, in all the states, panchayat is the basic unit of local government. The structure of Panchayati Raj institutions varies from state to state. In 14 states/UTs, the three-tier system exists while 4 states have two-tier and 9 states/UTs one tier. In Nagaland, Meghalaya, Mizoram, and Lakshadweep, Panchayati Raj institutions are established in accordance with the traditions and customs of their villages.

TABLE 21.2

Rural Development Institutions in India

	States/Union Territories	Institutions in					Total
		Rural Development	Agriculture and Allied	Animal Husbandry and Allied	Rural Industries	Others	
	(1)	(2)	(3)	(4)	(5)	(6)	(7)
1.	Andhra Pradesh	15	22	4	39	1	81
2.	Assam	16	2	—	12	1	41
3.	Bihar	16	12	38	53	1	129
4.	Gujarat	22	28	19	27	—	96

	(1)	(2)	(3)	(4)	(5)	(6)	(7)
5.	Haryana	2	10	1	74	—	87
6.	Himachal Pradesh	5	7	1	11	—	24
7.	Jammu and Kashmir	2	5	1	14	—	22
8.	Karnataka	22	22	3	84	—	131
9.	Kerala	15	12	3	42	—	72
10.	Madhya Pradesh	30	18	—	10	—	58
11.	Maharashtra	41	21	3	41	—	106
12.	Manipur	3	—	—	1	—	4
13.	Meghalaya	3	5	—	3	11	
14.	Nagaland	2	3	—	1	1	7
15.	Orissa	11	11	2	16	—	40
16.	Punjab	3	9	—	79	—	91
17.	Rajasthan	11	17	—	21	—	49
18.	Sikkim	—	2	—	1	—	3
19.	Tamil Nadu	16	16	9	49	—	90
20.	Tripura	2	1	—	2	—	5
21.	Uttar Pradesh	46	48	2	122	3	221
22.	West Bengal	19	19	8	30	—	76
Union Territories							
23.	Andaman and Nicobar Islands	—	1	—	—	—	1
24.	Arunachal Pradesh	2	1	—	1	—	4
25.	Chandigarh	1	1	—	2	—	4
26.	Dadra and Nagar Haveli	—	—	—	1	—	1
27.	Delhi	2	5	—	18	—	25
28.	Goa	2	1	—	7	—	10
29.	Mizoram	—	1	—	1	—	2
30.	Pondicherry	—	2	—	1	—	3

A Gram or Village Panchayat is a statutory body covering one or more villages with an average population varying between 1,000 to 3,000 people, and an average area of about six square miles. It is a body of elected representatives. The number of members varies from 5 to 31, but is 15 on the average. The Village Panchayat area is generally divided into wards, each ward returning its representative to the panchayat. In Assam and the Punjab, the entire village electorate elects all its members at one time. Reservation for women and for scheduled castes and scheduled tribes is provided for in most states. The members of panchayats are elected by a secret ballot in most states, while election by show of hands obtains in Assam, Jammu and Kashmir, parts of Madhya Pradesh, Uttar Pradesh and Himachal Pradesh. The Sarpanch (President) and Up a Sarpanch (Vice-President) are generally chosen by the panchas (members) from among themselves. The direct election of the Sarpanch is prescribed in Assam, Bihar, parts of Madhya Pradesh, the Punjab, Rajasthan, Uttar Pradesh and Himachal Pradesh. His term of office is five years in Kerala, Tamil Nadu and Uttar Pradesh, four years in Gujarat, Jammu & Kashmir, Maharashtra, Karnataka, Orissa and West Bengal, and three years in other states.

TABLE 21.3

Various Tiers of Panchayati Raj System (State-wise)

States/UTs having Traditional Councils of Village elders	States/UTs having only One-Tier System	States/UTs having Two-Tier System	States/UTs having Three-Tier System
1. Meghalaya	1. Jammu and Kashmir	1. Assam	1. Andhra Pradesh
2. Nagaland	2. Kerala	2. Haryana	2. Bihar
3. Lakshwadweep	3. Tripura	3. Orissa	3. Gujarat
4. Mizoram	4. Andaman and Nicobar Islands	4. Manipur	4. Himachal Pradesh
5. Sikkim	5. Sikkim		5. Karnataka
	6. Goa, Daman and Diu		6. Madhya Pradesh
	7. Dadra and Nagar Haveli		7. Maharashtra
	8. Pondicherry (only at block level)		8. Punjab
	9. Delhi		9. Rajasthan
			10. Tamil Nadu
			11. Uttar Pradesh
			12. West Bengal
			13. Chandigarh
			14. Arunachal Pradesh

Panchayat Samiti

The next tier in Panchayati Raj is the Panchayat Samiti. It is called Anchalik Panchayat in Assam, Panchayat Union Council in Tamil Nadu, Taluka Development Board in Karnataka, Kshetra Samiti in Uttar Pradesh, and Anchalik Parishad in West Bengal. The Panchayat Samiti is normally co-terminus with a community development block. In Karnataka, it comprises the taluka; in Maharashtra, some samitis cover two or three blocks. In West Bengal, there is an intermediary stage, called Anchal Panchayat, between the Panchayat and the Anchalik Parishad. The Anchal Panchayat corresponds to the former Union Board and has been allowed to continue in view of its historical associations. It is the Anchal and not the Village Panchayat that has taxation powers. The Anchal Panchayat takes care of the safety and protection of the area by appointing

TABLE 21.4

Panchayati Raj Structure in Different States

State	Bottom Tier		Intermediate Tier		Top Tier	
	Level	Body	Level	Body	Level	Body
Andhra Pradesh	Village or Group of Villages	Gram Panchayat	Block	Panchayat Samiti	Revenue District	Zilla Parishad
Assam	Do.	Gram Panchayat		(Abolished)	Sub-Division	Mohkuma Parishad
Bihar	Do.	Executive Committee of Gram Panchayat	Block	Panchayat Samiti	Revenue-District	Zilla Parishad (in 8 districts only)
Gujarat	Do.	Gram/Nagar Panchayat	Taluk	Taluk Panchayat	Do.	District Panchayat
Haryana	Do.	Gram Panchayat	Block	Panchayat Samiti		
Himachal Pradesh	Do.	Gram Panchayat	Block	Panchayat Samiti	Revenue District	Zilla Parishad
Jammu and Kashmir	Do.	Gram Panchayat	Block	Block Panchayat Board		
Karnataka	Do.	Village/Town Panchayat	Taluk Mandal	Taluk Development Board	Revenue District	District Development Council
Kerala	Do.	Gram Panchayat				
Madhya Pradesh	Do.	Gram Panchayat	Block	Janapada Panchayat		
Maharashtra	Do.	Gram Panchayat	Taluk/Block	Panchayat Samiti	Revenue District	Zilla Parishad
Manipur	Do.	Gram Panchayat			(Abolished in Nov. 1968)	
Orissa	Do.	Gram Panchayat	Block	Panchayat Samiti	Revenue District	Zilla Parishad
Punjab	Do.	Gram Panchayat	Block	Panchayat Samiti	Revenue District	Zilla Parishad
Rajasthan	Do.	Panchayat	Block	Panchayat Samiti	Do.	Zilla Parishad
Tamil Nadu	Do.	Village/Town Panchayat	Block	Panchayat Union/Council	Development District	District Development Council
Tripura	Do.	Gaon Panchayat				
Uttar Pradesh	Do.	Gram Panchayat	Block	Kshetra Samiti	Revenue District	Zilla Parishad
West Bengal	Do.	Gram Panchayat	Block	Panchayat Samiti	Do.	Zilla Parishad

Defedars and Chowkidars, while the development and civic activities are assigned to the Gram Panchayat.

Panchayat Samitis in most cases are indirectly elected bodies, the Sarpanchs of the constituent panchayats being its members. In Karnataka, the members are directly elected; and in the new Act of Madhya Pradesh, electoral colleges of panchas are provided to elect members of Janpada Sabhas. There is a provision for co-option of, or reservation for, women, scheduled castes and scheduled tribes and for special interests, such as co-operative societies and banks. The MLAs and MPs representing the constituencies, of which the Panchayat Samitis form part, are ex-officio members, generally without voting rights. The term of the Panchayat Samiti is concurrent with that of the Panchayat. Its President and Vice-President are selected from among the elected members. There are, however, slight variations in Assam, Madras, Maharashtra and the Punjab. In Assam, the election of the Anchalik Panchayat is direct; but an organic link with the Panchayat is established by making the elected members of ex-officio members of the panchayats. In Tamil Nadu and the Punjab, every panchayat has to elect from among its members its representatives on the Panchayat Samiti. Orissa provides for one of the panchas to be elected to serve on the Panchayat Samiti in addition to the Sarpanch. In Maharashtra, the councillors of the Zilla Parishad directly elected from the division in a block area become ex-officio members of the Panchayat Samiti.

Zilla Parishad

The highest tier is the Zilla Parishad, the jurisdiction of which generally extends over a district. In Assam, however, this generally corresponds to a sub-division, while, in Tamil Nadu, 13 districts have been demarcated into 21 development districts for this purpose. As in the case of the Panchayat Samati, the members of the Zilla Parishad are generally indirectly elected, with the Presidents of Panchayat Samitis, local MLAs and MPs as members. Provision is made for the co-option of women, scheduled castes, scheduled tribes and special interests, such as co-operative banks and societies and persons interested in rural development. MLAs and MPs have no voting rights in Orissa and the Punjab. In Gujarat, the Punjab and Uttar Pradesh additional members of the Panchayat Samiti are elected to serve on the Zilla Parishad. The only exception is Maharashtra, where a pre-determined number of councillors is directly elected from the electoral divisions in the district; but an organic link is established with the Panchayat Samiti by making the councillors members of the corresponding Panchayat Samitis. The term of office of the Zilla Parishad and that of the Panchayat Samitis is the same.

Functional Sub-Committees and Voluntary Organisations

For the effective implementation of the development programme, the village panchayat sets up functional sub-committees in such fields as agriculture, animal husbandry and cottage and small industries. Similar committees are set up at the block and district levels. On these committees are co-opted representatives of voluntary organisations and individuals with experience in specific subject.

These voluntary and associate organisations assist in the implementation of development programmes. Different "associate organisations" of such groups as women, youths, children, artisans and farmers, take up the responsibility depending on their organisational competence, for implementing development programmes on behalf of the statutory Panchayati Raj institutions. Voluntary organisations of all-India character or with state-wide ramifications work in collaboration with these representative institutions to implement the mutually agreed programmes. Members of both these types of organisations are co-opted as members of the functional sub-committees of the Panchayati Raj bodies at all levels.

Nyaya Panchayats

With the inauguration of Panchayati Raj system in the country, the Nyaya Panchayats were adopted as institutions for dispensation of justice and settle disputes at the grassroot level. Although provisions of Nyaya Panchayats exist in 15 states legislation, these institutions are functioning in eight states only. In states of Haryana, Himachal Pradesh and Punjab, the gram panchayats carry out the function of setting disputes in addition to the municipal and developmental functions. The composition of Nyaya Panchayats varies from state to state but generally they are based on a system of nomination or combination of election with nomination.

The working of Nyaya Panchayats have been evaluated by a number of committees and expert study groups. The relevant observations are as follows:

1. The committee on Panchayati Raj in Rajasthan was of the opinion that the Nyaya Panchayats were languishing for want of funds, secretarial assistance, adequate powers and people's faith in them.

2. The Maharashtra Evaluation Committee on the Panchayati Raj found entrustment of judicial functions to the Nyaya Panchayats "on the basis of democratic elections or otherwise" both "out of place and unworkable."

3. The Badal Team for Punjab felt that with a view to enable Gram Panchayats to devote greater attention to development work, judicial powers may be withdrawn from them.

4. Sahu Committee Report for Orissa felt that the Adalati Panchayat has not been able to discharge its duties as a full fledged village court.

Although the administration of speedy justice on a decentralised basis has its merits but the functioning of the existing Nyaya Panchayats have not been able to arouse interest and faith in them.

The Ashok Mehta Committee were of the view that Nyaya Panchayats should be kept as a separate bodies. The Committee were in favour of a qualified judge to preside over a bench of separately elected Nyaya Panchs. The elected Nyaya Panchs will not be entitled to seek re-election and they should serve in an area other than that from which they have been elected. Rural people desire a system of rendering justice by a competent authority, at more accessible location, quickly and at a low cost.

The Singhvi Committee is of the view that institutions of Nyaya Panchayats are a valuable aid to the development of social habits of self-government and rule of law. Nyaya Panchayats should be entrusted with the functions of mediation and conciliation in addition to adjudication. The Committee suggests that there may be a Nyaya Panchayat for a cluster of villages constituted by election or appointed from a special panel to be prepared of the purpose, in addition, each party to the dispute may be permitted to choose of Nyaya Panch from a panel to be presided by a professional judge as in the case of arbitration proceedings. Alternatively they may be elected be a consensus in primary panchayat units so far as possible. It is suggested that appropriate qualification and training may also be prescribed and a permanent staff for keeping records and for service of notices or summons should be appointed. In this connection, the Committee would like to consider the ill implications and ramifications of the recent recommendations of the Law Commission in respect of another variant of local judiciary of the form of Gram Nyayalayas.

The Gram Sabha

The extension of democracy of the people in the real sense should mean that the village panchayat should functions as an executive body to implement the policies and decisions of the Gram Sabha, comprising the entire adult population of the village. The Gram Sabha has an important role in activating the democratic process at the grassroots level, in inculcating community spirit, in increasing political awareness, in developing an urge for their development, in strengthening developmental orientations, in reminding about their duties to the country and their family and their rights, in educating the rural people in administrative and political processes and in enabling the weaker sections to progressively assert their point of view. Apart from the developmental programmes, the Gram Sabha can also discuss and decide the course of action in the direction of family planning and welfare, social evils and optimum utilisation of the vast human resources for their betterment.

The social sanction of the people will strengthen the hands of the Panchayats and act as a deterrent to arbitrariness. It will be particularly so when a Panchayat has to organise local manpower for community purposes, levy taxes or raise special contributions from the beneficiaries of a project, etc. The wider the consultation, the greater are the chances of the community effort. In fact, then effectiveness of the village panchayat, its strength and vitality would depend upon the sustained, intelligent and enthusiastic interest and co-operation of the village community in its affairs and activities. Accordingly, in almost all the States, the Gram Sabhas have been statutorily recognised and assigned specific functions to direct and supervise the activities of the village panchayats.

Functions

The functions of the panchayat may be classified under the following three categories:

    (i) Civic amenities,

    (ii) Social Welfare activities; and

(iii)   Development work.

Civic Amenities

Sanitation, conservancy, public health, street lighting, the supply of safe drinking water supply, and the maintenance of village roads, culverts, schools, etc., come under civic amenities, which are generally obligatory, while the other activities, which are optional, include the setting-up and maintenance of a library, a reading-room, a community hall, a playground and recreation centre, maternity and child welfare centres, cart and bus stands, and a burial ground. In regard to development works, the panchayats function generally as agents of the Samitis or Zilla Parishads. In the Union Territory of Delhi the ordinary civic functions of the panchayats, together with those of collecting taxes and making grants, have been entrusted to the Delhi Municipal Corporation. As a result, the panchayat has become a mere agency for the execution of local development work and the raising of public contribution for them.

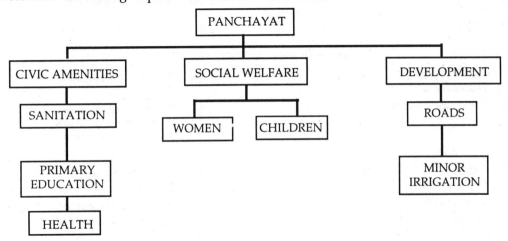

Fig. 21.4. Functions of Panchayats.

TABLE 21.5

Illustrative Functions of the Three Tiers of Panchayati Raj Structure

Zilla Parishad	Panchayat Samitis Taluka Board	Mandal Panchayat
(1)	*(2)*	*(3)*
Programme implementation of transferred functions	Functions assigned by Zilla Parishad in the	*Implementational (illustrative only):*
1. As indicated below: (a) Agriculture except research in universities (b) Animal	I. decentralised sector, e.g., Rabi, Kharif, Pig farms, Minor Irrigation, Health, Dispen-	I. (a) Fodder development activities with subsidised fodder cultivation (b) Land-shaping in the

(1)	(2)	(3)
Husbandry and Veterinary Services	series, Water Supply, Rural Roads, Tubewells, Sub-plans.	command area or water arrangement demonstrations
(c) Fisheries	II. Preparation of Block Plans	(c) Field channels demonstration
(d) Forestry	III. Co-ordination or Devetailing of	(d) Farmers' training
(e) Marketing	Panchayat Works where the	(e) Multiple cropping pattern demonstration
(f) Irrigation	Programmes Cover more than one Panchayat or	(f) Demonstration of drainage-cum-recycling programmes
(g) Health; Family Welfare	Taking up Directly till they	(g) Minikit distribution
(h) Education	Develop Capacities, Administrative	(h) Pisciculture demonstration
(i) Public Health Engineering		(i) Fisheries propaganda and fairs
(j) Communication		(j) Facilities for creation of coastal brackish water fishery development
(k) Industries		(k) Farm forestry
(l) Urban Development		(l) Soil conservation schemes
(m) Welfare of Backward Classes		(m) Rural housing and allotment of house sites for landless
(n) Social Welfare		(n) Assistance to hand-loom weavers
II. Planing Review, Monitoring and Evaluation		(o) Establishment of mulberry farms or gardens
		(p) Tissar collection or rearing projects
III. Co-ordination		(q) Assistance to handi-crafts with improved tools or collection for marketing
IV. Administrative and those flowing from organic linkages		(r) Health sub-centre construction
		(s) Recruitment and looking after health workers

(1)	(2)	(3)
		(t) Running adult literacy classes
		(u) Rural and link roads and culverts construction etc.
		(v) SFDA—identification and payment of subsidies
		(w) Family welfare projects
	II.	*Promotional (illustrative only):*
		(a) Organisation of literacy centres, balwadis, youth clubs, Mahila Mandals, voluntary organisations, etc.
		(b) Co-operation
	III.	*Procedural (illustrative only):*
		(a) Control of fairs and festivals
		(b) Registration of deaths and births
		(c) Construction and maintenance of Dharmashalas and Sarais
		(d) Opening and maintenance of public markets and slaughter houses
	IV.	*Municipal and Civic functions at village level:*
		(a) Water Supply
		(b) Health and hygiene
		(c) Lighting.

Control and Supervision

The Acts in many states provide for the control supervision and assistance of the lower tiers of Panchayati Raj institutions by higher tiers. Except in Madhya Pradesh, Madras and the Punjab, Panchayat Samitis have powers of scrutiny and approval of the budgets of the Panchayats. In all the states except Tamil Nadu, the Zilla Parishad scrutinises and passes the budgets of Panchayat Samitis. One of the functions of the Zilla Parishads is the co-ordination of the activities of Panchayat Samitis.

In the Third Five Year Plan, Panchayat Raj had been described as a part of interconnected democratic institution at the village, block and district levels, the primary object of which was to enable the people in each area in achieve intensive and continuous development in the interests of the entire population. The Plan empasised that it was of the utmost importance that there should be a clear recognition of the distinct role of federal co-operative organisations functioning at the state and district levels in the field of banking, marketing, processing, distribution, education and training. It laid down that Panchayati Raj institutions should promote the development of co-operatives and should endeavour to create a climate for community effort and their social functioning at all levels. At the Conference of State Ministers of Panchayats held in six districts in 1961, it was decided that the promotion of co-operation should be one of the ten test points of the success of Panchayati Raj. Panchayats therefore play an important role in the promotion and development of co-operative institutions within their areas.

Problems of Panchayats

Initially, the dominant classes had control of the Panchayati Raj institution; but, over a period , the dormant middle class and backward classes, realising the strength of their numbers, have changed the profile from what it was in the beginning. This is all well; but party politics and factionalism at the state level percolate to Panchayati Raj, defeating the partyless character of the Panchayati Raj institutions as they were originally envisaged.

At the Panchayat level, caste and class constraints are the hampering factors. Many panchayats, particularly in Saurashtra, helpless watch the bullies disregard the Panchayat. Such violations become difficult to check because candidates manipulate caste loyalties for their election and even indulge in terrorism .

In the circumstances, the effective functioning of the Panchayati Raj institutions is vitiated by wide economic disparities, social disabilities and caste loyalties. This is evident from the fact that there is too much politicisation of issues to the detriment of real development work.

There is one more drag on the smooth functioning of the Panchayati Raj institutions— the relationship between the non-official and the official.

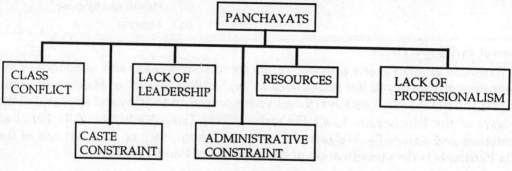

Fig. 21.6. Problems of Panchayats.

The Panchayati Raj institutions have to undertake and carry out developmental work within their jurisdiction. Their sources of income for this purpose include local cess, matching grants, plan grants, deficit adjustment grant and their own sources of revenue, such as professional tax, pilgrim tax, property tax, enterprises tax, etc. Because of planing at the national level and the rigid administrative framework that implements it, Panchayati Raj institutions are neither autonomous nor innovative in character. There is hardly any Zilla Parishad which, by its own efforts, had added to its revenue, apart from the conventional sources mentioned above. Though Zilla Parishads and Panchayats are empowered to raise their own resources by way of taxation on professions and trades, there is always an unwillingness on their part to impose any such levies because they have always an eye on their re-election. As a result, the developmental activities of the panchayats are hampered.

The Ashok Mehta Committee has thrown adequate light on the developments which have undermined the Panchayati Raj structures and made them ineffective. They are:

1. Except in Maharashtra and Gujarat, the PRIs were rarely given an opportunity to take up planing or implementational work on a sizeable scale.
2. Planning was entrusted to a body outside Zilla Parishad under the chairmanship of a minister.
3. Adequate and proper staff was not provided to the districts and blocks.
4. The plan allocation resources were tapered off.
5. PRIs were wilfully kept out of developmental work so that it never became stronger.
6. Bureaucracy role in dissociating the PRIs from the development process for its own benefits is equally great.
7. There was a lack of clarity in regard to the concept of Panchayati Raj itself and the objectives for which it should stand.
8. PRIs were dominated by economically or socially privileged sections of society and have such facilitated the emergence of oligarchic forces yielding no benefits to weaker sections.
9. Corruption inefficiency, scant regard for procedures and rules political interference in day-to-day administration, parochial loyalties, motivated actions, concentration of powers, and lack of services were inflicted a large number of panchayats.
10. In sum, the activities of PRIs were meagre, their resources base weak and the overall attention given to them niggardly. There was lack of political will to the PRIs.

Initially, the dominant classes had exercised control of the Panchayati Raj institutions, but over a period, the dormant middle class and backward classes, realising the strength of their numbers, have changed the profile from what it was in the beginning. This is all well; but party politics and factionalism at state level percolate to Panchayati Raj, defeating the partyless character of the Panchayati Raj institutions as they were originally envisaged.

TABLE 21.6

Problems of Panchayats

Administrative		*Non-Administrative*	
1.	Lack of bureaucratic response to PRI.	1.	Widening economic disparity in the villages.
2.	Poor and inadequate staff at grassroot level.	2.	Illiteracy of the elected members.
3.	Lack of technical support.	3.	Party loyalty.
4.	Unscientific plan process and lack of co-ordination.	4.	Groupism in villages.
5.	Corruption and favouritism	5.	Concentration of economic power with the rich farmers or traders.
6.	Lack of proper training to the elected members.	6.	Lack of leadership.
7.	Lack of missionary zeal amongst members and workers.	7.	Criminalisation of politics.
8.	Scant attention given to developmental activities.	8.	Uniformity of PRI is not suited to the country.
9.	Lack of awareness among workers.	9.	Lack of understanding of procedures and scant respect for rules.
10.	Lack of resources.	10.	Members work for their self-interest.
11.	Inadequate provisions of funds.	11.	Proper awareness is not there among villagers.
12.	Elections are not being held on one pretext or the other	12.	Vested interests have squeezed the democratic process.
13.	Lack of clarity about PRI's concept.	13.	Decline in value system.
14.	Lack of dedication of work.	14.	People have lost faith in PRIs.
15.	No career path has been drawn for PRI workers.		

The other reasons attributed to its dismal performance are:

(1) The election system introduced in the Panchayati Raj system has divided the villagers into parties/groups with conflicting interest.

(ii) Non-cooperation and non-participation of villagers in the development work.

(iii) There is lack of will, determination, dedication and missionary zeal amongst the members to take up development work.

(iv) Invariably funds are misappropriated.

(v) There is a problem of uniformity of PRI system.

(vi) The debatable issue is the unit of administration at the grass-root level. While over 60 per cent of inhabited villages have less than 1000 people. The question is whether a panchayat will be a viable unit of administration?

(vii) There is no coordination between the elected representative and bureaucracy.

(viii) Widening economic disparities in rural India have belittled the Panchayats.

Findings of the Administrative Reforms Commission

According to the Administrative Reforms Commission's findings, nearly 80 per cent of the villagers are dissatisfied with the Panchayati Raj because the "undesirable and unhealthy tendencies have the upper hand" in rural affairs, will "considerations of religion and caste taking the first place and qualification and sincerity taking almost the last place."

Another major reason is the restricted authority and paucity of funds. The state governments have not been very equitable in their relationship with the infant Panchayati Raj institutions. The financial resources granted to them have been meagre and inadequate. Adequate financial support has generally been denied to these institutions in most states, often even in respect of the "transferred" schemes and performances. Moreover, these institutions have shown little inclination to raise their own resources locally.

Apart from the paucity of funds, there has been a general apathy at the administrative and political level towards a strengthening of these bodies. Elections to those bodies have been repeatedly postponed; there is a state having the dubious reputation of postponing panchayat elections over a hundred times! Supersession of local bodies are too common. According to an able commentator: "Not much power can be exercised, holders of real power, at the central and state levels, have been reluctant to delegate authority." In fact, all the development programmes such as the IADP, CADP, DPAP, and so on—financed and operated by the Central Government—have no relation with Panchayati Raj institutions. In short, the higher level governments in India have been rather allergic to the concept of sharing the power with the lower level ones.

A review committee to Review the Existing Administrative Arrangements of Rural Development and Poverty (CAARD) was constituted on 25th March 1985 under the chairmanship of Dr. G.V.K. Rao, Ex-Member, Planning Commission, to review the existing administrative arrangements for rural development and poverty alleviation programmes and to recommend appropriate structural mechanism to ensure that they are planned in an integrated manner and effectively implemented.

The committee's important recommendations relating to Panchayat Raj are as follows:

1. Panchayati Raj Institutions (PRIs) have to be activised and given all the needed support so that they can become effective organisations for handling people's problems.

2. PRIs at the district level and below should be assigned the work of planning, implementation and monitoring of rural development programmes.

3. The block development office should be the sheet anchor of the entire rural development process.

A Plea for Integrated Administrative Structure

The L.M. Singhvi Committee (1986) concurs broadly with the recommendations made in the Report of the Committee to Review the Existing Administrative Arrangements for Rural Development and Poverty Alleviation Programmes (CAARD) in respect of integrated administrative structures for planning and development. The Committee considers it appropriate to underline that these administrative structures for planning and development should be dynamic and independent and should at the same time be integrated with institutions of local self-government losing their dynamism and independence.

The principal technical and administrative officers of various specialised departments along with their line formations should be part of the organisational and administrative structure of the Zilla Parishad. The District Development Commissioner would have to be the chief executive officer of Zilla Parishad. The District Development Commissioner should be entrusted with the task of assisting in coordinating the planning and implementation activities of various departments, agencies and institutions at the district level.

Officers of high calibre, proven competence and sympathy for Panchayati Raj institutions should be detailed to function as Panchayati Raj officials.

The Committee recommends that newer officials in the administration should be made to work in Panchayati Raj and rural development setting so as to sensitise our public administrations to the problems of rural India.

The Committee emphasises that the administrative structures should not be top-heavy and the administrative personnel should be made aware of the importance of Panchayati Raj institutions and their accountability to them generally.

The Committee is strongly of the view that substantial training, research and public education inputs should be provided to strengthen the Panchayati Raj institutions and the performance capabilities of those who are called upon to function as voters, elected representatives, administrative officials and voluntary workers in relation to Panchayati Raj institutions. Voluntarily institutions should be given the pride of place in providing these inputs. The Committee feels that this would be the most providing these inputs. The Committee feels that this would be the most productive and profitable investment in democratic institution building.

A model legislation within the framework of the proposed new chapter in the Constitution should be prepared with sufficient scope for appropriate local adaptations.

The Committee recommends the national and state level local self-government institutes, and centres for training at the district level, should be established and entrusted with training, evaluation and research responsibilities particularly in relation to Panchayati Raj and urban local institutions. The institutes and centres should also be clearing houses of information relating to local self-government and should monitor and report developments in that field.

The Committee is of the view that the proposed National Institute of Local Self-Government should, in respect of its research and evaluation functions, utilise universities, research bodies and voluntary organisations such as All India Panchayats Parishad which should have a consultative nexus with it and which would be an invaluable resource for dissemination of information as well as for proper motivation.

Revitalisation of Panchayati Raj Institutions for Democracy and Development

Accepting the recommendations of the L.M. Singhvi Committee (1986) of giving constitutional sanctity to PRIs as the third tier of government, the government introduced the Sixty-fourth Constitutional Amendment (1986) on May 15, 1989.

The objective of setting up local self-government for the rural areas is to break the bottlenecks and to straighten the kinks which were the outcome of the perpetuation of certain sordid vested interests. People to become partakers in the process of development is the aim of the new Panchayati Raj legislation. The salient features of the Act are:

As the Panchayati Raj institutions became weak and ineffective due to a variety of reasons, there was an urgent need to revamp the system. It is common knowledge that elections were not held regularly. Suppressions were a regular feature. Weaker sections did not have any say in its manning and running. The financial resources were grossly inadequate to take up any meaningful developmental work. The meagre devolution of powers made the system a mockery.

In order to eliminate these inadequacies and to enable them to function as units of effective self-government, the recent bill was introduced in the Parliament. It is now obligatory for all states to establish a three-tier system of Panchayats at the village, intermediate and district levels. For those states having a population of less than 20 lakhs, it is not obligatory to establish the intermediate level.

All seats in Panchayats, at all levels, will be filled by direct election. There will be reservations to ensure due representation in the Panchayats of the SC, ST and women categories. The tenure of office will be five years. In case of dissolution, there is provision to conduct election within a period of six months or reconstitute Panchayat for the remainder of the term. It also provides for the devolution by the state legislature of powers and responsibilities upon Panchayats with respect to the preparation of plans for economic development and social justice for the implementation of development schemes. It ensure sound finance for the Panchayats by securing grants-in-aid from the consolidated fund of the state as well as appropriating the revenues of designated taxes, duties, tolls, fees, etc. Finance Commissions may be set up in the states every five years to review the finances of Panchayats and recommend principles of apportion the taxes and assign grants-in-aid to the Panchayats from the consolidated fund of the state.

The ratio between the population of the Panchayat area and the number of seats should be the same throughout the state. Panchayats will be divided into territorial constituencies based on, almost equal, ratio between population and the seats. Only those directly elected members alone have voting powers in the meetings. The chairperson of the panchayat elected from amongst the elected members can be removed by two-thirds of such members present and voting. The number of reserved seats will be decided depending upon the size of their population, subject to a minimum of one seat for SC/ST. Thirty per cent of the total seats to be filled by direct election in every Panchayat shall be reserved for women and allotted by rotation to different constituencies.

It would prepare and implement plans for socio-economic development. Social justice will be the major guiding principle. The accounts shall be kept in such forms as desired by Comptroller and Auditor General (CAG) of India. The CAG shall cause the accounts to be audited and be submitted to the State Governor, who shall cause them to be laid before the state legislature. However, both the CAG and Election Commission have indicated that it would be difficult for them to estimate the likely additional work involved. There will be no other recurring or non-recurring expenditure.

The bill was adopted by the Lock Sabha on August 9, 1989 without much deliberation. The bill was defeated in the Rajya Sabha on 13.10.1989. The main objections to the bill were, there was no adequate consultation will all the parties and it aimed at sidetracking the states. They summed up that "this is a verdict against the bullying tactics of the Government." The Government made in an issue and announced the polls. At the polls, the Congress (I) party was not successful. The polls proved that it was a nasty step.

The bill is good in part, but it needs more discussion, deliberation and proper implementing machinery. The content as well as the means should be fair.

Summing Up

The organisation of the village as a social and political unit finds reference in Vedic literature and Jataka stories. Old inscriptions tells us how the village councils or assemblies were constituted, who were eligible to serve thereon and how they functioned. The village gramanee (headman) carried on the village government and the council or sabha of the village decided questions relating to village administration. The headman was always from the village and was not an officer appointed from outside.

These village organisations were not only self-sufficient economically but also were self-governed. Village panchayats in ancient times were developed, nurtured out of a necessity of protection from raids and economic survival in absence of adequate infrastructural facilities and development. It was in their unity and cooperation that there sustenance was possible.

Since then, the rural scene has seen sea change. The scale and scope of their activities diversified. Rural population has increased from little less than 100 million in 1901 to 615 million in 1989. Agricultural strategy has undergone a sea change. Rural industries and service sector has eclipsed. The ranks of agricultural labourers, marginal and small farmers has swelled. Joint family has eclipsed. The villagers and the villages are being increasingly drawn into ever-widening market economy. Administration innovations have also undergone changes with the implicit needs of the power structure. Today, villages are dependent on the cities for their supply of inputs and other basic needs, even for food. With the development of infrastructure and communication, villages have come under closer contact and demonstrative effect of urban areas.

In the changed context, the sole concept of village panchayat is not only feasible but also viable. What is needed is redesign of decentralisation. Moreover, India is a country of diversity and hence no one model suits the requirement of villages in India. So instead of one model, each state should evolve a pattern of village administration. What is needed is a positive approach, appropriate strategy, coordinated efforts cooperative approach and hard work to achieve the objectives.

Development work in future needs intricate designing and greater coordination at the state level. The entire rural development programme needs coordination at village or group of villages level. Panchayati Raj, a new system of local government came in as the logical answer to the new situation that emerged. Panchayati Raj meant the creation of the Gram Sabha as the crucial base of our growing democracy. The Gram Sabha consisted of the entire adult village population, the body of body men and women. Gram Sabha was to elect its executive, the Village Panchayat, to look after the day-to-day administration of the village. The Village Panchayat cannot go far in matters in inter-village development. Thus came the Block Panchayat Samiti at the Block level consisting of representatives of the Panchayats. The Panchayat Samiti was to take over the administration of all programmes of development at the Block level using the Block administration as its instrument of action. Subjects which went beyond the scope of the Block Panchayat Samiti and matters connected with the coordination of the activities of the Blocks were vested in the Zilla Parishad. Above the Zilla Parishad stood the state government. The State Government received its support and guidance from the Centre. Thus the Gram Sabha got linked with Lok Sabha in a single chain. The individual village could thus have the touch of the nation as a whole in every facet of its life and the nation could receive the echo back of the achievements, hopes and frustrations of the people in the process of development.

Politically speaking, it is a process of democratic awareness, making average villager more conscious of his rights and responsibilities towards the rural society than before.

Economically speaking, it is a collective coordinated and cooperative effort to improve the living standards of the people as well as improving the conditions of the villages.

Administratively speaking, it bridged the gulf between the bureaucratic elite and the people. Socio-culturally speaking, it generated a new leadership with pro-social change in outlook. It also helped rural people to cultivate and harness a developmental psyche. It is hoped that the Panchayati Raj will accelerate the developmental process in rural communities.

The Panchayati Raj is both an end and a means. As an end, it is an inevitable extension of democracy; as a means, it would continue to be responsible for discharging obligations entrusted to it by the people. Altogether, Panchayati Raj should contribute to a rich, rewarding harmonious and full vibrant live in rural India. It is a useful object lesson, for we all can learn to take unexpected difficulties and mistakes and weave them advantageously into greater pattern of our lives. There is an inherent good in most difficulties. Thus, Panchayati Raj has a bright future, if properly guided.

The primary object of a village panchayat is to strengthen the base of the democracy at the grassroots on the one hand and hand over the powers as well as responsibility to the people on the other hand so as to allow them to manage their affairs in the best possible manner.

What Panchayats should be...

"Independence must begin at the bottom. Thus every village will be a republic or panchayat having full powers. It follows, therefore, that every village has to be self-sustained and capable of managing its affairs. This does not exclude dependence on, and willing help from neighbours or from the world. It will be free and voluntary play of mutual forces... In this structure, composed of innumerable villages, there will be ever-widening, never ascending circles. Life wil not be a pyramid with the apex sustained by the bottom. But it will be an oceanic circle whose centre will be the individual always ready to perish for the village, the latter ready to perish for the circle of villages, till at last the whole becomes one life composed of individuals, never aggressive in their arrogance but ever humble, sharing the majesty of the economic cicle of which they are integral units. Therefore, the outer most circumference will not wield power to crush the inner circle but will give strength to all within and derive its own strength from it."

—*Mahatma Gandhi*

22

Rural Management

Introduction

The rural development programme calls for a concerted effort and a fusion of will and of skills in the political, administrative, professional and executive fields. Rural management, therefore, is an important aspect of integrated rural development. The managerial component of the task of improving the living standards of the rural poor is a very complex one and calls for gigantic efforts. The key to success lies in building up teams of trusted, dedicated and motivated people. An effort has been made by the Institute of Rural Management, Anand, to fill the managerial gaps in rural management. In a note, it briefly analyses its objectives and its utility in the implementation of the Integrated Rural Development Programmes (IRDP) in India.

In economic terms, it signifies a low propensity to consume rather than to save and less productive agriculture is the dominant occupation of the majority of the rural poor. In a typical rural family, insufficient resources arise from the fact that:

(i) The number of individual consumers in the household is larger relative to the production services the household is able to supply;

(ii) Lack of skills or educational attainments result in low quality as well as quantity of services relative to its own requirements;

(iii) Poor health and low productivity lead to a vicious circle of poverty-low income, poor health, low productivity and poverty;

(iv) Disability exists on an extensive scale.

The problem of poverty in the rural environment stems from the fact that the supply of labour competes for employment on an inadequate agricultural base, resulting in vast differentials in income from skilled and unskilled urban labour to unskilled rural labour. Unfortunately, poverty leads to a higher number of births and to increased poverty. The ability of a family to plan its size optimally is crucial from the long-run point of view of eradicating poverty. This apart, the structure of rural society, the landman relationship, the social relation between different classes, the inequitable flow of resources and benefits to and by the various socio-economic groups and individuals call for an integrated area approach for the rapid development of rural India.

Rural Development

In fact, rural development is often confused with agricultural development. No doubt, agricultural development is the basis of the development of the rural areas and of the industrial sector; but it is not an end itself. Agricultural development, or, to be more specific, agricultural productivity, is closely related to rural development. The health of the rural community and the quality of life deteriorates in proportion to the decline in agricultural and other allied activities. The term *rural development* is much wider than the term *agricultural development*. There are other sectors in rural areas, *viz.*, infrastructural development like roads, drinking water, housing, fuel, cottage and small-scale industries, possessing and marketing of goods, which play an important role in the overall economic development. Moreover, improvement in health, education, housing communication, etc., call for a planned approach.

Experiment in Rural Development

The concept of development is not a new one. Several pioneering experiments have been attempted by many eminent people in India. Although, poet Rabindranath Tagore sowed the seeds of a planned programme of development for the villages, it is Mahatma Gandhi who is responsible for the beginning of an integrated development of rural India. It was he who reminded us again and again that the soul of India lives in her villages and that in rural reconstruction alone lies the salvation of this country. That is why, the government since independence, has been experimenting with the concept of rural development.

The strategies for rural development have changed over the years. In the fifties, community development and national extension service block were started with the object of taking integrated development to rural areas. At that time, the development of agriculture and allied sectors was emphasised as the most important function of the national extension service. It was, however soon realised that the machinery devised for the purpose was not equal to the task of the programme of regenerating the rural economy, nor were the funds sufficient for this purpose. The achievements of the community development blocks, however, cannot be minimised. They represents the first organised attempt at lifting the centuries-old stagnant rural economy from the morass and inertia of a fatalistic outlook. They brought about visible changes in the social and cultural modes of the people and generated some hope in the masses living in the rural areas.

The major programmes for rural development under execution are:

    (i)   Community Development Programme
   (ii) Panchayati Raj
  (iii) Applied Nutrition Programme
  (iv) Extension Education and Training Schemes

  (v)   Small Farmers' Development Agency/Marginal Farmers' and Agricultural Labour Scheme
  (vi) Drought-Prone Area Programmes
 (vii) Tribal Development Agency
(viii) National Rural Employment Programme
 (ix)   Hill Area Development Programme
  (x)   Desert Development Programme
 (xi)   Food for Work Programme
(xii)   Command Area Development
(xiii) Jawahar Rozgar Yojana.

Integrated Rural Development

Conceptually, integrated rural development refers to the multi-faceted, multi-directional development of the rural economy by the fullest exploitation of local resources in men, material, land and water. The idea was first proposed in the central budget of 1976-77, and a beginning was made on the basis of local initiative and drive. The government acted as a catalyst to bring about a change, but it was the intrinsic strength of the economy itself which supported the services, and rising standards of living and sectoral economic activities. Environmental and infrastructural improvements can only be partially supported by outside help; it is the local population which has to pay for their maintenance and upkeep. No outside agency can sustain their economic activities of a village for any length of time. Hence, the importance of integrating all the economic activities on the basis of the local resources. The vast untapped rural labour force is a liability which has to be turned into an asset by harnessing it in fruitful and gainful employment. Full rural employment is the goal of integrated rural development.

In a rural situation, the following are likely to be the main elements:

  (i)   In the agricultural sector, the emphasis has to be on land reforms, the supply of inputs, soil conservation, water management, fisheries, poultry, dairy-farming, post-harvest technology, augmentation and harnessing of new sources of energy.
 (ii)   Cottage and small industries, including agro-industries management and marketing of the products.
(iii)   Health and Family Welfare, including environmental improvements.
 (iv)   Education, social education and cultural activities.
  (v)   Social Welfare Programme, including programmes for children, women and other weaker sections.

An integrated development plan, however, should be in consonance with local resources, local enterprise, and should be based on an intimate knowledge and understanding of local conditions, local needs and local possibilities.

The alleviation of rural poverty is the prime objective of the Sixth Plan. An increase in the productive potential of the rural economy is an essential condition for the solution of the problems of rural poverty. At the same time, recognising the constraints which limit the scope for higher growth rate in the medium-term, a more direct means of reducing the incidence of poverty and destitution would have to be employed. It is well-known that the hard core of poverty is to be found in rural areas. The poorest sections belong to the families of landless labourers, small and marginal farmers, rural artisans, scheduled castes, scheduled tribes and socially and economically backward classes. Households living below the poverty line have to be assisted with an appropriate package of technologies, services and asset transfer programme.

The strategy and methodology for accelerated rural development relate to:

(a) Increasing production and productivity in agriculture and allied sectors;

(b) Resources and income development of the vulnerable sections of the rural population by development of primary, secondary and tertiary sectors;

(c) Skill formation and skill upgrading programmes to promote self and wage-employment amongst the rural poor;

(d) Facilitating an adequate availability of credit to support the programmes taken up for the rural poor;

(e) Promoting marketing support to ensure the viability of production programmes and to insulate the rural poor from exploitation in the marketing of their products;

(f) The provision of additional employment opportunities for the rural poor for gainful employment during the lean agricultural season under the National Rural Employment Programme (NREP);

(g) The provision of essential minimum needs; and

(h) The involvement of universities, research and technical institutions in preparing a shelf of projects, both for self-employment and NREP, and in preparing strategies for the scientific utilisation of local resources.

Need for Professional Rural Managers

Increasing investments have been made in the rural sector to combat the massive problems of unemployment and poverty. A large number of rural development projects, addressed to the needs of specific groups of people, geographic areas and commodities, have bene implemented. Besides, the number of rural enterprises in the co-operative and public sectors have increased rapidly in the past few years. Professional rural managers are urgently needed in all these projects and enterprises.

Operation Flood II—with an envisaged total investment of nearly Rs. 485 crores over a period of seven years—will need around 400 fresh graduates in rural managerial cadres each year. This programme aims at helping some 10 million rural milk-producing families to set-up co-operatives in 150 districts in the country. Similarly, the setting-up of oilseeds producers co-operatives, with an investment of over Rs. 2,000 million will call for another 200 managers each year, at least until the mid-1980s. Programmes further envisaged include co-operativisation of fruits and vegetables, cotton, fisheries.

The present supply of graduates from the management institutions in India is inadequate to meet the demand for them. Moreover, almost all these management graduates are absorbed by the industrial sector. The rural sector, which so desperately needs professional managers, continues to suffer from an acute shortage. Besides, the rural areas, whose development has such an important place in our Five-Year Plans, face diverse socio-cultural and institutional problems which require specialised managerial resources.

The Institute: IRMA

The Institute of Rural Management, Anand (IRMA), was established in 1979 in Kaira District of Gujarat, with the active support of the Government of India, the Government of Gujarat, the National Dairy Development Board and the Indian Dairy Corporation.

IRMA is an autonomous body registered under the Societies' Registration Act, 1860, and is the first in India to undertake the professional education of young graduates in rural management.

IRMA is born out of a conviction that an all-around and sustained development requires specialised managerial manpower for the producers' organisations — and these are crucial for the development of the rural economy in India. IRMA seeks to generate appropriate managerial resources under management education and training, research and consultancy activities.

Objectives of the IRMA

   (i)   To impart education and training to young men and women so that they may manage income-generating and development activities for an on behalf of rural producers;

  (ii)   To offer training courses for policy-makers, directors, general managers and those in charge of specific managerial functions in rural enterprises and projects;

 (iii)   To conduct research in operating problems in order to help improve the management of rural enterprises and projects;

 (iv)   To undertake basic research into the processes of rural management to augment the existing body of knowledge; and

  (v)   To provide consultancy services to rural enterprises and organisations in the co-operative and other sectors in order to improve their organisational efficiency and effectiveness.

Programme in Rural Management

The Institute offers a two-year residential post-graduate Programme in Rural

Management (PRM). The programme aims at preparing outstanding young men and women for careers leading to management responsibilities in farmers organisations. It will equip its participants with those professional managerial skills and abilities which are essential for the management of rural enterprises and institutions that endeavour to bring about a change.

The distinctive feature of IRMA's post-graduate Programme in Rural Management is that it effectively blends education at Anand with field based training in village situation as well as in rural producers' organisations. Its aim is to build up practical, professional rural managers is reflected, on the one hand, in the strong application bias built into the courses, and on the other, in the emphasis placed on the two segments of field-based training to which nearly one half of the programme period is devoted.

The design of the PRM is based on the premise that it is as important for students of rural management to learn about the contextual realities in which they will have to work as it is for them to learn about management theories and concepts. Hence, in the Field-Study Section, which forms one part of field-based training, students have opportunities to study the conditions of village life and the functioning of rural institutions in their setting. In the Management Traineeship section, forming the second part of the field-based training, students are given an opportunity to appreciate the problems and conditions of rural enterprises and their functioning as organised systems working to bring about a change in rural India.

Two field-work modules of five weeks each are conducted under faculty guidance at sites spread all over India. For instance, for their first field—work module PRM 80-82 students were formed into eight groups and attached to the NDDB Spearhead Teams operating in Ahmedabad, Kolhapur, Guntur, Erode, Batinda, Rohtak, Meerut and Varanasi. Similarly PRM 81-83 students were located in four groups in villages in Banaskantha, Ujjain, Nalgonda and Madurai districts.

Training

The term *training* refers to the act of increasing the knowledge, aptitude and skill of a rural manager to do a particular job related to rural to rural development. It is concerned with imparting specific skills for particular purposes. That is why training forms part of the management development programmes in rural India. With the required shift in emphasis, the rural managers develop from *technical* to *human* and *conceptual* and *finally to conceptual skills.*

Trained personnel, led by a good leader, are essential prerequisites of a rapid development of rural areas. To manage the change we not only require managers, but those who would make a constant endeavour to improve—to improve themselves, to improve the effectiveness of their team and to improve the range and quality of rural services, so that their impact is felt by the teeming millions living in the rural environment.

TABLE 22.1

Profile of Management Process

Function	American	Indian
1	2	3
Planning		
Major objectives	Highly profit-oriented	Somewhat profit-oriented
Documentation of Objectives	Fully/partially documented	Partial/no documentation
Orientation	Medium term (2-5 years)	Short term/no planning (1-2 yrs)
Nature	Systematic, comprehensive	Limited/not detailed
Participation	Top and middle managers	Top managers, usually
Frequency of Review	Monthly	Monthly/ad hoc
Organising		
Layers of Hierarchy	4-7	5-8
Organisation Charts	Yes	Some/None
Authority Definition	Clear	Vague and ambiguous
Committee Usage	High	Low to none
Policy Decisions	Top and middle management usually formally stated	Top management—not formally stated
Staffing		
Policy Formulation	Top managers—parent company—formally stated—documented	Top managers—not usually formally stated — no documentation
Job Description	Detailed comprehensive need basis	Ad hoc little need basis
Recruitment		
Managers	Advertisement, Feelers, and campus interviews	Advertisements
Non-Managerial Cadres	Word of mouth, files and consultants	Word of mouth, files and consultants
Training and Development	Some in-company, job rotation, on-the-job, external management programmes, parent company plants	Job rotation, on-the-job, external management programmes
Compensation Systems		
Managers	Surveys, comparable managers in multi-national corporations	Ad hoc
Non-Managers	Collective bargaining	Collective bargaining
Promotion Criteria	Competence, training, education, experience	Seniority and experience
Directing		
Leadership Style	Authoritarian/Democratic	Authoritarian/Paternalistic
Middle Managers	Authoritarian	Authoritarian
Trust and Confidence in Subordinates		
Top Managers	Some	Some
Middle Managers	Some	Some
Trust and Confidence in Superiors		
Top Managers	High	Low
Middle Managers	High	Low
Interpersonal Relations	Somewhat co-operative	Somewhat co-operative
Decision-Making	Low	Low

1	2	3
Controlling		
Quality Control	Extensive parent company quality audits	Extensive
Budgetary Control	All Departments	Most Departments
Cost Accounting	Professional personnel	Professional personnel
Time/Motion Studies	Some	None/Some
Production-Setting Decisions	Committee/production manager	Top manager
Sales Setting Decisions	Committee/sales manager	Top manager/sales manager.

The format of this profile chart has been adapted from Boseman, G.F. and Phatak. A. "Management Practices of Industrial Enterprises in Mexico: A Comparative Study," *Management International Review*, 1978, 18(1), 43-48.

Objectives of Training

The main objective of training is to bridge the gap between the existing performance ability and the desired performance. The following are the main objectives of training:

(i) To impart to new entrants the basic knowledge and skills they need for the performance of definite tasks in a better way;

(ii) To assist the employees to function more effectively and efficiently in their present position by providing them the latest in formations and techniques and developing their skills in their particular field;

(iii) To build up a second line of competent officers and prepare them to occupy more responsible positions; and

(iv) To broaden the minds of senior manages so that they may correct the narrowness of the outlook that may arise from over-specialisation.

The Integrated Rural Development Programme is basically an attempt to launch a frontal attack on the problems of poverty and unemployment in the rural areas. With the objective of enabling the rural population to get maximum benefit out of the various schemes being implemented under the IRDP, it would be necessary to acquaint the beneficiaries with the latest technology in the relevant fields by evolving suitable training programmes. Keeping this objective in view, training of the beneficiaries, who are introduced to new schemes, new occupations or modern technology is an important component of the IRD Programme. The full cost of training of beneficiaries may be provided out of this programme. Training is envisaged both in the agriculture and allied activities as well as in industrial activities. Training in the agriculture and allied activities should however, be conducted only in courses organised in Gram Sevak Training Centres, Farmers Training Centres, Krishi Vigyan Kendras and Agricultural Universities. Training for setting up Rural Industries/Artisan activities etc. May be imparted in the ITIs, polytechnics, training schools run by the KVIC, All India Handicrafts Board or any other similar organisation of the Government of India or any other institution/organisation recognised by the concerned state government as capable of conferring the necessary skills on the participant.

Our main problem in fact, is training of personnel for rural development especially, the village level workers, the supervisor and others. Trained band of workers will bring a new direction to rural development, since these programmes call for great deal of organisational ability, skills of planning, efficiency for execution and consistency in monitoring the implementation. The infrastructure for imparting training comprises a net-work of institutions, namely the National Institute of Rural Development (NIRD), State Institutes of Rural Development (SIRD), the Extension of Training Centres (ETC), and other institutions of management development and rural management.

Training of the functionaries involved in the implementation of rural development programmes serves several purposes and its importance has been recognised at all levels. It helps in upgrading the professional competence of the functionaries, changing their attitudes and provides feedback from the field. Training of functionaries of both official and non-official agencies is essential for improving the performance in the field and accelerating the pace of rural development.

Accordingly, the training needs of various types of functionaries have been identified which are as under:

(a) Familiarisation with the broad objectives, strategy and targets etc., of special programmes like IRDP/DPAP/DDP/NREP/TRYSEM. The role of each programme has to be explained to the functionaries as well as the role of each functionary in the programme;

(b) A special course on IRDP for the implementing agencies. This would convey operational details on identification of beneficiaries, credit mobilisation, block level planning rural industries, component, monitoring and evaluation etc;

(c) A course on rural industrialisation and TRYSEM for functionaries of the industries and rural development departments, special programme agencies, organisation in the decentralised industrial sector and credit institutions. This would help in developing a co-ordinated perspective for all implementing agencies;

(d) Different training programmes on institutional financing, intended for various levels. Special accent has to be provided on orientation courses for branch managers an agents of banks. District level workshops to which collectors, project officers, district officials and bank managers are jointly called, need to be organised;

(e) Processing and marketing of agricultural produce;

(f) Marketing of products of rural industrial units;

(g) Management of rural enterprises;

(h) Financial management for project officer of special programme agencies;

(i) Accounts management for account staff of special programme agencies;

(j) Course on organisation of the rural poor;

(k) Project formulation, appraisal implementation, monitoring and evaluation of rural development projects;

(l)   Rural employment including NREP and others;

(m)   Block-level planning. This would be a detailed course on how exactly such a plan is to be drawn up;

(n)   Management of rural development projects;

(o)   Courses in training methodology and programme content for trainers of state and district-level institutions. Orientation courses also need to be organised;

(p)   Sectoral courses in sheep and pasture development, piggery development, dairy development, poultry development, irrigation management, watershed management, dry land technology, etc;

(q)   Joint courses for revenue and development functionaries and police officials with focus on the socio-economic development of the rural poor;

(r)   Basic services, minimum needs programme;

(s)   Voluntary action and people's participation;

(t)   Drought/emergency relief and their integration with on-going development programmes;

(u)   Women, child and youth welfare;

(v)   Welfare programmes for scheduled castes and scheduled tribes.

Institutions at Work

With the task in view various training centres, institutes in various sectors have been functioning in India. A state-wise and sector-wise detail of training institutions is presented. In all, there are 1,485 training institutions in India which are fighting with this gigantic task of imbibing skills in rural development personnel as well as target groups to make the rural development programme a success.

Hundreds and thousands of personnel from various levels are being trained from time to time by these institutes. With this, the task of implementation of schemes and programmes is being simplified day by day. Simultaneously the beneficiaries are being trained at various local-level institutions with the help of groups discussions, demonstrations etc. At state level, state Institutes of Community (Rural) Development and Panchayati Raj are imparting training to the lower and middle-level personnel involved in implementation of Rural Development Programmes.

Training of Beneficiaries

Besides the education of the families participating in the programmes about the objective of the programme and their responsibility towards the programme, they also need training to equip them with the skills and knowledge relevant to the economic activities selected by them. As most of the IRDP families live at the subsistence level, they are unlikely to be acquainted with better methods of production and management. Also, not having produced much for the market, they lack these skills. The attention paid to the training needs of the beneficiaries at present is grossly inadequate, it is often assumed, though very erroneously, that they do not need any training for carrying on the economic activities on such a small scale. There is no wonder many of the families flounder at the very beginning on account of lapses in management, which would appear to others to betray the absence of simple commonsense.

The viability of the programme will be greatly enhanced if the training aspect is diligently taken care of. The training needs of the beneficiaries should be identified at the stages of identification of the families and formulation of schemes. Schemes which require a greater training input than the implementing agencies are able to cater to are better shelved than implemented. The content of training should be carefully worked out, keeping its relevance and practicability and the level of the participants in view. Tips for efficiently managing the units and proper use of credit and other facilities should form an important part of training. Implementing personnel in various organisations should be developed as trainers of the IRDP beneficiaries. Simple manuals may be produced for the use of these personnel to enable them to impart worthwhile training to the beneficiaries.

The National Institute of Rural Development (NIRD) established in 1977 as the successor of the National Institute of Community Development set up in 1965 is functioning at Hyderabad with its regional centre at Guwahati as the apex institute for conducting training and research in the field of rural development.

The broad areas of its activity are:

* Social and economic well-being of rural communities.
* Institution building for rural development with particular reference to the evolving needs of rural development administration and management.
* Formulation of area-level plans for generation of employment and higher incomes for rural people.
* Promotion of human resources development and training.
* Transfer of technology appropriate to rural development.
* Dissemination through publication, of rural development information and knowledge.
* Issues relating to evolution of an egalitarian agro-industrial society.
* New strategies and policy formulation with regard to rural development.

The Institute attempts to translate into action the strategies and programmes of rural development in the national socio-economic growth process. Within each area, not only specific research studies are developed but training programmes, seminars and workshops with focus on specific topics are also organised. The research studies are action-oriented and are formulated in a pragmatic way so that they not only constitute a vial input for the various training programmes, but are also useful for policy formulation and programme implementation.

Community/Rural Development: Besides this institution, there are a number of other organisations like the State Institutes of Public Administration, State Institutes of the Universities, Institutes of Management, ICAR bodies etc. which are also conducting training and research in various aspects of rural development. This ministry has been supporting various seminars, workshops, training programmes, research and evaluation studies by giving financial assistance to such institutions.

Training of Rural Youth for Self-Employment (TRYSEM)

The National Scheme of Training of Rural Youth and Self-Employment (TRYSEM) was initiated with effect from 15th August, 1979. The main thrust of the scheme is on equipping rural youth with necessary skills and technology to enable them to take to vocations of self-employment.

Under the scheme, the target is to train about 2,00,000 rural youths every year in 5000 and odd blocks at the rate of 40 rural youths per block. The programme is an integral part of the IRD Programmes and constitutes that part of it which concerns the training of rural youth between age group 18-35 for self-employment avocations.

The selection of beneficiaries is based on income criteria, i.e. the family having income of Rs. 6,400 per year is considered for selection. The Priority in selection is given to the poorest families and only one beneficiary is taken from each family. Preference in selection is to be given to those who have entrepreneurial aptitude. Priority categories for selection are scheduled castes, scheduled tribes, ex-servicemen and persons who have attended the nine months course under National Adult Education Programme (NEAP). For women, a target has been suggested to the extent of one-third of the TRYSEM trainees.

During the four years of the Seventh Plan 5,61,676 rural youth have been given training under the TRYSEM programme, compared to 10,14,695 during the Sixth Plan. What is more important is that 3,09,744 trained youth are self-employed during the Seventh Plan against 4,78,396 in the Sixth Plan. More importantly, 48.1% belonged to SC and STs and 52% were women.

It is felt that the launching of various special programmes like DPAP/DDP/SFDA/MFAL/TRYSEM, etc. have created a need for continuous training of officials and non-officials who are involved in the policy planning and implementation of these programmes. It is sometimes possible to invite all the state level officers to National Seminars, Workshops, Training Courses etc. at the NIRD. But very often, the various constraints prevent officers from attending such programmes at Hyderabad/Delhi. To some extent, this difficulty has been obviated by conducting regional meetings. But this is no substitute for a regular training infrastructure at the state level, which could continuously organise training and research in the programmes and problems of a particular state/region.

This ministry has also launched upon an ambitious programme of preparing block level plans in selected blocks of the country. Ultimately, such plans have to be formulated for the entire country. In order to work out the methodology for the preparation of such plans and to give suitable training to state and district level officers, state centres proved valuable.

The dispersal of training facilities also removes the difficulty of communication as it is possible to organise programmes in the local languages and the training programmes are directly related to the situations prevailing in the states served by the training centres.

Functions

The main functions of the state centres will be—

(i) To conduct short-term training courses for the officials and the non-officials engaged in rural development and administration in the states;

(ii) To organise seminars, conferences and workshops for experts, academicians, administrators, researchers and non-officials on various problems of rural development and administration;

(iii) To undertake action-oriented researches on various problems of rural development and administration, so as to prepare case studies as inputs for the training programmes;

(iv) To serve as centres for the collection and dissemination of information regarding rural development and administration; and

(v) To provide consultancy service on problems of rural development and administration.

Training and Extension Support by NABARD

NABARD's basic objective to assist in bringing about integrated rural development calls for investment in human capital, besides that in tangible assets in the farm and non-farm sectors. This necessitates simultaneous action and the demand and the supply sides of credit. Firstly, to make credit delivery system more responsive to the needs of borrowers, it is necessary to upgrade the professional skills of officials working in the credit institutions through training. Next, the borrowers from rural areas have to be enlightened through a specially designed extension service on how to make efficient use of credit, a scarce resource, to rise their output and income and to repay the loans from incremental income.

Vikas Volunteer Vahini (VVV)

NABARD constituted VVV as an extension service for disseminating the five principles of 'Development through Credit' among rural masses. The five principles briefly are: (i) Credit must be used in accordance with suitable methods of science and technology; (ii) The terms and conditions of credit (techno-economic parameters) must be fully respected; (iii) Work must be carried out with the desired skill so as to realise optimum increase in the productivity and income; (iv) A part of the additional income created by credit must be saved; and (v) Local instalments must be repaid in time and regularly to facilitate recycling of credit.

The VVV consists essentially of small farmers, rural artisans and other persons of small means who have successfully put into practice the five principles of 'Development through Credit.'

The volunteers chosen, duly assisted by specialists or technocrats and a representative each from NABARD and commercial/co-operative banks, visit villages according to a programme drawn up by NABARD in close co-ordination with state government. During such visits the volunteers share with the village folk their own experience and propagate the message of 'Development through Credit' and repayment ethic. In each village visited by the volunteers, a NABARD Club is established with membership restricted to those who repaid their loans regularly and practiced the principles of 'Development through Credit.'

The VVV was inaugurated by the Prime Minister on 5 November, 1982 at New Delhi. A beginning was made by launching the programme in May 1983 in two districts of Tamil Nadu, viz., Madurai and Tiruchirapalli, which are now experiencing a scarcity of institutional credit due to increased defaults in repayment of earlier loans. In each selected district, 10 blocks and a cluster of 5 villages in each block were chosen. Under the second phase, the programme was extended during the year to 5 more blocks in these districts, covering a cluster of 5 villages in each block. Apart from organising a NABARD Club in each selected village, 12 volunteers were selected from each district to propagate the principles of Development Through Credit.' The banks and the state government evinced keen interest in the programme, with some of the banks offering to launch the programme, at their own cost in other districts were they had lead banks responsibilities.

With the experience gained and success achieved in Tamil Nadu, the programme was extended to the states of Gujarat and Orissa during the year. In Gujarat, 50 villages in five blocks of Sabarkantha district and 51 villages in 5 blocks of Rajkot district were covered. The programme evoked encouraging response on the part of the local population and officials of banks and state governments; it also motivated many defaulters to repay their old overdue loans. In Orissa, 55 villages in ten selected blocks of Ganjam district were brought under the programme.

For effective utilisation of the services of the selected volunteers, who were presented badges by the Prime Minister in November 1982, 29 Micro Pilot Projects (MPP) were launched in 18 states including the union territory of Delhi. Under these projects, volunteers were to operate in a cluster of 5 to 6 villages to help villagers in obtaining institutional credit for developmental purposes with a commitment to timely repayment. NABARD Clubs were also to be established for each cluster. Following the launching of MPP, a maintenance phase was ushered in by monitoring the activities of volunteers and holding regular meetings of members of NABARD Clubs. The focus of the VVV

Programme was extended to include preparation of village development plans and credit facilities for various economic activities, besides timely repayment. The main thrust was to bring about attitudinal changes in the users of institutional credit and propagating repayment ethic.

The launching of the main programme in three states and MPP in 18 states has created a favourable climate for institutional credit. Several banks operating in the project areas were prepared to take over the responsibility for the maintenance phase of the programme of the 332 clubs functioning in 18 states and one Union Territory in the country, 324 (97%) clubs are under decentralised maintenance by CBs, CCBs or RRBs having major loaning operations in the area.

Training

For upgrading human resource and institutional capabilities, National Bank accords high priority to providing training facilities for the officials of banks, state governments and other concerned institutions. Training programmes were accordingly conducted at the National Bank's Bankers Institute for Rural Development (BIRD), set up at Lucknow in September 1983, and at the College of Agricultural Banking (CAB) of the Reserve Bank of India, Pune, and several other regional centres.

BIRD ran two channels during the year with a total capacity of 54 participants for the Rural Development Projects Course (RDPC), mainly for the benefit of participants from RRBs. In view of the large training needs of RRBs, it has been decided to set up regional training centres in other parts of the country to supplement the training facilities at BIRD.

TABLE 22.2

Training Programmes Conducted or Founded by National Bank for Officials of Credit Institutions, Governments and Development Agencies

Programme	*Institutions*	*Number of Participants*
(1)	*(2)*	*(3)*
1. Rural Projects Development Course	RRBs	415
2. Refresher Rural Projects Development Course	RRBs	98
3. Rural Development Projects Course	CBs, RRBs, CCBs, RBI, Govt. Deptts.	517
4. Refresher Rural Development Projects Course	CBs, RRBs, CCBs, RBI, Govt., Deptts.	96
5. Animal Husbandry	CBs, RRBs, CCBs, RBI, Govt., Deptts.	126
6. Fisheries	CBs, RRBs, CCBs, RBI, Govt., Deptts.	51

(1)	(2)	(3)
7. Plantation	CBs, RRBs, CCBs, RBI, Govt., Deptts.	35
8. Horticulture	CBs, RRBs, CCBs, RBI, Govt., Deptts.	51
9. Non-Farm Sector (CAB)	CBs, RRBs, CCBs, RBI, Govt., Deptts.	107
10. Dryland Farming and Production of Oilseeds and Pulses	CBs, RRBs, CCBs, RBI, Govt., Deptts.	48
11. Wasteland Development Forestry Programme	CBs, RRBs, CCBs, RBI, Govt., Deptts.	40
12. Rural Branch Management and Credit Delivery	RRBs	255
13. Programme for Training in Rural Banking	RRBs	526
14. Internal Audit and Inspection Systems in RRBs	RRBs	119
15. Financing of Non-Farm Sector	RRBs	206
16. Trainers Training Programme on Methodology	CBs	12
17. Refresher Rural Branch Management and Credit Delivery	RRBs	93
18. Dryland Farming (BIRD/RTCs)	RRBs, CBs, Govt. Deptts.	46
19. Orientation Seminar for Non-official Directors of RRBs	Non-officials	36
20. Orientation Seminar for Senior Managers of RRBs	RRBs	34
21. Orientation Seminar for Co-op. Bank Officials	CCBs	52
22. Workshop on Mobile Job Trainers	RRBs	19
23. Orientation Seminar for Nominee Directors on Boards of RRBs	RBI	11
24. Orientation Seminar for Chairmen of RRBs	RRBs	41
25. Workshop on Wasterland Development	RRBs/Govt. Officials	17
26. Seminar on Plantation, Horticulture and Sericulture	RRBs/Govt. Officials	47
27. Technical and Non-Technical Programmes, Workshops and Seminars on various disciplines	CBs, DCCBs, LDBs, RRBs Govt. Deptts.	4,931
28. Various programmes conducted by JLTCs of 14 SLDBas with support from National Bank	SLDBs	8,869
		16,898

Special programmes were devised, with emphasis on effective management techniques, for the benefit of officials of the weak SLDBs in Bihar, Gujarat, Madhya Pradesh, Maharashtra and Tamil Nadu.

The National Bank continued to conduct special programmes on Rural Management and Credit Delivery (RBMCD) for Branch Managers of selected commercial banks (5), RRBs (20) and the major SLDs (14). The Bankers Institute for Rural Development (BIRD) and Regional Training Centres (RTCs) trained 255 officers of RRBs. On the other hand, 578 officers of SLDB were trained at the JLTCs. The training centres of CBs conducted the courses for their officers with the help of training module and faculty support provided by the National Bank.

The World Bank and the Training and Visit System

The training and visit system of agricultural extension, initially developed as a systematic programme by Daniel Benor, was first used extensively by the Bank of India in the early 1970s.

Agricultural extension, a system of supporting services aimed at making farmers particularly small-scale and subsistence farmers more productive, is being increasingly affected by the philosophy and methods of this approach. The experience with traditional extension work was quite disappointing. The reasons were varied-research did not take account local conditions; extension was biased toward men, when women played an important role; support services were inadequate; and so on. The key improvements offered by the training and visit system are the development of better links between farmers and extension workers, and between both of these and research; and the increased effectiveness of the extension worker.

The essence of the system is that it should be sufficiently flexible to be used effectively in any type of farming, under any conditions. Its aim is to improve the use of existing resources, concentrating initially on key improvements in major crops. In some areas, where farming practices are already efficient and appropriate, this has meant giving farmers technical advice on more productive crops or more appropriate types of fertiliser or seed. In others, advice on better farming methods—when to sow, how to weed—can produce dramatically better yields fairly quickly without much cash being paid out by the farmer. Quick and successful results are an important way of demonstrating the use of the system and in persuading more farmers to adopt it.

"System" is an appropriate name for the approach. Centered on providing farmers with relevant, clear, and sensible advice, which depends on close two-way contacts between farm families, extension workers, researchers, and administrators, it functions by allocating precise responsibilities and by and by timing activities carefully. The Chart I shows the line of command: not shown are all the links with research and time table of extension and extensional research activities, which are equally important. Village extension workers visit small groups of "contact" and other farmers at least once a fortnight, to teach them three or four carefully chosen recommendations about what to do over the next two weeks. Since farmers attending the sessions also pass the advice on to other farm families, one extension worker can reach from 500 to 1,200 farm families in this way. The extension workers—who generally spend eight days out of every two weeks on these visits-spend one day at a training session where subject-matter specialists teach them the recommendations of the next two weeks and discuss farmers' problems from the previous fortnight. When appropriate, these sessions are attended by representatives from supply and credit agencies who collect information on the support the farmers will be needing.

The subject-matter specialists divide their time, according to an equally structured programme, between these training sessions, research, and fieldwork—an important element of the latter involving adaptive trials on farmers' field to improve recommendations. The supervisors of extension field-workers also attend training sessions, in addition to spending at least eight days every two weeks in the field. At every level, contact is maintained between fieldwork and research, concentrating the system or making the extension work deal effectively with farmers' problems. The system embodies few new ideas, but by emphasizing key principles that are frequently neglected and by providing a resilient implementation system, it can have a significant impact.

Adopting the system for reforming the existing extension services is a major organisational effort. The key changes were to make the extension staff responsible only for extension work in a unified service and to put pressure on researchers to concentrate on the practical problems of the average farmer. As a result, technical recommendations are now available that can substantially increase farmers' incomes. The success of these recommendations for farming—both under irrigation and rainfed conditions—is well-known and proven; a number of them are also available for improving the productivity of small farmers in the rainfed areas with minimal investment on their part, as well as for raising productivity of large farmers.

To make its greatest impact, the system depends on all elements functioning well: extension staff need to be dedicated, capable of learning on the job, and respected; contact farmers need to be representative; research needs to provide the advice and improvements in technology and practices that are capable of increasing yields; supervisors need to monitor extension and research in the field; separate support facilities—to supply credit and inputs—must be available; and the distribution services and infrastructure must be in place to market the crops and provide the boreholes or the irrigation needed. In many areas, there are simply not the resources, either human or physical, to establish such a concentrated, inter-locking system. In these cases, it has to operate with more limited horizons to avoid the extension service losing its credibility.

The difficulties show that it had seemed perhaps deceptively simple to implement in the early days. While its main ideas are straightforward, its concentrated approach requires a radical change for extension work in most areas—in its focus on fieldwork, its procedures, and in the attitudes of staff at all levels. Once a system has been reorganised it has to be monitored and support continuously for improvements to be

CHART I

Organisation Pattern of the Training and Visit System of Agricultural Extension in India

Headquarters
The Director of Extension in the Department of Agriculture is in charge of administration, all technical and professional aspects, and effective implementation.

Subject-Matter Specialist

Zone Extension Officer
in needed for overall supervision when there are too many districts to be supervised directly by headquarters.

District Extension Officer
supervises 6-8 sub-district officers and is supported by subject-matter specialists

Subject-Matter Specialist*

Sub-division Extension Officer
guides and supervises 6-8 agricultural extension officers, and is in overall charge of the extension programme. He is supported by subject matter specialists.

Subject-Matter Specialist*

Agricultural Extension Officer
guides, trains, and supervises about 8 village extension workers

Village Extension Worker
is trained by the Agricultural Extension Officer and Subject-Matter-Specialist, and passes instructions on the farmers' groups in intensive and frequent field visits.

Contact Farmers

Farmer Groups

* *Subject-Matter Specialists-*
the link between extension work and research. They sit on technical committees at headquarters and district levels, visit research stations, and organise field trials with and train Agricultural Extension Officers and Village Extension Workers.

maintained. This can only be done by field supervision of extension work and farmers' responses, by monitoring the relevance of research work, and by training sessions—all of which require substantial commitment. Nevertheless, once established, the system has tremendous scope for self-sustained improvement. Given the needs of modern agriculture, suitably adapted to each set of circumstances, it seems logical way to ensure long-term progress.

Even though several institutes have been in operation for fulfilling the training needs of the rural development personnel and target people, there is every need to inculcate among the development officials a sort of responsibility and interest in implementing the programmes for the best of the target groups. In turn there is a dire necessity to educate the rural masses about various schemes and programmes, their utility and motivate them to accept and adopt such schemes for improving their standard of living. Even though the training to improve the skills of both the developmental personal and the target people is a must, it is also essential that both the target groups and implementors should work hand-in-hand and with an understanding of personnel development and national development. The selfless attitude among the developmental personnel at field level will be sure to give better results. Hence it is suggested by various eminent scholars that the personnel involved in implementation of rural development programmes should be imparted not only technical and administrative skills but also the importance of welfare of humanity so that they could consider the human values and help the poor for their better living standard.

Management Information System (MIS(

The combination of status and timely access to accurate and relevant information enables the programmer to function well in those roles of decision-making. Information is of great significance because the quality of managerial decisions is directly related to the information available to the decision maker. The better the information, the more conclusive it becomes in guiding decisions, whether confirming the existing choices or suggesting a search for new ones. This in turn emphasises the need for developing formal 'Management Information System' (MIS).

Stated simply, a MIS is a communication process in which information is recorded, stored and retrieved for decision-making in regard to planning, operating and controlling. In its simplest form, MIS, in the context of decision-making can be represented schematically (Fig. 22.2). The basic transformation underlying MIS is to proceed from "data to information." The term data may be defined as any bit of information, from the dust in the air to the flecks in the carpet to the latest inventory list. Information, on the other hand, is considered to be data processed to affect choice.

The organisational problem is to convert data into information. Only a proportion of data available in an organisation is of real management importance; much of it may be relatively valueless—some may even tend to create confusion. The rise of modern Electronic Data Processing (EDP) has both alleviated and aggravated the organisational dilemma inherent in having too much random data and too little ordered information. The chance that data will be missed has gone down, but that data will be lost or misinterpreted has gone up. It is, therefore, important that the information system identify the information needs of different level of management (top, middle and operating), the form in which it should be made available, the time and frequency at which it should be supplied, and the method of processing information to suit the requirements of each level. These aspects have been briefly discussed here. Moreover, some basic considerations in designing and implementing an MIS have been delineated.

Decision-making is an iterative process involving:

(i)   The recognition of the opportunity or the problems;
(ii)   Obtaining data;
(iii)   Understanding the information content;
(iv)   Seeking alternatives;
(v)   Evaluating them; and
(vi)   Choice and implementation.

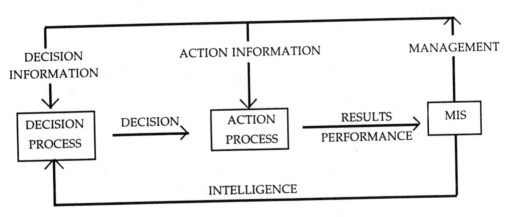

Fig. 22.1. MIS —An Overview.

Table 22.3 summarises the distinguishing features of three levels of management and the decision categories identified. Table 22.1(b) elaborates the information characteristics by the decision category.

At the strategic level, decision-making is largely a planning activity, and decisions are characterised by a great deal or Uncertainty and are future-oriented. Strategic decisions include establishing objectives, policy-making, organising and attaining an overall effectiveness of the organisation. The decision-making process is non-programmed—that is, it deals with ill-defined problems, usually complex and involving many variables, relies heavily on external information.

TABLE 22.3

Management Levels, Decisions and Information

Characteristic (1)	Top Management (2)	Middle Management (3)	Operating Management (4)
1. Planning	Heavy	Moderate	Minimum
2. Control	Moderate	Heavy	Heavy
3. Time frame	Long-term	Short-term	Day-to-day
4. Scope of activity	Extremely broad	Entire functional area	Single sub-function or sub-task
5. Nature of activity	Relatively unstructured, complex, many variables	Moderately structured, less complex, better defined variables	Highly structured straightforward
6. Type of decision-making	Strategic non-programmed	Tactical, mainly non-programmed	Technical, mainly programmed
7. Decision environment	Uncertainty	Risk	Almost certainty
8. Types of information utilised	(a) External information —Competitive actions —Customer actions —Availability of resources —Demographic studies —Government actions etc. (b) Predictive information (long-term trends) (c) Stimulated —"what if" information	(a) Descriptive —Historical information (b) Performance —current information (c) Predictive. —future information (short-term) (d) Stimulated "what if" information	(a) Descriptive —Historical information (b) Performance —Current information
9. Mental attributes	Creative, innovative	Responsible, persuasive, administrative	Efficient, effective
10. Departmental/divisional interaction	Intra-division	Intra-Department	Inter-department

Tactical decision-making pertains to short-term activities and the allocation of resources for the attainment of objectives. This kind of decision-making relates to such areas as the formulation of budgets, funds flow analysis, decisions on plant layout, personnel problems, product improvement and research and development. Tactical decision-making process has little potential for programmed decision-making. The decision rules are mostly ill-structured and not amenable to routine and self-regulation. Tactical decision-making relies to a greater extent on internal information.

Rural Development Activities: The Project Director, DRDA sends one monthly, five quarterly and one annual progress reports to the Secretary Department of Forests and Rural Development. The Assistant Project Officer(Monitoring and Evaluation) compiles the information received from various banks and other officials in the department and fills up the prescribed proforma. The selection of eligible beneficiaries under IRD Programme will be done by the DRDA officials, bankers and block officials in the presence of Village Officials and leaders. The APO (M&E) used to monitor and evaluate the different schemes with the available data and also by meeting the beneficiaries personally. A separate cell was established in the Secretariat under the guidance of a Director exclusively of IRD Programmes. The Deputy Director also monitors the IRD Schemes at state level and gives suggestions to the DRDA officials.

TABLE 22.4

Information Characteristics by Decision Category

Characters of information	Levels of Decision-making		
	Strategic	Tactical	Technical
Source	External	—	Largely internal
Scope	Very wide	—	Well defined, narrow
Level of aggregation	Aggregate	—	Detailed
Time horizon	Future	—	Historical
Required accuracy	Low	—	High
Frequency of occurrence of information change	Low	—	High
Frequency of uses of information	Infrequent	—	Very frequent

Note: From strategic to technical, the scale is a continuum.

The District Co-operative Officer sends six monthly, eight quarterly and one-yearly reports to the Registrar of Co-operatives. The three Divisional Co-operative Officers collect the data from Taluk Co-operative Officers working under their jurisdiction. They consolidate the information and send it to the District Co-operative Officer who in turn consolidates the figures and submits the progress report to the Registrar of Co-operatives. The monthly and quarterly proforma deal with targets and achievements of Co-operative Banks' activities, recovery of loan, sanction of loan, etc.

The District Lead Bank Officer sends three quarterly, two half-yearly and two annual reports to the Development Manager, Lead Bank Department, Hyderabad. He also sends credit reports to the Reserve Bank of India. A consolidated report will be presented in the District Consultative Committee meeting to be held quarterly. In this meeting the progress of different banks and various schemes will be reviewed which helps to plan the financial activities in the district.

The qualitative aspects of data primarily depend upon the skills needed for data collection and analysis and also on inter-personal interaction within the organisation and rapport with the personnel in the other organisations supplying data. Though training is a part of the activities in most of the departments, imparting of adequate skills for effective collection and analysis of data to those associated with these tasks, has not drawn the attention of trainers/ departments to the extent desired. The nature and duration of training should be identified based on the tasks assigned to a person and the level of functioning in the organisations.* So accordingly, it is suggested that for field-level functionaries (who are) responsible for data collection and reporting, periodical training meant for improving working knowledge—purpose of a scheme and its objectives, concepts used, field supervision, cross-checking of data supplied, etc. will suffice. The officials/persons at the higher level who are generally associated with survey designs, data analysis and supervising the work of field personnel, should be trained on design of surveys, statistical methods and also management practices (orientation courses) in order to discharge the functions/tasks more effectively.

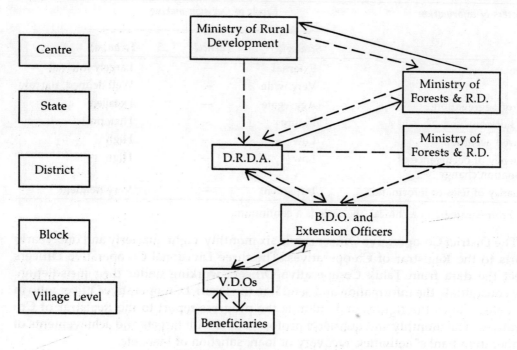

Fig. 22.2. Data Flows under I.R.D.P.

Besides training, the inter-personnel interaction in the organisation (to a desirable extent) and also with the concerned departments/agencies is expected to improve the

---

*It is expected that the training programme contents are related to the job chart of trainees to make the training meaningful and effective.

reliability of the data to some extent. In fact, such interaction provides an opportunity to the field staff about the current use of data (collected) and also make them appreciate the need for and utility of the data. Further, the officials at the higher level will be in close contact with the field situation (including problems of data collection) and thus may plan for their data needs more precisely. The training programmes are expected to facilitate such interaction of personnel (for mutual benefit) and this in a way helps in strengthening the organisation. The inter-departmental interaction will help in understanding the limitations of data and thus interpreting data accurately by the data-user department(s).

Importance of Motivation in Rural Development

Through the ages, psychologists and sociologists have concentrated their attention on the question, why do people behave in the way they do? The rural people should be motivated to participate in the development programme. They should be made to act in a certain way so that they may have the *motive* to do better for their own advancement.

What is Motivation?

The word *motivate* means to mover, to activate. Literally speaking, therefore, the motivational function of the rural worker should refer to the creation in the individual of a mental predisposition to perform the required activity and, thereafter, make him persist in it for the desired duration. Motivation, however, is internal to human beings— people are motivated by their own needs and not by others.

The programmer's function of motivation is, as such, concerned with working on these needs so as to influence behaviour in a desired or predetermined way. The findings of subsequent researches of Elton Mayo and Roethlisberger conclusively proved that work efficiency and output depended on the individual, as well as on the employees as a whole; and not wholly on the work itself or on the environment, but on several other psychological and motivational forces influenced by informal groups and by group cohesion. Later researches have further established that the employee's behaviour may not conform to the expectation of the work study forecasters mainly because the work has to be done by a human being, and the output of human energy is influenced by innumerable complex factors operating simultaneously on the system.

If a person's work *per se* adds to his or her happiness, then the job itself becomes the ultimate motivator. But for this to be so, the work must be valued and recognised as such. For the programmer/workers, this implies a continuing effort to underscore the importance of what the subordinate is doing in the overall context of the orgnisation. Motivation is a matter of human understanding — or the superior understanding the subordinate. If and when that state is achieved, it becomes a process of encouraging people to go, as far as possible, towards meeting their aspirations—their hopes and dreams. This requires giving them an opportunity to show what they can do. Their efforts must then be recognised and rewarded to the extent that this is possible within the system. They must be made to feel *wanted* within that system. This can be done by bringing home to them an awareness of the fact that their efforts do contribute to the organisation as a whole.

Motivation is not much different from friendship. A friend attempts to understand you and to help you, as far as possible, to achieve your aims. A friend is concerned about your happiness, and tries within the limits of his or her abilities to make you happy. A friend is someone who supports you and knows that he or she can count on your support in return. Above all, a friend is someone who will go out of his or her way to do things for you. The motive for this is nothing more than the knowledge that you would do the same for him or her. And so it is with mutual motivation in an organisation.

There are various ways to build motivation into a job which may be found in the voluminous literature on this subject. Writings on motivation tend to suffer from professional jargon, which psychologists and management experts employ in their attempt to be explicit.

Management by Objectives

The basic lack of motivation cannot be cured without scientific management effort. Motivation is that intrinsic power that makes things happen. We cannot merely create a programme with its apparatus of targets and statistical feedback proformas, and then sit back and wait for great things to happen. On the other hand, we cannot coax and cajole the extension staff to achieve the results, both quantitatively and qualitatively.

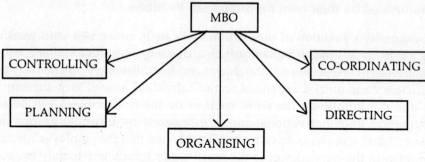

MANAGEMENT BY OBJECTIVES IN RURAL DEVELOPMENT
GOAL—INTEGRATED RURAL DEVELOPMENT
RESOURCES—MEN AND MATERIAL
ORGANISATION—VILLAGE PANCHAYAT

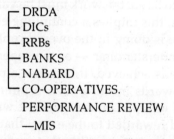

- DRDA
- DICs
- RRBs
- BANKS
- NABARD
- CO-OPERATIVES.

PERFORMANCE REVIEW
—MIS

Fig. 22.3. Rural Management by Objectives.

A call has been given in some quarters for the creation of a cadre of "rural managers." The answer lies in adopting the Management by Objectives (MBO) approach. It is a test of managerial competence to visualise and plan, and of executive skill to implement and achieve. It is perhaps the most effective means of integrating motivated individual effort into a composite and wholesome contribution to the overall objectives of the programme. It seeks to convert resources into results by planning, organising directing, co-ordinating and controlling activities and functionaries in any programme. It seeks to quantify and integrate objectives down to the individual engaged in any programme. In other words, the first requisite is that the programme must have specific goals or objectives which it must achieve. An objective is a managerial tool which sets the direction and pace of an activity to utilise resources optimally in order to produce results. It has to be distinguished from purpose, which is in the nature of the *raison d'etre* to the programme. In simple language, "objective" would mean a specific goal to be achieved in a given period of time in pursuance of the purpose of the programme. But objectives are not to be handed down in a spirit of authoritarianism. Instead, they should be fixed after discussion and mutual consultation at all levels, taking into account the long-term and short-term priorities at all levels.

Performance review is an integral part of the MBO process, for periodic performance reviews help in identifying the reasons for success or failure and in developing a definite plan of future action. These reviews can also throw up the inadequacies of the structure and provide guidelines for the modification of policies and practices. The focus in performance review in MBO is on the future; and an evaluation of past performance is important only as a source for ideas and the direction of future planning. Focus on performance-emphasis on improvement, future orientation and self-appraisal are essential features of this review. Self-appraisal not only increases such functionary's influence in the review process, but enhances the credibility of review results. An information system, designed to facilitate frequent reviews, has also to be developed.

Conclusion

Planning for an accelerated growth of rural areas requires planning for flexibility, both in respect of the human and non-human resources in a rural organisation and in the scope for a revision of plans. Organisations should be explicit in recognising the personal values and aspirations of its beneficiaries as well as its workers and administrators. A careful consideration should be given to the ethical aspects and to the organisation's obligations to society.

Progressive rural organisations/institutions that plan ahead provide promising job opportunities, set fair prices for their products, plan for a reasonable development of the rural environment in an integrated manner, and have a healthy regard for the interests of the community. It must be evident that however skilled the planner-executives are, the most important requirement of all is that of men who are wise enough not only to plan for others but to plan in a manner that would encourage others to plan for themselves. In the final analysis, this might well prove to be a very important guide to strategic management.

23
Agencies for Rural Development

Introduction

There is no dearth of agencies for rural development. At present, one could list out 44 agencies/institutions including 9 international organisations, who have been actively working for the rural development in India. The list is incomplete. Among these, co-operatives, commercial banks, regional rural banks have been working at the grassroot level. Under the multi-agency approach, the commercial banks (including Regional Rural Banks) have opened 31,148 rural branches as at end June, 1988 and 95,000 re-organised primary agricultural co-opertives are functioning in rural India. What is more, rural branches have mobilised over Rs. 15,000 crores of deposits and deployed over Rs. 10,000 crores in rural areas. In the present day context, it is expected that the banking system would be an instrument for bringing about socio-economic change/revolution in rural India through (i) reducing regional and sectoral imbalances; (ii) promoting growth and distributing justice; and (iii) harnessing science and technology for improving the productivity of rural assets—land, labour, livestock, water, forests, grassland, etc., and neutralising the liabilities of poverty, unemployment, indebtedness, etc. All these call for crystallising the role of specialised branches/units set up by banks.

Agencies

Besides, the financial and other agencies play a catalytic role in rural development. This apart, the corporate sector and the voluntary agencies have also engaged themselves in the task of rural development. In addition, a number of scientific and technical organisations like research stations of the ICAR, Agriculture Universities, Regional Research Laboratories, Krishi Vigyan Kendras, Community Polytechnics, Indian Institutes of Science and Technology etc. are located in various parts of the country. Mobilisation of resources and its deployment in agricultural, non-farm activities, rural artists, cottage industries, and integrated rural development is a continuous process.

Agencies for Rural Development

1. Central Government
2. State Governments

3. Village Panchayats, Panchayat Samitis, Mandal Panchayat, Nyaya Panchayat and Zilla Parishad
4. District Rural Development Agency (DRDA)
5. District Industries Centres (DIC)
6. Council for Advancement of Rural Technology (CART)
7. National Institute of Rural Development (NIRD)
8. National Co-operative Development Corporation (NCDC)
9. Primary Co-operative (Agricultural/Non-agricultural)
10. Primary Land Development Banks (PLDB)
11. Large-sized Multi-Purpose Societies (LAMPS)
12. Farmers' Service Societies (FSS)
13. Scheduled Commercial Banks (Branches in Rural Areas)
14. Regional Rural Banks (RRB)
15. National Bank for Agriculture and Rural Development (NABARD)
16. Rural Electrification Corporation (REC)
17. Agricultural Finance Corporation (AFC)
18. Internal Fund for Agricultural Development (IFAD)
19. Agro-Industries Corporation (AIC)
20. National Land Resources Conservation and Development Commission (NLRCDC)
21. National Land Board (NLB)
22. State Farms Corporation of India (SFCI)
23. Cotton Corporation of India (CCI)
24. National Dairy Development Board (NDDB)
25. National Committee on the Development of Backward Areas (NCDBA)
26. Khadi and Village Industries Commission (KVIC)
27. Rural Marketing and Service Centres (RMSC)
28. District Supply and Marketing Societies (DSMS)
29. Composite Rural Training Centre (CRTC)
30. Voluntary Agencies (VA)
31. Industrial Houses (IH)
32. Adult Education Centres (AEC)
33. Indian Dairy Corporation (IDC)
34. Institute of Rural Management (IRM)
35. World Bank (WB)
36. Agro-Industries Corporation (ADC)

37. Afro-Asian Rural Reconstruction Organisation (AARRO)
38. Centre on Integrated Rural Development for Asia and Pacific (CIRDAP)
39. Food and Agricultural Organisation (FAO)
40. United Nations Education, Scientific and Cultural Organisation (UNESCO)
41. World Health Organisation (WHO)
42. United Nations Industrial Development Organisation (UNIDO)
43. International Development Association (IDA)
44. Organisation for Economic Co-operation and Development (OECD).

Rural development is a part of the same process of economic development and social change. They have to go on simultaneously. Although, various agencies are working in this direction, the rural development programme lacks co-ordination and cohesion. Moreover, until and unless a strong will for development develops within the rural community the development process would not gather momentum.

The country is poised for growth and the rural environment is conducive for concerted action in improving rural standards. Financial institutions, particularly bank have been helping in multidimensional way in achieving this. The need of the hour is a co-ordinated action on the part of the government, corporate bodies, voluntary agencies and the banks. It is also important that efforts and resources deployed by various agencies do not overlap. In fact, each agency should supplement the efforts of others and treat the programme as a joint endeavour with one single purpose. The principal objective of rural development is the development of the rural people, particularly the rural poor. The three crucial inputs in rural development are the motivation of rural people, the relevant technology and management and implementation of the transfer for technology to rural poor.

Farmers' Service Societies

The government has been constantly striving to find out a solution to the problem of adequately meeting the credit needs of the rural sector through a proper institutional credit set-up. Since 1951, the central and state governments have been experimenting with varied programmes with the sole objective of eliminating rural poverty and raising the level of living in rural India. The promotion of Farmers' Service Societies (FSS) is one such effort, which was initiated in 1978 to meet the challenge. The need for a new rural credit institution of this type was felt because of the inadequacy of the conventional types of co-opertives and commercial banks, the continued neglect of small and marginal farmers and rural artisans, and the non-availability of package of inputs and customer services along with technical advice and complementary services under one roof to small and marginal farmers. The aim of the Farmers' Service Societies was to provide a national network of integrated credit services for an extensive modernisation of agriculture by fully utilising the talent, experience and resources already available with the co-operatives and commercial banks.

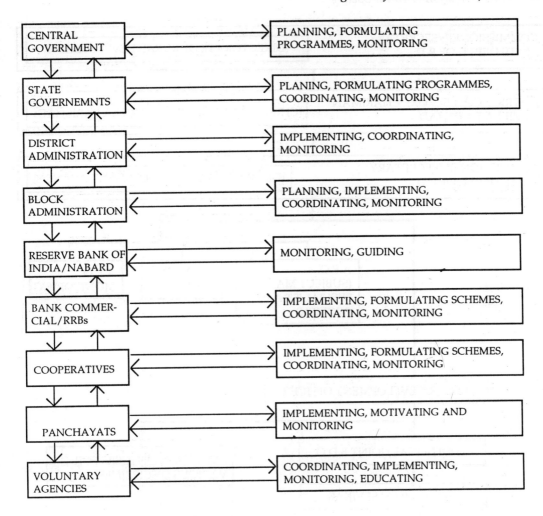

Fig. 23.1. Multiple Agencies for Rural Development.

Objectives

The objectives of the FSS are:

(i) To make the contribution of the small farmers, marginal farmers and agricultural labourers in the agricultural development quite meaningful;

(ii) To provide credit in the right amount at the right time for creditworthy schemes;

(iii) To supply inputs and services at reasonable rates at the right time;

(iv) To arrange for a fair market where the small man would get a reasonable surplus; and would be able to buy his requirements of fertilisers, pesticides, seeds, agricultural implements as well as consumer goods at a fair price.

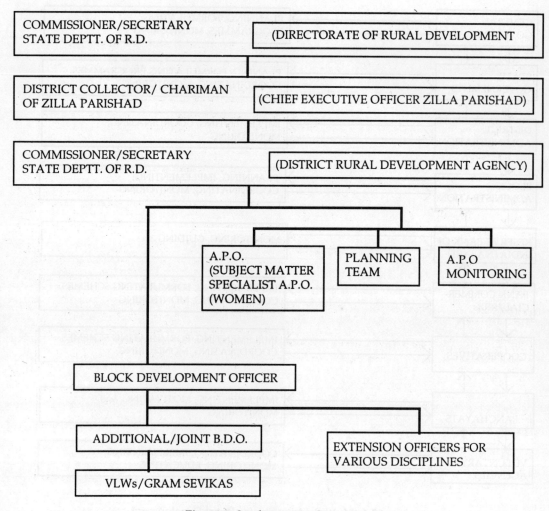

Fig. 23.2. Implementing Structure.

In addition the Farmers' Service Societies provide a package of inputs and customer services, along with technical advice and supporting services for storage, transportation, processing and marketing at a single contact point.

Genesis of FSS

The National Commission on Agriculture (NCA), which was constituted in 1970 to go into the various aspects of agriculture, considered the financial aspects of agriculture, and devoted much thought to a satisfactory agricultural credit policy. The Commission emphasised three basic goals of credit policy in respect of agriculture, viz.—

(i) It should provide a total system for building up and expanding all the activities and facilitate the modernisation of agriculture, including organisation of services and marketing and bringing about improvements in it;

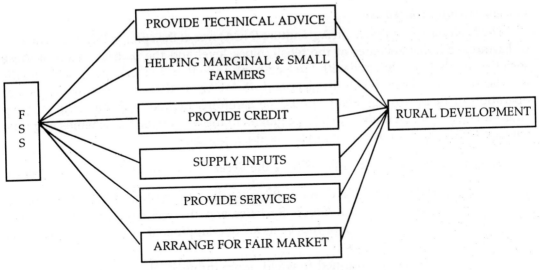

Fig. 23.3. Objectives of Farmers Service Socieites.

(ii)   It must have a comprehensive connotation of agriculture to make it almost co-terminus with rural development, covering all the production needs of rural households; and

(iii) It must facilitate and provide for linkages between finances and services for current inputs as well as for investment in land development, wells, pump sets and farm equipment.

In short, it implied an integrated rural development as well as an increase in rural production and productivity.

The co-operatives in the country has a very weak financial base, and uneconomic scale of operations and poor coverage; and they include a large number of formal societies. The National Commission on Agriculture was, therefore, of the view that efforts should be made to bring together small uneconomic societies and revive non-functioning societies by amalgamating them with the working ones so that they may become large-size societies which may reap the benefits of large-scale operations and offer integrated credit facilities. In 1971, the Commission, therefore recommended the Farmers' Service Societies (FSS).

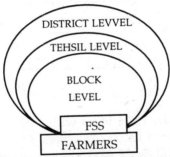

Fig. 23.4. Linkages within the District.

Phased Action Programme

The National Commission on Agriculture (NCA) was of the opinion that the formation of Farmers' Service Societies at the tehsil/block level and the district union of these societies, as also their linkage with the lead bank and other financial institutions might first be tried out in 46 SFDA districts and 41 MFAL districts. It recommended that operation of these arrangements should be carefully studied and that with suitable adaptations as a result of the experience gained in these districts, the schemes might be extended very year to cover more districts at a rapid pace.

A study on the working of the FSS by the Reserve Bank of India revealed that:

1. In certain status like Gujarat, Bihar Andhra Pradesh and Maharashtra, the Primary Agricultural Credit Societies and the FSS have been functioning side by side and there has been an overlapping of area of operation and duplication of work;

2. Large farmers continued to wield more influence than the weaker sections in getting benefits, quite contrary to the objective of the FSS and representatives of state governments and sponsoring banks did not take much interest in correcting this trend;

3. In many cases, the total amount of loan given to the weaker sections was found to be unsatisfactory;

4. In many FSS there were no technical personnel and hence no technical guidance was available;

5. In many states the overdues of FSS ranged from 20 to 40 per cent of the payments due; and

6. The non-credit functions, including provision of services like marketing etc., were fund to be limited in many FSS.

In the rural credit structure, the FSS have an important part to play at the base level. The sponsoring banks, the NABARD and the state governments have a responsibility to activise the FSS so that the weaker sections in the rural society get the benefits of integrated credit delivery system.

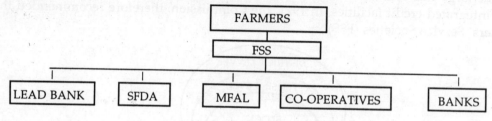

Fig. 23.5. Area of Operation of FSS.

During the year 1987-88, the 1,826 FSS's with a paid-up capital of Rs. 52.63 crores mobilised Rs. 12.25 crores, loaned Rs. 212.78 crores, 13.17 lakh borrowers of which, Rs. 187.34 crores was short-term and Rs. 25.44 crores long-term credit. The total outstanding credit stood at Rs. 336.42 crores consisting of Rs. 252.44 crores of short-term credit and Rs. 83.98 crores of medium- and long-term credit of the total outstanding credit, Rs. 115.72 crores or 34.4 per cent was overdue as on 30.6.1988.

The FSS owned 1,826 godowns, hired 675 godowns, and offered storage facilities in 1,562 godowns. Of the total 1,826 FSS 1,042 worked at profit, 686 at loss and 143 just balanced their budgets. The cost of the management of all the FSS aggregated Rs. 4.58 crores or, on an average, Rs. 24,500 per FSS. The FSS have brought about a socio-economic change in the areas of their operation, and helped the small and marginal farmers and rural artisans to raise their level of living above the subsistence level.

Organisational Structure

The organisational set-up of the FSS is a grand synthesis of all that is good in the co-operatives and commercial banks.

The FSS has threefold objectives:

(i) To have a sound capital base, (ii) To have a paid management with effective control of the government, the financing institutions and the members, and (ii) To extend a variety of services required by farmers under one roof.

In order to have a sound capital base the Reserve Bank of India now NABARD gives loans to state governments from its National Agricultural Credit (Long-Term Operations) Fund towards their share capital contribution to the FSS. The amount of share capital contribution is restricted to Rs. 50,000 to a FSS operating in an area covering a population of Rs. 10,000 and to Rs. one lakh for block level societies. In order that the FSS may avail themselves of the share capital contribution, they have to fulfil certain conditions, such as viability, financial linkage with central co-operative banks or commercial banks, appointment of full time managing directors and technical staff, adoption of model by-laws etc.

The activities of the FSS are managed by Boards of Directors, which consist of representatives of farmer members, financing institutions which may be commercial banks or central co-operative banks or original rural banks, and the state governments. There may be nine or eleven or thirteen members on the Board of Directors. In a set-up where there are eleven directors, one full-time paid director manages the day-to-day activities of the FSS. Of the remaining ten directors, five come from the farmer-members of the FSS, of whom three are small and marginal farmers and two are farmers of other categories. The remaining five directors are: a representative of the financing institutions, a Block Development Officer, an Assistant Director of Agriculture, an Assistant Director of Veterinary Services and an Assistant Registrar of Co-operative Societies. However, the designations of the directors coming from the various departments of the state governments may vary from state to state. From the composition of the Board of Directors it is evident that an effort has been made to protect the interests of all concerned with the activities of FSS.

The staffing pattern of the FSS, consists of a managing director, three extension officers with appropriate clerical support. The staffing pattern, however, may vary from FSS to FSS, depending upon its coverage, the composition of its credit and the area of its operations. Managing directors and extension officers are initially deputed by the state government. While the salary of managing directors is borne by the financing institutions for an initial period of three years, the state governments subsidise the salaries of the technical staff. The FSS also have cashiers-cum-salesmen to look after their dealings in such agricultural inputs as fertilisers, seeds, pesticides, agricultural implements etc.

Salient Features of FSS

Certain features of FSS distinguish them from Primary Agricultural Credit Societies (PACS). These features relate mainly to the area of operation, management, activities and the staffing pattern. The PACS generally cover three to five villages having a population of about 2,500 to 3,000 and having about 250 to 300 members. The PACS are managed by an elected board of directors who render honorary service and have paid secretaries to look after the daily accounting work. In many cases, even the secretaries are honorary. The PACS are linked to district central co-operative banks and ordinarily meet only the short-term requirements of agriculture. There is generally no supervision of the end-use of credit except for the disbursement of the component of the credit. As against this, the structure of the FSS envisages a wider coverage. There can be two types of FSS, viz., a small size FSS covering a population of about 10,000 and comprising 20 to

TABLE 23.1

Economic Features and Business Potential of the Farmers' Service Societies

Item	Block size FSS	Small size FSS
Area of operation	100 villages or a block	10 villages
Population	1,00,000	10,000
Number of cultivating households (50%)	10,000	1,000
Number of agricultural labour household (30%)	5,000	600
Average holding size	3 acres (1.2 ha)	3 acres (1.2 ha)
Assume 50% coverage of agricultural holdings in 5 years representing small farmers	15,000 acres (6,070 ha)	1,500 acres (607 ha)
Cropping pattern	2 crops	2 crops
Major crop	paddy	paddy
Average area to be covered per year	3,000 acres (1.214 ha)	1,500 acres (607 ha) in the first year itself
Scale of finance for HYV*	Rs. 350 in kind	kind component + Rs. 100 cash component

*The credit requirement is calculated taking only short-term financing into consideration. However, medium- and short-term mix depending on the need of the individual farm will be required in which case this would roughly equal to Rs. 1,350 per holding participating in the programme. Calculations are made on this conservative assessment.

30 villages, and block-level big-size FSS covering a population of about one lakh. However, the difference between the two types of FSS is only one of the area of operation and not of functions.

Administration

The affairs of the FSS are managed by a board of directors, of whom some are nominated by the various departments of the state governments and others are elected by the members. Besides, they have paid managing director and technical staff to look after the disbursement, supervision and end-use of funds. The FSS render short, medium- and long-term financial assistance and deal in agricultural inputs and implements. They also assist in the marketing of farm produce and extend loans against agricultural commodities whenever required. They offer a variety of other services, such as the collection of milk, the maintenance of chilling centres, the cultivation of demonstration plots, the maintenance of artificial insemination centres, the sale of articles of food and other rationed commodities, etc. Apart from these activities, the FSS accept current, savings and the deposits, and extend deposits, banking facilities to their members. The amalgamation of societies is one of the important aspects of FSS, which, from the point of view of achieving the required level of business, is quite significant because the main objective of the scheme is to establish an institution which will ultimately have an economic size and reap the benefits of paid management.

Advantages to Financing Institutions

The FSS offer distinct advantages to financing institutions, particularly to commercial banks. While extending credit through FSS, commercial banks have only to supervise the activities of the FSS. The FSS take the responsibility of preparing the seasonal credit-limit statements on the principles of co-operative finance and submit them to financing institutions. Separate credit-limit statements are prepared for the kharif and rabi seasons and for term loans. The credit-limit statements furnish the required data about the borrowers, such as total holdings, proposed cropping pattern, area to be benefited by the proposed loan, scale of finance for meeting cultivation expenses, the amount of loan asked for, the amount of loan which borrowers are eligible, the amount of loan recommended, security offered, the repayment schedule etc. The preparation of these statements is important, and the officials of financing institutions may make a preliminary scrutiny of these statements before they are processed by the Board of Directors of the FSS. Since these statements are passed by their Boards of Directors, the managers of financing institutions should normally have no difficulty in approving the credit-limit statements. In this way, the maintenance of individual loan accounts and follow-up and supervision of credit on the part of financing institutions are avoided. That is why even small branches of commercial banks can easily manage five to ten societies and have far more coverage than would have been possible through direct lending.

Apart from the advantage of larger coverage through the FSS, commercial banks can also reduce the operational cost of agricultural lending. The FSS have a better feel of the area of operation, for they have farmer-members on their board who can give them a better feedback about individual borrowers and also assist them in the recovery performance. Moreover, the FSS, being co-operative institutions, are vested with effective summary power which can be utilised, if necessary to recover dues from recalcitrant borrowers.

Apart from the advantages the FSS offer to the financing institutions, the FSS have the potential to develop themselves into community based organisations which, after meeting the financial requirements of the community, can develop the required infrastructural facilities which are the pre-requisites of the integrated development of the rural economy. In this way, they offer a unique opportunity to financing institutions for their effective participation in the rural development of the regions which are served by Farmers' Service Societies.

Marginal Farmers and the Rural Development

One of the common features of the agrarian economy of the less developed countries is the preponderance of small and marginal farmers. A large number of factors, economic, geographic and sociological, contribute to the proliferation of the problems of small farmers who subsist in precarious living conditions in most of these countries. It is a historical fact that over the years their problems have been aggravated with the rapid growth in population and the sluggish rate of growth in agricultural productivity. The sub-division and fragmentation of holdings and very little improvement in irrigation facilities have perpetuated the poverty of these people. The pathological symptoms of peasant farming are too well-known now to be enumerated here. Quite a few research studies have been published in recent years, analysing the problems of 'subsistence farming," "peasant farming" and other types of farm living in different parts of the world.

In most of the policy formulations adopted for a agricultural development in developing countries, the emphasis has been on huge investments in multipurpose irrigation projects and on land legislation aimed at changing man and land relations. In the capital-starved agricultural economics there are instances which show that the investment made by the state in these highly capital-intensive projects have not yielded the desired results, because the farmers, who are expected to make use of these irrigation facilities, do not have credit facilities, it is only the bigger farmers who have taken advantage of the new situation. Those who made use of the new farm inputs prospered. The big cultivators themselves became exploiters of the smaller and weaker section of farmers. Next to the village moneylender, the big cultivators and landlords were the major source of credit in the rural areas. The inevitable consequence of this financial dependence was that the differences between the big farmers and the small farmers, in terms of their economic prosperity widened considerably.

With use of hybrid varieties particularly in irrigated areas, the total agricultural production as well as farm income had almost doubled within a short span of time. Such a rapid transformation was possible only with the aid of the necessary farm inputs. The total cost of cultivation under modern farming is being fairly high, and the credit requirements of the farmers taking to modern farming have also increased. The availability of credit and other farm inputs became a bottleneck for small farmers. Most of them could not reap the benefit of the green revolution, which was ushered in large parts of the country. The green revolution no doubt created an additional demand for farm labour, for farming became a commercial proposition. A number of studies have been made on the benefits accruing to the rural society because of the green revolution. Some of the studies have no doubt shown that the benefits have percolated down to the agricultural labourer in the form of higher wage rates and additional employment. Some other studies have revealed that, on the sociological plane also, there have been some changes.

The government has introduced various schemes to boosting agricultural production during the last three decades. The Intensive Area Development Programme which has been introduced in some of the selected districts aimed at intensifying the agricultural operations through the extension of farm technology and the dissemination of knowledge of modern farming. The results obtained, at least in some selected pockets, are quite tangible. However, the beneficiaries are usually the big and medium farmers.

Credit was one of the major bottlenecks in the developmental process. As organised banking was reluctant to venture into agricultural financing, much hope was pinned on the co-operatives. The co-operative credit movement has been given all the necessary incentives because it was behind that if the farmers were to be rescued from the clutches of village money lenders, the institutionalisation of credit was an imperative need.

The co-operative movement, which has been in existence in the country for over eight decades, has done very little to ameliorate the economic conditions of small farmers. The problem of these farmers was one of competing with those big farmers who had the capacity and influence to secure co-operative credit and other benefits. Ever since these issues were categorically highlighted by the Report of All India Rural Credit Survey, efforts were made to rectify the shortcomings of the co-operative credit institutions. Yet the problem remained. The power structure in rural areas being what it is, the small farmers were helpless. The Study Team on Agricultural Credit constituted by the National Commission on Agricultural categorised them as the neglected partners in agricultural growth and recommended the establishment of Farmers' Service Societies. It may be noted here that the formation of Farmers' Service Societies, which offer him credit and supply all the inputs, is a step in the right direction—it revitalises co-operative societies and makes them a powerful instruments for the development of the farming community.

The data published by the National Sample Surveys through their various rounds have been one of the major sources of information on the concentration of land holdings on the one hand and the preponderance of the small farmers on the other. Recently, for the first, time an attempt was made to conduct an agricultural census in the country. The report contains data relating to the number of operational holdings, tenurial relationships and many other useful details. Of the reported 70.5 million operational holdings in the country, 50 per cent are classified as "marginal farms" of less than one hectare. These holdings, however, account for only 9 per cent of the total area of 161 million hectares. It has also been reported that the marginal and sub-marginal holdings have on an average, only 0.3 hectare of irrigated land. Another very important feature of the Indian farming situation revealed by the Agricultural Census is that, in the cropping pattern of the marginal and sub-marginal farmers, such food crops as paddy and jowar predominate. This is perhaps an infallible indicator of the subsistence character of small farming.

Apart from small farmers and marginal farmers, the agricultural labourers form a substantial part of the rural population. They occupy the lowest rung of the rural pyramid. Their living conditions are no better than those of marginal farmers. With the increase in the population in rural areas, the size of the agricultural labour force has increased almost proportionately or more than proportionately, whereas the rate of growth of employment opportunities in non-farm activities in the villages are lower than the rate of growth of the rural population. It is normally assumed that economic development would bring about a shift in the occupational pattern in favour of non-farming activities. But it is perplexing to observe that the available decennial demographic data indicate a trend which is quite contrary to this notion. A comparison of the number of persons classified as agricultural labourers in the 1961 census and 1971 census reveals that there has been an increase of nearly 80 per cent in their number during the decade. Even if we make allowances of definitional differences, it may be observed that there has been a remarkable increase in the number of agricultural labourers during the census period. Where rural unemployment manifests itself in many forms, any increase in the labour force is likely to aggrieved the situation rather than ease it.

The problems of marginal farmers and agricultural labourers are so deep-rooted in our rural economy that it is believed that they are beyond economic measured. They are considered as welfare problems and not as an economic proposition under the available technology. This is basically due to the reasoning that the size of a holding is considered to be an obstacle to the development of small farmers. However, the latest development in the field of crop genetics has belied this assumption. The new technological possibilities thrown open by the hybrid varieties have proved that the total yield per acre can be boosted up even on small farms by applying to optimum package of farm inputs. This possibility has led the farm economists to think that the small size of a farm holding is not necessarily a limiting factor in the improvement of the economic status of marginal and potentially viable farmers.

An Agency for Development

The plight of small farmers and marginal farmers attracted the attention of the planners and others during the Fourth Five Year Plan period. In the "Approach to the Fourth Five-Year Plan" (November, 1968), emphasis was laid on the necessity of improving the small farmer and his economy in the overall framework of objectives for the development of agriculture. It was said that, in the agricultural sector, besides providing the conditions necessary for increasing agricultural sector, beside providing the conditions necessary for increasing agricultural output by 5 per cent per annum, step should be taken to enable a large section of the rural population, including the small cultivators, the farmers in dry areas and landless labourers, to participate in the development and to share its benefits. It was thought advisable to promote separate agencies for accelerating the process of the development of small and marginal farmers because the existing schemes, aiming at overall agricultural development, would not, per se, improve their conditions. The All-India Rural Credit Review Committee, after making a review of the farm situation in the country with special reference to co-operative credit, recommended the formation on the Small Farmers' Development Agency. The reports said: "The marginal and sub-marginal cultivators have to be helped to raise themselves on the basis of the land, equipment and skills which constitute the resources available to them. The problem is, therefore, to make their farm business more efficient in technology and surplus in economic terms and to supplement their resources and knowledge for this purpose. This effort is obviously restricted to those cultivators who can be developed into surplus farmers if they adopt improved techniques on the basis of the support in terms of supplies, irrigation services, machinery, etc. Appropriate schemes have to be drawn up by technical experts with reference to the local resources and requirements, so that such cultivators can undertake specific lines of investment, adopt a suitable crop pattern, use modern inputs, and so on. It is to deal with this limited problem that we propose an institutional set-up in the form of a Small Farmers' Development Agency." This agency was expected to co-ordinate the activities of the developmental departments and credit agencies in order to ensure that the requirements of the small farmers were adequately met. The task of the agency included that of identifying the special problems of the small farmers and devising programmes by which the farm economy might be made viable. Another major task of the agency was to arrange for credit either from the co-operatives or from commercial banks, by providing the necessary incentives by way of subsidies. This proposal was accepted by the Government of India and the scheme was introduced in 1970. It was extended to 46 districts, where small farmers were found in large numbers. The central government made a provision of about Rs. 1.5 crores for each district over a period of 5 years.

Simultaneously with the implementation of the scheme for the development of small farmers, a separate scheme for the development of marginal farmers, and agricultural labourers was introduced. It was felt that the problems of the latter category of peasants were more acute and deep-rooted than those of the former and that they, therefore, required a separate treatment. The Marginal Farmers' and Agricultural Labourers' Development Agency was charged with the responsibility of enabling marginal farmers to maximise the productive use of their holding by suitable changes in the crop pattern, namely, taking to horticulture, animal husbandry, bee-keeping etc. The necessary credit for productive investment was provided by co-operative and commercial banking institutions, which were given the incentive of subsidies. The Marginal Farmers' and Agricultural Labourers' Development Agency was set up in 41 districts in the country, where the marginal farmers and agricultural labourers resided in large numbers. Besides the districts selected by the central government for the execution of this scheme, state governments also selected some districts for its implementation. The year 1971-72 was the first full year of the working of this scheme in most districts. In the initial stages, efforts were directed at the identification and enumeration of marginal farmers and districts after the formation of the development agency. The schemes formulated for implementation were put through in most of the districts with the active support of co-operative bank.

DIC—Instrument of Rural Development

Very often, banks are criticised for going slow in fulfilling socio-economic objectives to the desired extent. The assumption is that finance is the only constraint in uplifting the lot of the neglected sections of society and the backward areas. It is the common experience of banks that, in spite of sincere efforts, they cannot do what they are supposed to do, for either the required infrastructure is lacking or the projects are not viable. The District Industries Centres, therefore, provided the right type of set-up for the promotion of the development of rural industries and crafts. More such specially devised institutional arrangements are necessary if the flow of banks credit to rural areas and the rural poor is to increase. The problems of these areas are so many and complex that unless the various agencies come together and evolve a common strategy, banks alone would not be in a position to achieve much.

The advantage of promotion of cottage and small units are too well-known to be repeated. In fact, for a developing country like India, with large population, there is no choice other than the promotion of rural cottage small units. Considering that poverty and unemployment are the most pressing problems facing our country, even after three decades of planned economic development the promotion of the small and cottage sectors. If planned systematically, can work wonders. Japan has shown the way.

No single factor can be advocated as the most important determinant of the success of a small unit. There has to be a blend of entrepreneurship, managerial abilities, the period of work experience, technical know-how and educational background, among others. With the passage of time, small-scale industries are entering highly sophisticated areas of production. A single individual cannot normally be expected to possess all the abilities required for the successful running of the unit. For the self-sustained growth of small industries, it is essential they should be self-reliant as possible. The inner strength, can come to small units only from combined approach to their development involving the grouping of entrepreneurs from various disciplines to set up a given unit.

Against the background, the setting up of a District Industries Centre (DIC) in every district, eventually, holds a good promise of transforming the rural scene by promoting small, village and cottage industries. The major aim of making the district headquarters of focal point of decentralised development is that it can serve as a link chain between large cities and remote villages. It has also the advantage of checking the migration of the skilled rural population to cities. Under the DIC programme each credit is manned by a General Manager of the rank of Joint Director of Industries. He is supported by a team of seven functional managers who are specialists in credit, raw materials, machinery and equipment, economic investigation, research extension and training, marketing, handloom, khadi and village industries. The idea is to provide prospective entrepreneurs a package assistance under one roof so that it may be easier for them to set up new units.

The policy change, emphasising the need for the rapid development of cottage and small-scale industries in rural and semi-urban areas aimed at generating larger employment opportunities. Obviously, small scale industries, sustained by locally available resources, have to be encouraged. It is only by the establishment of such industrial units which absorb raw materials and other resources available in the local and adjacent areas and which reduce commodities generally consumed by the local people that economic activity can be accelerated. The industrial policy hitherto followed had led to the growth of a few industrial pockets without creating any impact on the surrounding hinterland.

The DIC Programme continues as a centrally sponsored scheme during the 7th plan period and government of India shares its expenditure with the state government on 50:50 basis. As end March 1989, the total number of approved DICs stood at 422 covering 431 districts in the country. Over the years, the scale and scope of their operations have undergone substantial changes, in response to the changes that have been taking place in the social, political and economic environments. During the year 1987-88, the 422 DICs identified 3,85,286 entrepreneurs, established 4,40,568 new units comprising of 3,28,316 artisans based and 1,12,252 small scale units, arranged for credit of Rs. 1,371.50 crores from financial institutions and generated additional employment 14.11 lakh persons. In order to make DICs more effective, more particularly as an agent of rural development, the organisational pattern of the DICs is being restructured keeping its conceptual base intact. DICs have been playing a pivotal role in providing opportunities for self-employment.

Co-ordinated Endeavour

The process of the generation of employment opportunities was a co-ordinated endeavour in which such financial institutions as commercial banks, voluntary agencies, such as business houses government agencies and local bodies participated simultaneously. Now that the commercial banks have been in the field for quite sometime, it has been recognised that the non-availability of financial assistance is not the only reason for the non-exploitation of local resources.

In fact, the outstanding credit extended by commercial banks for the small-scale industrial sector amounted to Rs. 12,290 crores or 14.9 per cent of the total credit extended by the banking industry covering about 24.15 lakh SSI accounts as at end June, 1989, as compared to this, in June 1969 (on the eve of banks nationalisation), outstanding credit to small-scale industry stood at Rs. 251 crores, which constituted about 7 per cent of the total outstanding credit of the banking system. From the above it is evident that banks have channelised a substantial portion of their incremental resources into this vital sector. The outstanding credit of the state financial corporations stood at Rs. 5,725 crores at the end of March 1989, showing a rise of Rs. 168 crores over the year.

The Lead Bank Scheme is deeply involved in district development throughout the country, and banks have gained sufficient knowledge of the district economy, their expertise and knowledge can be beneficially harnessed to make a success of the District Industries Centre. While preparing Lead Bank Survey Reports and District Credit Plans, banks have identified growth centres as well as economic activities having a potential for growth and expansion in each district. Based on the readily available data with banks the task of the DIC is facilitated in identifying prospective entrepreneurs, bankable projects and their locations. What is more important now is that the DIC should undertake promotional activities and motivate local manpower to come forward and take advantage of the facilities offered. For this purpose, the active involvement of voluntary agencies already working in the area is necessary. In other words, the target group should be clearly identified; and, obviously such a group would mainly comprise the weaker sections of the population. Care, however, should be taken to weed out entrepreneurs whose main objective is to make quick money.

An overview of the DICs and their operations generally shows a poor picture. In most cases, the DICs had become an information centre and did not achieve the objective of providing a complete package of services and support to prospective entrepreneurs from the one office. The major reason for this was the lack of various allied facilities which were outside the purview of the DICs. Entrepreneurs had to visit State Financial Corporations, raw material depots and sometimes even markets in distant towns or cities. The reluctance of officers to camp in rural areas which lacked the minimum physical comforts was another factor adversely affecting their performance. These could have been provided at a small cost while taking care to ensure that they did not smell of conspicuous consumption and was generally within the larger cultural landscape of the rural areas.

Council for Advancement of Rural Technology (CART)

Appropriate technology is now a widely accepted concept. Considerable work has been done in India for the development of appropriate technology in different sectors of the economy. For the rural areas the research has been done on a variety of problems in a number of institutions like national research institutes affiliated to the Council of Scientific and Industrial Research, Indian Institutes of Technology, the Khadi and Village Industries Commission, the Indian Council of Agricultural Research and its affiliated bodies, etc.

Set up as a Society in October, 1982, under the Societies Registration Act, the Council became operational in March, 1984 with the assumption of office of a full time Director General. The main objectives of the Council include:

(i) to act as the national nodal point for co-ordination of all efforts at development and dissemination of technology relevant for rural areas for sectors other than those covered by ICAR and its sister bodies;

(ii) to act as a catalyst for development of technology, appropriate for the rural areas, by identifying and funding research and development efforts by different organisations;

(iii) to strengthen existing institutions of research and develop or set up institutions, so that national level institutions on matters of purely on largely rural interest are built up;

(iv) to act as clearing house of information and a data bank;

(v) to disseminate knowledge on rural technology to manufacturers of machinery, tools, equipment and spare parts so that large scale production of technically improved machinery etc. is carried out in the private, co-operative and public sectors;

(vi) to act as conduct for transfer of appropriate technology to government departments public sector undertakings and members of the public;

(vii) to conduct or sponsor training programmes for trainers so that improved technology is passed on to the beneficiaries in the rural areas;

(viii) to carry out research studies, surveys, evaluation etc. on the use of appropriate technology;

(ix) to do all other such things as the society may consider necessary, incidental or conducive to the attainment of the above objectives.

In developing and transmitting appropriate rural technologies priority sectors in rural development with emphasis on poverty alleviation and the policy objectives appropriate to rural areas contained in the 1983 Technology Policy Statement of the Government of India have been kept in view. Transfer of technology to scheduled castes, scheduled tribes and other weaker sections of rural society like landless labourers and artisans, who require special assistance which is not immediately available now in the existing schemes, is given special attention.

Keeping in view the priority areas and on a quick overview of the development of rural technology, the more immediate concerns of CART are the following:

1. Post harvest technologies.
2. Water supply and water management.
3. Energy.
4. Rural Housing.
5. Village industries.
6. Health care and Sanitation.
7. Technologies of women.
8. Transportation.

As for special groups, particular importance is given to rural women and youth. The later group would be of two categories viz., rural youth with little formal education and young professionals.

To begin with, some related technologies have been selected and steps taken to disseminate them. So far 213 projects worth Rs. 666 lakhs for technology transfer have been assisted by the Council as a means to field test and disseminate suitable technologies. The projects are mostly aimed at the improvement of the rural people living below the poverty line. The projects are designed to achieve the following objective:

— Opportunity to upgrade one's skills.
— Utilisation of these skills in better rewarding activities.
— Humanisation of toil.

TABLE 23.2

Number of Projects Sanctioned by CAPART since Inception

Scheme	No. of Projects Sanctioned
Promotion of Voluntary Action in Rural Development	201
Organisation of Beneficiaries of Anti-poverty Programmes	583
Rural Technology	213
Central Rural Sanitation Programme	282
Accelerated Rural Water Supply Programme	184
IRDP	59
DWCRA	321
RLEGP	222

As may be evident from the list of projects, the life of a project ranges from 6 months to 3 years, the former being very few. Further as the projects were sanctioned only in 1984-85, it is premature to assess the results yet. The real impact can be evaluated only after the projects are either completed or have run for a sufficient time.

In addition to project assistance CART is taking stock of technologies already generated to upgrade the technological content of the ongoing rural development programme. A publication entitled Rural Technology Guide is being brought but by CART in English and in major regional languages and has been circulated to all DRDAs and Blocks as part of its task of information dissemination. In addition, publications of clippings from newspapers and journals relevant to rural technology are brought out once in two months. A journal is also being brought out by the Council.

Certain critical areas have been identified in which a major thrust could be given to extensive application of new technologies. Two such exercises have been initiated so far:

A meeting of experts on low-cost construction technology was held on 14.6.1985 to take stock of the present state-of-the-art and formulate a specific action programme for applications of such technologies to the massive rural housing project to be executed under RLEGP.

A session on handloom technology was held on 15.7.1985 in the specific context of the new textile policy with stress on modernisation of handlooms and swift and smooth transfer of technology to the handloom weavers.

A computer division has been established in the Council to facilitate quick and efficient collection, collation, retrieval and dissemination of essential data covering the entire gamut of rural technology. The system is also being utilised for project monitoring.

In addition, work on the preparation of a national directory of rural technologies has also begun. The directory is to carry 14 major components of rural technologies and the first volume is expected to be finalised shortly.

Work on the preparation of four documentary films on the development and successful adoption of useful technological inputs for rural development is underway for widespread screening through the Films Division circuit and the Directorate of Field Publicity. Video Films on nine CART assisted projects are also being made.

On the request of the Ministry of Education, a seminar was organised on 22.11.85 by the Council on the new education policy to identify levels at which vocational education should begin and their linkages with rural technology specially in the unorganised sectors.

In order to identify and develop an effective delivery system from out of the existing institutional infrastructure, the Council has participated/sponsored meetings at Madras and Hyderabad relating to District rural technological training centres; at Trivandrum and Simla in the state level seminar on adaption of advanced Technology for Rural Development and at Ahmedabad on transfer of rural technology through voluntary agencies. The Council also participated in a national level conference on application of science and technology for Rural Development at Porbandar in December 1985 workshop on science and technology for rural Madhya Pradesh at Bhopal in February 1986 and a convention for mass awareness of science and technology for rural areas at Durg in January 1986.

Peoples Action for Development (India) (PADI)

This is a voluntary organisation registered under Societies Registration act 1860 under the administrative control of the Department of Rural Development. The Minister of Agriculture is the President of the Society, Minister of State for Rural Development, the Vice-President and the Secretary of this Department, the Chairman of its Governing Council. It is responsible for promoting voluntary action as a supplement to government efforts in rural development. To this end, it assists a large number of voluntary organisations to implement viable projects for economic and social development of the weaker sections in the rural areas.

PADI has been canalising funds from foreign donor agencies for financing projects of voluntary organisations. From 1984-85 funds under Central Sector Scheme for Promotion of Voluntary Schemes and Social Action Programmes have also been made available to PADI for giving financial assistance to voluntary agencies. From 1985-86, PADI has started assisting voluntary organisations in implementing the following additional schemes with government funds:

1. Development of Women and Children in Rural Areas (DWCRA)
2. Accelerated Rural Water Supply (ARWS)
3. Low Cost Sanitation in Rural Areas
4. Rural Landless Employment Guarantee Programme
5. Organisation of Beneficiaries.

During the year 1987, 383 project proposals were received and PADI approved 101 projects worth Rs. 1,181.71 lakhs involving PADI's assistance of 394.82 lakhs. During the year PADI has released Rs. 193.07 lakhs including foreign contributions.

During the year Rs. 10.5 lakhs were received from foreign donors and Rs. 42.86 lakhs were released for financing projects out of foreign funds.

PADI organised 5 conferences during the year 1985. The conference of Co-ordinating Voluntary Organisations was organised in New Delhi in April 1985 and the conference of Voluntary Organisations on Development of Women and Children in Rural Areas was organised in New Delhi in June 1985. Regional Conferences of voluntary organisations were organised at Pune in August 1985, at Tirupati in September, 1985 and at Indore in November, 1985.

As an advance action to implement the scheme of organisation of the beneficiaries, PADI organised a camp of IRDP beneficiaries of Indore District at Kasturba National Memorial Trust, Indore on November 15, 1985.

Role of Industry

Although the involvement of business houses in rural development goes back to many years, it gathered some momentum in the seventies. The industrial houses have managerial skills and organisation competence which could be deployed in a co-operative endeavour with the government and voluntary organisation to improve the consumption levels of the poorest in the rural areas. Aware of the technical and managerial resources available with the industrial houses, the Sivaraman Committee, in its report submitted to the government in 1978, recommended the participation of the non-governmental organisations, especially industrial houses, in rural development. To encourage the industry to participate in rural development, the union government started giving them tax incentives. Accordingly, the expenditure incurred by business houses on approved programmes of rural development became deductible expenses items while computing their taxable profits.

Even before the announcement of tax incentives, many industrial houses, including Tatas, Mafatlals, and Hindustan Lever, were engaged in rural development work. Some big business houses have adopted village near their factories and undertook welfare and other service activities in these adopted villages. Fertiliser manufacturers, as part of their sales promotion strategy, provide extension services, free of cost or sale fertilisers at subsidised rate and supplement it with other input to farmers in adopted villages. Some business houses engaged in the manufacture of consumer goods based on agricultural raw materials put up pilot projects, the benefit of which are reaped by many farmers in the adopted villages.

Companies which have set up their own organisation to undertake rural development work go about it more systematically than others. These companies carry out village surveys to identify the economic activities and assess the scope for development. On the basis of these surveys, eligible target groups of beneficiaries and economic activities are identified and specific schemes formulated. Financial allocation is then made according to the priority assigned to various activities and availability of funds. So far, the response of private sector industry to rural development has not been overwhelming and the impact on the rural poor has been negligible. There are many medium sized industries which can be encouraged to participate in this work through appropriate incentives. The participation of industry and voluntary organisations can only supplement the efforts of the government towards alleviating rural poverty.

Industry can play an important role in the upliftment of rural areas. With the organisational and managerial expertise at its command, the industry can involve itself in the following areas:

* Programmes which directly improve the economic well-being of the people, such as propagation of cottage and village industries, improvement of agriculture, etc.
* Programmes aimed at transfer of appropriate technologies, revitalisation of village crafts and traditional technologies, etc.
* Programmes directed at improving the quality of life, such as health programmes, sanitation, educational programmes, recreational, etc.

The programme adopted shall be acceptable to the rural people and should not disturb the rural environment. It should be based on the utilisation of local raw materials, with minimum energy per unit consumption of production and, at the same time, fall within guidelines set by government. In other words, the industry should undertake only those programmes in rural area which are simple enough to be adopted by the people who have limited education, skills and resources. The projects and processes feasible at the village level are totally new to organised industry. Establishment of rural development cells by different industries may be a step in the right direction to cope up with rural problems. These cells should have sufficient managerial input and financial soundness to pack up the developmental programmes on a continuous basis. Admittedly, in several industrial units, there are such cells and functioning well. But there is a need to revitalise their functioning.

Role of Banks in Rural Development

Banks play a key-role in rural development. Wealth is created as a result of the application of human effort, Human effort compromises of the passive one and the active one. The banks, or more specifically, the banker who conceive rural development, plan it in all its detail, mobilise the material and human resources for the project and benefit by the integrated development of the command area of its operation. The characteristic of banking, therefore, are knowledge, vision, meticulous (micro level) planning drive, dynamism and translation of the plan into reality. A good banker is one who is capable of inspiring confidence in people, and has the ability to motivate them to work with him in fulfilling the socio-economic goals set by him. In other words, a good banker ought to be a good, progressive and dynamic leader of men.

Banks can give the right lead for rural development, as they are the respository of resources to accelerate the process of rural development. Besides making available the finance for development banks can play a catalytic role in developing infrastructure, transfer of technology and know-how guidance and above all education of the rural people of varied target groups.

Government has assigned a pivotal role to the banking system in developing the village economy. In the sphere of credit the major thrust of government's policy has been on ensuring availability of credit to all classes of rural borrowers, especially those belonging to the weaker sections, on terms better than the usurious rates charged by village moneylenders. With this end in view, government's endeavour has been to strengthen, through the Reserve Bank of India (RBI), the multi-tier co-operative credit structure, which primarily serves the credit needs of the rural areas. The RBI has, in addition, played an important role in co-ordinating the efforts of commercial banks and co-ordinating the efforts of commercial banks and co-operative credit agencies in rural development. The accent of government policy in regard to banks has been on ensuring their penetration into rural area. Emphasis has also been laid by the banking sector on evolving programmes for an all-round development of the village economy by providing credit to agriculture and village industries. In the endeavour to develop the rural economy, the efforts of commercial banks, State Land Development Banks and State Cooperative Banks, are complemented by those of the NABARD.

The banks' role perhaps is in terms of taking up those programmes which could provide employment to the rural labour. Generation of additional employment opportunities in the rural sector is somewhat difficult to achieve in a short period. Considering the magnitude of the growth in rural labour force, it is also necessary to find employment opportunities for at least a major portion of them in the non-agricultural sector. How exactly the banks can play their role in this process of employment generation depends upon their ingenuity in adopting suitable schemes for financing. For the development of skills among the rural youth for self-employment, the Government of India has introduced the programme of Training Rural Youth for Self-Employment

(TRYSEM). By co-ordinating their lending programmes, banks can contribute substantially in this sphere, if they have the conviction to implement their own programmes effectively.

Towards this end, banks who are involving themselves deeply in the formulation of credit plans for rural development, evolving strategies for development, visualising the growth process in the rural economy and planning for the development of credit facilities in accordance with the requirements of growth in addition to providing credit to agriculture and other rural activities on an increasing scale. Banks are, therefore, more suited to take up the challenging task of rural development. And, the activities of all other agencies have to be co-ordinated with the banks in the true spirit of integrated area development for eradication of mass poverty in rural India. Above all, rural people should rise above the present state of affair and strive hard to develop with the assistance and guidance offered to them. They should accept that rural development is aimed at improving the living conditions of the people living in rural area.

The commercial banks which are now actively engaged in rural credit have on their rolls technical persons (agricultural graduates) named in different ways as Agricultural Officers, Rural Credit Officers, Agricultural Finance Officers, etc. They are supposed to guide the farmer in all technical matters and supervise the credit. But it appears that these technical persons have to spend more time in processing the loan applications, disbursing of the loan amount and preparing periodical reports to be sent to the central office. In the process, considerable time is not devoted for technical service and supervision. Further, the technical staff is quite inadequate. Loan amounts reach the rural community without adequate technical assistance and proper supervision. Even though it cannot be concluded that all borrowers need technical assistance and all misuse the loan amount, yet, credit with necessary follow-up action is bound to yield better returns.

Provision of adequate and timely institutional credit is an important condition for rural development. But credit should not become a "hangman's noose" for the borrower. Nor should it jeopardise the interests of the banking institutions. To have an adequate impact on agricultural production the provision of credit should be accompanied by, and co-ordinated with, extension services and supervision. Co-operatives are better suited to exercise supervision, and effective supervision should be invariably treated as a legitimate function of the apex banks and central banks. As financiers of societies, they should take the necessary steps to ensure sound working of the primary credit societies and primary land development banks. Through proper supervision, the mounting co-operative overdues can be minimised. The government with necessary support should help the co-opertives to introduce suitably modified and supervised credit programme. To start with, such scheme may be introduced in places where co-operatives are functioning well and gradually extend the scheme to other places. The commercial banks may be insisted upon to have adequate technical staff on their rolls. It is paradoxical that agricultural graduates remain unemployed in some states, in a situation of inadequate technical staff, including extension personnel.

The Regional Rural Banks sponsored by the commercial banks may be utilised for introducing the supervised credit scheme. For effective implementation of the programme, well-trained persons should be employed as local supervisors. Young persons with high school education preferably from agricultural families with practical farm experience may be chosen for training to serve as credit supervisors. One year specialised training in agricultural economics with emphasis on farm credit, co-operative organisation, farm management, techniques of supervised credit, etc., in necessary. The technical aspects of farm operation such as crop choice, use of fertilisers, control of insects and plant diseases should be included in training courses. The Reserve Bank of India has to necessarily play a crucial role in helping co-operatives and commercial banks to introduce supervised credit scheme.

The credit-giving institution, while providing short-term credit to weaker sections, should take into consideration the normal credit requirements for consumption purposes. However, a greater proportion of the credit should be in kind. Further, it should examine carefully the technical feasibility and productive capacity of the proposed farming operation with the help of credit. Technical advice, if required, should be provided to the loan applicant at this stage to evolve a suitable plan. Follow-up action must begin with the release of the first instalment of the loan. The credit supervisor must work closely with the borrowers. He has to supervise and control the use of the loan amount throughout the crop year. The subsequent instalment of the loan amount should be released after the banks is fully satisfied with the proper utilisation of the loan amount. Tenant cultivators, agricultural labourers, rural artisans and other weaker sections should be made creditworthy by helping them to take to certain gainful occupations through supervised credit programme. Attention should also be given to marketing and it should be made obligatory on the past of the borrower to sell his produce with the knowledge of the concerned bank. The credit supervisors have to assist the borrowers in marketing their products. Even an element of effective supervision over credit will go a long way in using the credit for productive purposes and reap the benefits. A well thought out supervised credit system with organisational efficiency aiming at the benefit of the weaker sections immediately called for.

Micro-Level Planning

One of the solution suggested by economists is to adopt bottom up micro-level planning to achieve the positive results in the field of rural development. The micro-level planning is based on the socio-economic, political and administrative needs, problems and aspirations of the people, potentialities of the area, local skills and entrepreneurship and possibilities of development with the active participation of the local people. Micro-level planning emerged as an effective instrument in achieving the goals set at macro level through an integrated process.

The major objectives of micro planning are:

1. To cater to the basic needs of specific areas/people and develop/harness rural skills and entrepreneurship.

2. To solve problems of areas and regions of extreme backwardness through active participation in the rural development programme.
3. To share the benefits of planned development to the optimum extent.
4. To work towards removing inter and intra-regional socio-economic imbalances.
5. To create greater employment opportunities and strive to improve the quality of life of the rural poor.
6. To remove rural poverty and inequality in income and wealth.
7. To achieve goals of integrated rural development.

In this type of planning there is scope to integrate the varied schemes, programmes, sectors and policies at the local level on fixed priorities.

Conclusion

We would like the reiterate that rural development is a part of the same process of economic and social change. There are a number of programmes formulated by the government and the industry, voluntary agencies, etc. Banks have been implementing them by providing necessary financial assistance. There are multi-disciplined institutions for rural development. What is wanting at the present moment is the co-ordinated and sustained effort. What is more, it is necessary to bridge the gaps of inequalities in rural areas. This could be attempted by well-organised service co-operatives to give support to farming.

Towards this end, the corporate sector, banks and other financial institutions should invest sizeable portion of their profits towards increasing basic infrastructure like schools, hospitals, health centres and take up the onerous task of propagating family planning, planned parenthood and motivating rural people to achieve a higher living standard. Rural development is a human development programme and, therefore, it should be above party politics. The motto should be to help with all the might the down-trodden irrespective of caste, creed, sex, etc.

Rural development should be looked upon not merely as ameliorating the socio-economic conditions of the rural people but also as motivating rural people to take up the integrated development of rural areas. In this direction, the process of development should originate at the individual level then linking it to family and then to a group of families and the village. It should developed from bottom to top. The people's active participation will bring in a sea-change in the scale and scope of operation. The results are in terms of change rather than the sum of crores of rupees spent on a project without bringing any benefit to the concerned people. The experiments in rural development have remained more or less at the top. It is, therefore, necessary that emphasis should be laid on 'Planning' from the bottom and that the exclusive reliance, so far placed on the 'pyramid structure' approach, be given up.

In the ultimate analysis the desire for development, the direction this process takes and the momentum it gathers, depends upon the will of the people. Various institutions for rural development can help in harnessing the energies of the people, especially of the rural people as well as the student community and in providing institutional and organisational channels for their efforts. The environment in the country today is conductive for concerted action in improving rural conditions and rebuild rural civilisation.

ROLE OF CHANGE AGENTS IN RURAL DEVELOPMENT AND NABARD

What is a Change Agent?

The Change Agent has been considered as a catalyst and defined in different ways. By and large, he is a person what contributes to the spreading of new ideas and attitudes favourable for the adoption of change. A successful change agent is one who possess ability to give rational direction to the needed change to attain what is sought.

Importance of a Change Agent

The people trapped in illiteracy and poverty suffering from extremes of material and social depravation tend to lose impulses of awareness and motivation and this deprivation makes them weak, isolated, vulnerable and powerless. The change agent plays an important role in influencing these people towards social and economic change in terms of adoption of innovations.

Who is a Change Agent?

The next question which arises is as to who is a change agent. Robert Chambers in his book "Rural Development—putting the Last First" observes that most learning of rural conditions is mediated by urban vehicles and based on such perceptions, policies are framed for rural development. According to Robert Chambers, the persons who mediate with rural people are academic researchers, aid agency and technical co-operative personnel, bankers, businessmen, consultants, doctors, engineers, journalists, lawyers, politicians, priests, school teachers, staff of training institutes voluntary agencies and other professionals.

In a study reported by NIRD it was found that the village level worker was known to a large percentage of people as villagers contacted him most. The next important functionaries, in terms of contact with the villagers were the Block Doctor and the Block Development Officer. About 30 per cent of the respondents reported that they were in contact with these functionaries. About 19 and 16 per cent of respondents reported that they had contacted Agricultural Extension Officer and Co-operative Officer, respectively. Thus, it will be seen from the foregoing that in the case of Indian rural conditions, development functionaries at the grossroot level had a large contact with the rural people. Naturally, if follows that the quality of these functionaries will determine the extent and degree of change.

A.K. Danda and Danda in their study 'Development and change in Basudha' found that the perceived relationship between the extension officer and the farmers is an important factor. Programmes for development are likely to suffer as long as the extension officer is perceived by them as an outsider. For the success of a programme, his acceptance as a trusted person seems to be essential. It is thus amply clear from the foregoing that the quality of the change agent in rural areas is of the utmost important. It is said that if you educate a man, you educate an individual but, if you educate a woman, you educate the entire family. I would go a step further and say, if you motivate a grossroot change agent, viz., village level worker, agricultural extension officer, co-operative officer, etc. you succeed in motivating the entire village community. With the intensification and widening of the Integrated Rural Development Programmes throughout the country and introduction of ISB activities, the number of grassroot development agents has gone up. District Industries Centres and TRYSEM programmes have provided fillip to the development of non-farm activities in the rural area and diversification of rural economic activities have received impetus on an unprecedented scale bringing about a distinct change in attitudes of the rural population.

Other Change Agents Media

Apart from the local development officials, there are other change agents who influence is equally pervasive. Amongst the programmes which made impact upon the farmers in rural areas, it was found that the awareness of the fertiliser programme was found to be the highest amongst the rural people followed by the use of improved seeds, insecticides and improved ploughs. Further, illiteracy being high in our country coupled with high price of newspapers, newspapers cannot make much impact. But, by and large, people have more access to radio. Several studies have shown that the increased knowledge level led to the adoption of new ideas, innovations and this medium can be used to a large extent to spread the message of change. During the last few months, TV network has been expanded at an unprecedented rate and about 90% population is reported to have been covered by TV it has a much advantage over radio and therefore, community TV programmes are, and could be effectively used as a change agent.

Voluntary Agencies

Voluntary agencies are yet another important source as change agents. The Indian experience shows that there are around 1000 voluntary agencies engaged in rural development. Some of them have indeed done yeoman service to the rural community. Most of these organisations have sprung up under the charistmatic leadership of social or religious reforms and their ideology has served as the moving spirit behind these bodies. Christian Missionaries, Ramakrishna Mission are the outstanding examples. A high percentage of voluntary organisations is concentrated in the western and eastern regions of the country. This is, perhaps, due to the influence of freedom movement and social reforms which were organised in these areas instilling among the people a desire to organise social reconstruction. Here too, the integrated projects operating in neglected areas have shown better identification with the rural poor and served as catalyst of development.

Village Leadership

Village leadership is one more and rather important change agent. Leadership has been defined as the activity influencing people to co-operate towards achieving the goal. A person who displays such a quality or activity in the rural area can be considered as a leader. In rural areas, the people seek advice of such leaders for solving their day-to-day problems and thereby influence their activities. This relationship is based on trust and because of its informal nature, there is very little awareness of the existence of this type of leadership to outsiders. But such type of leadership can play an important role, in influencing the rural people towards social change in terms of adoption of innovation.

Ramesh Arora in his "Peoples' participation in development process" found that the fundamental problem of development in the Indian rural context is the inculcation of aspirations, building up of attitudes and development of a forward-looking, self-helping and action-oriented bent of mind which put together would constitute what may be called development psyche.

Our rural people though illiterate, possess robust common sense and are willing to take innovative ideas provided the risk/uncertainty element is less and immediate gains are visible. Roy and others in their study of 'Cultural Innovation Among Indian Farmers' observed that one of the major incentives to receptivity was the prospect to raise the standard of living.

The above views is corroborated by Paul Harrison in the "Third World Tomorrow—A report from the battle front in the war against poverty." He observes that ordinary people have great wisdom and strength and can accomplish miracles when their initiative is given its head. But, their energies require guidance and education. In the case of China, this was provided by the party which with its communication structure and its cadres in every block of houses or workshop became a superb instrument for mobilising the masses across a wide range of issues and for transmitting education, information and motivation on any particular campaign.

Agricultural Universities

The Agricultural Universities have also proved good change agents, wherever they have move out to farms with missionary zeal demonstrating as to what could be achieved with proper planning and adoption of a package. In short, the association of voluntary agencies together with the enlightened rural leadership coupled with dedicated extension workers and zealous farm demonstrators from the nearby agricultural universities can provide an excellent combination capable of triggering multiplier effect changing the agrarian landscape.

Bank Officials

There has been sea-change in the lending portfolio of the banks and agriculture, cottage and rural activities have come to be devoted greater attention under the policy directives. With the launching of IRDP, DRI and unemployed educated youth schemes, the role of the bankers at the grassroot as well as at the intermediate levels as change agents has increased by leaps and bounds. By and large, commercial banks have given a good account in assisting the rural sector and acting as change agents. The number of rural branches opened, amounts advanced and number of small accounts assisted are a testimony to the role played by bank officials, despite several handicaps faced by them. Several training programmes and workshops are held, time and again, to bring about attitudinal changes, in the rural bank officials. Regional Rural Banks have been set up, which employ local people to ensure better understanding of local issues and better rapport with the beneficiaries. NABARD has established a separate college. Bankers Institute for Rural Development (BIRD), at Lucknow, to improve the banking skills of RRB officials and train them for better involvement in rural lending. NABARD also conducts training programmes for commercial bank officials and finances training programmes of cc-operatives to ensure high quality of rural lending.

Importance of Non-officials

The role of non-officials is crucial in the functioning of co-operative credit institutions. Since they head the institutions and are responsible for their policy and management, they ought to execute their duties of office in a manner that would act as good precedent. They should motivate the borrowers to adopt modern methods of production and modern technologies to secure higher incomes and adopt modern management practices for continuous expansion. The example of Punjab which made rapid strides is essentially a case of motivation provided by the non-officials heading the credit agencies with support of extension agencies which moved out to the field with missionary zeal. We have heard of several leaders in the co-operative movement who have been able to raise the institution and the area to great heights. We have only to peep into the past of the co-operative movement in our country and of certain bigger cooperative projects like sugar co-operatives to flash to mind the shining examples of non-officials who could through their effective leadership and guidance transform the entire faced of the rural economy of their areas.

Action Learning

Yet another change agent who could influence the adoption of change in the rural area is the successful farmer. An example is better than a precept. The example of success of one of their own brethren would influence the rural people much more than the talk and persuasion by several development officers. Thus action learning i.e. adoption of innovation based on the experiences of other co-practitioners in the field is a very potent change agent.

The action learning is one of the most important and effective ways of learning. No professional, be a doctor advocate or a professor can become perfect in his field unless he works closely with and under the supervision of the professional possessing higher calibre. The great teachers of the world moulded the thoughts of those with whom they worked by their mere association. Gandhiji could create a galaxy of leaders by his association with them. If we look at the development of sugar co-operatives in Maharashtra, we realise as to how a few dedicated leaders at the initial stage were responsible for laying the foundation of the great sugar co-operative complex in the country. They belonged to the farm community, moved amongst the farmers and motivated them to join in the new experiment.

NABARD and its Role

NABARD has been entrusted with development of not only agriculture but also the entire spectrum of cottage, village and small scale industries in the rural area. In the years to come, non-farm activities will have to grow at a much faster rate to absorb the surplus manpower from agricultural rural sector and prevent its migration to urban areas. NABARD has, therefore, with a view to generating larger employment potential in rural areas, provided several new lines of credit for artisans activities covering handloom, coir, sericulture and village industries.

The studies conducted by the Xavier Institute of Social Service show that a single successful village entrepreneur can play a vital role in attitudinal changes. The successful rural entrepreneur contributes to socio-economic change in the village by starting tiny shop, services or industry. He exemplifies the scope for diversification of economic activities and reduces the dependence on agriculture as the sole source of livelihood. By his example, he demonstrates to the rural youth that it is possible to make a decent living in the village without having to depend on agriculture only. He generates employment for members of his family and others and in his own little way, he helps to solve the problem of rural unemployment. Being a person of local origin, he provides competition to unscrupulous business practitioners from outside. He helps in making money roll inside the village and generates more income and employment within the village and makes it more self-reliant. The extent to which a new local entrepreneur succeeds in his business, he helps the village people to improve their self-image. He contributes to the new ideas and attitudes favourable for the adoption of change. It is against this backdrop that greater emphasis has come to be laid on entrepreneurial development in rural areas.

At present, productivity of men and machines in the rural area is, by and large, low and needs to be raised to improve living standards and make the rural products competitive vis-a-vis the urban produce. The Technology Policy statement placed by the former Prime Minister on 3 January 1983, before the 70th Session of the Indian Science Congress, inter alia, states "Human resources constitute our richest endowment. Measures will be taken for the identification and diffusion of technologies that can progressively reduce the incidence of poverty and unemployment and of regional inequalities." NABARD has against the above backdrop constituted an Advisory Committee comprising well-known experts in rural development and technology for devising ways and means for improving productivity of the rural men and machines.

Small Industry Research and Development, Organisation of the Birla Institute of Technology, Ranchi, the Centre of Rural Development of the Indian Institute of Technology, Madras, the Council of Scientific and Industrial Research, have evolved and experimented with several new technologies appropriate to the rural environment and the scale of production. Some of these relate to brick-making, paper recycling, carpentry, welding, bakery, soap-making, garment manufacture, sheet metal working, electronics, agro-service centres, use of agro-wastes etc. The crying need of the hour is the appropriate agencies at the field level which could demonstrate the benefits of these improved tools and machinery to the rural people and motivate them to adopt them. The experience of a few voluntary organisations in this regard has been worth emulation. The Society of Rural Development, Ranchi, and Father Bogaert's Institute of Social Service, have been training, for sometime past, mostly school-leavers and tribal boys. By motivating them through entrepreneurial development courses, these agencies have absorbed the trainees in the traditional as well as non-traditional activities and achieved a success rate which will be envied even by some of the advanced technology institutes in the country. Such agencies are the real change agents and harbingers of rural progress and prosperity.

The National Bank for Agriculture and Rural Development firmly believes that the rural development process to be successful and be of lasting value has to begin with the development of man in the rural areas and especially of the one who is last in the scale and has to be put first for assistance. UNESCO document emphasises. 'Development must be designed, even at the humblest level, as a process of ensuring the advancement of man through his endeavours.' NABARD firmly believes that the village roots in our country can provide the foundations for a new style of development, capable of expanding material wealth without sacrificing social welfare and spiritual values, which the West has suffered in the process of industrialisation. It is in this direction that it has tried to direct its efforts for improved loan recovery and credit absorption in the rural area. To accelerate this process of development of human resources in the rural area, the Task Force on Tiny Industries constituted by NABARD has, inter alia, recommended setting up of the "Rural Entrepreneurial Development Institute" to train the trainers for rural entrepreneurship as well as to co-ordinate the activities of various agencies engaged in entrepreneurial development in the country. This Institute, when set up, would be a national-level body motivating the change agents at the grassroot level.

24

The Village Level Worker in Action

A Day to Day Record of Ten Day's Work[1]

This study embodies a day to day record of the Village Level Worker's activities for ten consecutive days in Rajput Village. The activities of the VLW were observed very closely for three weeks, and at the end of each day during this period he was interviewed to obtain a verbatim record of his activities during the course of the day. For this reason he speaks in the first person singular in the pages that follow. Participant observation by a member of our research team was simultaneously carried on the ensure substantial accuracy in the accounts given by the VLW, and to obtain the responses and reactions of the people with whom he had worked. The characteristic responses and comments of the people are appended to each day's record. Some of the problems emerging from this study are discussed in a concluding comment.

1 November, 1854

Got up at 5.30 a.m. and went to the Co-operative Seed Store. Picked up dibblers. Accompanied by the Kamdar of Seed Store (an employee of the Co-operative Department, S.C.D.) I went to Bhamula Singh. I had met him last night and had arranged with him to have a dibbling demonstration in his field early in the morning today. But when we went to him at the appointed time he said that he was going to another field, and that he would not be able to have the demonstration in his field today. We arranged with him to give this demonstration day after tomorrow.

Next we went to Kabul Singh. I had spoken to him earlier and had arranged with him to have a demonstration tomorrow. We asked him to have it today. He agreed.

Accompanied by Kabul Singh, his three sons, two servants and the Kamdar, I went to his field. This is at a distance of about a mile from his house. The dibbling demonstration was given on half a *bigha*[2] of land earmarked for this purpose. Ten to twelve other agriculturists had assembled there. These included Prithvi Singh and Bhamula Singh who occupy a position of some importance among the agriculturists of the village. Several others also came; but most of them stayed only a few minutes, and returned to their work after seeing the method of dibbling. One of the agriculturists asked: 'Do you like this method yourself? Don't you think that it is very slow?'[3] I explained to the people the advantages of the dibbler. They did not look convinced. One of them said, 'If we adopt this time-consuming method of sowing we shall require twenty times the labour and time that we normally need for our sowing. That would be the end of our agriculture! How can we afford to waste our time experimenting with your fancy ideas?' Others nodded in agreement. His argument was not new; others had expressed the same doubts many times before, I told them 'You are right. If you sow all your wheat by this method you will surely be wasting your time. This method is recommended only for seed multiplication — for improving the seed and for maintaining its quality. That is why I ask you to select healthy grains from your seed for these demonstrations. That is why I ask you to work diligently on a small piece of land. This plot is not meant to give you wheat for domestic consumption or for sale; but you will have excellent seed for next year's sowing.' They did not appear to be wholly convinced. I asked them to see the seed from the demonstration plot after it was harvested. I added, 'That alone will be a convincing proof of what I have said just now.'

After the demonstration I measured three of Kabul Singh's fields for fertiliser demonstrations. I measured one more field for a half-field demonstration (Punjab 591[4] *vs.* local variety of wheat). Many people still believe that the local *(desi)* variety of wheat is better and this necessitates demonstrations of this nature.

Immediately after this I went to Tara Chand's fields for selecting suitable plots for demonstration purposes. I could not select any of his fields as they all are of an irregular shape and are more than a mile and a half from the village.

Returned home at 11.30 a.m. I had an appointment with the Cotton Supervisor (an employee of the Agriculture Department, S.C.D.) at 12.30 p.m., so I had a hurried bath and lunch. At 12.30 p.m. I went with the Cotton Supervisor to Malkhan Singh. He had sown the improved variety of cotton last year and we wanted to buy some of it for seed. I explained to him our requirements and asked him to sell us at least a part of the improved variety of cotton. He refused. He said, 'We need it for making cloth.' I tried to persuade him by suggesting that we were anxious to multiply the seed of the improved variety to popularise it and that it was for this reason that we needed the cotton from him. He said, 'Our womenfolk will never agree to do so.' After some more arguments he agreed to sell it on the condition that we shall obtain for him an equal quantity of cotton of the local variety.

In the hope of buying some more cotton of the improve variety I went with the Cotton Supervisor to G.—a nearby village. This village is located two miles from R.[5]— the village where my headquarters are. We left at about 2 p.m. Met Budh Singh, Hardeva Singh and Mangat Ram in G. For the last three or four days I had been trying to persuade them to sell their improved cotton crop to us. They were reluctant at first, but later agreed to sell it because of my personal influence and pressure. Krishan, however, refused to sell it on the ground that his family needed it for making cloth. He thought that the womenfolk would not be willing to part with it under any conditions. The cottonseed itself was needed by them to feed the cattle.

Later I vaccinated thirty to thirty-five people. Parents of very young children (of six months or less) objected to their being vaccinated; vaccination of adults is now regarded as normal and necessary. Today I vaccinated only adults. This work was continued up to 5 p.m. Back in R. I saw the college nursery,[6] and gave instructions regarding watering the beds.

Returned home. Received a note from APO (Agriculture, S.C.D). This upset me very much. It was authoritarian and aggressive in its tone from beginning to end. It was addressed to me without the usual 'Shri.' All though he had addressed me as *tum* (used for inferiors, S.C.D.) and not with the more courteous *aap*, although I think that there is a government directive making the use of the latter compulsory in government correspondence. I was reprimanded for not being in R. when he visited. This was most annoying. Had he found me in the headquarters he would have said, 'Have you no work to do? Field-staff are supposed to be out most of the time.' Now that he did not find me here he said, 'Why does he go about wasting his time with the Cotton Supervisor? He should take more interest in his own work.' I could not be present in R. as I had no advance information regarding his visit. The letter contained his orders asking me to give fertiliser demonstrations immediately. The APO desired that seven bags of super-phosphate and twelve bags of mixture should be used in these demonstrations. This was an order from above. I was never consulted about it. I had not even been given advance information regarding it, and so I could not speak to the people and persuade them to have these demonstrations. Further, I was scolded for not giving seed-drill demonstrations. This seed drill is in a village about three and a half miles away from R. How can I bring it? I do not have a pair of bullocks. Why could the office not send the Project tractor to bring the seed-drill to R. Now I shall have to use pressure on someone to lend me his pair of bullocks. The letter ended with a severe warning that drastic action will be taken against me if I do not comply with his orders.

When I was returning from the college nursery Tara Chand shouted, 'Today—— came.' (He twisted the name of the APO in a derogatory way). I asked, 'At what time? I did not know his programme.' Tara Chand said, 'Today he was wild. In Tikka Singh's house he said in the presence of several people that you had no business to go out with the Cotton Supervisor. He said that he will suspend you if you do not improve your ways.' What am I to do? If I had not co-operated with the Cotton Supervisor there would have been the complaint that the VLW was not functioning as a multi-purpose man and was not co-operating with other development officials; and when I did co-operate, here I am being warned that I will be sacked.

Between 6 and 6.30 p.m. I completed my office records.

At 6.30 I had my evening meal.

Between 7 and 8 p.m. I attended the *keertan*.[7]

At 8.15 p.m. I met Mulhad Singh and arranged with him to give a half-field demonstration — Punjab 591 *vs.* N.P. 710.[8] He has promised to take me to his fields with him at 5.30 a.m. tomorrow and to carry the seed in the bullock-cart.

Work to be done:

    (i) Write the diary.[9]
    (ii) Make demonstration maps in the diary.

Villagers' Comments: Kabul Singh : 'This man, the VLW, is very sincere. He works hard. He asked me to have a demonstration in my field, and I could not refuse ... To tell you the truth so many people come to us these days and ask us to do all kinds of things. Take this demonstration with that wooden thing—what do they call it? (He was referring to the dibbler, S.C.D.). First of all we have to select fat, healthy grain one by one. This takes a long time. Who has the time to do it? Then we have to prepare a plot specially for sowing. Then we have to use that — the dibbler—to make rows of small holes and sow each grain individually. He says that we shall get better seed next year. Maybe he is right. But is the government going to give us the money to hire the additional labour required? No. The government only wants taxes.'

Q. 'If the experiment succeeds this year will you try it next year?'

K.S. 'Yes, if the government asks us again. We cannot give all our time to these things, and the labour we hire has no patience for these methods. We cannot keep an eye on them all the time, and when left alone they will perhaps do it the way they have done so far.'

Q. 'What do you think about the other two demonstrations the VLW is planning?'

K.S. 'I do not know what he will do. He will perhaps try some new manure (chemical fertiliser). These are good for a short time; they immediately increase your yield. But they sap the fertility of the soil.'

Q. 'What about the new wheat?'

K.S. 'We have tried it for several years. It is better in appearance, and also stands rain and frost better. It brings a better price too. Some people say that its yield is larger, but my impression is that it is the same as that of the local variety. But the local variety is better in taste. From the point of view of health there is nothing like it.'

2 November, 1954

Mulhad Singh kept his appointment and came to my house at 4 a.m. I went to his field located at a distance of about a mile from the village. I had arranged to give three demonstrations there.

The first one was to be a half-field demonstration. A field of about six *bighas* was divided into two equal halves; in one part we have sown Punjab 591 and in another the local variety of wheat. The second one was a manure demonstration. For this a field with an area of approximately five *bighas* has been divided into three parts. In one part we have put super-phosphate today. For the time being the other two parts have been left as they are. A further supply of fertiliser is awaited which will probably include the other manner to be used for the demonstration. The third one was a varietal demonstration. The area of the field in which this demonstration has been given is approximately four *bighas*. This has been divided into four parts. In one part, we have sown Punjab 591, in another N.P. 710, in the third, the local variety and the fourth part has been reserved for a dibbling demonstration (seed to be sown in Punjab 591). This will be given tomorrow. These three demonstrations took more than three hours. No other agriculturists were present when these demonstrations were given.

At about 8 a.m. I came home and left immediately for G. on my bicycle. I reached there a little after 8.30. Here I had an appointment with Budh Singh. I had promised to meet him at dawn in his fields but was late. However, he was waiting for me. For the dibbling demonstration we needed the assistance of about five boys. As they were not present near the field we had to go to the village to fetch the boys. We came back to the field at 9 a.m. With the help of a standard dibbler, in half a *bigha* of land specially selected seeds of Punjab 591 wheat were sown. The following agriculturists were present to observe the demonstration—Buddhu, Surat, Manohar, Chandarbhan and Loti. The boys assisting in the demonstration were supposed to be receiving training in the technique of dibbling. The demonstration continued up to 1 p.m. I returned to R. at about 1.30 p.m.

After taking my midday meal I vaccinated twenty students of the primary school. I left R. at 3 p.m. with a bullock cart borrowed from Shyam Singh (student). This was in response to the 'most urgent' orders of the APO. The project seed drill was at B-N, a village situated at a distance of about four miles from R. I met the APO for Social Education and Public Participation on the way. I told him that I was going to B-N to bring the seed drill. He asked me to proceed. I reached B-N at 5.15 p.m. The VLW was not present. The seed drill was in charge of an agriculturist who at first refused to hand it over to me. I was disappointed. I pleaded with him to give me the machine. He wanted a letter of authority. I showed him the APO's letter. He wanted to keep it. This I did not allow him to do. In the end he gave the seed drill to me after obtaining a receipt to that effect from me. I returned to R. at 7.30 p.m. Then I went to the *keertan*, spent a few minutes there and returned home to take my meal. After resting for a few minutes I went to meet the APO (Social Education) at the residence of the Principal of the local Intermediate College. I looked up the Extension Teacher (Agriculture) later, and asked him to accompany me for the seed drill demonstration tomorrow. Left the APO at 9 p.m.

Work to be done:

(i) Write the diary.
(ii) Enter in the register the names of persons vaccinated.

Villagers' Comments: Mulhad Singh: 'Government is taking keen interest in our welfare these days. The VLW is different from other officials. He is humble, and wants to improve things in the village.'

Q. 'What do you think of the new seed?'

M.S. 'What can I think? If the government thinks that it is good, it must be good.'

Q. 'Do you think that it is better than the local variety'?

M.S. 'Yes. It resists disease much better. It can stand frost and rain, and there is more demand for it in the market.'

Q. 'What about yield?'

M.S. 'I cannot say. Some people say it is more, others say it is not.'

Q. 'Some people say it is not as good in taste.'

M.S. 'They are right. It is not half as good. If the *roti* is served hot it is more or less the same, but if we keep it for an hour or so it gets as tough as hide. No, it is not as good in taste. People say that we all become very weak if we eat this wheat.'

Q. 'What is your experience?'

M.S. 'Many more people suffer from digestive disorders these days. Our children have cough and cold. Perhaps it is because of the new seed and sugarcane. It may be that the air has been spoilt by the wars.'

Q. 'And what about the new fertiliser?'

M.S. 'They increase the yield; there is no doubt about it. But they probably destroy the vitality of the land and also of the grain.'

3 November, 1954

I got up at 5 a.m. and went to the college building to meet the Extension Teacher (Agriculture). I had to chalk out a programme with him to go to Tikka Singh's field situated at a distance of about a mile. Accompanied by Tikka Singh, his two sons and two servants, I reached there at 6 a.m. The Extension Teacher tried to start the seed drill, but the machine was not in order. It was releasing more seed than was necessary for the operation in hand. The machine had to be stopped. No one other than Tikka Singh, his sons, and his servants were present on the spot. We had to return to the college building to arrange for a bullock-cart to bring back the machine. I went along with the bullock-cart to the field and brought it back at 7.30 a.m.

Accompanied by Tara Chand and six students I went to the fields of Mulhad Singh for a dibbling demonstration. These fields are about a mile and a half away from the village. There I gave the dibbling demonstration. Five other agriculturists were present at that time; three from R. and two from Gs. — another nearby village. Before starting the demonstration I explained to them the advantages of dibbling. One of the persons present on the spot raised the point that this method was not suitable for fields or more than two *bighas*. I explained to them that this method was to be adopted only for improving the seed and for increasing the supply of the improved seed. The demonstration was given on one *bigha* of land and was completed at 11.15 a.m.

After this I came back to the college building with a view to meeting the Extension Teacher who unfortunately was out. Then I returned to my house for the midday meal.

After the meal I went to the midwife and told her that the APO, Social Education, wanted to see her. Then I went to this APO and discussed with him the possibility of visiting T-D, a nearby hamlet, but this could not be done as he had to see the midwife.

At about 2.30 p.m. I went to the Seed Store to obtain twenty-seven seers of superphosphate for Isam Singh. He accompanied me. Then we went to his field which is at a distance of about a mile and a half from the Seed Store. There we measured the field and divided it into three equal parts. In one part, we put superphosphate and left the other two parts unmanured for the time being. In the second part, we shall put another fertiliser when the field is about to be irrigated. The third part will go without any chemical fertiliser. Two agriculturists, Surjeet and Roddha, were present there. They were asked to take advantage of this plan. They expressed their willingness to do so and assured me that they will see me after preparing their fields.

After finishing this demonstration I returned to the tube-well at about 5.30 p.m. and spoke to the operator about completion of *pucca* channels. I requested him to expedite the work and suggested that papaya trees should be planted around the tube-well.

Then I went to see the vegetable plots of Gaje Singh. I noticed that he had planted his vegetables very close together. I asked him to do some thinning and he agreed. After this I went to the fields of Isam Singh and saw his nursery. I found that the leaves of most of the plants had fallen off and only the bare stems were left I told him that it would be no use keeping the plants any longer in the field.

Returned home at about 5.45 p.m. Took my meal, and accompanied by the APO went to the Pradhan at 8 p.m. to seek his help in finding a suitable house for the midwife. As the Pradhan was indisposed this had to be postponed till the next morning.

After this we went to see the girls' primary school teacher who was ill and sat with her for about fifteen minutes. On our way back we met the new Ayurvedic doctor and inquired from him about the *hawan*[10] to be performed tomorrow. Then we returned home.

Work to be done:

Write the diary.

Villagers' Comments:

The seed drill—

Tikka Singh: 'They ask us to buy all kinds of new machines. Everyone said that this machine was very good. You saw how good it was? It refused to work from the very start. It is always like this with these machines. You know Prithvi Singh, the man who owns that big tractor. To buy the tractor they had to sell their bullocks. It gave them no end of trouble. They had to spend a lot of money on its repairs, and all their field operations were delayed. And finally they had to hire bullocks to complete their work. These machines are not dependable.'

Dibbler—

Mulhad Singh's comments are largely the same as those of Kabul Singh (see record of the first day).

Chemical fertilisers—

Isam Singh: 'Why will it (i.e. the chemical fertiliser) not be useful? A well-fed man is always stronger than one who is half-starved. It is the same with the soil.'

Vegetables—

Gaje Singh: 'We do not grow vegetables. This man (the VLW) wanted us to grow them this year, so we have sown some. A goldsmith takes minute care of everything when he is making ornaments. Do you expect us to do the same in agriculture? The government wants us to grow vegetables, and we accept what they say. But now they expect that lines should be straight (i.e. sowing should be done in straight lines) and plants should not be too close together. Perhaps they will order us to water the plants every two hours. We have other work too.'

4 November, 1954

I got up at 5 a.m., and met Isam Singh. I had arranged to give a dibbling demonstration in his field. This had been fixed up yesterday, but today he told me that as they planned to do their sowing in another field it would not be possible for them to go out for the demonstration in the morning. He wanted me to give the demonstration in the evening, but I thought that it should be done the next morning as soil is humid only during that part of the day. I arranged with him to give a varietal demonstration in the evening.

After this I came to the Seed Store accompanied by the APO (Social Education). It was decided earlier that we should go together to the Project headquarters where I would inform the APO (Agriculture) that the seed drill was out of order. But the APO (Social Education) now assured me that he would send the APO (Agriculture) to R. to attend to the machine. So I dropped the idea of going to the headquarters and instead went to the field of Kabul Singh. It was 6.30 a.m. The field is at a distance of about a mile from the village. I had to give a superphosphate demonstration. The field was kept ready. I divided it into three equal parts. As in other demonstrations, superphosphate was put in one part and the other two parts were left as they were for the time being. The area under this demonstration is three *bighas*. The demonstration ended at 8 a.m.

Then I went to see the Extension Teacher of the local college. I saw the fields in which he has sown improved varieties of wheat. He has sown Punjab 591 in one plot and N.P. 710 in the other. He got the improved seeds from the Co-operative Seed Store.

Accompanied by the Extension Teacher I came to the college. We saw the seed drill and found that its chain was out of order. The machine was releasing more than the required quantity of seed. We waited for the APO (Agriculture) but he did not turn up. The Extension Teacher asked me to get the chain repaired at the Project headquarters. As suggested by him I went there on my bicycle. I went to the house of the APO (Agriculture) to inform him about the machine and to get further instructions from him about the necessary repairs. To my disappointment I learned that he had left the place on an inspection tour yesterday. Then I went to the shop of Natthu Mistri, got six joints of the chain replaced and returned to R.

While coming back to R. I met the Field Teacher (Social Education) to whom I handed over a note for the APO (Agriculture) about the break-down and repair of the machine.

I reached R. at about 3 p.m. I missed my midday meal. I handed over the repaired chain to the Extension Teacher to fit to the machine.

At about 4 p.m. I left to meet some of the Jatia Chamars living in one part of the village. On my way I met Kanhaiyya Julaha[11] who wanted to know about the help the Project could possibly render to his caste. I told him that they could get improved machines for weaving and could also obtain necessary raw material on the fulfilment of certain conditions. I suggested to him that the Julahas should have a Co-operative Society of their own.

I reached the quarters of the Jatia Chamars at 4.30 p.m. and convened a small meeting. I explained to them the facilities given to the Harijans by the CDP. I told them that if they were willing to pave the lanes the Project would grant them 50 per cent of the amount needed as a government subsidy. They could also construct model houses, dig new wells, and repair old wells, on the same condition. Then I told them that medicines were being distributed by me free and that they could see me whenever they needed them. They were also informed that there was a midwife in the village and that they could avail themselves of her services free of charge when required. Further, I explained to Baru, who happened to be an agriculturist, that he could get a loan for agricultural improvement and extension of irrigation.

They were glad to meet me and expressed their interest in the Project activities. I was assured co-operation in all the activities. About twenty-five people were present in the meeting. I was told that they have already applied for financial help towards the repairs of their wells. I informed them that money had been sanctioned for this purpose and that they could now start the work. I assured them that the CDP share of the expenses will be given to them very soon.

They demanded that they should be allowed to acquire the premises near the community well. This had been used by them for holding the meetings of their caste *panchayat*[12] for a very long time, but had now been taken possession of by Rjput Zamindars[13] (Chakhu and Kashmira). They expressed their desire to construct a *chaupal*[14] for community purposes. They told me that they had done much work in connection with the cleaning and paving of lanes when the Chief Minister of U.P. had visited the village.

Some of the Jatia Chamars wanted credit facilities. I suggested to them that they form a Co-operative Society and explained its many advantages. They promised that they would meet together and think this over. I returned with the impression that they will take keen interest in community development work and co-operate in it.

I returned to my house at 6.30 p.m. to get some agregene. I gave some of it to Kabul Singh and Tikka Singh. I explained to them that this disease resistant drug was to be mixed with the seed. At about 7 p.m. I went home to have my evening meal. Later I joined the *keertan* group[15] for an hour or so.

Work to be done:

Write the diary.

Villager's Comments:
Chemical fertiliser—

Kabul Singh: 'The VLW said that the government is giving some *English manure* (*angrezi khad*, i.e. chemical fertiliser) free, I agreed to take it. He has given me very little. He has put it in only one part of the field, not in the whole field. If the government distributes fertiliser why does it not give it in sufficient quantity?'

Help to weavers—

Kanhaiyya: 'We hear that the government wants to help the village people. What has it done for us? He (the VLW) asked us to form a Co-operative Society. We are very few and are illiterate. Even if some of us can read and write that is not enough. We shall never know the rules and regulations of the Society. If we have a *babu*[16] (manager or clerk) he will eat away all our profits.'

Q. 'What about getting machines and raw materials?'

K. 'Who will give us machines? And who will give us raw materials? The government wants us to satisfy so many difficult conditions. Unless we have influence we cannot get anything.'

Help to Jatia Chamars—

Kirpa: 'The Government comes to us only when it wants us to do some work for them; otherwise never. We do not have enough eat and they ask us to build new houses. Why can they not give us land? Why can they not lend us money to build houses?'

Nakli: 'Everything is for the moneyed people. Will the *doctorni* (lady doctor, reference was to the midwife) come to us without money?'

Q. 'Did she ever refuse?'

Another person (name not recorded): 'We shall not say that. She comes to our quarters. But will she give us the same services she gives to the moneyed people? Can we buy her expansive medicines?'

Q. 'What about forming a Society?'

Laughter.

Kirpa: 'We do not have even parched gram and you want us to wear gold ornaments.'

5 November, 1954

Last night I had been to the *chaupal* of Bharat Singh. Kalu Singh, Malkhan Singh, Shyam Singh and Bharat Singh were present there. I had taken some agregene with me for Kabul Singh. As he was not there, I handed it over to Bharat Singh to be given to Kabul Singh on his return and explained it uses and advantages to all the people present there. It was decided that a demonstration will be given in one of the fields of Isam Singh and that agregene mixed seed will be sown in a part of a field belonging to Shyam Singh. A varietal demonstration was also fixed for today in the fields of Tikka Singh.

I got up at 4 a.m., and went to Shyam Singh's field at a distance of about a mile from the village. I was accompanied by several agriculturists. First I measured the field. Its area is about four *bighas*. I divided it into four equal parts, and sowed the agregene mixed wheat seed in one part.

After this I measured the nearby field of Tikka Singh. Dividing it into two equal parts I gave a varietal demonstration of Panjab 591 and local wheat. Among those present at the time were Baru, Buddhu, Bhagirath and Sadhal. I tried to persuade them to have a free trial of chemical fertiliser in their fields. Their response was not encouraging.

One-third of one of the fields of Isam Singh was prepared for a dibbling demonstration. Surjeet Singh, Tirlok Chand, Tikka Singh and Isam Singh were present. We selected healthy grains from the seed and the demonstration was started. This continued up to 12.30 p.m. In the course of this demonstration one of the agriculturists suggested that in his opinion it might be better to have an iron dibbler instead of the wooden one now in use. I explained to him that the dibbler had been evolved after very careful research by the Director of Research, U.P., and that the wooden dibbler was inexpensive and easy to make.

I came back to the village and contacted the Tube Well Operator in connexion with the question of providing water to the fields above the channel level. He said that this will have to wait until the next year. He appeared to be helpless in the matter and could not make a definite promise.

I reached home at 1 p.m., and took my midday meal. Soon after, Bharat Singh, Kallan Singh, Malkhan Singh and Shyam Singh came to me to take fertiliser from the Seed Store. Two of them went to get bullock-carts from their houses, and Bharat Singh accompanied me to the Seed Store. A Jatia Chamar met me on the way and told me that he had a complaint to make and that he would like to speak to me privately. He told me that his brother had been malhandled and beaten by Malkhan Singh (a Rajput Zamindar). I consoled him and asked him to suggest politely to Malkhan Singh not to repeat this thing in future. I told him not to tell anyone that he had met me in connexion with this dispute. I requested Bharat Singh to use his good offices in this matter. He assured me that he would speak to Malkhan Singh.

Fertiliser and agregene were supplied to the agriculturists from the store and they left. Bharat Singh and Shyam Singh told me that they were going to their fields and that they would like me to go with them. They proceeded with the bullock-cart. As I had to go to the school, I promised to join them later.

I returned to the school at about 3.30 p.m. and got the vegetable plots irrigated. Then I saw the experimental plot of Balbeer Singh who teaches Agriculture in the local college. I suggested to him that they should put dung manure in the beds, and that in some of the beds they should sow Panjab 591. I also suggested that some improve barley could be sown by the method of dibbling. He agreed to do so. I then met the Extension Teacher in connexion with the seed drill. He informed me that he had fixed the repaired chain on the machine but it had broken again. This made it impossible for us to give a seed drill demonstration. Then I went to the fields of Shyam Singh and Bharat Singh at about 4.30 p.m. These fields are about a mile and a half from the village. There I measured two fields of Bharat Singh and divided them into three parts. Fertiliser was applied in one of the parts in my presence. Later explained to Bharat Singh and five or six other agriculturists present on the spot the method of preparing good dung manure. I told then the advantages of green manuring, and advised them to grow *sanai*, *moong* (type 1) and *dhencha*. Then I divided a three *bigha* field, belonging to Shyam Singh, into three parts and put superphosphate into one part. I divided another one *bigha* plot into four parts, and handed over some agregene to Shyam Singh and asked him to mix it with the seed and then sow the seed into one of these parts.

It was already dark. I returned home at about 7 p.m. I had my meal. I went to the *keertan,* and then met Tirath Singh with a view to arranging a varietal demonstration of barley in his field tomorrow.

Work to be done:

(i) Write the diary.

(ii) Make diagrams of the field demonstrations given in the course of the day.

Villager's Comments:

Agregene—

Kabul Singh: 'He (the VLW) has sent some medicine. It is to be mixed with the wheat seed.'

Q. 'Why?'

K.S. 'I don't know.'

Shyam Singh: 'We have sown some seed mixed with a new medicine.'

Q. 'Why?'

S.S. 'Because the VLW asked us.'

Q. 'In what way is the medicine useful?'

S.S. 'I do not know. Perhaps it protects the crops from disease.'

6 November, 1954

Getting up at 5 a.m., I went to Tirath Singh and Kabul Singh. I took then to the Seed Store and got for them barley K. 12 and barley C. 251. Then I went to their fields situated at a distance of about two furlongs from the village. In area these fields are six and one and one-half *bighas*. I got both these fields divided into three equal parts for giving a varietal demonstration of the improved varieties of barley along with the local variety. Tirath Singh, Ramchandra, Jagmal, Mamraj Singh, Kabul Singh and Naseeb Singh were also present there. After the demonstration I explained to them the advantages of sowing *berseem* which makes an excellent fodder crop. I also did some propaganda in favour of planting papaya and banana.

From there at about 9.30 a.m., I went to the school and handed over some barley seeds, C. 251 and K. 12, to the agriculture teacher. These were meant for a dibbling demonstration. In the nursery I saw the beds of lemon, *karonda* and *galgal*. The *karonda* seeds had sprouted, but the other two did not show any signs of life. I instructed the gardener to water the beds with a sprinkling can.

I went to the Seed Store again at 10.30 and met the Co-operative Supervisor to obtain the receipts of fertiliser distributed to cultivators so that I could enter their names in the register. There I met the VLW of Gs. and had a talk with him regarding the work in progress in his village. I returned to the village in half an hour and met Fateh Singh in connexion with the repairs to his well. He promised that he will get model sanitary repairs done to his well. Then I came home to have my midday meal.

At about 12.30 p.m., I went to Kabul Singh for completing the *sawai*[17] bonds. There I examined his buffalo which was suffering from a disease locally known as *nakkassa*. I suggested to him a local treatment consisting of boiled *tira* and pieces of raw bottle-gourd to be given to the animal at regular intervals. I asked him to inform me about the condition of the buffalo in the evening.

Then I went to the seed Store. It was 1.30 p.m., and I was thinking of distributing fertiliser to some of the agriculturists. At the Co-operative Supervisor had gone on tour I could not do this. The APO (Co-operatives and Village Organisation) arrived from the Project headquarters in the meantime. I told him that the seed drill was out of order again and that no further demonstrations were now possible.

After the APO had left I went to a meeting of the weavers at 5.30 p.m. When I went there about twenty persons were present. Some more joined a little later. I explained to them the aims and objectives of CDP and the duties of the VLW. I told them that they could get free medicines from me. Then I spoke to them about the advantages of co-operative organisation. I told them that CDP would be willing to give them subsidies and technical advice for improving rural sanitation, for paving village lanes, for repairs to wells, and also for installing community hand pumps.

I told them that financial help could be given to their caste (weavers) for buying improved implements and looms. The weavers put forward their difficulties and demanded a cheap and adequate supply of yarn and improved handlooms. They were asked to form a Co-operative Society so that these facilities could be made available to them. They told me that they were having great difficulty because of the pond (*johad*) near their living quarter. This pond generally overflows in the rainy season. They promised to contribute some money towards the construction of proper drains and requested help from CDP in this respect. I told them that I would approach the Rajputs of the neighbourhood so that they may also make some contribution and thereby lessen the burden of the weavers. I promised them that I shall try to obtain a one-third subsidy from CDP funds for this purpose. They assured me that they will contribute substantially in the form of *shramdan*. Next, they told me that they were experiencing great difficulty in obtaining good drinking water as the Rajputs did not allow them to use the nearby well. They said that the water in their own well was brackish. I suggested to them that either they could get a community hand-pump installed in their locality, or I would try to persuade the Rajputs to let them use their well. This well needs some sanitary repairs, and I have obtained an assurance from the weavers that they will contribute reasonably towards it if the Rajputs allow them to draw water from it. The meeting came to an end at about 6.30 p.m.

After the meeting I was taken to a child said to be suffering from enlarged spleen and fever. When I saw him he had no fever I assured the patents that I shall get the child examined by the Co-operative Society doctor.

Next, I went to the *chaupal* of Teja Singh. Mangat Singh, Dhoom Singh, Bishan Singh and Manchand were present there. I asked them if they had sown *berseem* and planted papaya trees. They said that they were not thinking of sowing any *berseem*. I explained to them its advantages. One or two people hesitatingly said that they may try it this year. Teja Singh expressed his willingness to plant bananas near his fields adjoining the village.

I returned home at 8 p.m. and had my evening meal.

Work to be done:

(i) Write the diary.

(ii) Complete the demonstration register.

Villagers' Comments:

Improved barley seed—

Tirath Singh: 'I am trying this new barley for the first time. We have tried new wheat and sugarcane before. The VLW says that this type is better than the local variety.'

Q. 'Do you think it will be better?'

T.S. 'How can I say anything now? We must first see the results.'

Berseem—

Tirath Singh: 'We have heard about it, but have not grown it so far.
If I get any seed from the government I will try it.'

Help to weavers—

Kanhaiyya: 'He (the VLW) came again. He talked about our forming a Society. I do not think we shall ever form one. Even if we do, I am sure it will fail. We are not used to working that way. We asked him to do something about the pond. He wants us to contribute money, and to work ourselves. What is the government doing?'

7 November, 1954

I got up at 5 a.m., went to Kallu Singh, and accompanied him to his field situated at a distance of about four furlongs from the village. After measuring the two plots of four and five *bighas* earmarked for this demonstration, I divided each of them into three equal parts. In the five *bigha* plot I gave a mixed fertiliser trial. I applied forty-two seers of mixed fertiliser in one art and sixty-three seers in the other, and left the third part as it was. In the other plot of four *bighas*, I applied twenty-one seers of superphosphate in one part, leaving the other two parts as they were. Parts 1 and 2 will get a dressing of chemical fertiliser when they are ready for irrigation. In the third part only the usual manure will be used. Kartar Singh, Kallu Singh, Bishambhar Singh, Chamela Singh and others were present on the spot to watch this demonstration. The purpose of the trial was explained to them. One of them inquired as to why the ratio of fertiliser in different fields was different. I told them that it was being done to determine the quantity most effective for the soil of R. Their attention was especially drawn towards the great utility of dung manner. They were told that if one member of the family attended exclusively to the collection and proper preparation of this manure, he would be doing a real service to the family by adding greatly to the yield of the fields. I then suggested to them that they should plant papaya and sow *berseem*. They promised to do so.

I returned to the village at about 9 a.m. Accompanied by Kallu Singh, I went to the *chaupal* of Prithvi Singh. Pratap and Lakshman were also sitting there. I asked them if they were planting any papaya trees. Prithvi Singh and Lakshman Singh promised to plant fifty each within three or four days. They were also advised to sow *berseem*. They replied that they would sow *rij* and not *berseem* as the latter is believed to be 'cold.'[18] I told them that *rij* was good for horses, and that *berseem* was to be preferred for milch cattle. They said 'yes' to me, but did not look convinced. I told them of those who had benefited from this experiment. On this they agreed to grow some *berseem*.

After this I went to the Pradhan[19] at about 11 a.m., to seek his help in finding a house for the midwife. He promised to take me in the afternoon to the house which he had already suggested to the APO (Social Education). Then I returned home for lunch. Soon after the meal I went again to the Pradhan. He asked me to call the midwife also so that she too could see the house. The Pradhan informed me that the accommodation he had in view was an independent house and not a part of another house. I went to the midwife and informed her about this house. She did not like the idea of living in a separate house. So we decided to put a tin partition in the room in which she is living at present, to separate the cattle-shed from the portion used by her.

Then I went to the Dhunias (an occupational caste which cards cotton) and called a meeting. This was at 1.30 p.m. About ten persons were present. Prominent among them were Baru Singh, Keshao, Umrao and Majeed. I explained to them the aims and objectives of the CDP and asked them to take advantage of it. They were also informed about the medicine chest, containing medicines for most common ailments and ordinary diseases which has been supplied to me by the Project. These medicines, I assured them, could be had free of charge, and they could unhesitatingly approach me for them whenever they needed some.

I explained to them that they could get carding and jinning machines if they formed a Co-operative Society. This could facilitate, accelerate, and economise their work as well as costs. They assured me that they would give careful thought to the proposal and see what they could do in the matter.

Five families wanted to have a community hand-pump. They requested financial assistance for this. I promised them that I would discuss this matter with the Dy PEO, and if possible they will get the assistance. The meeting concluded at about 4.30 p.m.

Some of the Dhunia leaders said that they would hold another meeting to discuss their needs and problems and would like me to attend it. I assured them that I shall always be available for consultation and for working out the details of any plans they may have in mind.

While returning from the meeting Latour Singh met me at the *chaupal* of Fattu Singh. He informed me that his bullock was ailing, and suggested that I should examine it. I accompanied him to his house and examined the bullock. Latour Singh and Amar Singh were also present. The bullock looked very weak. It was not eating anything and was having loose motions (bowel movements). Both were symptoms of indigestion. I wrote down the following indigenous prescription: *Chiraeta*—2 *chhataks,*[20] *Sounth*—2 *chhataks*, plain salt—2 *chhataks*, Ajwain—1 *chhatak, Kali Jeeri*—2 *tolas, Hara Kasees*—2 *tolas, Kattha (burnt)*—2 *tolas*—to be pounded and mixed, and given in one ounce doses twice a day. I explained to the people the symptoms of several diseases of the cattle and also the methods of their treatment.

Then I called on the Co-operative Society doctor and took him to Kanhaiyya Julaha whose boy seemed to be suffering from enlarged spleen. The doctor declared him all right. The doctor also examined the daughter of Fattu Julaha. She was suffering from enlarged spleen. He asked them to get medicines from the dispensary.

At about 6.30 p.m. I returned home. After my meal I met Mula Singh regarding the irrigation of fields above the channel level.

Work to be done:

Write the diary.

Villagers' Comments:

Fertiliser and manure—

Kalla Singh: 'He has put some manure in the fields: one part has been left as it is, in another part a small quantity of fertiliser has been applied, and in the third part a still larger quantity has been applied.

Q. 'Why this difference?'

K.S. 'He wants to prove that by putting in more manure we can get a better yield.'

Another person present, 'As if we do not know!'

Q. 'What about cow dung?'

K.S. 'We know its utility and have been using it. But how to collect it? Our womenfolk cannot go about collecting it. No Rajput will sent his daughter-in-law with a basket to collect cow dung.'

Papaya and *berseem*—

Prithvi Singh: 'He has asked us to grow papayas. I think I will plant a few. We do not eat them very much—they do not taste good. And women think that they are inauspicious .... *Berseem* is believed to be cold, it does not give strength to the cattle. But we can try. Maybe it is as good as the VLW says.'

8 November, 1954

Getting up at 5 a.m., I went to the fields near the tube well and examined the germination of wheat. In many fields it appears to be promising. I also examined the fields in which fertiliser demonstrations have been given. The germination in these fields was found to be excellent.

Returned home at 6.30 a.m. Had bath. Went to the college to meet the DPO. As he was busy I went to the school nursery. I directed Mangal, the gardener, to apply chemical fertiliser to some of the plots. In the meantime Mula Singh and Umrao Singh came there. I advised them to take some vegetable seedlings from the nursery and plant them in their backyards. They were shown the papaya seedlings that were ready, and were advised to plant them in the backyards or in the fields. They promised to do so.

At about 8.30 a.m. I returned to the village. On my way I met Sakat Singh. He told us that he wanted pea and gram seeds. I immediately took him to the Seed Store and got him the required seeds. There I found that about twenty-seven pounds of potato seed was still lying unsold. I persuaded Sakat Singh to buy that seed, and gave him detailed instructions regarding the correct method of sowing and manuring it.

Returned home at 10.30 a.m. Did some routine writing work which took about an hour. After finishing this I had my lunch.

At 1 p.m. I went to a nearby hamlet to give a fertiliser demonstration in the fields of Mussaddi Singh. This took two hours.

They I returned to R. and went to the locality of Jatia Chamars. I took with me the medicine chest. On the way I inquired from the Julahas if they needed any medicines. Fifteen persons took medicine for cough, two for ringworm, two for boils, and one each for constipation and fever.

After distributing the medicines I spoke to them. I asked them to attend the *keertan* and the adult education classes at the Panchayat Ghar. They were advised to start work on the two wells for their locality, money for which had been sanctioned by the CDP. They promised to start work on the wells soon. They assured me that they will send four or five persons from their locality to the Panchayat Ghar for learning to perform the *keertan*, and will then start a *keertan* centre in their quarter.

I returned home at 7 p.m., and went after a while to the Principal to inquire about his health. After half an hour I came home and had my evening meal. Then I went to the *keertan*, and there listened to the story of a greedy and untruthful person who wanted to amass wealth by unfair means and who met a deserving end.

From the *keertan* I returned home and did some routine work.

Work to be done:

Write the diary.

Villagers' Comments:

Medicines—

A Jatia Chamar: 'He came to us with medicines for the first time. It will be a great help if he can give us free medicines whenever we need them.'

Q. 'What medicines did he give?—*desi* (indigenous) or English (western)?'

J.C. 'We do not know. As he (the VLW) is a government official the medicine must be English.' (In point of fact most of the medicines in the medicine chest supplied to the VLW are Ayurvedic.[21])

Q. 'What medicines do you like?'

J.C. 'What we can get? We are to poor to be able to afford a doctor's fee. English medicines give quick relief.'

Keertan—

Ramma: 'They ask us to join the *keertan*. Will the Rajputs ever allow us to sit with them?'

Interviewer, 'They say they will.'

R. 'There is a saying. An elephant has two sets of teeth—one that he shows, another that he uses. They may say whatever they like, but they will never let us sit with them.'

9 November, 1954

I got up at 4.30 a.m. today and went to the half-field demonstration plot near the Seed Store. In this field G.P. 25 and the local variety of gram had been sown sometime ago. The germination was fairly good. Then I went to Ridka's field where improved variety of potato seed, supplied by the CDP, has been sown. The germination was satisfactory in this field also.

Having seen these two fields I returned to my house for a bath. About twenty minutes were spent in prayer. Then I went to Malkhan Singh. He was sitting in his *chaupal* with Prithvi Singh, Kabul Singh, Shyam Singh, and some others. I asked Kabul Singh and Shyam Singh to accompany me to their fields for the demonstrations we had planned earlier. We three reached the fields at about 8.30 a.m. The distance from the village to the fields is a little more than a mile.

A fertiliser demonstration was given in the field of Shyam Singh, and then it was repeated in the field of Malkhan Singh. The distance between these fields is about a furlong. When the demonstration was being given in the field of Shyam Singh, Malkhan Singh and his servants were also present.

This is how I gave the demonstration: I divided the plot into three equal parts by measuring it with a tape. In the first part I applied supersulphate and in the second, mixed fertiliser. No fertiliser was applied to the third plot as we intended to keep it as a 'control plot.' It was decided to apply uria or more mixed fertiliser at the time of irrigating the field.

Four *bighas* of land are under the first demonstration. The second demonstration given in Malkhan Singh's plot of about three acres followed the pattern of the first.

Later, in the field of Khadak Singh, I gave a half-field demonstration. I divided a plot of two *bighas* into two equal parts. Panjab 591 was sown in one part and in the other the local variety of wheat was sown. This was done with a dibbler.

I then proceeded to the field of a Mali.[22] This field is at a distance of about six furlongs from the field of Khadak Singh. Potatoes had been sown in this field. Mixed fertiliser had been applied in two parts of this field while the third part had been left without any fertiliser. The proportion of fertilisers in the three parts of the field had been 1½ : 1 : 0. In part one, which had been given a larger dose of fertilisers the germination was excellent. In the second .part, in which only a limited quantity of fertiliser had been applied, it was better than the germination in the third plot which had no fertiliser. The third plot, being the 'control' plot, had been manured in the usual way, but without any chemical fertiliser.

At about 10 a.m. I came back to the *chaupal* of Prithvi Singh. Partap Singh (Patwari),[23] Chhanga Singh, and some others were sitting there. I spoke to them about the proper care of cattle. I also explained to them some of the modern methods of cattle breeding. I also told them about the new methods of feeding the cattle. They appeared to feel that what I had told them was right and useful. I then emphasised the importance of a balanced diet for the cattle. This was very necessary if they wanted to keep their cattle healthy and free from diseases, I told them. Turning to the point of cattle breeding I asked them to improve their livestock by taking certain precautions in their village. The first thing that I asked them to do was to get all the scrub bulls castrated. There are three stud bulls in the village — one pedigree and the other two of local breed. For improving their cattle stock it was necessary for them to allow only the pedigree bull to operate.

Then I asked them to plant papaya trees in the courtyards of their houses and in their gardens. In this village I did not find anyone refusing to do so on the ground that it was inauspicious to have papaya trees near the house. In G. most people had refused to plant papaya trees on this ground. Persons present at Prithvi Singh's *chaupal* agreed to plant papaya trees. I asked Prithvi Singh to grow onions and cabbage in his field. He showed willingness and agreed to accompany me, whenever I was free, to attend to this work in his field.

I then went to J-K, a part of the village which is practically an independent hamlet, and met Nathu Singh, Isam Singh, and Musaddi Singh in the *chaupal* of Nathu Singh. I suggested to them that they have a separate primary school for their locality. Nathu Singh liked the idea but feared lack of support from the CDP officials. I asked him to write an application and hand it over to me. He said that he would consult the other elders and influential people of the locality and would let me know their final decision.

While we were talking I noticed that there were three or four heaps of cattle dung on the open ground. Explained to the people that they should cover these with earth. This was necessary if they wanted to get full advantage of the nitrogen in the dung. I told them that animal dung contains nitrogen which helps greatly in adding to the fertility of the soil, and that due to the heat of the sun most of this nitrogen escapes if the dung is left uncovered. Winds also sweep away a part of this valuable manure. In the rainy season water washes away what is left of it. In order to avoid this loss I asked them to dig pits of $8 \times 6 \times 4$ or $12 \times 8 \times 4$. These should be covered with earth regularly. Explaining the disadvantages of open manure heaps I told them that such manure is often responsible for crop diseases. When such manure is put in fields it is easy for the white ants to ruin the crops. I felt that they were convinced about what I had said. They promised to act on my suggestions.

I came back to my house at about 1 p.m. With about five *tolas* of agregene from my house I went to the *chaupal* of Daroga Singh. His father, Musaddi Singh, was in the house. I handed over the agregene to him and instructed him to mix it well in twenty seers of wheat. I came back to my house and had my midday meal.

After this I called on Baru Singh, Parsa, Haridwari, and Kirpa who were all present in their houses. I sat for sometime with Jadgish (one of the boys who was injured in a collision between a truck and a train). I had a brief talk with him and asked him about the condition of his injuries. From his talk it was clear that he was nervous, so I consoled him. I also had a talk with Parsa. I suggested to him to sow *berseem* and explained its advantages at some length. But he was reluctant to try it. A detailed explanation was necessary to convince this man. In the end he agreed to sow *berseem* in one *bigha* as an experimental measure. Before leaving his house I told Parsa that I had medicines with me and that anyone in need could come to me.

I went to the Cornell Project House at 3 p.m. and had a talk with Dr. Dube regarding problems and difficulties of the VLW. Left Dr. Dube at 6.30 p.m.

Returned to my house, had my meal, and attended the *keertan*. After this I went out again to meet Shyam Singh. He was in his house. I asked him to be in readiness for a dibbling demonstration in his field early tomorrow morning. He agreed.

Work to be done:

   (i)   Write the diary.

  (ii) Prepare statements for the meeting to be held in the Project headquarters tomorrow.

 (iii) Demonstration Register to be completed.

 (iv) Medicine Register to be completed.

The following statements are needed for tomorrow's meeting:

   (i)   Copy of the diary.

  (ii) Survey report.

 (iii) List of people who bought potato seed (improved).

 (iv) List of Rabi[24] demonstrations.

  (v) List of persons to whom fertiliser was given free.

In the preparation of all these statements at least three hours are required. It may be completed by 1.30 a.m.

Villagers' Comments:

Fertiliser demonstration—

Malkhan Singh: 'These English manures (chemical fertiliser) are good, but you have to weigh them like medicines. We are not used to it. They you have to water the fields at regular intervals, and they need a lot more water. There is nothing better than cow dung, but we never have enough of it. These foreign manures are also good, if we can learn to be careful with them. They are especially good for the new varieties of sugarcane and wheat.'

Improved cattle—

Prithvi Singh: 'Who does not want improved cattle? I will be very proud if I own some. People go to the Panjab to buy them. We have contributed money to buy these large bulls. But what are we to do with the scrub bulls: Many people leave bulls[25] with a religious motive in return for a request granted by supernatural powers. You cannot castrate them. Who would go in for the sin of castrating a sacred bull?'

Compost—

Nathu Singh: 'Don't think we do not know about compost. We know its utility. We do not want manure to lie in heaps in front of our houses. But what shall we do? Our women (i.e. Rajput women) cannot carry manure to a distant pit outside the village or near our fields. Labour is difficult to get. Chamars are now swollen-headed. They do not want to serve us, and we cannot depend on them. They will carry the manure from our houses, and for a few annas throw it in the pit belonging to someone else.'

School—

Nathu Singh 'We need one very badly. In fact, we have employed a private teacher who runs a school in the *chaupal* of C.S. It is difficult to get things from the government. Officers are slow, and oblige only those who have "pull." We shall approach the government for a separate school.'

Berseem—

Parsa: 'The government is asking us to do too many things. If they give me this new seed I will grow it. We are afraid that we may be charged heavily for it, or next year they may ask us to return the seed with interest.'

10 November, 1954

Got up at 5 a.m. Picked up the dibbler and went to the house of Shyam Singh. The following were present in his *chaupal:* Bharat Singh, Roopchand, Bhagmal, Chaman Singh and Girwar Singh. I spoke to them about the importance of animal manure and told them how they could have more manure for their fields. In front of Shyam Singh's house there was a large refuse heap which was uncovered and unprotected. I pointed this out to them and added that they were wasting valuable manure. I told them that the best way to protect manure is to deposit it in a properly dug manure pit and to keep it covered. I then added that the nitrogen content of the heap lying in front of the house could be preserved considerably by covering it with earth. We started work on the manure heap. In ten to fifteen minutes the heap was covered with earth. Then I spoke to them about the utility of *berseem* as a fodder crop and asked them to grow it in their fields. They told met that they have been growing *rij* or *rijka* (known locally as *lusan*) and were not particularly anxious to change from it to any other fodder crop. So I had to deal at some length with the comparative merits and demerits of *berseem* and *rijka* for milch cattle. They agreed to experiment with *berseem* on a limited scale.

We then got ready for a dibbling demonstration to be given in one of the fields of Shyam Singh. I collected six boys of the primary school and took them along with Shyam Singh and his sons to the fields. There I selected a one *bigha* plot for the demonstration. I got it ploughed. We got straight lines drawn in one plot, the distance between two lines being twenty-seven inches. Then with the aid of the dibbler, assisted by school students, I gave the demonstration.

I then hurried to the nearby field of Musaddi Singh to give a mixed fertiliser demonstration. Then I returned home and had my meal.

Today was the day of our fortnightly staff meeting. Equipped with my records and reports I left for the Project headquarters on my bicycle. On the way I gave a superphosphate trial in a three and a half *bigha* plot belonging to Fattu Singh. After this I rushed to the Project headquarters, reaching there at 11 a.m.

The meeting started punctually at 11 a.m. The new DyPEO spoke to us about the reallocation of work. He said that it was felt that the work-load of the VLW was rather heavy and as such he was making an attempt to reduce it by relating the other development staff, such as Panchayat Secretaries and Cane Supervisors, more closely to Project activities. I was informed that from now on I shall have to look after only R. and the hamlet of T-D. G. which had so far been under my charge was now transferred to the Panchayat Secretary.

The DyPEO exhorted us to work with devotion and sincerity. It was announced that the village showing greatest enthusiasm and maximum achievement in respect of Project activity will be awarded a cash prize of Rs. 100. The prize money will be handed over to the Gaon Sabha. The VLW concerned will be recognised for his meritorious work by a special entry in his service roll.

Under the revised administrative set-up, groups of villages have been placed under the charge of different APOs. They will be in overall charge of all development work in these villages.

It was announced that a Refresher Training Camp was being organised at J-J. This was to be attended by all the VLWs as well as by the Panchayat Secretaries and the Cane Supervisors. The duration of the camp was to be one week. The VLWs were asked to provide two statements about the agriculture demonstrations given by them. The details regarding these statements were also given. We were asked to prepare the statements in the meeting itself but when we pointed out that the statements involved considerable work we were allowed a week's time to forward them to the office.

Plans of action for the future were discussed. The decision that amonium sulphate, groundnut cake, and bone meal could now be given as *taccavi*[26] to the agriculturists on 5½ per cent interest was announced. We were asked to prepare statements evaluating the results of *kharif* (crops sown in the rainy season) demonstrations. We were directed to enter the best agriculturists for the *rabi* (crops sown in winter) competitions. Prizes are awarded at different levels, such as, Gaon Sabha, Adalati Panchayat, Tahsil[27] and District. We were asked to start work in connexion with the planting of community orchards. I was asked to give more attention to the college nursery. We were directed to sent in our reports on kitchen gardens within a week. I was informed that agriculturists in my villages could get *taccavi* loans for Persian wheels and also for boring wells. We were asked to prepare a statement showing the area of land under cultivation, with particulars regarding land under irrigation from tube-wells and from other sources. We were also informed that people could now get loans for buying good breeds of cows and buffaloes. A loan of Rs. 300 for a cow and Rs. 500 for a buffalo could be advanced; to be repaid in ten equal six-monthly instalments. All VLWs were asked to get one 'foot bath' for the cattle constructed in each village under their charge. These are to be constructed at a central place on the way the village cattle generally pass. The foot bath containing disinfectant in the water is expected to protect the cattle against hoof and mouth disease. It was clearly pointed out to us that the only subsidy CDP was willing to give for this was three bags of cement per village. Bricks and labour were to be supplied by the villagers themselves. White Leghorn eggs were to be made available at a subsidised rate of two annas per egg. If anyone wanted them to be hatched in the incubator at the Project headquarters the approximate cost of each chick would be eight to ten annas. We were asked to promote actively the programme of getting model sanitary repairs effected in the village wells, and to give priority to the paving of village lanes. We were asked to supply particulars regarding *akharas*[28] in the village. The meeting ended at about 7 p.m.

I stayed for the night at the Project headquarters.

Concluding Comments

The aim in this study has been to give an intimate picture of one Village Level Worker in action, and to bring into sharp focus some of his activities and problems. Although it is not possible to make many broad generalisations from observations extending over only ten days, some reflections and a few tentative conclusions may be hazarded.

True to the original conception of his role the VLW has been functioning as a multi-purpose extension agent. As the CDP programme centres mainly round agricultural extension most of his time and energy naturally go into this work. Nevertheless, he has given a reasonable part of his time to other items of CDP activity, such as sanitation and medical care, and care of cattle health. He has also made some effort at mass contact with a view to finding out the 'felt needs' of the people and to popularising knowledge of the aims and objectives of the project. His success in getting items of DCP programme accepted—wholly or partially—can be attributed to his patience and perservance in trying to educate the people to accept the plans and practices offered by the CDP. His own observations and comments by the people illustrate the degree of initial reserve, hesitation, and reluctance with which the village greets his new ideas and innovations.

The VLW understands the necessity for administrative co-ordination, and has been co-operting with the village level officials and field staff of other development departments. As the record shows he gave considerable time to the Cotton Supervisor in one of his visits. However, the fact that this gesture on his part was not well received by the APO (VLW's immediate superior) deserves to be noted.

On the whole the work-load of the VLW is rather heavy. For effective multi-purpose functioning it is necessary that he should have a much smaller area under his charge. From the record it will be clear that while he did agricultural extension work in all the village under his charge, his other activities were confined only to R. which happens to be his place of residence. He could distribute medicines only in R. Attention to cattle health, as well as participation in youth welfare activity and CDP sponsored recreation programmes too, were possible only in this village.

The VLW's immediate superiors do not appear to be very tactful in their dealings with him. Instead of trying to build up his prestige in the village they inadvertently help to lower it. From the record of the first day it will be seen that the APO (Agriculture) criticised the VLW publicly in his absence, and asked the village people to convey warnings to him that he would be discharged. The general tone of his letter to the VLW, mentioned in the first day's record, reveals a glaring lack of understanding of VLW's role. The denial of the elementary courtesy of addressing a co-worker with *shri* and *aap*, and the warnings and threats of dismissal are not in tune with the theory of extension work which demands utmost harmony, co-operation and team spirit for the successful execution of the programme.[29] In this particular instance the VLW does not appear to be at fault. Treatment such as this in which the VLW is dealt with as a subordinate of low status and no consequence frustrates the man in the field and kills his zest for work. It is essential that calculated effort should be made to curb this 'boss mentality' so that a healthy team-spirit may be created.

Another point elaborated further elsewhere[30] may be briefly mentioned here. From the record of the last day one will get the impression that in the staff meetings there is only a 'one-way communication'; the officers do the talking, the VLWs do the listening. To generate more life into these staff meetings and to build up the VLW's self-respect, the VLWs should be encouraged to participate more actively in the deliberation and decisions of these meetings. They should be expected not only to put forward their difficulties, but also to make suggestions for improving the methods of work, something that is not being done at present.

Finally, from the general response of the people it will be evident that the community development projects are viewed largely as a sort of government 'drive' and not as vital democratic movement of the people themselves. They expect the government to do much for them, but have a deep-seated scepticism regarding its methods and motives.

REFERENCES

1. The observations reported in this study were started in the fourth week of October 1954, and were continued upto 14 November 1954. For reasons of space, activities covering only ten days are described here. The VLW, who got used to being observed by us in the first week and went about his work more or less normally afterwards, has earned our gratitude by his understanding co-operation. For practical reasons he must remain anonymous.

2. The local measurement of land. The size of a *bigha* differs in different parts of Uttar Pradesh. In this region a *bigha* is about one-fifth of an acre.

3. The process is very slow. The dibbler is a simple wooden implement with several rows of pointed wooden pegs at a distance of approximately ten inches from one another. When it is pressed into freshly ploughed soil it makes small holes in the earth in which the selected seed is sown.

4. An improved variety of wheat developed by agricultural research in India.

5. R. refers to the village where the headquarters of the VLW are located and where this record was obtained. It is a large village with a population of more than 5,000. The Rajputs are the dominant caste and the largest landowners in this village. Earlier in this volume it has been called 'Rajput Village.'

6. R. has a Higher Secondary School or Intermediate College. In conjunction with CDP this institution has started a nursery where vegetable seedlings and small plants of fruit-bearing trees are raised. The nursery is subsidized from DCP funds.

7. Community singing of religious and devotional songs organised by CDP.
8. Another improved variety of wheat.
9. The VLW is required to maintain a diary of his activities.
10. Burning incense and making sacrificial offerings. This doctor had just moved in from a neighbouring village and had planned this ritual to inaugurate his practice in the village.
11. The Julahas are the Hindu caste of weavers who work the traditional handloom.
12. Traditional council of elders.
13. Landlords.
14. The place where men sit, smoke, and usually sleep at night.
15. This group has been organised as a part of the social education programme of the CDP. It meets after the adult education class for community singing of devotional songs.
16. Clerk. This term is also used for educated people who hold minor government positions.
17. Bonds pledging return with 25 per cent interest.
18. It is common to describe foods as 'cold' or 'hot,' i.e. as cold-producing or heat-producing.
19. Literally 'head' or 'chief.' He is the presiding officer of the elected village council, and its chief executive officer.
20. Local measure of weight. Sixteen *chhataks* make one seer.
21. The indigenous system of Indian medicine.
22. A caste of gardeners and vegetable growers.
23. Keeper of land records, a minor government official.
24. Crops sown in winter.
25. Bulls are regarded as sacred. It is believed that Shiva, a great God of Hindu Trinity, uses a bull as a mount. Calves dedicated to the gods grow into bulls and are not regarded as the property of any individual. They graze freely around the village.
26. Loans advanced for agricultural improvement.
27. Administrative subdivision of a district.
28. Village wrestling pit where people take exercise and practise wrestling.
29. It may be added that in the traditional administrative organisation of India the relations between a government employee and his official superior were generally governed by a rigid protocol, and the former had to behave as an inferior even in social matters. Political leaders viewed this as an undesirable inheritance from British rule—something quite out of tune with the aims of free India. In the orientation and training programmes for rural development workers great emphasis was laid on the necessity of discarding the out-of-date superior-subordinate mentality, and on developing a healthy co-operative team spirit.
30. Appendix I.

25

The Village Level Worker and Changing Village Environment

I

The Village Level Worker represents a new type of public servant in the administrative organisation of India. Without question he is part of the vast body of government officials who run the affairs of the state, but in his case a special effort has been made to train him in ideals and methods of work which are remarkably different from those of the traditional bureaucracy. As a multipurpose rural social worker he is given special training and orientation courses so that his general approach and methods of work in the field may be different from and superior to those of the other government officials who have operated without much success on the village level in the past. The VLW is expected to function in the village not as a minor government official, but as a friend and well-wisher, and to a certain extent as a leader, of the village people. He is expected not only to promote ready-made plans and programmes but also to help constructively in formulating them. He is expected to study the *felt needs* of the people and to strive to work for their satisfaction. More than this he should endeavour to create progressive needs in them.

In conception, his role is that of a generalist, but he cannot function effectively without adequate specialisation in several branches of development activities that he sponsors and guides in the villages under his charge. He has to take the initiative in several matters, and has yet to keep himself sufficiently in the background so that he may not even inadvertently obstruct the emergence of a new leadership in the village. In fact, he is expected to work in such a way that his own services may eventually become unnecessary, and in such a manner that habits of group and co-operative action will take such firm roots in village life that development activities may become self-sustaining and self-supporting. The task is indeed challenging and demands special aptitudes and personality traits. The VLW is a new and emerging role in Indian village life. Although it has gradually defined itself in limited spheres, in part it still largely remains vague. The VLW himself is not very clear about his exact position, role, functions and responsibilities. Notwithstanding their general training in extension methods and practices the VLW's superior officers and co-workers on the village level do not possess a clear conception of his role. Indeed, the emphasis in different VLW training centres is on different things, and as a result of this trainees come out of these centres with different views of their role. The village people also have not been able to make up their minds about this new type of government functionary. To some extent they distrust him as they distrust all minor government officials, but they are not totally unaware of his somewhat unorthodox methods of approach and work, and do not lack in appreciation when they get help and advice from him. As the key figure of development effort in India village life the VLW deserves a close and careful study. In this study an effort will be made to examine and understand this role with particular reference to one Community Development Project Block in one of the western districts of the State of Uttar Pradesh.

It has been mentioned earlier that this Community Development Project Block was formally inaugurated in October 1953, although preparatory work in regard to it had started a little earlier. Out of a sanctioned strength of twenty multi-purpose VLWs with training in extension methods, the Project started with only seven. Gradually, as trained people became available they were appointed to this project. At the close of the first year of project activities there were eighteen such VLWs on the staff. About this time, with a view to reducing the work load of the VLWs, the Panchayat Secretaries who had undergone extension training courses of shorter duration were taken under partial CDP control, and, in addition to their own departmental work, were assigned to multi-purpose extension work in a few villages. The Cane Supervisors too were allotted some duties of this kind. This study, however, is concerned only with regular multi-purpose VLWs; the other development officials also functioning in this capacity have been touched only in passing.

With a view to understanding the VLW's problems and difficulties and evaluating his emerging role, he was approached and studied from several angles. An effort was made to understand and analyse the VLW's own understanding of his role through participant observation and through interviews in which a loosely structured schedule-cum-interview guide was used. A record of the daily activities of two VLWs was kept in two project villages for a number of days. In order to understand their views on the subject the Project officers and the village people were interviewed both formally and informally. Ranking of project VLWs on the basis of specified criteria of success and specified aptitudes by the Project officers adds considerably to our comprehension of their view of the VLW's role, problems and difficulties.

To begin with, we shall examine the general background of the VLWs of this Project, and will follow this by an examination of their ideas of the basic aims, methods and programmes of planning and development, their views on the relative success or failure of the different parts of their multi-purpose training, their opinions regarding intra-project and inter-departmental official relations, their criteria for the success of a VLW and the self-evaluation of their own work. The basis for the observations that follow has been provided by the response of the VLWs to different questions in the key schedule administered to them in long, private interviews.

II

Out of seventeen[1] multi-purpose VLWs working in the Project seven are in age group 31-35, six are in group 20-25, two are in group 36-40, and there is one each in group 26-30 and 41-45. By caste six of them are Brahmins, five are Jats, three are Rajputs and one each are from Kayasth, Siani and Kurmi castes. Educationally they represent different grades: two have passed the Intermediate examination, seven have graduated from High School, one has studied up to High School, six have passed the Diploma examination in agriculture, and one has passed the secondary vernacular examination. Six VLWs have additional qualifications, four having passed some vernacular examinations and two having undergone co-operative training. All but one are married. Six live with their families in their respective headquarters, ten have to live away from them for one reason or the other. None of them is divorced or separated from his wife and one is a widower. One important reason why so many cannot have their families with them is that living arrangements for them are not satisfactory. The government has not provided them with quarters, and it is not easy to rent houses in the villages. Consequently they often have to go on leave to see their families and relatives because of family affairs and emergencies, and this involves interruption of CDP work on the one hand and considerable expense to the VLW on the other.

Out of the seventeen VLWs in the Project three are direct recruits, the rest were serving in some development department of the State government at the time of their recruitment to their present job. Before coming to their present positions six of them were in the Co-operative Department, four in the Panchayat Raj Department, two in the Agriculture Department, and one each in Prantiya Raksha Dal[2] and the Civil Supplies Department. All have undergone six months of multi-purpose extension training. Eight of them were trained in an institution of western U.P., run according to the teachings of Mahatma Gandhi, where the accent is on mass contact and constructive work, five in an agricultural school of western U.P. where the emphasis is more on agricultural extension, one in an Etawah training centre with a comparatively balanced training programme, and one in another Gandhian institution of eastern U.P. Nine of them had volunteered for the VLW job, while eight were nominated and sent for training by their parent departments.

The motives which actuated them to accept this job were diverse. Three candidly said that they needed some employment and applied in response to advertisements for the post of VLW, four accepted it because of the possibility of an immediate raise in salary. Others had different reasons, ranging from a desire to work for the uplift of the nation to an eagerness to contribute to India's agricultural prosperity. In leaving their parent departments most of the departmental VLWs were conscious of the fact that they were going to be a part of an important national experiment. Of the fourteen departmental selections, four held positions carrying salaries in the range of Rs. 50-75, five in Rs. 76-100, one in Rs. 100-25, three in Rs. 126-50, five in Rs. 151-75. In their new positions ten get salaries ranging from Rs. 100-10, five from Rs. 111-20, one from Rs. 121-30, and one from Rs. 141-50. Thus among those who were in government service before, ten received an increase in their salaries. In five cases the rise is slight and in the other five it is appreciable. In four cases people had to accept a slight loss in transferring to their present positions. In one case this loss is considerable. Where there has been a reduction in salaries the individuals have presented their case for readjustment of salary, and have been waiting a long time to learn the outcome of their representations.

All the seventeen VLWs were born and brought up in villages, but three of them have spent a considerable part of their lives in towns and cities. Four of them are from the eastern part of U.P., that is, from a rural background somewhat different from the one in which they are working at present. The rest are from western districts, four being from the district in which the project itself is located. With the exception of those from the eastern districts they speak the same dialect as the people of the project area. There is general agreement among them that the caste of a VLW, in actual practice, does influence his work materially. Some characteristic responses from them are: 'One is more successful in a village of one's own caste.' 'Thakurs respect me because I am a Brahmin.' 'Higher castes are listened to by all, while an untouchable may be able to influence only the untouchables.' 'An untouchable could not have functioned effectively in a Rajput village.'

The VLWs have a fairly clear idea of the basic aims and main objectives of the Community Development Programme. In verbalising these aims, nine said they were 'to raise the standard of living in the village', five emphasised 'inculcating a spirit of unity and co-operation', three mentioned 'creating social equality and new values', and two laid stress on 'welfare and development of the agriculturist'. Among other objectives mentioned by them are: 'improving the moral standard of the country', 'providing jobs for the unemployed', and 'co-ordinating development activity on the village level'.

Regarding the questions of what the functions of a VLW should ideally be and what they actually are, they were less precise and definite. In response to the first, eleven pointed out that multi-purpose development activity should be their main work. Some elaborated their answers further to say that their job was to understand local *felt needs* and to get targets fixed on their basis (5), developing local initiative (2), helping the villagers (2), and changing the views of the village people (1). In regard to their actual duties they also said that they were multi-purpose extension agents and were doing many-sided development work in the villages. But at least eleven added with some bitterness that in doing so they had to carry out the orders and wishes of their officers and had to achieve targets fixed by those at the top. Two said that flattering their superiors and going out of their way to please officers had become one of their most important duties.

Their view of the VLW's role is clear. Fifteen of them said that they thought of themselves as friends of the village people offering advice to them when it was needed, and three thought that they were leaders and innovators in the village. Six of them added that notwithstanding their own view of the role they could not forget the fact that they were minor government officials who had to carry out the orders of their superior officers. In response to the question as to what the job of a VLW actually is, fourteen said that it was to achieve targets fixed at the top, one said that his job was to discover felt needs of the people and on their basis to help in the determination of CDP targets, and still another said that his job was to convey the demands of the village people to higher government officials. One thought that his job was both to discover felt needs with a view to fixing targets, and to achieve targets fixed by the higher project officials.

With regard to their general approach, fourteen thought that they were in the village to help the people to help themselves, while three phrased it in terms of helping the village people. Two out of the three who said that they were in the village to help the people were of the opinion that ultimately their job should be to help the people to help themselves.

The Village Level Workers appear to have a clear conception of what the villagers generally think of their role and what they expect them to do. Eight of them thought that village people expected help in village development work from the VLWs, three said that they were generally regarded as well-wishers and helpers of the people, two said that the people expected help from them in getting money (government loans and subsidies), and two said that they were thought of as spokesmen of the villagers before higher officials. Of the remaining two, one said that the villagers did not clearly understand what the VLW's functions were and consequently did not expect anything definite from him, while another said that villagers had fantastic expectations and wanted him to produce miracles in a short time.

In regard to their view of the expectations of higher CDP officials fourteen said that above all officials expected them to achieve the targets which they fix from time to time. Six thought that officers expected them to work hard for village development, three thought that they were expected to obey orders, and one thought that the officers expected them to popularise development work.

Almost all the VLWs claimed to have discovered a number of felt needs in the villages under their charge. The list of these felt needs is long and varied and includes the need for organising sanitation drives, provision for more irrigation facilities, paving of village lanes, construction of school buildings, supplying of improved agricultural implements, seeds and fertilisers, consolidation of land holdings, organising co-operative societies for promoting rural industries, making provision for grazing facilities and cattle care, making model sanitary repairs to wells, construction of roads, finding work for the unemployed, and appointing trained midwives.

On the question of their contribution to the establishment of CDP targets fifteen said that they did not contribute to it at all, one said that his contribution was meagre, while only one said that the suggestions of the VLWs were generally accepted.

All the VLWs realise that they are agents of change in the communities in which they are working. According to them the following are some of the important changes introduced by them (the figures in brackets indicate the number of VLWs who claim to have introduced them); introducing improved seeds (11), giving demonstrations of modern agricultural practices (10), introducing green manuring (8), popularising chemical fertilisers (7), introducing the dibbler (7), organising village sanitation drives (5), paving village lanes (5), popularising vegetable growing (4), introducing new agricultural implements (4), constructing school buildings (3), introducing the practice of interculture (3), introducing the Japanese method of paddy cultivation (3), organising adult education classes (2), digging compost pits (2), popularising secondary vaccination (2), starting co-operative societies (2), organising *shramdan* drives (2), constructing *panchayat* offices (2), planting orchards (2), digging model wells (2), organising a community centre (1), organising a maternity centre (1), starting a youth organisation (1), organising a centre for leather curing (1), making drinking water available for the untouchables (1), introducing inoculation of cattle (1), starting a nursery (1), organising community singing of religious songs (1).

The VLWs have tried to evaluate the success and acceptance of the different items of development programmes sponsored by them. A good response from people was reported in respect to the following items: agricultural demonstrations (6), improved seeds (5), green manuring (5), village sanitation drives (3), paving of village lanes (3), introduction of chemical fertilisers (3), use of the dibbler and new agricultural implements (3), vegetable growing (2), construction of school buildings (2), maternity centre (1), games and sports (1), compost pits (1), co-operative societies (1), leather curing industry (1), *shramdan* (1), construction of *panchayat ghar* (1), planting orchards (1). In their view, the people's response was not enthusiastic in respect to the following items in their respective areas: Japanese method of paddy cultivation (2), vegetable growing (1), community centre (1), adult literacy class (1), paving of lanes (1), model sanitary repairs to wells (1), and nursery (1). About the following items it was reported that the village people were neither too enthusiastic nor completely cold: improved seeds (3), dibbling for seed multiplication and practice of interculture (2), vegetable growing (1), green manuring (1), games and sports (1), agricultural demonstrations (1), chemical fertilisers (1), orchards (1), Japanese method of paddy cultivation (1), and new agricultural implements (1).

Most of the VLWs reported that they did not devise any specific programmes for the non-agricultural people. These people, however, benefited from general community activities such as sanitary drives, adult education classes, and youth welfare organisations. In one centre a co-operative society of the Jatia Chamars has been organised for curing and tanning leather along modern lines. Another VLW reported some effort on his part to start a co-operative society of local weavers. The general consensus of opinion was that because of the high priority given to agricultural extension and to some other items of the development programme they did not have the time, incentive, or encouragement to devise and stimulate special programmes for the non-agricultural people. Some

VLWs reported that they had contacted people with a view to persuading them to join the cottage industries and handicraft classes that are being planned and will be started at the Project headquarters under the auspices of the CDP.

Regarding the success or failure of their multi-purpose VLW training, fifteen said that they had benefited from it, while two thought that they had not. The latter were inclined to feel that there was such a wide gap between the theory they had been taught in the training centre and the realities they were experiencing in the field that their training was practically useless. In answering the question as to how they had benefited from this training some said that they 'learned new practices and techniques', while others said that it 'influenced my personality and way of thinking'. The following reported gains may be mentioned especially: widening of general knowledge (6), learning effective techniques of mass contact (4), training in extension methods (5), and developing idealism, obtaining training in improved agricultural techniques, learning dignity of labour, and obtaining training in animal husbandry and cattle-care (1 each). In regard to the relative success or failure in the presentation of different items in the training programme the following were considered particularly successful: agricultural extension methods (11), social education (6), co-operative organisation (5), techniques of mass contact (4), horticulture (3), and practical work and extension methods (4). Among items in the training programmes which were regarded by some not to have been effectively and successfully taught were the following: *panchayat* organisation (4), co-operative organisation (3), social education (2), horticulture (1), animal husbandry (3), and handicrafts and cottage industries (2). One complained that there was no practical emphasis in the training, and another remarked that subjects other than agricultural extension were not given adequate attention.

Notwithstanding the weaknesses and drawbacks of the training programme to which they called attention, fourteen VLWs thought that it changed their outlook towards life and national affairs, and only three held a contrary view. However, in view of their practical experience most of them feel that some aspects of their training programme were unrealistic. Two complaints heard most frequently from them are about the treatment which they receive from higher CDP officials, and about the planning from top down which characterizes much of the development activity in the project. The training centres emphasised that methods of work in CDP would not follow traditional bureaucratic lines and that the relationship between VLWs and higher project officials would not be a superior subordinate relationship. Yet their field experience has showed the VLWs that the administrative set-up of CDP is not radically different from that of other government departments, and that the APO, and DyPEO, rather than helping and guiding them were often inspecting their work. Another unrealistic aspect of their training, they think, was that it laid great emphasis on grass roots planning. Time and again in the course of their training they were told that plans will grow up from village people, whereas in reality they had the frustrating experience of finding that the plans invariably came from the top and had to be carried down by them to the village people. Other complaints voiced by the VLWs were that the timely support, supplies, and co-ordinated effort promised to them in the course of their training were seldom available to them in the field.

When asked to indicate the spheres of work in which they felt that they were well-qualified and adequately trained, two said that they had the necessary equipment for all aspects of CDP work, others felt that they were well qualified in some fields and somewhat inadequately equipped in others. Agricultural extension work leads the list of subjects in which VLWs feel competent and well trained (11). The setting up of co-operatives is second on the list, six VLWs regarding themselves well versed in this branch. Other items on the list are: mass contact (3), social education (2), *panchayat* organisation (3), horticulture (2), and public health and sanitation (1). In enumerating the areas of CDP work in which they did not feel confident about the adequacy of their training, nine expressed diffidence over practical work in the field of animal husbandry, especially in performing castration. Most of them felt that their training in this respect, consisting in many cases of only one demonstration of castration to a large group of trainees, was insufficient and their attempts to do such work could even be dangerous. Other items in this list are: social education (2), *panchayat* and co-operative organisation (4 each), public health and sanitation (2), horticulture (1), cottage industries (1), and accounting and maintenance of records (1).

The VLWs appear to have definite ideas on the subject of the group or groups of people in the village through whom they can work most successfully. Thirteen showed an unmistakable preference for 'successful cultivators with no factional affiliations'. Two said that they had to work through 'men with official connexions and political influence' because they considered it a good policy to keep them pleased, but six regarded this group as a nuisance. Five VLWs said that they had to consult 'important village leaders' and 'leaders of factions' because their co-operation is necessary for the success of development measures. Two said that they avoided such people as much as possible, one found them unhelpful, and two thought that they were helpful. Fourteen VLWs were definite in their opinion that successful cultivators of the 'middle group', those who were neither very rich nor very poor, were most helpful to them in their development work. Others listed the following as helpful: Harijans (1), very rich and very poor people (1), economically poor agriculturists (1), educated young men and school masters (1), and influential people (2). The general consensus of opinion appeared to be that since the agricultural extension programme was the most important single item on the project schedule it was best to work mostly with the middle group of agriculturists. Among those who obstructed development work on the village level 'leaders and men with official contacts' were regarded as the worst by eleven VLWs. Other obstructionists mentioned by them are: conservative elements in the population (3), petty officials (1), and educated people (1).

When they were asked whether they thought that force should be used under certain conditions to get the CDP programme accepted, nine answered in the affirmative and eight in the negative. Two of those who supported some use of force doubted if its results could be long-lasting. One who rejected the use of force by the VLWs said that some pressure could be useful for land consolidation and village sanitation if the State made necessary enactments. Nearly all who supported use of force wanted it to be limited and as far as possible legal.

Eight VLWs said that village people had started coming to them regularly for advice, six said that people came occasionally to them but that the VLW himself had to go to them mostly, three said that they had to go to the villagers only for explaining new things but for their normal requirements the people themselves came to them, and one said that people were not approaching him for any help.

Nine VLWs said agriculturists were the ones who most frequently came to consult them, and six mentioned poor people in this connexion. Manual workers, educated people, and Harijans were among those mentioned by others as appearing quite often with requests. Once again it was pointed out that persons belonging to the same caste as the VLW tended to cluster around him in the village, and generally gave him their unqualified support.

In respect of their official relations thirteen VLWs said that their officers—APOs and DyPEOs—treated them like 'subordinate officials', three said that they were treated like 'younger brothers', and one said that they were treated like a 'combination of younger brother and subordinate official—something between the two'. Regarding their general relations with other village level development staff sixteen said that their relations were good, only one regarded them as unsatisfactory. However, the same could not be said about co-operation. Only five found the other village level officials co-operative, twelve complained of lack of co-operation. The VLWs, however, could not enumerate the points on which there was lack of co-operation between them and the other village level development staff. Much of this lack of co-operation is attributed by them to the narrow departmental outlook of the other officials, who are jealous of the VLWs because of their higher emoluments and who see in them a challenge to their established position of superiority in the village. Inactivity, red tape, and lack of effort at co-ordination from the top were mentioned as other factors responsible for lack of co-operation from other officials. The Patwaris from the Revenue Department and Cane Union officials were specifically mentioned as being unco-operative.

The frequency of visits by higher CDP officials such as APOs and the DyPEO differs from centre to centre. Some centres are visited quite often while others are left relatively untouched. The key centres are, of course, visited more than other villages and APOs have to go to different villages more often than the DyPEO. Regarding visits by APOs, one VLW said that they came nearly once a week, two said that they came 'frequently', three said that they came once a fort-night, nine said that they came once a month and one said that they came once in two or three months. Regarding the DyPEO the responses were as follows: once in fifteen days (1), frequently (2), once a month (3), once in two to three months (2), and rarely (9). Analysis of orders, instructions, suggestions, and guidance given by these officers to VLWs during three visits preceding our interviews shows that these tours are more for routine inspection and for on-the-spot inquiry than for actual field guidance. Four VLWs reported having received some practical suggestions from these officers in their tours, and only three said that they were helped by them in planning field demonstrations.

On the subject of freedom of expression in staff meetings eleven said that they were permitted practically no freedom, while six claimed that they could express themselves in these meetings without any check or hindrance. Many of those who said that they had reasonable freedom of speech appeared to be doubtful about its effectiveness. Twelve said that they could speak freely in minor advisory committees; five said they could not.

With only one exception all the VLWs said that they could not contribute effectively to the formulation of CDP targets. Some pointed out that they were discouraged from doing this when they first tried to do so and have since learned to accept targets as given by the higher officers. There were practically no spheres in which they could act on their own initiative, for they needed permission, sanctions, or orders for doing nearly everything. Only one VLW was satisfied with the measure of support and co-operation given from project headquarters, three thought that the attitude of higher officials was 'generally helpful', and thirteen complained of absence of adequate and timely support. Several concrete instances were given in making this last point. In many cases VLWs promised certain things to villagers on the basis of assurances from higher officers, but were eventually let down by the officers who went back on their assurances. Frequent delays, supplies of poor seeds (to be distributed as improved types) and charging of prices higher than prevailing market prices for seed and fertilisers were some factors which hurt the rapport of VLWs in the villages. Officials did nothing to improve matters when these deficiencies and the consequent difficulties were pointed out to them. Ten VLWs thought that they could work more efficiently if they had powers to incur limited expenditure on approved projects within their respective fields. Some expressed the view that they should become fully multi-purpose and should have the powers and functions of Panchayat Secretaries and Cane Supervisors also. Two said that they did not need any additional powers, two did not understand how VLWs could be given more authority, and one said that a VLW was a servant of the people and as such did not need any 'authority'.

On the subject of the VLW's work load fourteen thought that they were overworked; three were of opinion that their work load was reasonable. Thirteen could not say if any part of their work was unnecessary, two regarded *panchayat* work as unnecessary, and two opined that frequent census work and surveys which they were called upon to do involved a waste of their time. One suggested that there should be fewer villages and a considerably smaller population under a VLW's charge. It was pointed out that sometimes they had to do menial work such as running errands for higher officials. Their multifarious activities kept them so occupied that they did not even have time to read newspapers and books. Twelve of them thought that they had to do too much routine work; five, on the contrary, regarded the amount of routine work as normal and not unusually heavy. Of the twelve who complained about the large amount of routine work, four mentioned *panchayat* work and two mentioned census work in this connexion. It was pointed out that even printed forms were not supplied to them in sufficient quantity, and on occasions they had to buy their own paper and spend a great deal of time drawing up the additional forms required. When asked to make suggestions regarding the sharing of their work load with other village officials, eight had no suggestions to offer, six suggested that Patwaris should do the survey and census work which is at present being done by the VLWs, two suggested that Patwaris should help them in keeping records, and that Panchayat Secretaries should be called upon to share their development work. Almost all approved the multi-purpose concept of VLW, and rather than give up a part of their work to others wanted their field of operation to be limited to smaller population units in the interest of effective and efficient functioning.

When asked to indicate *their* test of a 'successful VLW', they mentioned a variety of personality traits, characteristics and achievement tests. Ten thought 'selfless dedication to service and hard work' as well as 'ability to co-ordinate social work' to be the ultimate test of a successful VLW. Other responses concerned character, good behaviour and ability to get along with villagers (4), identifying oneself with villagers and reducing their difficulties (3), gaining the confidence of villagers (4), success in changing people's outlook (2), and impartiality (2).

The question as to what type of a VLW was regarded successful in actual practice brought diverse answers, but all had one common feature, namely, that the yardstick used by the village people and by the higher CDP officers was different. According to the village people a successful VLW has one or more of the following characteristics; willingness to do hard work (5), consideration for village people and understanding of their problems (4), ability to fulfil promises (2), honesty (2), success in achieving targets (2), and impartiality, character, tactfulness, ability to speak well, simplicity, and ability to gain the villager's confidence (1 each). The officers allegedly use a different measure. Ability to achieve targets (7), flattery (6), ability to speak well (2), hard work (2), obedience (1), and tactfulness (1), are according to the VLWs interviewed, the qualities that determine their success in the judgement of their officers.

When asked to indicate one or more qualities which in their opinion were a measure of the success of a VLW they indicated a variety of characteristics: honesty and truthfulness (10), capacity to do sustained hard work (9), humility (6), impartiality (5), consideration and understanding (4), determination (4), will for service (3), ability to gain confidence of the village people (4), ability to keep one's word (2), ability to explain project objectives (2), ability to interact well (1), and knowledge of the job (1).

In evaluating their own work twelve VLWs claimed that they were most successful in agricultural extension work. Among other areas of CDP work in which they claimed outstanding success are: village sanitation (1), mass contact and public participation (1), social education (1), sports for village youth and children (1), planting of orchards (2), formation of village co-operatives (2), stimulation of a public health programme (1), and irrigation (1). Among the areas in which they thought that they either failed or were only partially successful they mentioned the following: sanitation (8), public health (5), public works (4), animal husbandry (2), adult and social education (4), horticulture (1), *panchayat* organisation (1), irrigation (1), and *shramdan* and community activities (2). All of them thought that they were benefiting the community and the country. They believed that their utility lay in their work in the fields of increasing food production, in promoting rural sanitation, in initiating welfare programmes, and in adult and social education activities. When they were asked to indicate the items on their schedule which they expect will persist for at least five years after the termination of community development projects, all VLWs, with only one exception, said that new agricultural techniques introduced by them are most likely to become a part of the people's life. According to them other achievements of lasting significance are: co-operative societies (2), tube wells and irrigation facilities (2), village sanitation (4), recreation programmes (2), school (1), methods of cattle care (1), roads (2), paving of village lanes (3), libraries and reading rooms (2), and changed outlook towards life and a general attitude of co-operation in village development (2).

When asked to indicate their worries and difficulties most of them felt that conditions under which they could operate with dignity and self-respect have still to be created. When dignitaries and important guests visit the villages, far from being accorded a place of some respect and honour, the VLWs are relegated to a humble position and have to run errands. Officers often rebuke them in public, and as a result their prestige suffers. No effort is made to build up their prestige in the village, nor are the people encouraged to look upon them as their friends and leaders in village development work. Not one of the VLWs interviewed recounted that his work was praised by high officials in public.

Then there is the question of incentives and rewards. Most VLWs have to labour at their present jobs harder than they had to work in their parent departments, and that too without a paid assistant[3] but they are not rewarded by rises in salaries, cash awards, or even public and official recognition of their accomplishments. They realise that in this task of national reconstruction they will have to work hard and that they cannot expect financial rewards for every little thing that they do. Nevertheless they do want some recognition for particularly meritorious work. In one or two cases when rewards were definitely promised for achievement in specific items of project work they were never given to the winners. For instance it was pointed out that two prizes for best work in promoting the orchards plantation programme have not yet been given to the VLWs who showed outstanding success in this field. A third problem that worries the VLWs is that of in-service training. No refresher courses or training camps have been organised for them, and the supply of literature giving them latest information regarding the different aspects of their work has been very meagre. Most of the VLWs who went on sightseeing tours to other projects appeared to think that they did not benefit much from such trips. Finally, there is the great question of the future before them. Departmental VLWs feel that chances of promotion were better for them in their parent departments. With the policy of making direct recruitment to the posts of APOs and ADOs, both direct and departmental VLWs feel that the chances of their promotion are very considerably reduced.

III

What do the other project officers such as the Assistant Project Officers (APOs) and the Deputy Project Executive Officer (DyPEO) think about the VLW—his role, problems, and difficulties? In answering this question we shall rely mainly on material obtained in formal and informal interviews with two DyPEOs—one formerly an officer of the co-operative department, and another a revenue official who before coming to this Project earned a reputation for himself for making success of another Project, and two APOs—one formerly an information officer and now in charge of social education and public participation, and another originally from the co-operative department and now in charge of co-operatives and *panchayat*. All these officers have had training in extension methods.

In regard to the relative merits of direct recruitment compared to nominations from other development departments to the VLW posts, the general consensus of opinion appears to be that direct recruitment could be useful if it was made through fair and open competition on the basis of desirable personality traits and aptitudes and could be followed by intensive job training for an adequate period, say eighteen months or two years. It was felt that in the recruitment of VLWs factors other than those of merit and aptitude were beginning to play some part, and that this tendency led to the selection of persons who had neither the temperament nor the personality for the kind of work which they were called upon to do.

For direct recruits a training of six months is not regarded as adequate. It is felt that in several branches of CDP work they therefore come rather ill equipped. Another characteristic of a number of young direct recruits to the job is that they enter it with somewhat impractical idealism and have a tendency to become frustrated when they find that things do not necessarily develop as they wish them to. On the whole they are weak in maintenance of accounts and routine official records.

The departmental VLWs, on the other hand, are more seasoned and practical, but often lack the idealism, sense of dedication, and higher motivation demanded by the job. Their values and attitudes are influenced to a certain extent by the orientation courses and extension training that they get, but in a large number of cases the old methods of work and norms of thought which they acquired in their parent departments either persist or are easily revived. They are good in routine work, but some tend to concentrate more or 'show projects' that on substantial work. In point of honesty some may not be above reproach as they cannot easily give up the habits acquired by them in previous government service. When nominating persons for VLW jobs departments have in many cases suggested people whom they wanted to be rid of, without any consideration of their suitability for the new assignment. It was the opinion of those interviewed that policy and methods of recruitment need revision, that from both sources individuals should be taken only after proper screening, and should be given more effective training.

Among departmental personnel selected for VLW jobs, those from agriculture and co-operative departments have proved most successful. On the whole university graduates have not proved a success as VLWs. Their superior ways, manner of speech and dress, and constant desire for promotion to a higher post befitting their academic qualifications, stand in the way of their applying themselves whole-heartedly to the job. Persons having passed the matriculation or an equivalent examination, preferably with training in agriculture, are generally best suited for this work. All of these officers expressed an unmistakable preference for workers with a village background. Present salaries of the VLWs were considered adequate, although it was felt that there was great disparity in the gain to personnel recruited from different departments, Panchayat Secretaries jumping up from a salary of Rs. 60 a month to Rs. 110, but senior agriculture and co-operative people receiving no proportionate gain. It was felt that there were unreasonable delays in making legitimate salary adjustments, and that some system was needed under which especially meritorious services could be rewarded with enhanced salaries. As a general rule people work best in the section of the country from which they come, where they do not differ from the rest of the people in dress, speech and food. And it was recognised that a VLW could function more efficiently in a village which was predominantly populated by persons of his own caste.

There is general agreement that the concept of a multi-purpose VLW is useful, but the officers interviewed feel that it may not be expedient to saddle him with the work of a Patwari or Lekhpal also. As an experimental measure VLWs have been given Panchayat Secretary's work for a limited area, while Panchayat Secretaries have been given VLW's development work for one or more villages under their charge. Project officials are watching the results of this experiment. They favour withdrawal of all other village level development staff from the Project villages. They feel that there is fair understanding among the VLWs of the basic aims and objectives of the community development projects, and also of their own functions and responsibilities. They understand the VLW's role as that of 'a friend who offers advice when it is needed' but emphasise that initially the VLWs will have to think of themselves as leaders and innovators. It is realised that the ideal would be for the VLW to discover local felt needs and for the Project to formulate plans accordingly. Yet out of concession to the realities of the day it is felt necessary for the VLWs to achieve targets fixed from above. The officers point out that individual projects have very limited autonomy, the budget structure and directions from state headquarters determine their time schedule and main lines of activity to a very great extent. Under these conditions a VLW can have relatively little freedom of action and is often under pressure to achieve the targets given to him. As regards the general approach of the VLW the higher officials feel that he must endeavour to help the people to help themselves, but they argue that today they may have to use persuasion bordering almost on pressure. They expect the VLWs to work with devotion and sincerity and realise that their job involves hard labour without adequate compensation. As they are themselves under constant pressure to show concrete results to their superior officers and visiting dignitaries, they have to ensure that VLWs achieve results that can be seen.

Regarding *felt needs* of the people they think that the important ones among them are well-known and that no special effort is required to bring them to light. VLWs can, of course, call attention to specific local needs and demands. There are certain areas in which people express their needs but the project can do nothing; for example, it cannot undertake consolidation of land holdings or start any major irrigation works. As there is very limited flexibility in the programme, it is difficult to have individual projects for each village, and consequently the VLWs cannot contribute materially towards determining the CDP targets. As planning so far has tended to come from the top to the bottom the autonomy of the individual projects has been considerably restricted. Regarding innovations sponsored by CDP and people's response towards them, it was pointed out that their acceptance was slow and extremely cautious, but the indications are that the tempo will increase.

About the job training programme of the VLWs the general consensus of opinion was that it has not been as successful as it ought to have been. Organisation of many of the training centres leaves quite a bit to be desired; while some parts of CDP work are adequately covered in the job training, others are only superficially touched upon or are practically ignored. In general, training in improved agricultural practices is satisfactory, but the same cannot be said about animal husbandry, and public health and sanitation. Departmental VLWs are naturally strong in the work of their respective departments. It is doubtful if these training programmes succeed in changing the fundamental outlook of the trainees towards life and national affairs, or if they give them the technical knowledge of all that they are supposed to do in the villages, but they do leave the training centres with some idealism, and this in itself is a welcome addition to their mental equipment.

The officers realise that it is necessary to have a core of individuals in the villages of the project area conscious of planning developments so that people may take upon themselves an increasing share of responsibility for development work. But they frankly admit that such a leadership is at present nowhere in sight. Village councils (Gram Sabhas) are split into factions, and not many office bearers of such bodies could be described as selfless and public-minded. Men of influence often come forward with unusual requests for favours, and want certain advantages for themselves to the exclusion of others. There are certainly some individuals who are interested in development work for patriotic motives, but their number is not very large. Village Level Workers should work as far as possible with those who are interested in agricultural improvement and village development, but for practical reasons they cannot avoid 'leaders of factions' and 'men with political connexions'. It is true that some people from these classes have tended to treat the VLWs as servants, and when irregular favours were not granted to them they put obstacles in the way of community development work. Only a few people go to the VLW for advice as yet, but their number is gradually increasing. On the subject of the use of pressure and force the opinion was almost unanimous that only legal coercion should be exercised and that too after proper education of the masses.

We have pointed out earlier that the VLWs feel quite strongly that they are not treated well by some of their superior officers. The officials admitted that such complaints are not without foundation, and that some officers not properly oriented in extension methods have tended to make unnecessary displays of their authority. The VLWs are entitled to be treated well but this will not eliminate all supervision and pressure to show results. Many of the VLWs may abuse autonomy and equality if these are accorded to them. They are younger brothers, not in a western family, but in an Indian joint family. They are entitled to courtesy and consideration, but if they fail in discharging their responsibilities they cannot claim exemption from rebuke. Equality and respect have to be earned, the officers said, and added that those who work well are treated almost as equals. Those who are slow and lethargic naturally have to account for their failings, and have no right to resent criticism.

In the normal course of their duties the APOs and DyPEO have to do some inspection and to make on-the-spot inquiries. It is a fact that they have not been able to give much field guidance to the Village Level Workers, but this can be explained partly by their preoccupation with other activities in the initial period of the project.

With regard to the co-operation of the VLWs with the staff of other departments it was pointed out that initially they could not get along well with Panchayat Secretaries and Cane Supervisors. The former got less salary and were consequently jealous of the VLWs. As they could manipulate village politics they sometimes put obstacles in the way of a VLW's work. Where there was friction the VLW could not utilise the *Gaon Sabha* for his purposes for want of support from the Panchayat Secretary. The Cane supervisors regarded themselves as more important than the VLWs, and as they could oblige people during the cane season they favoured key figures in the village in order to build up their own position and prestige as against that of the VLW.[4] Patwaris and Lekhpals lacked development consciousness, followed traditional bureaucratic methods, and refused to do even minor things without specific orders from superior revenue officials. This involved delays and caused resentment among the VLWs who could not make headway in any ventures connected with land unless they got copies of land records from the Patwari or Lekhpal. These officials have considerable local influence, are aware of the trends and developments in village politics, but are paid very much less than the VLWs. As project officials can approach the Patwaris or Lekhpals only through Tahsildars of the revenue department such delays at present seem to be unavoidable.

Regarding freedom of expression in staff meetings and the VLW's contribution to over-all programme planning and setting of targets, it was pointed out that they had reasonable but limited freedom to express themselves but could not contribute much to over-all programme planning because the project was under pressure from above to undertake specific lines of action decided at the State level. In explaining why freedom of expression in staff meetings must be limited it was pointed out that they almost always had a very heavy agenda. The meetings started at 10 a.m. and continued till 5 or 6 p.m. often with only a short break. This necessitated imposing time limits on the VLWs when they started explaining their problems and points of view at length. It was true that VLWs were sometimes handicapped by lack of timely support and supplies, but this was not always the fault of the project officers. Financial regulations were very rigid, parts of the CDP programme were inflexible, and the project staff itself had very little control over the quality and even the quantity of materials supplied by State headquarters. It was a vicious circle; when the officers were disappointed in some request or expectation by their superior officers, they had to disappoint those who were working under them. It was not always wise or practical to protest against decisions and actions of State headquarters. Because of this it is necessary that careful checks be employed by State headquarters when sending improved varieties of seeds and equipment to the project. The officers consider it impractical to give any drawing and spending powers to the VLWs even for approved projects in the villages under their charge. For many more years to come supervision of their work and strict financial scrutiny and control cannot be avoided.

With regard to the work load of the VLW it is felt that he certainly has to work hard, but his work load cannot be described as excessive. By giving some development work to the Panchayat Secretaries efforts have already been made to reduce the VLW's area of operation. It is realised that the VLWs have to attend a number of staff meetings and also have to do considerable routine work, but almost all of it is necessary and cannot be eliminated. At the present stage it may create administrative and practical problems if the VLWs are asked to do the work of Patwaris or Lekhpals, and the latter are asked to do any multi-purpose development work in addition to their present duties. In the life of this project this experiment may prove undesirable.

IV

To the village people the role of the VLW is not very clear, for they have not been able to decide whether to regard him as 'a minor government functionary' operating on the village level or as 'a social worker and leader'. While these two roles are clearly understood in their separate aspects by the village people, the VLW—who appears to be a cross between the two—often puzzles them. It is generally well-known that the VLW is a paid government employee and people with some education and urban contacts also know that in respect to salary and official status he occupies the lowest position in the official hierarchy of the planning and development department. However, his methods of work are somewhat unorthodox and mark him out from other village officials who still follow the traditional methods of work. The VLW is definitely much less authoritarian than other officials who have hitherto operated on the village level. Unlike others who appear on the village scene periodically (and for work connected with one department only) the VLW lives in close and continuous touch with the people of the village or villages under his charge and takes interest in several branches of development activity. In his manner of dress and speech, too, he is different from other government officials, and often speaks the language of social workers. The realisation that a government servant can also function as a social worker and agent of reform is emerging very slowly, and at the time of the present study the appreciation of this possibility was confined largely to the rural *élite*.

Speaking for the Project area as a whole the people may be divided into four groups on the basis of their view and understanding of the VLW's role:

(i) The rural *élite*, consisting mostly of people of higher status and higher income groups, who have some education and urban contacts. Most people in this category belong to upper castes, but it also includes other educated people who are active in village and inter-village politics.

(ii) The agriculturists. This group includes most of the land-owning agriculturists who are not active in village or inter-village politics. Some of the persons classed in this category are 'opinion leaders' in certain phases of village affairs but they generally keep away from village politics, which is directed by persons of group one.

(iii) Artisan groups and occupational castes. This group includes a large number of castes whose economy is integrated with the general agricultural economy of the village. In traditional rating this group occupies a middle status, neither very high, nor very low. A major part of the subsistence of its members is obtained through the practice of their traditional crafts, and they generally do not accept work commonly regarded as 'menial labour'.

(iv) The low status, low income groups. This class includes the 'untouchable castes, and people who earn their livelihood by humble occupations and menial labour.

It has been suggested earlier that the first group has some degree of understanding of the VLW's role. Some individuals of this group read newspapers and attend meetings where social, political, and development questions are discussed. They are the ones most exposed to the agencies that communicate modern ideas to rural areas and their urban contacts keep them generally better informed about national and regional developments than the other sections of the village population. It is from this group that most of the members of the different advisory committees associated with CDP are drawn. Thus, this is the group best acquainted with the aims and methods of the community development movement in the village population. But this also happens to be the most status conscious group. Rather than working with the VLW, whose status is the lowest in the development organisation, people from this group seek to associate more with the 'officers' whose status is higher. As some of these people have contacts with or access to political leaders, officers have to be particularly careful in their dealings with this section. On the whole this group has a patronising attitude towards the VLW, and generally has tended to dictate what he should do. Some persons of this group have openly regarded the VLW as a kind of personal servant and have used pressure to secure his services for their own advantage. Others among this group have felt that the VLW should work in consultation with them and should generally accept their approach to village problems. VLWs have found their position rather difficult when they are subjected to conflicting pressures by rival factions in the *élite* group. Too close an association with this section has alienated some VLWs from the rest of the community, and as a consequence of this has limited development activity to a fraction of the village population. In some cases VLWs made a determined effort to remain uninfluenced by this group and to work with all sections of the village people, but most of them soon found that this policy did not pay. The officers evaluated the work of the VLWs mostly on the basis of the opinions of these people, and were reluctant to resist their pressure because of the political connexions of this section. The VLWs had therefore to exercise utmost tact in handling these people. It was necessary to keep them pleased, and at the same time to check their undue interference in development work. On the whole the VLWs have found working with this 'enlightened' group most trying.

Of the other three groups the VLWs have had most contact with the second and the fourth, and not so much with the third. As agricultural extension and Harijan welfare had definite priorities in the schedule of project activities, this was natural. To most of the agriculturists the VLW appeared to be a combination of representatives of the agriculture and co-operative departments, and they viewed him as just another official, although of a more friendly type. The under-privileged Harijan group is conscious of the fact that the State is taking certain measures for their economic and social uplift, and they have tended to view the VLW as an official specially appointed for this purpose. However, they were somewhat disillusioned to find that he was spending most of his working time with agriculturists, and that, being landless, they naturally could not benefit much from his services in this field. However, there were other areas of work in which the VLW came in contact with them. The general view of this group is that the VLW is a government official, who has, among other obligations, the duty to look after the welfare of the under-privileged section. The third group has felt the impact of the CDP activities the least. While they are aware of the presence of the VLW they do not quite understand why he is there nor do they know what possible help and advice they can get from him.

It must be emphasised here that the presence of the VLW is not known to all the people in the second, third, and the fourth groups, and their understanding of his duties and functions is comparatively restricted. In a field survey of people's reactions and general response to its activities at the close of the first year of the CDP's life, an effort was made to find out how widely the VLW and his achievements were known. For this purpose intensive inquiries were made in two villages. In Rajput village, a large settlement with a population of over 5,000, a stratified random sample of 10 per cent of the families living in the village was drawn, and the head of the family, or, if he were not available the next oldest adult male, was interviewed. In Tyagi Village, a smaller CDP block village with a population of about 750, 50 per cent adult males were interviewed. Out of 114 persons interviewed in Rajput Village fifty-six had heard about the Project, fifty-eight had not. Among these forty-four knew M, the former VLW, who had worked in the village for about seven months, and only twenty-two knew T, who had recently taken charge and had been in the village for only about three months. Out of this sample only fifty-nine said that they had met the VLW. The VLW had sought the co-operation of only forty-eight of these people in his development activities in the village. The picture is somewhat different in Tyagi village, the second and smaller settlement. Out of 117 persons interviewed in this village, seventy-four had heard about the Project and forty-three were not aware of its existence; here ninety-five knew the VLW, eighteen did not. In this sample the VLW had met ninety-three people although he had sought the active co-operation of only twenty-four people. In both the villages the *élite*-agriculturist group as well as the low status, low income group knew the VLW and his activities much better than the artisan group. The village population as a whole were best acquainted with his work in the spheres of organising sanitation and *shramdan* drives, secondary vaccination, and inoculation of cattle. Knowledge of his activities in other fields was confined to limited sections only.

Lately a number of spectacular and impressive activities were concentrated in Rajput village and they are likely to have increased the general awareness regarding the Project and its work. In the case of Tyagi village, because of politically conscious leadership within the village, the tempo of development activity has been greater than in other villages of comparable size. But the figures above refer to the months of October and November 1954, when the project had been in operation for only one year. In villages other than the select two dozen 'key villages' where intensive work was being done, because of less concentrated nature of project activities the VLWs had probably reached a much smaller percentage of the village population at the same period.

In the final analysis the general response of the village people to a VLW depends to a large extent on his personality and individual qualities and his initial successes and failures. His understanding and tact in grasping the local situation is of considerable importance too. The general attitudes of the village people as well as the internal organisation of the village, especially the pattern of its leadership, also materially govern his ultimate acceptance and success or failure. While the village people look to the government, rather than to themselves, for active measures in the direction of village development and economic reconstruction, they have an intense suspicion and distrust of the petty government official. Initially the VLW had to start with this handicap. His approach, coupled with considerable development propaganda, has modified this way of thinking on the part of the villager to a slight degree. But people are still somewhat sceptical about the whole business, and nothing frustrates the VLW more than evidences of general apathy and distrust in those among whom he works.

V

To conclude, we shall briefly examine some of the problems and considerations emerging from this study.

In order to ensure the success of the large-scale plans of rural community development it is necessary that personnel for the VLW posts should be selected on the basis of certain desirable personality traits and aptitudes. In view of the very special and diverse nature of their work, it is also essential to provide the right kind of training for the persons selected for this job. The training programme should not only orient the trainees in the principles and methods of extension work, but should be designed to give them a reasonable degree of proficiency in all the important areas of their multi-purpose activity. The training should inspire them with an urge for dedicated national service, but the VLWs should not leave their training centres with an impractical idealism, for they will need a good deal of realism in facing a multitude of perplexing problems and tangled situations in the field. Their training would remain incomplete if this sense of realism is not imparted to them.

A series of problems arise when the VLW enters his field of action. Here his success will depend upon a number of factors, many of which are outside his control. In the first place it is necessary for him to understand and accept the programme which he seeks to promote in the area under his charge. Secondly, he should be happy and well adjusted in the total official organisation of the project. In the absence of understanding, sympathy, and timely support from his colleagues and official superiors, his well-intentioned programmes can be wrecked. Thirdly, the people among whom he is working should also understand and approve his programmes, for the ultimate success of the development programme as such will depend upon the final acceptance of its ideology by the village people. The success of the CDP team can be gauged by its success in devising meaningful approaches to overcome the different types of resistances offered by the people to the acceptance of the development ideology and programmes.

Those responsible for formulating the plan have generally been aware of some of these prerequisites and vital factors governing the successful implementation of the programme, and have, therefore, devised a number of measures which are calculated to ensure proper recruitment and training and to secure suitable working conditions for the VLWs. The theoretical basis of their approach could not be fully tested against the empirical experience of the field in the first phase of the life of the projects. As data emerging from the experience of individual projects are now accumulating, it is possible to make a preliminary evaluation of the emerging role of the VLW.

In view of the above considerations we may ask if the VLWs of this project are of the right type and with desirable aptitudes and personality traits? Have they been adequately equipped for their job by their training?

Development literature lists a wide range of qualities and aptitudes desirable in a VLW. For example, a Handbook of the Uttar Pradesh Government on 'Principles of Extension Work' (*Prasar Karya ke Siddhanta*) enumerates five essential, and twenty-seven desirable attributes in a VLW. The essential qualities are: honesty, self-confidence and optimism, knowledge of the different areas of his work, sympathy, and will for sustained hard work. The list of desirable aptitudes and personality traits is long and varied, and includes, besides the five essential qualities listed above, the following: desire to acquire new knowledge, an instinct for correct on-the-spot decisions, ability to communicate ideas and plans clearly, resourcefulness, foresight, capacity to draw people to him, enthusiasm, courage, organising ability, love of physical labour, capacity to inspire others, practical common sense, friendliness, patience and tolerance, selflessness, developed sense of co-operation and team work, willingness to hear other's points of view, habit of giving only those promises that one can fulfil, simplicity, spirit of service, and physical endurance. It will indeed be futile to look for all these qualities in every VLW of all the projects. In this study an attempt was made to rank and evaluate the VLWs on the basis of ten specified aptitudes.[5] and eight specified criteria of success.

On the basis of personal observation and the people's reactions, we are inclined to agree generally with the evaluation and ranking of the VLWs of the Project by the officers. In this ranking, three of the seventeen VLWs were graded poor, twelve average to good, and two outstanding. In ranking them according to specified aptitudes, the officers found that the VLWs of the Project as a group were strong in understanding village customs and social organisation, and in 'co-operativeness' (with other project staff). They were good to average in the following: 'ability to gain confidence of the villagers', 'willingness to work with all castes and economic groups', and 'knowledge of extension principles and methods.' As a group they were weak in the following: 'initiative', 'emotional attachment to village people,' and 'interest in developing village initiative and leadership'. Ranking them according to specified criteria of success the officers found the group as a whole strong in 'personal acceptance by the villagers' and in 'developing balanced village programmes fieldwise'. They were good to average in 'enlisting people's participation in public works', in 'bringing programmes to all groups in the village', 'in stimulating individual villagers to adopt recommended improved practices' and in 'contributing to over-all project programme planning'. They were judged to be weak in two areas—in 'educating villagers to reasons why improved practices are better than traditional ones' and in 'developing local initiative and leadership'.

While the general level of the VLWs is, on the whole, satisfactory, it appears that they were not too carefully screened at the time of their selection for this type of work. Departmental recommendations or an all too brief interview do not appear to be the most satisfactory methods of recruitment to a pivotal job like that of the VLW. Even a simple testing for desirable aptitudes and personality traits would have excluded the selection of at least two out of the three VLWs rated as 'poor' by the officers in the ranking referred to above. The tendency of departments to get rid of undesirable individuals by their transfer to CDP must be deplored, and the tendency to use official and political influence in the matter of selection to these jobs must be guarded against. Proper screening and testing of all the applicants, and their selection only on the basis of necessary qualifications and desirable traits and aptitudes is necessary. For this it is essential to devise suitable tests, and apply them vigorously. The necessity of recruiting a large staff in a very short time is often mentioned as a reason for the lack of greater care and caution in the selection. It is realised that officials were under pressure, and that the rapid expansion of development activities made unexpected demands on them. But unplanned developments in a department of planning appear to be somewhat paradoxical. A more accurate anticipation of personnel requirements can greatly help in reducing the possibility of the selection of undesirable individuals to these posts. It should be borne in mind that a wrong type of person in a VLW post can be more harmful than a failure to fill the place.

In the absence of a full and intimate knowledge of the operation of the VLW training programmes a balanced evaluation of their success cannot be attempted here. However, on the basis of the experience with the VLWs of this Project a few general observations can be made. It appears that the different training centres have somewhat different orientations, and on the whole the programmes offered by them are not as balanced as they might be. It is not suggested that a rigid uniformity should be insisted upon, but it is perhaps necessary to ensure that certain areas of work which are basic for the VLW as an action man get adequate attention in all centres. While the partial success of the training programme is not denied, especially in the field of orienting trainees in extension methods and in imparting to them a sense of idealism, it has to be noted that in certain fields the trainees leave the centres wholly unequipped or but partially equipped. It has been noted that some VLWs were extremely reluctant to perform vaccinations because they felt that their training for this work was inadequate. Performing castrations was unusually difficult for some because their training for this work consisted of one or two hurried demonstrations by a non-resident instructor. Direct recruits to the job found that their training in accounting procedure was insufficient. Other comparatively weak areas of training have been mentioned earlier. It has also been observed that the organisation of some of the training centres and their programmes bore the imprint of hurried and insufficient planning. One further observation may be made here. It appears that the trainees were not sufficiently sensitised to likely field situation. For example, they were not familiarised with areas where they could expect to meet unexpected resistance from the people even in respect to things that would be apparently beneficial to them. They were not told that the established bureaucratic tradition of administration can still be a strong influence in the actual functioning of the CDP, notwithstanding the efforts on the part of the government to orient their planning officials in modern methods of extension work. Most of the VLWs were not prepared to meet with opposition and an unsympathetic attitude from the rural *élite* in general and from the politically influential sections in particular. Inclusion of suitable case studies in the training programme based on actual experience of work in the field, will perhaps give a more balanced perspective to the trainees and will prepare them better for 'the shocks' they are likely to get in the field.

Three general suggestions may be offered in this area. First, it is desirable to attempt an evaluation of past and current VLW training programmes. Secondly, on the basis of accumulated experience it is necessary to evolve more balanced training programmes, possibly of a longer duration. Thirdly, it will be useful to benefit by the experience (the success as well as failure) of the VLWs in the field. Carefully prepared case studies, based on this experience, can be helpful not only to future VLWs in training, but also to more seasoned development workers both in the field and in higher administrative positions.

From observations and materials presented in Sections II and III of this study, a number of questions emerge that concern the adjustment and functioning of the VLW in the official organisation of the Community Projects. Some of the minor problems, such as lack of suitable residential accommodation and unusually long delays in making salary adjustments and payments of travelling allowances, should not detain us. However, it is necessary to point out that delays in respect to the latter cause very considerable hardship to the VLWs. Since they are usually persons with modest salaries and practically no outside resources, it is difficult for them to wait endlessly for such payments. In one case a VLW did not get his transfer T.A. for eighteen months in spite of constant reminders. In another instance, a VLW got disgusted with the delay in salary adjustment, and rather than work for a smaller emolument in CDP, decided to quit it in favour of his parent department. Some cutting of red tape, elimination of routine office formalities, and tightening of general office administration are indicated.

The major problems in this area are: (a) the creation of atmosphere in which a VLW can function with some initiative and independence, (b) the building up of his 'prestige', (c) the provision of adequate incentives for him to work to the best of his abilities, (d) the arranging for his in-service training, and (e) the evolving of administrative practices and organisation under which the VLW can get timely support and help. Most of these problems are closely interrelated.

Bound by a rigid organisational framework and fixed targets, the VLWs feel that they have very limited independence and scope for initiative, and officials concede that this indeed is so.

In respect to his 'prestige' the VLW meets with the first challenge from his own immediate official superiors. While officials generally explain their authoritarian tone as a direct consequence of the pressure on them to 'show results', it cannot be denied that most of them have an inner conflict of values in respect to this matter. Their short training in extension methods and principles does not make them sufficiently alive to the fact that their task calls for a pattern of intra-department ordering of relations different from the one in which they were nurtured. It has not been realised that the concept of team-work as accepted by development ideology, necessitates a change in the superior-subordinate relationships that largely characterise the bureaucratic structure of India. The prevailing view among officials appears to be that the new approach is too doctrinaire, theoretical, and impractical, and that in the long run only traditional methods work. Assertion of official superiority and authority at every possible point frustrates the VLW who was given to believe in his training that in the Community Development Projects the climate of work would be basically different. The officials' view of the VLW's role and position is easily taken over by the rural *élite* and influential village leaders who inter-act with officials on a basis of equality. Soon they begin to treat the VLW as a minor government official of no consequence. Little, if any, effort has so far been made to build up the position and prestige of the VLW in the villages where he operates. As a result of the operation of these two factors, within the project administration there is a regrettable tendency toward a one-way communication: higher officials fix targets and issue directives, the VLWs try their best to realise them in action.

This raises the question of incentives for more and better work. A rigid schedule, externally determined targets, and lack of opportunity for individual initiative, coupled with authoritarian supervision and general public apathy do not provide adequate incentive for originality, innovation and dedicated work. The realisation that impressive 'show projects' earn better dividends than educational efforts to change people's ways of thought, alters the perspective in which the VLW views his role. To the detriment of the basic aims of the community development movement, he consequently begins to concentrate on the spectacular in his activities. The busy officers and visiting dignitaries like to *see* things happening, and the practical, worldly-wise VLW who has a few showpieces to offer is likely to get their approval. But even then his individual work is rarely commended in public. Often, he does not want a special reward, but denial of recognition, when recognition is due, certainly frustrates him.

In their day-to-day activities the VLWs often find that they cannot get the support necessary to redeem promises and carry out plans. At the time when they are under pressure to create interest in a certain seed for which there is really not much demand, supplies of it are often not received in time and the VLW loses prestige when he cannot fulfil promises made to villagers on the strength of assurances given by his officers. In the course of our investigations we came across a number of cases which demonstrate the plight of the VLWs in situations of this kind. In trying to dispose of a certain quantity of seed, the VLWs in desperation had to make appeals directly opposed to the aims and principles of extension work. For instance, the VLWs were asked to sell a supply of improved seed of corn which had been received too late for the season's sowing. As it is there is very little demand for this seed in the area for it is not grown there on any large scale. The VLWs had to go from door to door begging people to buy the seed for domestic consumption if for nothing else. The villagers naturally did not like paying more than the prevailing market price, and since it was 'improved seed', it was considerably dearer than ordinary corn for domestic use. We know of three VLWs who were similarly under pressure to sell a certain quantity of potato seed. It was not only received too late for sowing, it was of an inferior quality (some of it being actually deteriorated) and was priced much higher than comparable or even better seed in the market. As a last resort the VLWs had to appeal to the rich villagers to help save their jobs by buying this seed even though it was not needed. Notwithstanding these appeals they could not thrust all the unwanted seed on unwilling villagers and had actually to pay the price of the unsold seed from their own salaries.

Without multiplying examples we can pass on to another but related problem. In some cases the seed received by the Project headquarters was obviously of an inferior quality. It was evident that its use would not produce the desired and promised results. Yet VLWs were asked to distribute it in the area. The VLWs took it to the villagers who, after considerable pressure, accepted it with great reluctance and scepticism. The yield justified their misgivings. In the following year the VLWs found it difficult to sell more seed, though this time it was certainly excellent in quality. There are many examples, too, of lack of fulfilment of promises, wherein the VLWs promoted items in the project schedule, but felt let down when the promised supplies and subsidies were not received in time.

In passing it should be noted that considering the area and population under the charge of a VLW his work load is rather heavy, and this results either in his working with one section of the population only or in emphasis on a few items of the project schedule and the neglect of others.

The problems delineated above require a critical re-examination of the entire range of questions in this area. If an expert in the field of public administration is called upon to devise necessary adjustments on the basis of observed facts and accumulated experience, it may not be difficult to make suitable modifications in administrative organisation and procedure of the Community Development Projects.

Traditional stereotypes and attitudes of the development officials (DyPEO, APOs) have shown a persistence that cannot perhaps be altered by brief orientation courses in extension methods. Much more will probably have to be done in this respect. Under actual service conditions steps could be taken to bring home to them the realisation that the content of extension training programmes is not all 'sentimental nonsense.' It has been pointed out earlier that tight schedules and fixed targets, coupled with the insistence on 'showing results', curb the autonomy of the individual projects and, while limiting the scope for initiative and innovation, tend to attach undue importance to impressive looking but often superficial achievements. While a certain degree of rigidity in the budget and work schedule of the projects cannot be avoided, it is desirable to have a sector in which the individual project, and within the project individual VLWs, can exercise initiative on the basis of specific local felt needs.

The question of investing necessary prestige in the office of the VLW needs careful attention. In the popular estimation status and salary often go together, but it would perhaps be Utopian to suggest that the salaries of the VLWs should be measurably enhanced at the present time. Fortunately there are certain intermediate roles, such as that of the school master, which carry a status for above that warranted by the salary of their post. With persistent effort there is no reason why acceptance of a VLW in a similar role cannot be secured. Some useful steps in this direction would be to accord to the VLW a place of honour in meetings attended by important officials and political leaders, to grant constant public acknowledgement of the importance of their work, to ensure less public demonstration of authority and superior status by his immediate officers, and to provide for suitable public honour to outstanding VLWs. It would not be difficult to secure the co-operation of the press in publicising the achievements of deserving VLWs. Some of them might even be considered for exceptional recognition through a suitable award by the President of the Republic. Such honours have recently been instituted, and the inclusion of a VLW in the lists of those so honoured would emphasise in a dramatic manner the importance of his role and position in new India.

Considerable thought has been given to the problem of providing incentives for the

VLWs to work better, but so far no definite principles have been formulated. It is perhaps not desirable to have too many cash awards for minor achievements, but they should not be completely ruled out as a means of recognition for exceptionally meritorious work in specific areas. Accelerated increments in salary and promotion to higher posts should be given according to set principles which take due account of exceptional achievements of the VLWs. In this sphere, it will be necessary to guard against judging the VLWs mainly on the basis of 'show projects'. In evaluating their work consideration should be given to their success in developing a balanced village programme, in carrying it to all sections of the population, and in developing local initiative and leadership.

It has been observed that facilities for in-service training of the VLWs are practically non-existent in this area. A supply of useful literature, technically sound but simply written, could with profit be made available to them regularly. Apart from a set of seven useful extension handbooks published by the U.P. Government, the VLWs of this Project got no other development literature. Even these handbooks were made available to them only after they had been in the field for more than a year. They were not familiar with the publications distributed by the Community Projects Administration in Delhi. What was more surprising was the fact that *Grama Sevak*, a periodical publication of CPA, which is a journal of the VLWs, by the VLWs, for the VLWs, was not known to any of the VLWs of this Project. While some of these publications have been written and produced with imagination, their distribution is unsystematic and unsatisfactory. This requires organisation. Refresher courses and short training camps for VLWs need to be organised, but this must be done with forethought and careful advance planning. With imaginative planning the annual sight-seeing tours of the VLWs could be turned into positive educational experiences, but the way they are handled at present makes them of very doubtful utility. According to the evaluation of the VLWs who have participated in these trips they are 'a waste of time and money'. In many instances 'people conducting them around the other projects did not know what they were showing them'.

In order to ensure that the concept of the VLW's multi-purpose functioning becomes meaningful, it is desirable also to examine the questions of his work load, his area of operation, and timely official support for his activities. This perhaps is the most important single area that calls for systematic investigation. In this sphere, however, the social analyst can only point out the need; specific recommendations call for technical competence in the field of public administration. The experience of this Project shows that if the VLW's area of operation cannot be reduced to consist of a population of about 3,000 per VLW, he should at least be given technical help in specific items of project activity. The field teachers have been associated with the VLWs in organising social education activities; similar help from public health workers may also be considered. The VLW would still remain in over-all charge of the area, but just as he is helped by the Field Teacher in devising and executing social education programmes he could be helped by a public health man in that field of specialisation.

Similarly, it would be useful to have an agency or channel through which difficulties in programme planning and execution could be transmitted to the Community Project's Administration. State authority is both necessary and desirable, but a higher authority should be able to correct it when it errs. Project officials find it hard to criticise State level decisions, and even have to yield to the point of distributing defective seeds out of season or of undertaking action plans which they know for certain are not needed in the area. A suitable mechanism to avoid such pitfalls has yet to be evolved.

Finally a word about the personal acceptance of the VLW and through him of the development aims and programme by the village people. It is in this area that the concept of a multi-purpose extension agent and social worker is undergoing its supreme test. Deep-rooted scepticism of government-sponsored welfare measures and distrust of the official are hard to eradicate, and only years of patience, perseverance, and hard work can bring about a change in this outlook. Experience shows that village people tend to magnify failures and underrate successes in experiments of community development. VLWs have often spoken to us about the icy silence of the people concerning their successful projects and of their mirthful caricatures of their small failures. A few ill-planned initial projects can cause irreparable damage to development work. It may not be true of the area to say that nothing succeeds like success but it is certainly true to say that nothing fails like failure. Choice, planning, and execution of initial projects, therefore, call for very great caution. Initial contacts of the VLW and Project officials materially affect the general response of the village people towards their work. As community development activities cover a wide and diverse range of decision-making, the policy of working with and through the so-called leaders of the village and men of influence may be fatal to the project objectives. The movement must remain broad-based, and should for its success approach the very sources where decisions of different types are made. The blessings of influential men, or even endorsement by a village body like the *Gaon Sabha*, may fail to take the programme to the people. In the area under study the agencies of decision-making are diffused: problems of everyday life are discussed and opinions are formed in informal friendship groups, and in gatherings of kinsfolk. A successful VLW will penetrate these groups, and will work with heads of households and caste groups. An unusually large part of Project activities concerns individuals and their families rather than the village as a unit. The educational objectives of the projects can be best attained by this approach, for it is conducive to an intelligent acceptance both of the VLW and of his programme by the people. Co-operation and support of village leaders is necessary for larger projects requiring the participation of village as a whole, but even in such activities persuasion through the VLW is more valuable than the pressure of village leaders. Problems of communication and of the development of effective contact techniques call for deeper sociological and psychological analyses, and deserve high priority in evaluation and planning research.

The concept of a multi-purpose village level worker is indeed useful, and has to a considerable extent proved its merit and utility in the field. It is, however, an emerging role in Indian village life—one that is still evolving and being defined. The course of its evolution and its final form can still be directed and controlled, and it should be the policy of the administration to channel it in the most appropriate direction. Empirical case studies and critical evaluation of its development will point out the areas where more thinking and planning are needed to ensure its final emergence in the form which seems most desirable. As a pivotal figure in the movement for rural community development the VLW merits wider studies both from sociological and public administration viewpoints.

REFERENCES

1. At the time of this research one of the eighteen VLWs was transferred to another Project, leaving seventeen subjects for this study.
2. A government sponsored voluntary organisation of village people for military training.
3. In their previous jobs they had paid assistants who carried out their instructions and did most of the hard work involving manual labour.
4. They did so by allowing influential people larger quotas at shorter intervals for the sale of their sugarcane to the mills.
5. The criteria used in this ranking were the same as those used by the programme Evaluation Organisation in the ranking of VLWs all over India.

26

The Attack on Poverty

The questions we will look at here are how rural development can be improves, and the main economic sectors which must be considered in order to widen the growth process and its impact on the poor.

The Conduct of District Operations and the IAS

In spite of the defects in the increasing number of rural institutions introduced or expanded in the 1950s, there has been a further proliferation of agencies and programmes since 1970. 'At the field level...multiplicity of functional departments and agencies has led to virtual balkanisation of the field,' writes Mohit Bhattacharya.[1] Despite the many efforts to stimulate development from below, 'there is a lot of spurious decentralisation all around such as looking to sanctions and approvals upward, almost at every step. 'Often during our survey, in state capitals and district towns we heard similar comments from experienced civil servants. As a senior IAS officer told me. 'What we need are some simple ideas upon which to build rural development.'

Let us try to look at some of the possible improvements. To begin with, the size of districts varies a great deal,[2] although it has considerably increased everywhere in terms of population. There has been, in states where districts are particularly big (in terms of population, as in Bihar) a trend to bifurcate them. This needs to be systematically encouraged, in almost all states, as a number of officials pointed out to me both in Delhi and in the provincial capitals. The whole process of rural development is becoming increasingly complex in every sense of the word: social economic and technical. Thus it is necessary to work with a unit which is really manageable and controllable from district headquarters.[3] At the same time it would be better to have smaller states. For decades, it has been suggested that the enormous state of Uttar Pradesh should be bifurcated. I remember some leading officers in Madras (in 1964), saying that the smaller size of their state after the 1956 changes had proved helpful for planning and management. While there is much good sense behind such ideas, the issue is so heavily loaded with politics that it may not be possible to implement such a change in the near future. District bifurcation though by no means simple from a political point of view, is less difficult to realise.

The next step deals with district leadership. As we have observed wherever a good IAS collector is in command, the district administration works more swiftly. In many states, however, the collector is not directly involved in development tasks. Perhaps the ideal solution would be to have a District Magistrate or Collector who is directly and primarily concerned with developmental tasks, and is a generalist in development, seconded by a first class agricultural officer, well trained, well paid and with enough prestige attached to his rank. Both these officers could directly control and run the main agencies. This is very different from the present situation in which the Collector has five types of responsibilities: law and order, revenue distribution of certain commodities, development and relief operations in cases of emergency like floods and drought. In addition he is chairman of various committees involved in development. He also acts as a co-ordinator for the different departments engaged in development. He could perhaps be relieved of some of these functions (law and order, and land revenue for instance) handling only the occasional serious and important matter in these areas, other activities being left to his subordinates.

While our conclusions remain the same today as they were in the 1960s, one must raise several questions with regard to the future. Are the new generations of IAS officers of the same calibre as their predecessors? I do not have enough direct evidence to answer this, but in the opinion of one of the most senior and experienced officers, the best candidates joining the IAS are as good as ever; however, between the top people and the average he thinks there is a wide gap. The latter are of poorer calibre than their predecessors, for several young people today are less attracted by the IAS. They prefer to enter business, scientific research and other professions. There is also the question of seriously falling standards of university education. The IAS does not train its officers sufficiently in economic, financial and banking problems. On the other hand, with the recent sending of probationers to villages, the service has improved as far as training in rural development is concerned. The Planning Commission has recently decided to adopt another method (this was adopted by Maharashtra in 1962) by which, in addition to the Collector or District Magistrate, another IAS officer of equal rank and status should have complete authority and responsibility with respect to development work.'

The efficiency of the administration is also highly dependent on the political leadership. At present, the quality of the local politicians in several states is fairly low because of a number of factors: poor qualifications and lack of experience,[4] intrigues and rivalries. All in all, political leaders often do not demand enough from their officials and this encourages a lack of rigour at administrative levels. Politicians also sometimes prefer to have a senior IAS officer as Collector because the latter is likely to be more amenable to political pressures, IAS officers also, in certain cases, look down on political bosses in the districts or in the states if they feel the local party leaders are poorly educated. People also speak of a growing tendency among IAS officers towards careerism and opportunism, which is connected with 'the danger of posting and promotions becoming matters of patronage,' as B.B. Vohra states in a very critical article. Such a risk goes hand in hand with a 'search for security'.[5] Apart from this, there is also the fact of corruption.

B.K. Nehru, one of the most respected ex-ICS officers speaks of similar problems: 'The forces which erode the efficiency of the administration have been in operation in the States for a much longer time than at the Centre.' He adds that it is necessary to remove political influence from the civil service, to improve its economic position to such an extent that it becomes impervious to financial pressures and financial inducements and thirdly, to restore to it once again its professional integrity.'[6]

In spite of these weaknesses, India still enjoys several advantages in this regard in comparison with other developing countries. A number of IAS officers now in senior positions in New Delhi and in the states are competent, quick-witted and fully dedicated to their country and their work. Besides a number of them are thoroughly familiar with the basic technical aspects of agricultural problems.[7] On the other hand, there are cases where the generalist approach goes too far. For instance, I know of an ex-Secretary of Irrigation in a state, whose previous experience (in foreign trade in New Delhi) had nothing to do with his job, and of a Secretary of Agriculture who had previously been with the Ministry of Defence.

The reader may well ask why we are emphasising the role of the IAS so much. We will revert to that matter in the next chapter. Here it is enough to point out the following facts. All attempts at peoples, participation through co-operatives, community projects and Panchayati Raj have yielded disappointing results both in terms of economic development and social justice. The slow rate of economic development has been confirmed by numerous examples, while that of social justice is unavoidable since such institutions are bound to remain in the hands of medium and upper farmers.

Some dedicated and able cadres (and these do exist)[8] can 'have things done' and more effectively protect the interests of the poor. Among such people are civil servants who constantly tour their districts, meet the villagers and listen to them; we have seen a number of such officers during our surveys and subsequent visits. Of course, even an able Collector supported by a first-class agricultural officer will not achieve miracles, mainly because the tasks are so enormous, but such a team would nonetheless bring about a definite improvement. One would not then hear the frequent complaint made by farmers who, after expressing some grievance, add the usual *koi nahin sunta* ('nobody listens').

As we have seen district planning is becoming increasingly complex. The earliest attempts to improve it go back to the preparation of the Third Five Year Plan (1961-66). Nearly twenty years later, the question has still not been solved. There are comparatively well-run districts such as Thanjavur, but too often district officers are of relatively low calibre and are given no lead by the Collector. The Dantwala Committee on block level planning recommends 'pooling together the available planning skills at the district level instead of scattering this scarce resource in several blocks.'[9] Such a team should visit the blocks at frequent intervals to help them prepare their own plans. It is clear that these guidelines will be easier to implement by means of a small hard core of officers as outlined above. These officers could, by dint of their ability and character, compensate for at least some of the shortcomings of their subordinates. The improvement of district planning, which also requires similar efforts at the state and central levels, would, of course, boost economic growth. But, what is less obvious, it will also have social implications and value for the poor, as will be emphasised below.

Indirect *Versus* Direct Attacks on Poverty

It is obvious that a direct attack on poverty through collectivisation leading to a greater equalisation of incomes and power remains a very remote hypothesis, unless some unforeseen events occur in the not-too-distant future. Also, the target group approach can be expected to contribute only in a limited way to the eradication of poverty. Should one, therefore, talk as some Indians do, of the lack of a political will? I would be more inclined to say that politicians are simply aware of the balance of power within villages and that it is in their interests not to upset this drastically.

When considering an indirect attack on poverty there seems to be more scope for strengthening trends observed in relatively progressive areas where growth favours the poor as well as the rich. With a stronger district organisation, a wide range of measures can be pushed through. We have already dealt, in the previous chapter, with the social value of updating land records and consolidating holdings, wherever possible.

Proper water management is one of the priorities in terms of irrigation and drainage. As far as the farmer is concerned, considerable progress has been achieved. Gradually minor irrigation and quick result-oriented schemes have been encouraged with outstanding results in several regions. Efforts are being made to speed up major irrigation works. A number of very alert senior civil servants like B.B. Vohra have played a highly positive role in this.[10] In the draft of the present Five Year Plans (1978-83), Raj Krishna, as member of the Planning Commission, has had the opportunity of implementing the ideas he has been advocating for many years. The problem is to go even faster and provide more assistance, particularly in terms of qualified personnel, to states like Bihar, Assam, Orissa and parts of U.P. where progress remains slow. Drainage is equally needed and, in this connection, I wonder whether the extreme urgency of a more massive effort is always understood by policy-makers.

Such a water-oriented policy has an obvious economic value, but its social consequences are no less important. As we saw in many districts where the untapped potential for irrigation remains considerable, a farmer with even 0.5 hectares of land properly irrigated and drained can, with the help of additional inputs, considerably improve his income. At the same time, he becomes less vulnerable to pressure or exploitation by big landowners. Besides, having more work to do on his own land, he creates employment opportunities for landless labourers.

Then comes the supply of other inputs. Before thinking of credit and subsidies to small and marginal farmers, the most urgent goal is to ensure an ample supply of appropriate seeds, chemical fertilisers and pesticides at a reasonable price. This automatically wipes out many malpractices and other cases of abuse, the victims of which are always the small, and marginal farmers. Since they carry little weight in rural institutions, in times of shortage they are the first to suffer. Shortages leading to black marketing compel them to pay high prices if they can afford them, or prevent them from buying at all. During our last survey, we found substantial improvements in the supply of chemical fertilisers and seeds, with the result that, unlike in 1963-4, we rarely registered complaints. The same could not be said of cement, which was rationed,[11] and for which, too often, a *bakshish* had to be paid. In other cases the cement delivered was mixed with sand.

Agronomic research and adequate seed multiplication need further improvement, although much has already been done. This involves research institutes and agricultural universities. The latter, created in practically every state during the 1960s, often with Americans support, have uneven records. The positive role of the Punjab Agricultural University of Ludhiana is well-known. The same can be said of Pantnagar U.P. Agricultural University. Its research, seed multiplication and extension activities were boosted by one of the finest IAS officers, D.P. Singh.[12] Unfortunately the situation has deteriorated in the last few years and in some states one hears that these universities have become a hotbed for politics or that research is not sufficiently oriented towards local problems. Certain researchers also tend to seek assignments abroad, especially in U.N. agencies.

The problem of improving seeds supply also needs to be considered[13] and here again conditions vary from state to state. In fact, the whole of India must get used to what has happened in the Western world, namely, a continuous process of releasing new seed varieties and multiplying them.

Research in wheat has made a fair amount of progress; the situation is now improving for rice, but the same cannot be said of pulses and oilseeds. As regards the former, some new and better varieties (green gram, *mung* beans), which mature in sixty days instead of ninety, could play an important role as a third crop between the rabi and kharif. Experiments conducted with farmers have yielded 500-700 kilograms per hectare, which is usually higher than traditional varieties. Besides, such crops, enrich the soil in fixing nitrogen from the atmosphere. They do not need chemical fertilisers if phosphate has been used for previous crop. Maize, which is a kharif crop, could be sown with greater profit in the rabi in several parts of Karnataka or Maharashtra, if not in the north-west. Some very encouraging success has been achieved in eastern U.P. and Bihar in the last few years.

Sorghum and bajra grown in poorly rain-fed areas face difficulties, yet there is room for some progress[14] through the use of new seeds, treating them against pests and sowing them early. It is surprising that so little has been done so far for oilseeds (particularly groundnuts) especially when there is a deficit of vegetable oil at the all-India level due to which oil imports are growing. Attempts to introduce soyabeans have not yet produced any striking results. On the other hand, sunflower seems to be rather promising in Maharashtra. Cotton needs increasing attention. Research in new varieties is moving ahead, but one major problem is that the rains are often very poor and there is a lack of irrigation; yields are therefore bound to remain low. Today, they are often around 100 kilograms per hectare in Maharashtra, while the highest yield in the country was 360 kilograms (lint) in Punjab (in the year 1978-79).

Sugarcane, another cash crop, has not been greatly helped so far with new varieties. It is true that the relatively cold winter of northern India does affect yields negatively, but more can be done as, even today, in many districts of eastern U.P., farmers are not yet using the better varieties of sugarcane introduced in the 1930s in western U.P. (Special mention must be made, however, of a new variety—COJ 64—released by Dr. J.C. Kanwar of the Punjab Agricultural University, which has pushed the average yield for Punjab from 39 tons per hectare in 1971-72 to 56 in 1977-78, with a sugar recovery rate of 10.8 versus 8-9 per cent with old varieties).[15] Tapioca has known a sharp expansion in Kerala under a very suitable climate, but its potential has not been fully exploited elsewhere. In other areas, we have seen how potatoes are progressing. Here again, the next steps are not so simple. The bumper crop of 1977-78 led to the crisis of a surplus, which, because potatoes are a perishable commodity, was aggravated by the lack of cold storage facilities. Prices fell sharply and this discouraged farmers from pushing potatoes further.

Then come the new crops. In the hills of Orissa, they are experimenting with wing beans, a plant cultivated in Papua and Burma. The pods, leaves, seeds (which contain 17 per cent oil) and roots are rich in protein and in vitamins. Aquaculture and fish enjoy a large untapped potential. Interesting schemes such as the raising of prawns in brackish ponds near the sea in Thanjavur have been started. Vegetables have expanded considerably in the last thirty years, first around the big cities[16] and then in the vicinity of district towns. Today smaller towns have begun to be surrounded by a vegetable belt, but much more can be done deeper in the countryside, provided it is well connected by road to enable quick delivery to markets. The same applies to milk promotion and sales as well as to fruit. All these subsidiary activities are of particular importance for small or very small farmers. They all require a good water supply management. The question is not to innovate, but to speed up existing trends, or encourage them wherever they are still sluggish.

Intermediate, Alternative and Low Cost Technologies

Indian farmers are engaged in a process of semi-technical change, combining several old techniques with key new inputs such as pumps, chemical fertilisers, pesticides and, less frequently, tractors. Like other Asian peasants, they are trying to follow a new road towards agricultural progress which is neither the traditional pattern nor a copy of some Western blueprint. In this process there is scope for further innovation in the field of intermediate technology. Biogas plants can help but, as we have seen in several places, they are too expensive and only medium and upper farmers can afford them. Cheaper devices are being introduced, but small farmers will find even these too expensive.[17] In addition, the smaller farmers lack enough cattle to feed the biogas plants, and social relations in the villages are such that we cannot expect much from collective and jointly-owned units. It is also important to note that what is left from biogas in terms of manure, though better than normal manure, cannot replace chemical fertilisers. And such devices can very seldom be used for energising tubewells. The biogas unit cannot be built in the midst of the fields since this would mean that farmers would have to transport their cattle manure, which is usually near their houses where the cattle are kept. Bamboo tubewells, though promising, are not always an answer to steel pipes. Bamboo pipes have been a success in certain regions (as in parts of Bihar) but not in others.

Research is progressing in solar energy but often, as in the case of engines and pumps, the present models are still too expensive. No large-scale application of solar energy looks promising for the immediate future but, according to Dr. Ved Prakash, 'There is no reason why direct use of solar energy cannot be undertaken exclusively within the next fifteen years.'[18] Another interesting field of research is being opened, particularly in Tamil Nadu, which seeks to reduce the quantity of inputs like chemicals fertilisers or pesticides while increasing their efficiency. For instance, when steeping sprouting seeds of paddy in Carbandazim (Banstin) solution for fifteen minutes, 'the control obtained is equal to spraying twice with chemicals against bacterial leaf-blight'. The cost of treating one hectare drops from Rs. 250-575 for field spraying to Rs. 9. By applying di-ammonium phosphate at the rate of 2-3 kilograms for 40 square metres, it is possible to either cease applying chemical fertilisers to the main field or to reduce them to 30 per cent, while getting the same or higher yields as with full applications to the main fields. The costs are cut to nearly half. The placing of nitrogen fertilisers five centimetres below ground level can also save half of the chemical fertilisers normally recommended for the same yield.[19]

These examples gives us an idea of what can still be done in all these matters, and of the enormous social content of this research. The first problem is one of initiative— which is still seriously lacking in several states (here again I wish to emphasise the high calibre of a number of senior officers I met in Tamil Nadu). The second problem is to find new devices or new techniques which are so cheap that small, or at least medium, farmers can afford them.

Small Industries and Trade

In spite of all that has been written of the bias in favour of large-scale industry, there has been a tremendous expansion of all sorts of medium, small and tiny industries, including workshops equipped with only one or two machine tools. Here again progress is extremely uneven, as we observed when travelling through the country. The growing emphasis on the small sector is welcome, but where it is just starting, as in eastern U.P., Bihar, Assam, Orissa and wide tracts of central India, it may take time to gather momentum because the Punjabi model cannot be transplanted so easily in a different set-up. Trade is also penetrating deeper, beyond roadside villages to others less well-connected, especially in the progressive areas. This needs more encouragement, just as the promotion of growth centres does. Both sectors help diversify the rural economy, increase the total volume of production and widen employment opportunities.

Roads and Electricity[20]

Compared with many developing countries, India had a relatively good start at the time of Independence and the progress achieved, in terms of road construction, has been impressive. People who have covered around 40-50,000 kilometres by road since the early 1950s, as we have done, are struck by the growing density of roads and the increasing number of asphalted roads leading to villages. Yet this is not enough, as the economy is becoming more demanding than ever. Typical are the villages around Mirpur which, like many others, are still a few kilometres away from a good road, and consequently put to a fair amount of inconvenience regarding transport. Then, as we saw in Palamau, there are areas which are even more isolated.[21]

Rural electricity did not cover even one per cent of the villages at the time of Independence. By the beginning of 1981, 250,000 (45 per cent of all villages) had been electrified; and as many as 4.1 million pumps, tubewells and pumpsets were relying on electricity. In some states such as Punjab, Haryana and Tamil Nadu, practically all the villages are electrified.

These data represent remarkable achievements and yet, power crises and shortages have assumed really dramatic proportions since 1979.[22] Irrigation suffers a great deal and tractors and pumps relying on oil engines have been hit by the lack of diesel oil. The whole small industries sector—flour and rice mills, threshing machines, engineering workshops, small pump manufactures, etc.—has either had to operate at less than optimum strength or has often even ceased operations altogether. As will be explained below, the crisis has several causes and affects practically all sectors of the economy.

The National Process of Rural Development

The different sectors of rural economic life reviewed so far present us with the basic framework of the national process of rural development. In addition to major crops, secondary agricultural activities (vegetables, fruit, fish, animal husbandry, milk) play an increasing role. Trade and small industries are expanding. Agricultural and non-agricultural activities require an increasingly wide and efficient network of transport and communications as well as electricity. To these priorities are to be added social programmes such as those for family planning, drinking water supply, health and education.

It is clear that the present stage of India's rural life is already miles ahead of the stereotyped image of closed and isolated villages which Charles Metcalfe described in the early nineteenth century: 'Village communities which are little republics, having nearly everything they want within themselves and almost independent of any foreign relation.'[23] It is beyond the scope of this work to discuss the validity of Metcalfe's statement (which has been contested by certain historians) even for the nineteenth century, but it is clear that, in spite of the renewed popularity of the concept of self-reliance under the Janata Government and international influences, the ideal of the self-sufficiency of the village is totally unrelated to the actual facts of life. As we have seen, with the population pressure being so heavy, the only way is to have an increasingly open village economy, linked with the outside world: a fast growth of yields per hectare involving the proper selection of new inputs (and not the copy of some Western or Soviet model), and the active promotion of non-agricultural activities, some relying on the advanced technologies of large factories, others on the various intermediate technologies used in small factories.

In order to achieve a relatively harmonious development of these interdependent factors of growth, one needs to plan and manage the district economy better, and to make sound use of government and private forces. Yet this is not the end because these goals are closely connected with planning at the national and state levels.

National Planning in Electricity

Since our intention is to study rural development, we will consider here only the sectors which have a direct impact on the process described above.[24] As regards infrastructure, especially road building, the use of trucks and buses, no new measures seem necessary. Electricity, on the other hand, is a major concern, requiring, as many Indians emphasize, extraordinary and drastic efforts. In several respects, this is a typical crisis of growth since India's progress has been enormous: consumption has increased from 6.6 billion kilowatt hours in 1950-51 to 76 billion in 1977-78, capacity from 2.3 million kilowatts to 26 million. One must, however, underline that the growth rate has been falling from a yearly average of 11.1 percent for the decade 1960-61 to 1970-71, to 6.6 per cent for 1970-71 to 1977-78.[25] For many years there has been a power shortage, but it took a really dramatic turn for the worse in 1979. Climatic factors have affected hydro-electric plants negatively in periods of drought as in 1979, or positively as in 1978 when the monsoon was very heavy. On the other hand, the same 1978 monsoon adversely affected thermal power stations that year, due to the flooding of coal mines.

Other major factors can explain the crisis too. Coal[26] is still supplying many electric plants but production is far from satisfactory; management, labour troubles, ageing equipment and shortage of rail transport, all explain why production has stagnated at around 105 million tons from 1976-77 to 1979-80, though in 1980-81 it increased to 119 million tons. Shortcomings in planning and constructing new electrical plants are no less responsible for the crisis. The Second and Third Plans (1956-66) achieved two-third of their targets for installed capacity, the Fourth Plan of 1969-74 only 47 per cent. Performance improved to 75 per cent in the following years. Other troubles, such as the increases in oil prices and the several months—long embargo on oil transport from Assam, have made the situation worse.

State electricity boards and the management of power plants are facing similar difficulties which have been aggravated by strikes and other troubles since 1976. For instance, in Uttar Pradesh, thermal generation fell by 50 per cent in December 1979 due to an agitation provoked by power engineers. In Bihar—and the case is not exceptional—the existing installed capacity of the Electricity Board is 730,000 kilowatts, but since several units are old and subject to frequent breakdowns, the present capacity varies from 350 to 400,000 kilowatts, while the peak demand is 600,000. When it can, the Electricity Board receives assistance to the extent 100,000 kilowatts from the neighbouring states. This assistance is not regular and is inadequate.[27]

The total network relies on over one million circuit kilometres of transmission and distribution lines, including 28,000 kilometres of transmission lines at 200 kilowatts or over. Here again expansion has not been smooth. Management and operations face several short-comings as observed in the field: malpractices, falling voltage, break-downs, etc. Several networks have expanded gradually instead of being planned from the beginning, so that high voltage transmission lines are lacking—which leads to heavy losses of power over long distances. To remedy this situation would require considerable redesigning of systems. There is also a tendency, on the part of able officials and engineers, to concentrate more on increasing the existing capacity instead of improving maintenance and operations.

One can thus say that the present crisis is due to a number of factors such as lack of discipline, mismanagement and labour trouble in the coal mines at certain times as well as the price of oil and the unrest in Assam. As a result, many industries were affected and had to work at less than optimum capacity. Several key industries such as chemical fertilisers, cement and steel were hit. In 1980-81, the production of cement was 18.5 million tons as against a potential production of 22.66 million tons; nitrogen factories produced 2.15 million tons instead of the potential 2.84 million; steel ingots were 9.12 million tons as against a potential 11.4 million. Part of this deficit had to be made up by additional imports, thus eating into the country's foreign exchange reserves.

The Renewed Debate on Agriculture and Industry[28]

With the advent to power of the Janata Party in 1977, the old debate which had arisen just after Independence—namely, should one give priority to agriculture or industry—was revived and the Five Year Plans were criticised for laying excessive emphasis on industry at the cost of agriculture.

In fact, the problem is not one of a choice between the two but of proper interdependence or linkage. We have seen how agriculture has become dependent on several key industrial inputs. On the other hand, a large sector of industry depends for its survival on agricultural goods, which it processes. Finally, in terms of incomes and the demand for consumer goods, there is a close link between an expanding agriculture and industry. In this context, what is to be criticised is not industrialisation *per se*, but its content. Greater emphasis should have been placed on certain industries directly supporting agriculture. The most glaring example is chemical fertilisers. Starting practically from scratch in 1950-51, production reached 344,000 tons in 1965-66 and 3 million tons in 1980-81.[29] In one sense this meant a substantial rise, but India still imports more than one million tons of nitrogen fertilisers and a substantial quantity of phosphate fertilisers. The performance through the Five Year Plans has been as follows:

Percentage of Targets Achieved in the Production of Chemical Fertilisers

1951-56	71
1956-61	18
1961-66	19
1969-74	24
1974-78	71

In addition to power shortages, other difficulties delayed the construction of new plants. The situation is only partly improving[30] and several new plants are under construction, but one can imagine how much easier things would have been if greater efforts had been made between the mid-fifties and the mid-seventies.

The picture is not very different for cement, which is urgently needed in all fields of economic life. From 2.73 million tons in 1950-51, output reached 10.8 million in 1965-66. It went up to 18.8 million in 1976-77 and then levelled off at 19.3 million during the next two years and fell to 18.5 million tons in 1980-81. Steel follows a similar trend: 1.1 million tons (finished steel) in 1950-51, 4.8 million tons in 1965-66, 7.1 million in 1976-76 and then a decline over the next two years down to 6.6 million in 1978-79. Here also, the power shortage is not the sole factor inhibiting production.

It is also important to look at industries that depend on agricultural goods. There are too many 'sick mills' in the textile and sugar industries. This does not stimulate agricultural growth and leads to low industrial productivity and high prices. In certain cases the mutual dependence between farmers and mills affects the farmers negatively.[31]

Several more examples can be given of the need for greater efficiency and linkage between both sectors. All these problems explain why manufacturing industries declined by 2 per cent during 1979-80. Over and above all this, and related to it, was large-scale deficit financing and the return to a high rate of inflation (about 20 per cent in 1979) which, in previous years, had been considerably controlled.

Since 1980-81, the situation has improved. Industrial production increased by 4 per cent, and in 1981-82 it went up by 8 per cent. There was some improvement in the supply of electricity and rail transport, but it will take several years to overcome the present shortages. Agriculture picked up in 1980-81, as well as in 1981-82.

Price Factors

Money plays an increasing role in rural development: more wages in cash, greater use of cash inputs, a growing share of agricultural production entering the market, rising investments and increasing purchases of goods. Thus, the relationship between monetary production, costs, and prices of agricultural produce has become a very sensitive issue, which requires constant watching. We have seen cases where farmers need more or better price incentives to induce them to push certain crops. Apart from this, the situation is fluctuating—a glut of sugar brings prices down, a sharp increase in potato production is followed by a fall in prices. Farmers know how to raise their voices, but the task of the government is not easy and it continues to grow with the increasing diversity of the monetised sector in rural life.

These observations, made during our field study in 1978-79, were amply confirmed in the following two years, which shows how complex these issues have become today. For decades, traders in grain, cotton, sugar and oilseeds were the main pressure groups, lobbying at the local and national levels with politicians in power. Today, while this set of factors remains, others have appeared: direct action or agitation by farmers, not only the big ones (who may, at the same time, be traders as well), but also medium and small farmers. The initial movement began under the leadership of Sharad Joshi, an ex-international civil servant posted in Geneva, who later returned to India. From Maharashtra the movement spread to the north-west and the south[32] where several serious incidents occurred. This new situation is, in itself, a sign of the advance made by Indian agriculture. Similar problems were faced by farmers in Europe—even in a country like Switzerland, agitating farmers took to direct action and created several 'incidents'.

To set up proper price relationships between inputs and outputs is an extremely complex technical task. If political interference is added to such a situation, it becomes still more difficult to find solutions. Thus, India will have to learn how to live with such problems. One cannot expect instant and correct answers in all cases.

Towards A.D. 2000

The first question I would like to look at here is that of population. The 1981 census has counted a total of 684 million people. The decennial rate of increase of 24.75 per cent over the 1971 figure is hardly below the rate for 1961-71, which was 24.8 per cent. It is, however, interesting to note that in several states with more than 200 million inhabitants, the growth rate is coming down. In most cases this is due to a fall in the birth rate. At the national level the birth rate is estimated at 36 per thousand (41 in 1971). As to the death rate, it is clear that it remains fairly high (14-15 per thousand) compared with several other Asian countries. It can be expected to fall in the coming decades. Drastic efforts are therefore required in the field of family planning in order to compensate for the fall in the death rate and to bring down the rate of population increase.

It is interesting to note that, although the idea of birth controls is much more widespread in towns and villages today than it was years ago, implementation varies greatly from state to state. In Maharashtra, Tamil Nadu, parts of Andhra and Kerala, progress is obvious. In U.P. Bihar, Rajasthan, Orissa and some other states propaganda has never been very active except during the Emergency. Today a growing number of town-dwellers understand the logic behind family planning in view of the overall cost of living, the cost of educating their children and the problems of finding jobs.

In villages a large number of medium and relatively small farmers understand that when their holdings are divided between several sons, the latter will face all kinds of hardship. On the other hand, it is true that tiny landholders and landless people may find an advantage in having a few more children, since labour is the sole source of income in such families and the more children there are, the more the potential labour power. However, as we have observed in the field, the fertility of these couples is rather low and infant mortality is still very high. It is highly desirable, thus, to speed up family planning programmes without committing the excesses of the Emergency. This is a problem the seriousness of which cannot be underestimated. According to the Census Commissioner, if much greater efforts are put into family planning than have been done so far, it is possible that the population will not exceed 950 million in the year 2000. If this is not done, reaching the billion mark is not an impossibility.

It is obvious that India's rural economic potential is far from being fully tapped; consequently, even without drastic political and economic changes, growth can expand further and affect a larger number of the poor. In this connection the first question is that of water management. The old canal systems need substantial improvement in order to increase water supply, prevent loss through seepage and possibly increase the time period over which irrigation is provided when water supply and water sources are not perennial. In the mid-1970s, B.B. Vohra estimated that 16 million irrigated hectares could improved thus.[33] There are also areas where the replenishment of ground water is not reliable, which could lead to decreased irrigation. In certain cases deeper tubewells solve the problem, but this cannot be the answer everywhere.

There is also the important question of additional irrigation. From 20 million hectares (gross) so far, the ultimate potential of ground water is assessed at 35 million hectares. But one must bear in mind the fact that, at the beginning of 1975, 63 per cent of the territory was not yet covered by systematic hydrogeological surveys. It is significant to note that differences ranged from 75 to 80 per cent in Bihar, Orissa, Maharashtra, Madhya Pradesh; they came down to 9 per cent in Haryana and 17 per cent in Punjab.[34] It is amazing that in a developing country as advanced as India, such an elementary and crucial task has not yet been completed.

These data confirm that there is still a large untapped irrigation potential in the eastern region, in many parts of which poverty is particularly acute. Most of these areas have good, if not excellent, alluvial soils which can easily hold two crops a year of wheat and paddy, or two of paddy, the wheat yielding 2,000 kilograms per hectare and the paddy 4,000. For several years discussions have been held about the creation of a national water grid to connect the Ganges basin (which has an excess of water) with the Deccan rivers which are more susceptible to a low flow of water. One of the biggest obstacles in this is to take the grid across the Vindhyas. The latest proposal envisages pumping at a maximum height of 130 metres instead of lifting the water to 400 metres as earlier planned. Such a grand scheme, if achieved, could further enlarge the irrigation potential. However, it will take several decades for it to be completed.

No less urgent a problem is that of drainage. At present 25 million hectares are flood-prone, but as many as 20 million of these can be protected. These data, given in the Draft Five Year Plan 1978-83, probably exclude many tracts of lowlands suffering from excess water even under normal rainfall conditions. Then there are 6 million hectares which are affected by waterlogging, and 7 million which are saline or alkaline due to various factors such as the 'capillary rise from subsoil bed of salt, indiscriminate use of canal water, ingress of sea water'.[35]

On the basis of present achievements, it is clear beyond doubt that progress in water management can pave the way for progress in other inputs such as new seeds for cereals, chemical fertilisers and, when required, pesticides. The National Agricultural Commission has made the following forecasts for the year 2000:

	1971	2000
	(in million hectares)	
Cultivated area (net)	140	150
Cultivated area (gross)	165	200
Irrigated area (net)	31.3	61
Irrigated area (gross)	38.5	84
Foodgrain area	123	123
Cash crops	28	45
Horticulture	5	13
Plantations	2.3	2.8

Source: National Commission on Agriculture, pp. 304-5 of their report.

Present condition confirms these national assumptions: wherever grain yields go up, farmers tend to reduce the area devoted to grain in favour of cash crops. The acceleration of progress in irrigation implies that the targets envisaged for 2000 can be achieved. In 1980, they reached 52.6 million hectares gross. The commission assesses the supply of chemical fertilisers at 14 million (nutrients) in A.D. 2000, nearly three times the 1978-79 level of 5 million. This implies that there will be a tremendous effort to build new plants, and to operate old and new ones more efficiently than is being done now, because imports can cover only a very small part of the total supply that has been forecast. The target seems rather difficult to attain, unless very exceptional measures are taken and implemented over the long term. But it deserves consideration as one of the top priorities for the country.

Losses due to rodents, insects, diseases and weeds have never been scientifically assessed on an all-India basis. Following one of the most conservative guesses, such losses represent 20 per cent of the crops, particularly food crops. Though the use of pesticides is progressing, especially in advanced areas, more has to be done to include other methods such as biological control and the eradication of rodents with simple traps, as is being done in the Krishna delta. On the whole, the complex tasks needed for a sound control programme require more efforts than have been made so far.

The Commission envisages a production of 230 million tons of foodgrains for the year 2000 (132 million in 1978-79, a good year). Practically all the increases are to be achieved through higher yields.

| Main Foodgrains | Forecast for the year 2000 | |
	Yields (tons per hectare)	Area (in million hectares)
Wheat (irrigated)	3.4	15
(unirrigated)	1.5-2	3
Rice	2.8-3.5	32 (24 million irrigated)
Maize	2.6	9
Jowar	1.2	17
Bajra	1.2	12
Pulses	1.5	25

Source: National Commission on Agriculture, pp. 242-51 and 304 of their report.

The targets, in terms of yields, seem too high. For wheat the already advanced irrigated areas can perhaps reach these targets. Late starters will not. The estimates for non-irrigated wheat appear fairly doubtful. For rice, what has been seen in the advanced areas of south India makes 3.5 tons per hectare (about 5 tons per hectare in terms of paddy) appear plausible. Even if water management improves drastically in eastern India, an average figure of 2.8 tons (4.2 in terms of paddy) as given for U.P., Bihar, Madhya Pradesh, seems far too high, especially as today these states have not even been able to attain one ton of rice per hectare in many areas.

For jowar and bajra, which are bound to remain largely rain-fed, the target seems very optimistic if we keep in mind that today they range from 200 to 700 kilograms per hectare. An average yield of around 700 kilograms per hectare seems reasonable. To treble, if not more, the present yields of pulses, seems extremely ambitious, although we must wait for the results of the new varieties that are presently being released. It may be safer to expect not more than 1,000 kilograms per hectare.

To sum up, the targets set for wheat and rice can certainly be attained with irrigation, but they may take longer than expected. For rain-fed crops in dry areas, such high average yields do not seem practicable for biological reasons, unless new scientific discoveries take place.

Could one reach the 230 million ton target by devoting more area to foodcrops at the cost of other crops? Even if the latter were done, it seems that the target is too high. In the last few years, the growth trend has tended to level off, partly because of already high yields in advanced areas and partly because of slow progress in poor but potentially rich districts of Eastern India. It seems that to reach even 200 million tons in A.D. 2000, considerable efforts would be needed in the overall agricultural policy and in the support of industries.

To produce is one thing, to consume is another. India managed to have a surplus of 22 million tons of foodgrains in 1979, in spite of mal-nutrition in several parts of the country. The main reason is that in areas of slow growth, the income of the poor has hardly improved; hence they cannot buy and eat more, thereby absorbing the surplus of the advanced areas. To avoid or discourage such trends, it is imperative to bring about, at least in areas opened upto irrigation in the future, a more balanced pattern of growth. As we will see below, this is by no means easy at this stage.

In the field of cash crops the Constitution envisages sharp increases in areas and yields:

	Area (in million hectares)	
Crop	1971	2000
Oilseeds	16.3	25.5
Sugarcane	2.6	5.0
Cotton	7.6	11.5

Source: *National Commission on Agriculture*, p. 304 of their report.

According to the National Commission on Agriculture, average groundnut yields should increase from 0.7 tons per hectare to 1.5, sugarcane from 42 tons to 82, cotton lint from 120 kilograms per hectare to 460. Here again, targets seem too high in terms of areas and yield,[36] though one can expect substantial increases in both. Any forecast on the expansion of horticulture is very risky since actual figures are even less reliable than those for the main crops.

Even if we assume that the birth rate will fall more rapidly in coming years, it is obvious that the fairly large number of farmers who live reasonably well now on 1.5-2 hectares of irrigated land will in the coming generation, have to manage on half that amount, if not less. Those plots which are already small will become smaller, which means that not only will their owners need to increase their yields, but they will also have to work harder in non-agricultural pursuits.

What will happen in dry, semi-arid zones that are not fit for irrigation? (These cover around 47 million hectares in 84 districts.) A clear answer is difficult to give. No matter what can be achieved with better dry farming techniques, yields beyond 500-1,000 kilograms per hectare are very doubtful and double cropping is, of course, out of the question. These areas are less heavily populated but, compared with land resources, the balance is tight. This underlines the greater need for efforts in better communications and non-agricultural activities.

Finally, we must consider the political leadership. A great deal has been written on its impact on development and the needs of a strong and stable government. Such statements are much too sweeping. As many Indians have pointed out, it is doubtful whether, in the near future, India can enjoy a government which follows absolutely clear-cut and rational policies. The network of forces and interests at the centre and in the states compels her to make compromises, untidy bargains which hinder a smooth economic policy. At the same time, this type of political life has thus far kept India out of major and dramatic crises whereby the future of the nation is at stake, unlike countries such as Iran, Afghanistan and Pakistan.[37]

'We finally muddle through', remark some Indians, and a friend went even further: 'We have become like Italy, we can manage even with a poor government.' Such statements need some qualification. As the collapse of the Janata Government demonstrated, there are limits to 'muddling through'. The deterioration of law and order, the growing labour unrest, the student disorders[38] and lack of decision-making, had, at that time, assumed dangerous proportions. Secondly, in the case of rural development, we can broadly consider two kinds of problems. As confirmed in western U.P., even political instability has not prevented a widespread process of development because local conditions have been favourable. These areas have had a relatively good start, enterprising castes, and minor irrigation that relies on tubewells. In Punjab also, the breakthrough in new seeds occurred at a time of great political instability.

On the other hand, in many parts of India, especially in the region that extends from eastern U.P. to Assam and Orissa, individual farmers and private trade cannot overcome the most fundamental obstacles to development such as water management (which requires major and medium works of irrigation), drainage and flood control. Unstable governments, political leaders who are more interested in local feuds than in public works, as well as a weak administration have a grave and negative impact on such schemes. Such conditions have existed in U.P., Bihar, Assam and Orissa for nearly two decades now. Unless some exceptional local leaders at last take over, how can things really improve? Fortunately, a number of other states, especially in the south and in Maharashtra and Gujarat, have faced much better conditions so far.

Towards New Horizons

Not only is India changing but so also is its image abroad. At last a growing number of foreigners are realising that it is not only a country of sadhus, holy cows and beggars. What is becoming increasingly clear is the will to use the socio-economic forces of the country more efficiently, the economic assets developed so far, the large stock of available talents.

Such aims, which fit well with the perspective of this book, face severe obstacles. A number of warnings have been issued in recent times about existing and future dangers. As L.K. Jha, an experienced civil servant, has emphasised in his book *Economic Strategy for the 80's*: 'We are passing through not just a bad patch in our economic progress, but a deeper social, political and moral malaise, the seeds of which lie in the malfunctioning of the economic system as a whole. Indeed the very quality of individual and national life is in jeopardy.' B.K. Nehru, a man of great calibre, like L.K. Jha, issued another warning in *The Roots of Corruption* (1981) in which he spoke of the deterioration in the political scene. Many similar opinions could be quoted, which give us an idea of the challenge faced by India's government.

Several positive factors may gradually counteract these defects. Mrs. Gandhi has gathered around her a number of very competent civil servants, who do not believe in dogmas but in efficiency. After thirty years of red tapism, economic controls, an inefficient public sector, which together hindred the economy and led to all kinds of malpractices and corruption, definite steps are being taken in order to stimulate productive forces in the well-founded hope that they will also affect the conditions of the poor. Mrs. Gandhi has given the first indications of changes being made in the right direction, as an increasing number of Indians acknowledge, but these may need further efforts if they are to make a greater impact on the economy.

Such a down-to-earth policy belongs to the art of the possible. In the socio-political and economic context of India, one does not see any other way out.

REFERENCES

1. M. Bhattacharya, 'Administrative and Organisational Issues in Rural Development', *The Journal of the Indian Institute of Public Administration*, No. 4, 1978.
2. Total number 405 in 1980-81.
3. Among the many factors which explain development in pre- and post-partition Punjab and later, was the relatively small size of the districts.
4. In one medium-sized state, three ministers knew only their native language, which was not Hindi, in 1978.
5. B.B. Vohra, 'Time for New Norms', *Seminar*, October 1978.
6. B.K. Nehru, 'The Role of the Civil Services in India Today', Seventh Govind Ballabh Pant Memorial Lecture, April 1980.
7. This of course does not mean that they can replace agronomists, but that they know and understand enough to design and implement suitable policies with the assistance of specialists.
8. Some people object that too many IAS officers are not interested in district life and prefer to be in a state or in the central secretariat. There are certainly cases like that, but one still finds a number of young cadres who are prepared to spend several years away from big towns and paper work.
9. *Report of the Working Group on Block Level Planning* (New Delhi, 1978), p. 7.
10. For over a decade he has been advocating a stronger water policy. See B.B. Vohra, *Land and Water Management in India* (New Delhi, 1975).
11. There have been ups and downs in the supply of cement since the 1960s.
12. D.P. Singh later dealt with the National Seeds Corporation until December 1976.
13. The National Seeds Corporation has been going through various troubles since 1977.
14. Indian research institutes as well as the U.N. International Crops Research Institute for Semi-Arid Tropics (ICRISAT) at Hyderabad, are active in these fields.
15. M.S. Gill, 'Punjab—The Continuing Miracle', *NCDC Bulletin*, Nos. 3-4, 1979.
16. Even in 1950, a town like Poona, in Maharashtra, had a poor supply of vegetables.
17. The investment cost for some of the devices used earlier varied from Rs. 4,000 to Rs. 5,000. The latest devices cost Rs. 2,000-3,000. In both cases 5 head of cattle are required to make the plant economical. More than 80,000 biogas plants were operating in India in 1980-81 (*Nouvelles de l'Inde* No. 214, October 1979).
18. *Kurukshetra*, June 1977.
19. J.H.S. Ponnaya, *Low Cost High Efficiency Technology for Rice* (Madras, 1978).
20. All data come from Tata Services, *Statistical Outline of India, 1980* (Bombay, 1980).
21. *Road network:*

	1950-51	1975-76
	(in thousands of kilometres)	
surfaced	157	533
unsurfaced	243	843
	400	1,376

Railways 53,200 kilometres in 1950-1,60,700 in 1977-78.

22. Although serious problems have always existed, they reached a peak in 1979 and after. During the summer of 1981, tubewells in parts of Bihar were getting electricity for only one hour a day. The situation improved in the latter part of 1981-82.

23. Quoted by B. Cohn, 'Structural Change in Rural Society', in R.E. Frykenberg (ed.), *Land Control and Social Structure in Indian History* (Wisconsin, 1969).

24. Many publications have dealt with national planning and agriculture. See, in particular, the fine analysis by John W. Mellor, *the New Economics of Growth, A Strategy for India and the Developing World* (Ithaca, 1976).

25. The rate seems to have risen again in 1978-79 by about 10 per cent, installed capacity 29 million kilowatts. Further improvements in 1982-83.

26. Coals mines were nationalised in 1973. Thermal power stations (including oil and gas) supply more than 50 per cent of the country's electricity, hydro below or above 40 per cent, nuclear around 2.8 per cent.

27. *Overseas Hindustan Times*, 6 and 14 December 1979. On the whole, the crisis is worse in northern India than in other parts. One factor may be the poorer management of state electricity boards here than in other parts of the country.

28. For the following data, see *Economic Survey*, 1981-82, and *Statistical Outline of India*, 1980.

29. In terms of nutrients, N. (nitrogen), P_2O_5 (phosphoric acid).

30. Although utilisation of the existing capacity remains rather low—57 per cent in 1970, 58 per cent in 1978.

31. Farmers in U.P. may have to wait six months, if not more, before they are paid for their work by certain co-operative sugar mills.

32. Barbara Harriss studied these problems in a very fine paper entitled 'Agricultural Mercantile Politics and Policy—A Case-Study of Tamil Nadu', paper presented at the Seventh Conference of European and South Asian Studies. London, July 1981. See also G. Deleury, 'Societe traditionnelle en Inde, le poids des castes', Paris, *Croissance des Jeunes Nations* (May, 1981).

33. Op. cit., p. 40.

34. *Fifth Five Year Plan 1974-79*, p. 95. The situation is worse in many other developing countries.

35. National Commission on Agriculture, *Abridged Report* (New Delhi, 1977), p. 209.

36. The yields of the table correspond to a total of 250 million tons, while the Commission takes 230 million. Yet even that quantity involves very high yields.

37. Each of these countries faces a different type of crisis, but all the crises are extremely serious.

38. The growing deterioration of the educational system (which becomes worse every year) is not felt too strongly in certain circles since senior jobs are still in the hands of people who were educated in the early years after Independence. But the impact will soon be more noticeable. In the long-term, this is a matter of major concern.

27

Rural and Sustainable Development

Rural Development: The Indian Experience

Rural development, variously examined, may simply be understood as a trinity of economic growth, judicious distribution of benefits and accessibility to improvement opportunities, to fulfil the needs and aspirations of the rural inhabitants, who are heterogeneous and hierarchical in many respects.

An attempt has been made here to critically analyse and understands the multidimensional complexities of the Indian experience of rural development in terms of conceptual frame, strategies, and numerous development programmes with specific reference to land reforms and consequences. Planned institutional transformations, based upon such analysis and understanding however, suggest and alternative approach towards greater agrarian reforms and better rural development.

Viable Strategies

Rural development in India remains basically political oriented and operates through power structures at the national and local level. The model of rural development strategy is essentially an 'improvement approach.' During the pre-independence period, the attempts made in community development were by and large, scattered in character. The individuals with missionary zeal and various agencies—both governmental and non-governmental, have tried to improve the quality of life of the people in areas and communities marked by backwardness and isolation.

Some of the community service oriented agencies, which undertook development activities in India, are:

1. Government sponsored ones through the appointment of commissions and committees, viz., Grow More Food Campaign.
2. Individuals associated with the Government bodies—Brayne's effort in the state of Punjab Mayers' attempt in the hilly terrains of Uttar Pradesh.
3. Non-governmental organisation like the YMCA's Marthandam experiment.
4. Individuals not associated with the Government like the attempts of Mahatma

Gandhiji at Sevagram, Wardha, Sabarmathi and that of Poet Laureate Rabindranath Tagore at Shantiniketan and Sriniketan.

The dawn of independence paved the way for launching of the Community Development Programme (1952) on a national scale in the direction of making rural life oppulent through elimination of rural socio-economic problems. The National Extension Service (NES) blocks were created to route the community development activities, NES blocks became the administrative machinery conduits/of for the implementation of community development programmes. Later on approaches galore as part of the strategy taking the programmes to the village door-steps.

The major approaches pursued in community development by the Government at the Central and States were:

1. Gandhian approach
2. Project approach
3. Area approach
4. Sectoral approach
5. Self-sufficiency approach
6. Growth centre approach
7. Integrated approach
8. Decentralised planning approach
9. Target group approach
10. Minimum needs approach
11. Participatory rural appraisal.

Rural Development Programmes

Following the approaches and the notion of the national level community oriented programmes and defined area projects, the Government of India initiated a plethora of development programmes since the First Five Year Plan (1951-56). These programmes range from generalised programmes like the C.D.P. and N.E.S. to agricultural-specific development programmes like.

1. Intensive Agriculture Area (IAAP)
2. Intensive Agriculture District (IADP) and
3. High Yield Varieties (HYVP)
4. Extension programmes like Laboratory Training to Land Visit.
5. Area development programmes such as
   Command Area Development (CADP),
   Desert Development (DDP),
   Drought Prone Area (DPAP), and
   Hill Area Development (HADP).

6. Target Group Specific programmes like

   Antyodaya

   Integrated Rural Development (IRDP)

   Integrated Tribal Development (ITDP)

   Small Farmers Development Agency (SFDA) as well as

   Marginal Farmers and Agricultural Labourers (MFAL).

7. Employment programmes like

   Crash Scheme for Rural Employment (CSRE)

   Food For Work (FFWP)

   National Rural Employment (NREP)

   Pilot Intensive Rural Employment (PIREP)

   Training of Rural Youth in Self-Employment (TRYSEM)

   Employment Guarantee Scheme (EGS)

   Rural Landless Employment Guarantee Scheme (RLEGP) and

   Jawahar Rojgar Yojana (JRY).

8. Social Welfare programmes like

   Applied Nutrition (ANP)

   Integrated Child Development Service (ICDS)

   Mahila Mandal (MM)

   National Adult Education (NAEP) and

   Yuvak Mandals (YM).

Most of these programmes were merged into the Integrated Rural Development Programme (IRDP) with and avowed objective of the creation of income generating opportunities through employment to the rural poor in elevating them above the poverty line.

Impact

Over four decades of experience with multiple rural development programmes hardly have made any change in the uneven rural socio-economic relationships dominated by the powerful and privileged sections of society. The hiatus between their objectives and implementation has been widely observed. In fact, all programmes operating in such organisational and legislative set-up were not to upset the existing structure. It has not only served the interests of richer farmers, but their power stood in the way of effective implementation.

Thus the politico-economic games of rural development relying heavily on the statutory agencies and organisation failed in its primary objectives, as it could not provide conducive conditions for the growth of sustained, synchronous and overseeing grass-root institutions. It remained confined to monitoring and overseeing of poly-centric and somewhat amorphous efforts by uncommitted bureaucracy at several local and district levels, regional and autonomous units by-passing such efforts of mobilisation for participatory development.

As a result the programme benefits failed to percolate to the target segments in their objective of raising above the poverty line by income generating assets. To rectify the sorry state to affairs in rural development transactions, a critical look a fresh for result oriented achievements need to be taken by those at the helm of affairs in policy making, bureaucracy academic level, politicians, local leadership and voluntary bodies with a view to enliven the programme, in making rural development quite meaningful.

Alternative Strategy

The strategies adopted in rural development have so far not diversified the benefits to the vulnerable segments of rural society. The rural institutions established with a view to decentralise have not accelerated the wider participation of people in the planning and implementation levels, to usher in rural development. The institutional approach had so far resulted in mismanagement and lack of benefits to the needy, neglected and weaker segments. Implementation of the programmes of poverty alleviation for the promotion of rural development warrants an alternative strategy. It is strongly felt that the people's participation in various stages of development is the sine-qua-non for meaningful and balanced rural development.

The alternate and appropriate strategy towards effective implementation of rural development and rural poverty alleviation would be

1. Revival of the Gram Sabha.
2. Revitalisation of the Panchayat Raj Institutions.
3. Micro-level resource and need-based development planning.
4. Involvement of people in the planning and implementation infrastructure of programmes.
5. Participatory Rural Appraisal.

The suggested alternate strategy could go a long way in planning and implementing of the programmes with effective participation of the people through Panchayat Raj for balanced and meaningful rural development.

Sustainable Rural Development

India being a country of villages in beset with numerous socio-economic problems affecting the well-being of the people. The living conditions in rural life manifest a pathetic scene in all walks of social life. In contrast, the traditional rural society in spite of problems like transport, communication, education, health etc., the life was comparatively full, rich and prosperous. The rural areas, on account of agricultural prosperity in the traditional society, promoted and overall development in their midst. There was self-sufficiency self-reliance and self-dependence for anything on Indian soil. In view of such conditions, the rural society was autonomous in every respect and managed its affairs to the fullest satisfaction of the people.

Such traditional character of abundance and prosperity could not last long. The agricultural prosperity was affected due to the failure of monsoon leading to backwardness in the rural economy and the living conditions of the people, with proliferating socio-economic problems like unemployment, poverty, indebtedness, migration, illiteracy, drop-out from school, ill-health squalor, poor sanitation and public health and environmental pollution. The worst sufferers however were the people belonging to the weaker segments, glorified later as the downtrodden. With a view to mitigate their sufferings in bringing back to their original, rich prosperous and autonomous life, there were certain attempts made in this direction during the pre-independence movement. These were scattered and sporadic, in nature, throughout the country. The community development programmes launched in the year 1952 had the following aims, objectives and approaches:

1. Economic development through community organisation.
2. Economic growth with equitable and distributive social justice.
3. People's participation at various stages of planning, implementing and evaluation.
4. Need-based development planning.
5. Government and non-government agencies to assist both at the national and international levels.
6. Balanced development of rural communities.
7. Proper utilisation of the vast unexploited country-side resources lying dormant.
8. Encouraging villagers to become self-reliant, responsible citizens, quite capable and willing to participate effectively with some knowledge and understanding of nation-building activities.
9. Inculcating a spirit of self-help amongst them through development activities in village Panchayats and cooperative bodies.
10. Improving and modernising traditional agricultural practices essential for augmenting agricultural productivity.
11. Extending the principles of cooperation by making the rural families credit-worthy.
12. Attacking the problems of hunger disease, squalor, illiteracy, unemployment by peaceful means.
13. Elimination of inequalities.
14. Mobilising ample employment opportunities.

Impact of rural development over the years have left massive underdeveloped pockets despite four decades of planning. It called for a drastic change in our planning process. The development must be based on the felt needs of the people and promoted on the resources of the people and areas. Only then will our development attempts be sustainable in the villages and ameliorate the socio-economic conditions of people. The participatory approach however, needs to be strengthened, where the rural people must be effectively associated in all the phases of development. So that they could become the effective participants rather being passive onlookers.

Participatory Rural Appraisal (PRA) as a strategy in rural development ensures integrated development through the effective participation rural people in planning development evaluation of the incremental income and elimination of their problems. The salient features of PRA are as follows:

1. Mobilisation of people on a common forum for planning and development based on felt needs.
2. Preparation of a village resource-map.
3. Involvement of local people, leaders and institutions like industrious youth, women, elders in the government machinery.
4. Reliance on the knowledge and skills of the people.
5. Exchange of information among those people involved in comprehensive planning, implementing and monitoring activities.
6. Providing a structure for local aspirations in achievement of goals.
7. Chalking out of a list of the projects, on priority basis seeking support from government and village organisations.
8. Planning for sustainable development with village leaders and institutions.
9. Adopting a multi-disciplinary approach involving social scientists like sociologists, economists, geographers, cartographers, population experts, scientists, development administrators etc.

The distinctive feature of PRA about the knowledge articulated is generated through interviews, investigation, mapping of resources, diagramming of prioritised development needs, presentation and analysis of problems. Moreover, PRA is built upon the premise that rural people are capable of solving their problems by giving priorities, with vast knowledge.

Of the approaches presented in the preceding paragraphs for sustainable rural development Participatory Rural Appraisal (PRA) works better through the mobilisation of people with instant solution upon the felt needs. It involves the people, development machinery of the government, financial and academic institutions. Therefore, for making the rural development programme more sustainable, effective and meaningful, PRA has to be considered as an *alternative strategy* in making rural life oppulent and prosperous, realising the goal of economic growth with equitable social justice.

Role of NGOs

Development, defined variously relates to the improvement, growth, increase, increment—are the different facets of development. Development generally signifies improvement at the initial stages from undesirable state of affairs to a desirable one in any field of social living. It is development in the economic sphere irrespective of the field of application—whether social economic or otherwise, but it should be sustainable in the long run for the well-being of the people in the areas concerned.

Development attempts initiated in the rural areas in the past four decades resulted in improvement in the topography but the development of infrastructure in rural areas, by and large with least impact was discernible in the socio-economic aspects of rural living. The socio-economic conditions of the rural masses remained more or less at the same level in contrast to the pre-independent scenario.

The pre-independent rural India was marked by physical segregation from the under-world, cutting off the villages due to lack of transport and communication. Though agricultural production was least people were able to manage and make a living in villages. Irrigation was managed by the community upon water harvest schemes, particularly through percolation ponds, tanks etc. The farming families had lives took to meet the operational requirements in agriculture, but were self-reliant, self-dependent with prosperity in other areas of rural living. In addition, the people were known for unity, fraternity, peaceful co-existence and interdependence, which promoted their social solidarity.

On account of limitations identified with their habitation there had limited contacts to the outside world, except their participation during festivals of importance elsewhere on certain occasions. The independent conditions in agriculture were more preserved, when the farmers produced their own seeds, manure with complete involvement in agricultural production and lift irrigation. Hence, farming families in the rural areas sustained on agriculture owing to the abundant production of subsistence crops.

The cost of cultivation of various crops too remained comparatively low and return from cultivation was more than the investment. Consequently the farm families had surplus production and the net returns from agriculture were rather profitable which led to prosperity in rural socio-economic life.

Such condition of prosperity and self-dependence witnessed during the pre-independence era gradually withered with the onset of innovation, modernisation, mechanisation, application of science and technology to realise the objectives of increasing food production. Innovations in farm practices with Green revolution mechanisation and HYVP have created not only imbalanced development among the agriculturists but led to rural unrest.

With a view to accelerate the process of development in problem-ridden areas, the planning process was set into uplift the socio-cultural and economic conditions of the rural people. Several strategies and approaches (sectorial, integrated, target group, minimum needs, decentralised planning, PRA etc.) had been adopted in the process to make the benefits of planned development reach the poorest of the poor. In such realised programmes (Area specific, Target group, Employment, Social Welfare), the targets failed by and large, to effect rural transformation and community ties. Consequently, such of the rural poor for whom programmes were intended either remained where they were or reaped the benefits only marginally upon limitations at various levels. The stronger forces in village life have appropriated the benefits in the name of the weaker ones. Consequently, the gulf between the rich and poor had widened further.

We are now faced with a piquant situation of simultaneous existence of skyscrapers and developed pockets on the one hand and poverty-stricken people and under-developed pockets on the other. This has ultimately caused the emergence of the imbalanced development of areas and people at large.

In a social welfare state, it is the bounden duty of the government to mitigate the sufferings of people and develop their areas of living. In view of the limitations identified with the government i.e., the resource crunch and the problems of benefit percolation through government machinery, the Non-Governmental Organisations (NGOs) are encouraged to supplement the efforts of the governmental agencies in the task of integrated rural development.

The NGOs could effectively participate in the process of planning, implementing, monitoring and evaluation of rural development programmes by tapping assistance from within and outside the country. Since the promoters of NGOs are familiar with the local conditions, people, environment, problems, administration, they are relevant to the present state of impasses and fit into rural development transactions.

In such transactions, the government on an experimental basis could short list certain NGOs having long standing service, development worth and entrust the task for realising the quality of development. Once the government is convinced of their quality of service in rural development, their trials may be extended to larger areas by involving more NGOs.

The areas of service which may be entrusted to the NGOs to achieve sustainable development in rural areas are:

1. Agriculture and related land development activities
2. Irrigation systems—Minor and medium types
3. Innovation—diffusion in agriculture development
4. Agricultural extension education
5. Education—Formal, non-formal, adult-population education, functional, literacy-programmes.
6. Employment generation—skill development through training.
7. Health and family welfare—family planning propaganda—motivation—research and training, rural health centres, dispensaries etc.
8. Development of the weaker segments particularly of women, SC, ST, SF, MF, AL, RA.